Stormtroopers

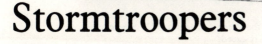

Stormtroopers

A Social, Economic and Ideological Analysis,
1929–35

CONAN FISCHER

Lecturer in History, Heriot-Watt University

London
GEORGE ALLEN & UNWIN
Boston   Sydney

George Allen & Unwin (Publishers) Ltd,
40 Museum Street, London WC1A 1LU, UK

George Allen & Unwin (Publishers) Ltd,
Park Lane, Hemel Hempstead, Herts HP2 4TE, UK

Allen & Unwin, Inc.,
9 Winchester Terrace, Winchester, Mass. 01890, USA

George Allen & Unwin Australia Pty Ltd,
8 Napier Street, North Sydney, NSW 2060, Australia

First published in 1983

British Library Cataloguing in Publication Data

Fischer, Conan
    Stormtroopers.
1. Nationalsozialistische. Deutsche Arbeiter-Partei. *Sturmabteilung* –
History
I. Title
943.08′5   D253.7
ISBN 0-04-943028-9

Library of Congress Cataloging in Publication Data

Fischer, Conan.
    Stormtroopers, a social, economic, and ideological analysis, 1929–35.
Bibliography: p.
Includes index.
1. Nationalsozialistische Deutsche Arbeiter-Partei. Sturmabteilung.
2. Germany – Politics and government – 1918–1933.   3. Germany –
Politics and government – 1933–1945.   I. Title.
DD253.7.F57 1983   943.085   83-2550
ISBN 0-04-943028-9

Set in 10 on 11 point Plantin by Computape (Pickering) Ltd,
North Yorkshire
and printed in Great Britain
by Mackays of Chatham

Contents

Preface

I am deeply indebted to many friends, colleagues and institutions for their encouragement, advice and assistance during the preparation of this book. Professor Volker Berghahn, Professor Francis Carsten, Mr Ian Connor, Professor Klaus Hildebrand, Dr Klaus-Peter Hoepke, Professor Peter Hüttenberger, Professor Michael Kater, Dr Lothar Kettenacker, Dr Hsi-Huey Liang, Dr Tim Mason, Dr Jeremy Noakes and Dr Peter Stachura very kindly provided assistance and advice during an earlier stage of my researches. Dr Ingrid Buchloh supplied me with detailed information on the Nazi movement in Duisburg and Dr Lawrence Stokes provided extremely informative material concerning the SA in the town of Eutin, Holstein. Professor John Röhl, Mr Anthony Nicholls and Dr Richard Bessel offered particularly useful advice on an earlier draft of this work. Dr Ian Kershaw, Dr David French and Dr Bill Knox have advised and assisted me in numerous ways over the past few years. The present script was read painstakingly by Dr Jill Stephenson to whom I am grateful for her many helpful suggestions. My especial thanks are due to my doctoral supervisor, Dr Hartmut Pogge von Strandmann who has provided help and encouragement from the outset and given invaluable advice on the present script.

The staff of the archives and libraries visited were most helpful and sometimes took a great deal of time and trouble in giving invaluable guidance. As well as scholars and archivists, many other people helped towards this book in a variety of ways. Among these was Captain (ret.) Walther Stennes who kindly allowed me a very informative interview concerning his period as commander of the eastern German SA. I am indebted to the SSRC, the former Anglo-German Group of Historians (now part of the German Historical Institute, London), the Volkswagen Foundation, the German Academic Exchange Service and the British Academy for funding my extended stays in Germany while conducting research on the SA.

My greatest thanks go to my wife for tolerating the intrusion of Hitler's stormtroopers into her home over several years. She has provided advice and encouragement far beyond the call of duty.

Of course any shortcomings contained within this book remain my responsibility alone.

Edinburgh
February 1982

For Mary

Abbreviations

ADGB	Allgemeiner Deutscher Gewerkschaftsbund
AG	Aktiengesellschaft
BA	Bundesarchiv Koblenz
BDC	Berlin Document Center
Bez	Bezirk
BHStA	Bayerisches Hauptstaatsarchiv München
BL	Bezirksleitung (KPD)
BMW	Bayerische Motorenwerke
BVP	Bayerische Volkspartei
DAF	Deutsche Arbeitsfront
DNVP	Deutschnationale Volkspartei
EKKI	Exekutivkomitee der Kommunistischen International
Ge	Geheime Staatspolizei (Gestapo)
GLAK	Generallandesarchiv Karlsruhe
Gr	Gruppe (SA)
GStABD	Geheimstaatsarchiv Berlin-Dahlem
GStAM	Geheimes Staatsarchiv München
HHW	Hessisches Hauptstaatsarchiv Wiesbaden
HJ	Hitler Jugend
IfZ	Institut für Zeitgeschichte
KJMV	Katholischer Jungmänner-Verein
KPD	Kommunistische Partei Deutschlands
LAS	Landesarchiv Speyer
NHStA	Niedersächsisches Hauptstaatsarchiv
NS	National Socialist/nationalsozialistisch
NSBO	Nationalsozialistische Betriebszellen-Organisation
NSDAP	Nationalsozialistische Deutsche Arbeiterpartei
NSDFB	Nationalsozialistischer Deutscher Frontkämpferbund
NSV	Nationalsozialistischer Volkswohlfahrt
NWHStA	Nordrhein-Westfälisches Hauptstaatsarchiv
OG	Ortsgruppe (NSDAP)
OGL	Ortsgruppenleiter (NSDAP)
OSAF	Oberster SA-Führer/Oberste SA-Führung
Pf	Pfennig(e)
Pg	Parteigenosse (NSDAP)
PND	Polizei-Nachrichtendienst
PO	Politische Organisation (NSDAP)
RF	Rotfrontkämpferbund
RGO	Revolutionäre Gewerkschaftsopposition
RM	Reichsmark (RM 1 equalled 1s sterling in 1933)
RW	Reichswehr
SA	Sturmabteilung

SAA	SA-Anwärter
SAG	Staatliches Archivlager in Göttingen
SAM	SA-Mann
SAR	SA-Reserve
SB	Staatsarchiv Bremen
SM	Staatsarchiv München
SPD	Sozialdemokratische Partei Deutschlands
SS	Schutzstaffel
Sta	Stahlhelm
Stu	Sturm (SA)
Stuba	Sturmbann (SA)
Stuf	Sturmführer (SA)
Tru	Trupp (SA)
Truf	Truppführer (SA)
TTC	Technical Training Company
TU	Trade union
USPD	Unabhängige Sozialdemokratische Partei Deutschlands
VLS	Voluntary Labour Service
WAC	Women's Action Committee
WHW	Winterhilfswerk
WRS	Winter Relief Scheme (WHW)
ZK	Zentralkomitee (KPD)

Glossary of German terms used in text

Abitur:	Highers, A-levels
Adolf Hitler Spende:	Adolf Hitler (Welfare) Appeal
All gemeine Fortbildungsschule:	General continuation school
Bayernwacht:	Bavarian Guard – paramilitary wing of the Bavarian People's Party
Berufsschule:	Trade school
Bonzen:	Big-wigs
Einwohnerwehr:	Citizens' Defence League(s)
Fortbildungsschule:	Continuation school
Freikorps:	Free Corps
Frontbann:	Cover organisation for the banned SA, 1924–5
Gau:	Nazi administrative region
Gauleiter:	NSDAP regional leader
Gausturm:	SA formation of sub-group size
Geselle:	Journeyman
Gestapo:	Secret police
Gleichschaltung:	Assimilation (of institutions by the NSDAP from 1933)
Grenzschutz:	Frontier Guard (volunteers organised by the army for defending the eastern frontier)
Gruppenführer:	SA general
Gymnasium:	Grammar school
Handwerker:	Skilled worker, artisan
Hilfskasse:	Assistance fund
Hilfswerklager:	(SA) welfare camp(s)
Inhaber:	Proprietor
Kampfbund gegen den Faschismus:	Militant League against Fascism
Kaufmännischer Angestellte:	Clerical or sales employee
Kernstahlhelm:	Core Stahlhelm
Meister:	Master craftsman
Mittelschule:	Middle school
Mittelstand:	Middle classes
Mittelständler:	Member(s) of middle classes
Mittlere Reife:	O-grades or O-levels
Oberführer:	Senior SA general
Obergruppe:	SA corps
Oberscharführer:	SA sergeant-major
Obertruppführer:	SA senior warrant officer
Ortsgruppe:	Local NSDAP unit of organisation

Pfalzwacht:	Palatine Guard – paramilitary wing of Bavarian People's Party in the Bavarian Palatinate
Realschule:	(approx.) modern high school
Reichsbanner:	SPD-dominated Republican paramilitary formation
Reichstag:	Weimar Parliament
Reichswehr:	German army
Rottenführer:	SA corporal
Saalschutz:	Meeting-Hall Guard (forerunner of SA)
SA *Anwärter*:	SA probationer
SA *Mann*:	SA private
Schar:	Smallest SA unit
Scharführer:	SA sergeant
Schufo (Schutzformationen):	Activist units of Reichsbanner
Selbsthilfe:	Self-help
Sonderaktion:	Special Action – NS campaign to provide work for Nazi veterans after 1933
Stahlhelm:	Steel Helmet – monarchist paramilitary formation
Standartenführer:	SA colonel
Stosstrupp Hitler:	Hitler Assault Troop – forerunner of SS
Sturm:	SA Company
Sturmabteilung:	Storm Section (the German abbreviation, SA, is always used in English)
Sturmbannführer:	SA major
Sturmführer:	SA lieutenant
Sturmmann:	SA lance-corporal
Tannenberger:	Member(s) of right-wing Tannenberg League
Technische Schule:	Technical school
Truppführer:	SA sergeant-major
Untermenschentum:	Sub-humanity – a Nazi term used to describe those considered racially and socially inferior
Verband/Verbände:	Right-wing paramilitary association(s) of the Weimar era
Volksschule:	Elementary school
Wandervögel:	Nationalist youth group
Wehrstahlhelm:	The active Stahlhelm formations
Winterhilfswerk:	Nazi Winter Relief Scheme – money raised for welfare purposes through voluntary subscription
Zentrum:	Centre Party – the party of German Catholics outside Bavaria

1 *Introduction*

The NSDAP rose to prominence in German politics over half a century ago, but despite the passage of time, the debate over the causes and character of Nazism and its wider historical significance continues unabated, not least because of the sheer enormity of the phenomenon. Any analysis invites examination of other elements in German social and political life and comparison with other political systems and ideologies, sometimes tainting them, at least implicitly, and often exposing the raw nerves of current ideological standpoints.

The social background of the NSDAP's adherents has been central to this debate, since, by the early 1930s, the Nazi movement enjoyed substantial popular support. This alone did not bring Hitler to power, but it was certainly a necessary precondition for his success. Even before the republic collapsed, observers noted the NSDAP's attraction for sections of the lower middle class, particularly the peasantry and small proprietors of non-urban Protestant Germany, and salaried employees.[1] The NSDAP undertook its own survey of party members in 1935, the results of which, although treated with caution, are broadly accepted. These confirmed its attraction for the lower middle classes. While under half the population could in a broad sense be so defined, of the party's members 55·1 per cent were lower middle class by the same token in January 1933 and 57·8 per cent in January 1935. Similarly, a substantial section of the Nazi electorate stemmed from lower-middle-class backgrounds, although the exact proportions remain debatable. The NSDAP fared less well in recruiting workers. Although 46 per cent of the population were so defined, the proportion of workers in the party was 31·5 per cent in January 1933 and 30·3 per cent in January 1935.[2] In the electoral arena the relative level of working-class support for the NSDAP was possibly lower still.

If these figures are generally accepted, their significance remains controversial. There have been isolated attempts to demonstrate strong working-class support for Nazism,[3] but the main debate has centred on whether National Socialism is definable as a lower-middle-class movement, or whether its basis of support was sufficiently broad to invite its characterisation as a populist mass movement.

Advocates of the former interpretation acknowledge that their argument faces difficulties. Conceptual problems attach to the term 'lower middle class' as its limits are not immediately clear and the class lacked sufficient social and economic coherence for identical interests to prevail. Furthermore, among the Catholic third of the lower middle classes there was relatively little support for Nazism, at least until 1933.[4] None the less it is argued that the crises of the Weimar era squeezed, or appeared to squeeze, much of the lower middle class between big business and organised labour and that the Protestants, at least, responded by supporting Nazism in the early 1930s.[5]

Other historians place greater emphasis on differences within the lower middle class. White-collar staff were not especially predisposed to vote Nazi,[6] although the same group was over-represented within the party itself.[7] Furthermore, while much has been made of the NSDAP's attraction for the peasantry, peasants were heavily under-represented within the party membership nationally.[8] Regarding the lower middle class's social coherence, the working-class backgrounds of many clerical staff has been noted,[9] while the small peasantry, it is argued, possibly shared more in common with other manual occupations than with the rest of the lower middle class.[10] The NSDAP's ability to gain a third of its membership from the working class is also regarded as significant. No one disputes that the NSDAP was relatively unsuccessful in recruiting workers, at least in those constituencies where the SPD had traditionally done well, but the demographic structure of German society meant that in absolute terms the NSDAP had gained 267,423 workers as members by January 1933 even if that did only represent 31·5 per cent of party membership.[11] In the same month the KPD had a membership of barely 300,000[12] which was not exclusively working class.

This socially diverse party was, therefore, arguably 'a catch-all party of protest'[13] which, as Moore puts it, cannot be forced 'into the sociological straitjacket of mere lower-middle-class resentment'.[14] Such a party simultaneously faced great risks and enjoyed great potential. During the mid-1920s the NSDAP, still recovering from the effects of the failed Munich putsch and operating in a period of relative economic prosperity, failed to attract mass backing, but its increasingly successful political exploitation of the rural economic crisis in Lower Saxony during 1928 and 1929 showed its capabilities.[15] With the onset of the depression it came into its own. The conventional parties were ill-placed to appeal to a plurality of interests during a crisis. They had originated in the imperial era (or before) when, given the absence of a fully developed parliamentary system, parties operated predominantly as pressure groups for specific interests, be these the organised labour movement, agriculture, big business, Roman Catholicism or whatever. Despite the constitutional advance represented by Weimar, the parties were slow to change, while the NSDAP with its radical, nationalist rhetoric and a compelling, dynamic leader could appeal to many voters in a defeated, partially occupied country which had slid into rapid economic decline. In contrast with those of other parties, the NSDAP's adversaries were sufficiently narrowly or sufficiently vaguely defined to leave ample potential support across a broad sweep of society and the NSDAP succeeded in rapidly occupying any vacant political ground. The maintenance of this diverse support was another matter. Once the depression showed signs of easing in late 1932, support for the NSDAP wavered as people began to revert to former loyalties or simply failed to vote. Furthermore, as the Nazi movement's confidence faltered, the contradictions inherent in its range of policies and electoral promises became evident and took their toll. Hitler assumed office with his movement in disarray, at the invitation of conservative politicians who planned to exploit the NSDAP's considerable (if declining) electoral strength to conduct conservative policies. Instead, by giving Hitler the chancellorship, they provided the Nazi movement with the one success which could – and did – rally it in 1933.

The diversity and breadth of the Nazi movement has prompted some historians to question whether the organisation displayed essentially similar characteristics throughout Germany during the years of its political offensive. Buchloh's study of the NSDAP in Duisburg demonstrates that Hitler avoided detailed interference in issues concerning economic policy, which allowed 'the local NS-organisations sufficient maneouvrability to orientate their propaganda and activities to the specific political and socio-economic attributes of the town'.[16] This meant mobilising working-class as well as lower-middle-class support and here the Nazi movement succeeded. Looking elsewhere in Germany, Nazism assumed various forms socially and ideologically which partly reflected the political flexibility demonstrated by Buchloh. Where mass support was obtainable from an impoverished peasantry – as in Schleswig-Holstein – the NSDAP succeeded in mobilising such support.[17] In Westphalia, where workers comprised more than half the economically active population, the NSDAP took care to woo their support, not without success.[18]

The NSDAP's *relative* failure among the working class nationally is better explained by the political character of a section of that class – industrial employees – than by characteristics inherent in Nazism itself. Much of the industrial working class had long been organised within the trade union movement (usually socialist, but sometimes Catholic) and within the SPD, or sometimes the Catholic Centre Party. It would require a certain *naïveté* to expect the destruction of such loyalties within a couple of years by the NSDAP, but there were openings for the Nazi movement even among people associated with this group. The young, and particularly the jobless young who had little personal experience of working-class politics, were an obvious target for the Nazi Party. Among the quarter of the working class employed in crafts and small firms where unionisation and political organisation had made less headway, it seems that the NSDAP fared reasonably well electorally.[19]

Thus Nazi strategy and, consequently, support varied from place to place. The NSDAP might conceivably have further enhanced its appeal by using particular sections of the movement to appeal to particular social groups. Next to the party the Storm Troops (Sturmabteilung) or

SA represented the largest Nazi formation until 1933 and was actually larger than the party during 1933 and 1934. The party itself was aggressively dynamic, but the SA even more so. It was instrumental in taking politics into the streets and market-places of Germany in an age when the mass media were insufficiently developed to feed it into every home. Its youthful, often unemployed members who could devote substantial time and energy to the Nazi cause both provided publicity through marches and rallies and spread it through proselytisation and leafleting. Like Fascism in general, Nazism employed violence to underpin its political message (at times violence seemed to be the message itself) and here, too, the SA was indispensable. In a violent age the NSDAP itself needed protection from political opponents, especially the KPD, and the SA provided this. More important, the SA disrupted rival political groups' campaigns through endless petty fighting, intimidation and, occasionally, terror on a grander scale. Even during the late Weimar period the SA could sometimes virtually force the SPD and, in places, the Centre Party underground. These long-established parties might retain existing support in such circumstances, but, leaving aside their reluctance to find a common, effective, platform on which to fight Nazism, the physical possibilities of attracting fresh support were limited, even at a time when both electoral participation and the size of the electorate were increasing. After Hitler's takeover, the SA had a further vital service to perform. It provided the government with an informal but devastatingly effective means of removing public institutions which hindered the concentration of power at the centre (such as some state governments) and of removing rival political organisations, notably on the left. In short, the new government was able to combine centralised coercion with localised, populist insurrection embodied largely in the SA.[20]

Most histories of the SA have bypassed any detailed discussion of its social character and hence neglect any new insights that this might provide into the appeal and character of Nazism during its rise to power. It has usually been assumed that the SA simply represented the younger and more dynamic adherents of the Nazi movement.[21] None the less, these studies have revealed much about the SA's early political history. To summarise briefly here, it was formed in August 1921 when the NSDAP reorganised its paramilitary wing, the Saalschutz, and renamed it the Sturmabteilung (SA). Under the nominal command of a Freikorps officer from the Brigade Ehrhardt, Klintzsch, and under the effective leadership of a Reichswehr officer, Röhm, the SA provided protection for the Nazi leadership and for party meetings. However, Röhm in particular strove to create an independent, military role for the SA.[22] Hitler had misgivings about this, partly because of the inherent threat to his authority, but also because Röhm's radical, activist leanings were not to his taste. Thus in 1923 the conservative Göring was appointed SA commander, while the forerunner of the SS, the Stoss-trupp Hitler was established as a numerically small, but élitist counter-weight to the SA[23] – a role it was to retain right up to the Röhm purge of mid-1934.

None the less, the SA played a central part in Hitler's abortive Munich putsch of November 1923, which led to its banning nationally. Despite this it survived under the name Frontbann, and Hitler's resolu-tion to seek power through the ballot box after the Munich fiasco (the so-called policy of legality) did not prevent him from appointing Röhm as Frontbann commander in April 1924. Perhaps predictably the two men failed to agree on the role of the revived SA when, in February 1925, Hitler sought to shape it as a propaganda unit closely tied to the party.[24]

Röhm resigned as leader and was replaced in May 1926 by Pfeffer von Salomon, who apparently favoured a political role for the SA rather than a military one. However, Pfeffer came increasingly to share his predecessor's outlook[25] and by August 1930 felt obliged to resign his command because of Hitler's insistence on party supremacy within the Nazi movement.[26] Under Pfeffer the SA had begun to assume the characteristics which brought it a prominent part in national political life during the early 1930s. The original SA had consisted largely of the war generation, containing many former Freikorps members, but during 1927 it began to be regarded as a vehicle for working-class recruitment, largely through street marches in working-class areas.[27] Goebbels, in particular, projected the image of the SA as a working-class body, with, apparently, young and unemployed workers being particularly attracted to the SA.[28] In terms of size, too, the SA's character altered as the economic crisis deepened. It grew from a relatively small, protective troop into a paramilitary force of perhaps 30,000 men by August 1929[29] and 60,000 men by November 1930 with a national rather than a primarily Bavarian membership as had earlier been the case.[30]

When Pfeffer resigned SA–party relations were clouded by financial problems as well as by endemic disputes over SA autonomy and activ-ism. Hitler was particularly concerned about the SA's sometimes destructive activism which endangered his (admittedly cynical) presen-tation of the Nazi movement as a legal and responsible, if dynamic and anti-republican, force.[31] Hitler's personal misgivings about the SA were shared by the authorities who intervened intermittently to restrict SA activities. In July 1930 the SA was banned from wearing uniform in Prussia, but the ban, which applied to the wearing of brown shirts, was circumvented easily by the wearing of white shirts – or no shirts! – and consequently was soon dropped.[32] This compared ominously with the permanent and more effective ban imposed on the KPD's paramilitary wing, the Red Front, in 1929. A more determined effort was made to curb the SA nationally when the Minister of Defence, Groener, banned it totally on 12 April 1932. The move was short-lived, for the right and the army argued that the ban, in effect, favoured the SPD and KPD Verbände (more to the point, they were anxious to make a deal with Hitler) and their opposition precipitated Groener's resignation on 13 May and the rescinding of the ban by the new, arch-conservative von Papen government on 15 June.[33] In any case, neither the Prussian uniform ban of 1930 nor the national ban of 1932 disrupted the SA very greatly. Both were half-heartedly imposed and the manifest disunity among its opponents actually heartened the SA which believed it could weather anything the authorities inflicted on the organisation.

Röhm was reappointed leader of the growing and increasingly assertive SA in January 1931. After Pfeffer's resignation Hitler appointed himself supreme SA leader and made Wagener his chief of staff, but perhaps because he doubted the acceptability of this arrangement to the SA,[34] or perhaps because of personal doubts over his own ability to handle the body,[35] Hitler replaced Wagener with Röhm, choosing in him the man whom he felt could best direct its violent activism along lines more or less acceptable to the NSDAP.

By January 1931 the 100,000-strong SA was almost too much for Röhm. The mutiny of some north German SA leaders under Stennes in April, which followed a crisis in the Berlin SA during the previous autumn, was symptomatic of the SA's impatience with the electoral road to power and the consequent supremacy of the party within the Nazi movement.[36] The mutiny was contained quickly enough and the SA expanded seemingly inexorably to contain 290,941 members by January 1932 and 445,279 members by August.[37] However, the realisation within SA circles in the autumn that the electoral road had failed and that a Nazi electoral setback was imminent caused both a decline in SA strength[38] and a growing propensity within the SA to resort to greater violence and to increasingly radical political acts, the most famous being the co-operation between the SA and KPD during the Berlin transport strike in November 1932.

The appointment of Hitler as Reich Chancellor in January 1933 saved the SA. Its membership soared from around 425,000 to over 2 million within a few months[39] as many of Germany's male unemployed sought to share in the fruits of Hitler's political victory. Material benefits – not least jobs! – were expected, but the SA as a whole also expected that a violent reckoning with Nazism's enemies, whether of the left or the right, would follow the Nazi electoral triumph of March 1933. The party, they found, thought differently. It wished to work with the army, with industry and with the political right.[40]

If general histories of the SA are largely in accord on the above points, studies specialising on the post-takeover crisis in SA–party relations, which culminated in a purge of SA leaders in July 1934, have pinpointed problems in historians' treatment of the SA. These studies, particularly that of Bloch,[41] seek to explain the SA's significance within the wider framework of interwar German history by examining a broader range of socio-economic and political forces which contributed to the decision to purge the SA. Several studies of Nazism have treated the SA similarly, and again substantial disagreement has arisen. At once the SA's social composition becomes important. Fest portrays the SA as an essentially petit bourgeois band of *déclassés* who demanded restitution for the hardships and upheaval inflicted on them by Germany's defeat, and particularly by the economic collapse of the early 1930s: 'desperadoes in search of a pension'.[42] This interpretation is reflected in earlier and later studies which describe the frenetic, vacuous activism of the displaced lower middle classes within the SA. They sought, it is argued, recompense for their socio-economic decline and loss of self-esteem, and sought particularly revenge on the organised working class whose relative emancipation during the Weimar era they, in their destitution, resented bitterly.[43] If Schweitzer would agree with this description of the SA's social background, his perception of its implications differs. In the SA's call (repeated, he feels, by many rank-and-file Nazis) for a 'second revolution' in 1933 and early 1934 he detects the relatively constructive, if unrealistic, wish to return to a pre-capitalist, corporatist order, against which big business, the traditional conservative élite and the senior Nazi Party leadership stood.[44] Other works, which characterise the stormtroopers as unemployed working class, present a radically different interpretation. Weissbecker regards the stormtroopers as victims of Nazi demagogy which was allied with big business.[45] Kele places the SA within a working-class Nazi camp locked in a struggle for supremacy with middle-class elements of the Nazi movement around the time of Hitler's takeover.[46] Diels's account of the same era concentrates on Berlin where, he argues, an SA socially indistinguishable from the Berlin KPD and Reichsbanner was both revolutionary and socialist. Therefore although its nationalism and extreme activism distinguished it from the left, he argues, it was well out of step politically with the Nazi Party and the SS.[47]

Specialised studies of the Röhm purge in 1934 also reach substantially different conclusions depending on differing perceptions, implicit or explicit, of the SA's social profile. Left-wing studies produced by exiled resistance groups after the purge regarded Hitler's blow as the emasculation of a strongly working-class body which, particularly after the Nazi takeover, reflected in its opposition to Hitler's policies popular discontent with the new regime.[48] Postwar studies have varied in their conclusions. Krausnick relates the purge largely to the struggle between the SA's leaders and the army for control of the armed forces.[49] To Gallo it signified the elimination of Nazism's revolutionary wing.[50] Bloch's study wavers between perceiving the SA as a body destitute, unemployed workers led by equally destitute members of the middle classes which, to a certain degree, represented working-class interests, and regarding it as essentially lower middle class in its composition and outlook.[51]

The tendency of historians to break off in mid-1934 is perhaps unfortunate. The SA's significance in high politics may have vanished, but the problems posed by its mass membership remained. In the months following the purge a more compliant leadership struggled to resolve the SA's problems as, helped from March 1935 by the reintroduction of conscription, it was scaled down steadily in size. By the end of 1935 the nature of effects of this readjustment were clear.[52]

Therefore some historians have presented the SA's history in essence as one strand within that of a broadly lower-middle-class movement. For them the SA's role in high politics, including Röhm's dispute with Hitler over the army's future, was very important. Rank-and-file discontent is typified as petit bourgeois resentment and suspicion over the growing accommodation between Hitler and traditional conservative interests. Others, regarding Nazism, at least implicitly, as a mass movement, believe the struggle between party and SA signified a breakdown of the socially diverse coalition of interests which helped Hitler to power. Regarding the SA's rank and file, all would agree that the organisation of hundreds of thousands and then millions within the stormtroopers had its price: the recruits demanded a reward for their commitment. Disagreement centres on the precise nature of these demands. To resolve this question one must establish who the stormtroopers were.

The contrasting interests, hopes and fears of different social and denominational groups during this period make the investigation of the SA's social composition indispensable if its politics are to be fully understood. The problem lies less with the leadership, whose social profile and politics have attracted considerable and often systematic attention,[53] than with the ordinary stormtroopers. Discussion of the latter has usually been subsumed into consideration of the SA as a collective entity with social and political differences between stormtroopers and their leaders noted briefly and often implicitly. This does the historical importance of the ordinary stormtroopers an injustice. The SA's mobilisation of mass support rivalled the party's for a time, and while Hitler's personality coupled with the Leader Principle ensured the domination of the Nazi movement by its leaders, it would have been nothing without its masses. The character of the SA's membership was particularly important because SA recruits were volunteers and free to leave the organisation, although admittedly after January 1933 not without risking official displeasure.

A series of quantitative surveys has provided recently a partial response to the problem by seeking to establish the SA's social profile, albeit without usually distinguishing between leaders and men.[54]

However, the incompleteness of surviving SA membership records, the different approaches adopted, and the contrasting interpretations of basic results obtained have produced glaring disagreements which probably cannot be attributed simply to regional or other variations in the SA's social composition. Not only is this particular issue essentially unresolved, but the studies in question make no claims to be comprehensive analyses of the social and political history of the SA as a mass organisation. Thus the history of ordinary stormtroopers in their own right remains largely unwritten and this book hopes to help fill that gap.

Notes

1 For instance: S. Neumann, *Die Parteien der Weimarer Republik*, 4th edn (Stuttgart, 1977), p. 78. First published as *Die politischen Parteien in Deutschland* (Berlin, 1932).

2 Reichsorganisationsleiter der NSDAP (ed.), *Partei-Statistik. Stand 1. Januar 1935* (Munich, 1935), Vol. 1, p. 70. 'Lower middle class' defined as salaried staff, independent artisans, independent shopkeepers and merchants, civil service and farmers.

3 M. H. Kele, *Nazis and Workers. National Socialist Appeals to German Labor, 1919–1933* (Chapel Hill, NC, 1972) is one of the more recent such works.

4 E. Fröhlich, 'Die Partei auf lokaler Ebene. Zwischen gesellschaftlicher Assimilation und Veränderungsdynamik', in G. Hirschfeld and L. Kettenacker (eds), *The 'Führer State': Myth and Reality. Studies on the Structure and Politics of the Third Reich* (Stuttgart, 1981), pp. 255–69; T. Childers, 'The social bases of the National Socialist vote', *Journal of Contemporary History*, vol. 11, no. 4 (1976), pp. 27, 40: table 1B.

5 K. D. Bracher, *The German Dictatorship. The Origins, Structure and Consequences of National Socialism*, trans. J. Steinberg (London, 1973), pp. 195–204. S. U. Larsen (ed.), *Who Were the Fascists? Social Roots of European Fascism* (Oslo, 1980) argues similarly for a wide range of European fascisms, the German variety included.

6 Childers, 'Social bases', pp. 23, 28, 30.

7 *Partei-Statistik*, pp. 58, 59, 61.

8 ibid.

9 Childers, 'Social bases', p. 30. See also: G. Eley, 'The Wilhelmine right: how it changed', in R. J. Evans (ed.), *Society and Politics in Wilhelmine Germany* (London, 1978), pp. 122–3, where Eley notes that politically the white-collar staff were divided between left and right.

10 B. Moore, Jr, *Injustice. The Social Bases of Obedience and Revolt* (London, 1978), pp. 408–10.

11 *Partei-Statistik*, p. 70.

12 W. Tormin, *Geschichte der deutschen Parteien seit 1848* (Stuttgart, Berlin, Cologne and Mainz 1968), p. 210.

13 Childers, 'Social bases', p. 31.

14 Moore, *Injustice*, p. 411.

15 J. Noakes, *The Nazi Party in Lower Saxony, 1921–1933* (Oxford, 1971), chs 6, 7.

16 I. Buchloh, *Die nationalsozialistische Machtergreifung in Duisburg. Eine Fallstudie* (Duisburg, 1980), p. 181.

17   R. Heberle, *Landbevölkerung und Nationalsozialismus. Eine soziologische Untersuchung der politischen Willensbildung in Schleswig-Holstein 1918–1932* (Stuttgart, 1963).

18   D. Mühlberger, 'The sociology of the NSDAP: the question of working class membership', *Journal of Contemporary History*, vol. 15, no. 3 (1980), pp. 493–511. Very recently Hamilton has reinforced the impression of extreme political opportunism within the NSDAP, with the movement varying its message to suit particular social groups. Hamilton demonstrates that this paid handsome dividends electorally among the well-to-do, among whom in many urban areas the relative level of support for National Socialism was high. R. F. Hamilton, *Who Voted for Hitler?* (Princeton, NJ, 1982).

19   Childers, 'Social bases', pp. 25, 31, 42: tables VII–B, VII–C.

20   Bracher, *German Dictatorship*, pp. 252–71; J. Diehl, *Paramilitary Politics in Weimar Germany* (Bloomington, Ind. and London, 1977), pp. 286–92; J. Klenner, *Verhältnis von Partei und Staat 1933–1945. Dargestellt am Beispiel Bayerns* (Munich, 1974), pp. 37–8.

21   For instance: A. Werner, 'SA und NSDAP. SA: "Wehrverband", "Parteitruppe" oder "Revolutionsarmee"? Studien zur Geschichte der SA und der NSDAP, 1920–1933 (Dissertation, Friedrich Alexander Universität zu Erlangen, 1964); H. Bennecke, *Hitler und die SA* (Munich, 1962); C. Bloch, *Die SA und die Krise des NS-Regimes 1934* (Frankfurt-am-Main, 1970). Bloch, in particular, does note a high incidence of unemployment in the SA, but in all books discussion of the SA's social character does remain general and, usually, implicit. M. H. Kater, 'Zur Soziographie der frühen NSDAP', *Vierteljahreshefte für Zeitgeschichte*, vol. 19, no. 2 (1971), pp. 154–5.

22   Bennecke, *Hitler und SA*, p. 69.

23   Bloch, *SA*, pp. 13–15.

24   Bennecke, *Hitler und SA*, p. 120.

25   Bloch, *SA*, pp. 24–5; Bennecke, *Hitler und SA*, p. 135; P. Hüttenberger, *Die Gauleiter. Studie zum Wandel des Machtgefüges in der NSDAP* (Stuttgart, 1969), p. 66.

26   Bennecke, *Hitler und SA*, p. 152; Hüttenberger, *Gauleiter*, p. 67; Noakes, *Nazi Party*, pp. 182–3.

27   Bennecke, *Hitler und SA*, p. 126.

28   Kele, *Nazis and Workers*, p. 123.

29   Bennecke, *Hitler und SA*, p. 140.

30   Werner, 'SA und NSDAP', pp. 544–52.

31   ibid., pp. 461, 473.

32   Bennecke, *Hitler und SA*, p. 146.

33   G. A. Craig, *The Politics of the Prussian Army, 1640–1945* (Oxford, 1975), pp. 446–56.

34   Bloch, *SA*, p. 34.

35   Bennecke, *Hitler und SA*, p. 149.

36   Werner, 'SA und NSDAP', pp. 463–4, 531.

37   ibid., pp. 544–52.

38   Bundesarchiv Koblenz (BA), SA Archiv (NS23)/337. SA der NSDAP. OSAF Führungsamt. München, 3.9.1935.

39   M. Broszat, *Der Staat Hitlers. Grundlegung und Entwicklung seiner inneren Verfassung* (Munich, 1969), p. 256. This growth pre-dated the absorption of some right-wing *Verbände*, notably the Stahlhelm, into the SA.

40   Bloch, *SA*, pp. 51–2, 78; Broszat, *Staat Hitlers*, pp. 257–8; K. Gossweiler, 'Der Übergang von der Weltwirtschaftskrise zur Rüstungskonjunktur', *Jahrbuch für Wirtschaftsgeschichte*, vol. 2 (1968), pp. 55–116; R. J. O'Neill, *The German Army and the Nazi Party, 1933–1939* (London, 1966), p. 43.

41   Bloch, *SA*.

42   J. Fest, *The Face of the Third Reich*, trans. M. Bullock (London, 1972), pp. 209–11, 217–23. Quotation, p. 223.

43 W. S. Allen, *The Nazi Seizure of Power. The Experience of a Single German Town. 1930–1935* (Chicago, 1965), pp. 74–5; Bracher, *German Dictatorship*, pp. 344–5 – but see pp. 238, 272 where Bracher speaks of SA success in attracting the unemployed working class; I. Fetscher, 'Zur Kritik des sowjetmarxistischen Faschismusbegriffs', in G. Jasper (ed.), *Von Weimar zu Hitler, 1930–1933* (Cologne and Berlin, 1968), p. 157; K. Heiden, *Der Fuehrer. Hitler's Rise to Power*, trans. R. Manheim (London, 1967), p. 431; T. W. Mason, 'Labour in the Third Reich 1933–1939', *Past and Present* (1966), p. 113; W. Sauer, *Die Mobilmachung der Gewalt*, Vol. 3 of K. D. Bracher, G. Schulz and W. Sauer, *Die nationalsozialistische Machtergreifung. Studien zur Errichtung des totalitären Herrschaftssystems in Deutschland 1933/34* (Frankfurt- am-Main, Berlin and Vienna, 1974), pp. 233–55.

44 A. Schweitzer, *Big Business in the Third Reich* (London, 1964), pp. 3–5, 35–7, 75–6, 113–19, 125.

45 M. Weissbecker, 'Nationalsozialistische Deutsche Arbeiterpartei (NSDAP) 1919–1945', in D. Fricke *et al.* (eds), *Die bürgerlichen Parteien in Deutschland. Handbuch der Geschichte der bürgerlichen Parteien und anderen bürgerlichen Interessenorganisationen vom Vormärz bis zum Jahre 1945*, Vol. 2 (Leipzig, 1970), p. 403.

46 Kele, *Nazis and Workers*, pp. 148, 182–6, 217–18.

47 R. Diels, *Lucifer ante Portas. Zwischen Severing und Heydrich* (Zurich, 1949), pp. 152–8.

48 K. Bredow, *Hitlerrast. Die Bluttragödie des 30. Juni 1934. Ablauf, Vorgeschichte und Hintergründe* (Saarbrücken, 1935), pp. 29–37; O. Strasser, *Sonnabend 30. Juni: Vorgeschichte, Verlauf, Folgen* (Prague, date unknown), *passim*; *Weissbuch über die Erschiessungen des 30. Juni 1934* (Paris, 1935), pp. 35–73.

49 H. Krausnick, 'Der 30. Juni 1934 – Bedeutung – Hintergründe – Verlauf', *Aus Politik und Zeitgeschichte – Beilage zur Wochenzeitung, 'Das Parlament'*, Vol. 25, no. 54, 30 June 1954.

50 M. Gallo, *Der Schwarze Freitag der SA. Die Vernichtung des revolutionären Flügels der NSDAP durch Hitlers SS im Juni 1934* (Cologne and Hamburg, 1972).

51 Bloch, *SA*, pp. 37–8, 45–6, 68, 146.

52 See pp. 87–9, 90–2, 130–2, 218.

53 M. Jamin, 'Zur Rolle der SA im nationalsozialistischen Herrschaftssystem', in G. Hirschfeld and L. Kettenacker (eds), *The 'Führer State': Myth and Reality. Studies on the Structure and Politics of the Third Reich* (Stuttgart, 1981) is the most recent contribution. Ms Jamin has also carried out a fuller social analysis of the SA's leadership, 'Zwischen den Klassen. Eine quantitative Untersuchung zur Sozialstruktur der SA-Führerschaft' (Dissertation, Rühr-Universität-Bochum, 1982), which was passed after the completion of this book.

54 Specifically on the SA: R. J. Bessel and M. Jamin, 'Nazis, workers and the uses of quantitative evidence', *Social History*, vol. 4, no. 1 (1979), pp. 111–16; C. Fischer and C. Hicks, 'Statistics and the historian: the occupational profile of the SA of the NSDAP', *Social History*, vol. 5, no. 1 (1980), pp. 131–8; M. H. Kater, 'Ansätze zu einer Soziologie der SA bis zur Röhm Krise', in U. Engelhardt *et al.* (eds), *Soziale Bewegung und politische Verfassung* (Stuttgart, 1976), pp. 798–831; P. H. Merkl, *The Making of a Stormtrooper* (Princeton, NJ, 1980), which discusses principally SA and SS members who joined the Nazi movement before 1930; P. H. Merkl, *Political Violence under the Swastika. 581 Early Nazis* (Princeton, NJ, 1975), esp. pp. 581–99, which discusses the same material as found in *Stormtrooper*; M. H. Kater, 'Zum gegenseitigen Verhältnis von SA und SS in der Sozialgeschichte des Nationalsozialismus von 1925 bis 1939', *Vierteljahresschrift für Sozial- und Wirtschaftsgeschichte*, vol. 62, no. 3 (1975), pp. 339–79; M. H. Kater, 'Sozialer Wandel in der NSDAP im Zuge der nationalsozialistischen Machtergreifung', in W. Schieder (ed.), *Faschismus als soziale Bewegung* (Hamburg, 1976), pp. 25–67; L. D. Stokes, 'The social composition of the Nazi Party in Eutin, 1925–32', *International Review of Social History*, vol. 23, pt 1 (1978), pp. 1–32.

2 The SA and German Society: Problems of Interpretation

The complexities of Weimar society impinge on any discussion of the SA's social background and of its membership's aspirations. Germany's rapid industrialisation had created new social forces, but by no means destroyed the old, a process partly reflected in the contrasts between different regions' socio-economic structures. The economic crises of the Weimar era, and particularly the increasing levels of unemployment among social groups from which the SA recruited, complicated the picture further.

Between the censuses of 1882 and 1925 the balance of activities within the German economy had altered considerably even though in absolute terms the numbers engaged in all main economic sectors (with the exception of servants) continued to grow. Agriculture was still the largest single employer in 1882, occupying 42·2 per cent of the working population, but by 1925 this proportion had declined to 30·5 per cent. Industry and crafts displaced agriculture as the largest sector, with its share of the working population rising from 34·3 per cent in 1882 to 42·1 per cent in 1925. Perhaps even more significant was the emergence of a sizeable modern tertiary sector with the proportion of the working population engaged in commerce and communications rising steeply from 8·6 per cent in 1882 to 16·4 per cent by 1925, while the proportion in public service rose slightly from 5·7 to 6·7 per cent. Domestic servants were fading from the scene, with their representation declining from 9·2 per cent in 1882 to 4·3 per cent in 1925.[1] The less detailed 1933 census, taken in the depths of the depression, revealed an acceleration of these trends, with the exception of the industry and crafts sector. This, perhaps disproportionately affected by the depression, declined relatively and absolutely.[2]

There were considerable changes in the internal structure of individual sectors, including industry and crafts. Even in 1848 the craft guilds had decried the threat posed by industrialisation to their economic viability and to the whole lifestyle attached to the guild economy. During the imperial era factory-based industries, accompanying technological change and a progressive concentration of ownership and control, forced the craft sector, relatively speaking, into rapid retreat.[3] However, if this sector was in relative decline, its proprietors remained sufficiently numerous to form a potentially considerable political force, particularly if combined with other members of the lower *Mittelstand* such as shopkeepers, innkeepers, the peasantry and petty officials. The first signs of a distinctive political response from this group emerged even before the First World War,[4] and in the Weimar period the belief that this numerically strong group was being squeezed unjustly between an 'amoral capitalism' and organised labour found more definite political expression.[5]

Ironically, the crisis within the crafts sector during the Weimar era ceased to represent structural decline. Instead it formed part of the general economic crisis which, in the early 1930s, hit larger firms just as hard. The crafts sector had adapted to industrialisation in two ways: through the modernisation of production methods – notably the increasing use of electricity – and through a growing tendency to complement big industry rather than compete with it. Processes unsuited to the production line – many of modern, precision-made components – allowed some craft areas to flourish, while others found a new role servicing and repairing the products of the second industrial revolution, or were themselves a product of this revolution.[6] Outside the cities agriculture remained dependent on a relatively large artisan sector. Therefore despite increasing capital concentration among larger firms and despite the introduction of increasingly impersonal, rational production processes in the factories, a quarter of individuals in the industry and crafts sector remained active in crafts in 1925.[7] Looked at slightly differently, about a third of those in the industry and crafts sector worked in firms employing 10 or fewer people, another third in medium-sized firms employing between 11 and 200 people, and only a third in big firms occupying 201 or more people.[8]

Of course, the despair in the crafts sector during the final years of Weimar was profound, but sometimes historians have tended to over-play the image of this sector as a relic of the pre-industrial era, the death of which was accelerated by the economic crisis of the early 1930s. Furthermore, while many craft enterprises were operated by the pro-prietor alone, over 1·5 million skilled workers and apprentices out of a total labour force of 9·78 million in industry and crafts were engaged in crafts.[9] This substantial number of workers did not exist in an idyllic world of cuckoo-clock manufacture far removed from the realities of modern economic life. Instead their firms were often linked closely with industry and many used their experience and training in the rapidly modernising crafts sector as a preparation for skilled jobs in industry.[10]

Of the other economic sectors less need be said. Agriculture suffered from chronic indebtedness and falling prices, and from a chronic frag-mentation of land tenure, despite the existence of large estates (particu-larly in the north and east of Germany). However, agriculture remained a large employer and, as modernisation aided a recovery in output after the war, its overall significance within the Weimar economy began to increase.[11] In absolute terms, the numbers engaged in farming and forestry rose from 7·13 million in 1882 to 9·8 million in 1925 which allowed agriculture to retain considerable political significance.[12] The structure of employment within agriculture differed markedly from that in industry which implied that farming's political behaviour would also differ. Farm labour, for instance, was seldom unionised and, with exceptions, tended not to vote SPD. In industry and crafts 1·79 million employers and managers occupied 1·46 million salaried staff, 9·78 million workers and 0·22 million members of their own families, while in farming 2·2 million employers occupied 4·79 million members of their own families (predominantly females), but only 2·61 million workers and a mere 0·16 million salaried staff.[13] Therefore, away from the large estates the agricultural working class was much more fragmented than its counterparts in many non-agricultural sectors.

Internal developments in the rapidly growing commerce and communications sector resembled broadly those in industry and crafts. The proportion of persons occupied in larger firms increased until the mid-1920s, although over a third of employers and employees remained in firms occupying three or fewer persons. As in industry, the proportion of smaller firms and of the workforce employed in them increased somewhat during the depression as jobless ex-employees tried to make their own way and some existing firms contracted.[14] The commerce and communications sector also resembled industry and crafts in occupying many more employees than employers and members of their families, but in the former sector salaried staff rather than workers were prevalent. Thus 1·99 million proprietors, managers and members of the professions occupied 2·22 million salaried staff, 1·44 million workers and 0·41 million members of their own families.[15] In the administration and health sectors, too, salaried staff were prevalent.[16]

Therefore no one type of economic activity could be described as typical or dominant in Weimar Germany and, certainly, no single sector represented a homogeneity of interests even between members of the same social class within any sector. This in itself could complicate any assessment of the SA's social character and the difficulties are emphasised further when German society is considered class by class rather than by economic sector. According to the 1925 census, 45·1 per cent of the economically active population of 32 million were workers or wage-earners who formed the largest single group within society, but not an absolute majority. Three further groups, each of similar size, followed: proprietors, the professions and executives (including senior civil servants) who were classified as independents (17·3 per cent), members of proprietors' families helping in the family enterprise, classified as assisting family members (17·0 per cent), and salaried staff and civil servants up to middle grade (16·6 per cent). Servants formed a further 4·1 per cent of the working population.[17] When the male population alone is considered (from which, of course, the SA recruited) things appear rather different.

Servants (0·1 per cent) and assisting family members (6·3 per cent) largely disappear, while independents (21·7 per cent), salaried staff and civil servants (18·7 per cent), and workers (53·2 per cent) feature more prominently.[18]

The 14·4 million-strong working class was concentrated quite heavily within the industry and crafts sector (67·9 per cent), with 11·1 per cent working in agriculture and most of the remainder in commerce and communications. The other two main social groups were distributed more evenly between economic sectors. Of salaried staff and civil servants 27·6 per cent worked in industry and crafts, 42·1 per cent in communications and commerce, 21·8 per cent in administration, and the rest elsewhere. Of independents, about 40 per cent worked in agriculture, 32 per cent in industry and crafts, 22 per cent in commerce and communications, and the rest elsewhere. The other sizeable group, assisting family members, was concentrated overwhelmingly in farming.[19]

Therefore the social structure of any community could, and did, vary greatly according to the type of economic activity prevalent within it. Although the working class was strong nationally, in agricultural regions, in particular, it was very much weaker and often outnumbered by independents and assisting family members. Similarly, if salaried staff showed well nationally, in rural areas they could be all but absent, while their presence was particularly marked in urban areas. This process is illustrated in rough-and-ready fashion by comparing urban Berlin with the tiny, rural Prussian province of Hohenzollern. In Berlin the working population comprised: 15·4 per cent independents, 2·2 per cent assisting family members, 30·5 per cent salaried staff and civil servants, and 45·9 per cent workers. In Hohenzollern, by contrast, independents constituted 26·7 per cent of the working population, assisting family members 39·1 per cent, salaried staff and civil servants only 6·7 per cent, and workers only 25·5 per cent.[20]

It follows that in relative terms the working class and salaried employees were represented most weakly in smaller communities (of under 10,000 inhabitants) while independents and assisting family members were represented most strongly in these same communities. The reverse was almost true of cities of 100,000 inhabitants or more, but the strongest relative working-class representation was actually in communities of 10,000 to 20,000 and the weakest relative independent representation in communities of 50,000 to 100,000. However, it would be mistaken to regard the working class as an essentially urban phenomenon, even if among other social groups relative strengths tended to reflect absolute strengths. In fact, over 50 per cent or 7·46 million of workers lived in communities of under 10,000 and only 28 per cent or 3·97 million in cities of over 100,000.[21]

The social composition of different age groups further illustrates the complexities of interpretation. Among the male population the great majority of independents were older than 30, while among assisting family members the opposite was true. Workers were concentrated heavily in the age range 14 to 30 with a considerably lower relative representation in older age groups. Only salaried staff and civil servants were spread fairly evenly through all age ranges. Therefore, the male working population aged 20 to 30 was 63 per cent working class, 20 per cent salaried employees and civil servants, 7 per cent independents, and 10 per cent assisting family members. At age 40 to 60 it was only 42 per cent working class, still 20 per cent salaried staff and civil servants, but 37 per cent independents, and 1 per cent assisting family members.[22] Thus, it would be mistaken to regard any of the broader classes as caste-like groups which had little or no personal contact with one another. Not only did intergenerational mobility occur, but a certain degree of mobility within an individual's lifetime.

The complexity of Germany's interwar social structure was also accentuated by legislation concerning salaried employees shortly after the founding of the republic. Many public employees who had been occupied as wage-earners before the war found their status upgraded to that of salaried employee in Weimar. The jobs were often menial and with a growing tendency to routinisation and rationalisation throughout the economy, were becoming more so.[23] None the less, the employees concerned were classified by the census as salaried staff and, consequently, have been regarded generally as lower middle class. As any division within the salaried staff group between the working and middle classes would inevitably be arbitrary and even misleading, the historian is best advised to apply universally the label 'lower middle class'. Even so, many salaried staff held jobs (sometimes manual) little different from those considered working class,[24] had grown up and lived in communities considered working class, often joined socialist trade unions and often supported the SPD – generally regarded as a workers' party.[25] By the same token, some wage-earners – classified by the census as workers – in small workshops in rural areas experienced lifestyles more akin to a patriarchal, pre-industrial economy and had never supported the SPD.

Therefore, while the core of any class can be identified relatively easily – in the working class's case the several million urban and industrial workers – problems arise at an extremely broad margin and involve millions of individuals. Too purist a definition of any class threatens to produce an ideal type seldom found in reality, while any broader definition threatens to produce a group which possesses relatively few common interests. To be sure, a large block of working-class, although not exclusively industrial working-class, Germans supported the SPD and, from 1919, the KPD (and for a time the USPD), and lived in communities where most people did the same. Furthermore, they belonged to clubs and organisations run by the SPD or KPD. In a sense they had become a society within society – not least because of the rejection and even persecution of socialism in the imperial era. However, about half of the working class did not vote for the left[26] and if workers are regarded simply as those supporting the KPD and SPD while supporters of the NSDAP became, virtually *a priori*, members of the middle class as some historians have implied,[27] any further discussion of the social bases of political parties becomes superfluous and the realities of political behaviour in twentieth-century Germany are distorted.

Changes within the core of the working class have also created problems. There is general agreement that the nature of work altered during the 1920s. The rationalisation and streamlining of production methods and the growing propensity to regard workers and even salaried staff as factors of production without regard to their moral worth became widespread. The role of the skilled worker within some industries diminished and here growing numbers of skilled men were occupied in routine, semi-skilled tasks, although Preller reminds us that this rationalisation aided job mobility within and between factories. The skilled worker was no longer tied to a specific process in a specific works, as had sometimes been the case previously.[28]

A fiercer debate has centred around the living standards and lifestyles of the working classes. One body of opinion, as represented by Geiger, has pointed to evidence of upward social mobility within the Weimar working class and argued that with increasing public welfare expenditure, the overall living standards of workers were rising to the point where sections of the working class were adopting a more middle-class lifestyle.[29] Thus Kater, who accepts this interpretation, has classified skilled workers both in crafts and industry as lower middle class in his work on the SA and on Nazism generally.[30] He regards the rump working class as distinctly a minority in society.[31] Other writers, notably Kuczynski, have pointed to falling real wage rates during much of the 1920s and reached the opposite conclusions. Kuczynski argues that even the best-paid workers, such as the Berlin bricklayers, sometimes faced months when their wages fell below subsistence level and that for the majority matters were often considerably worse.[32] Similar debates have surrounded working conditions among salaried staff, although here the problems are of a more relative nature.

As will be seen, the depression created infinitely more miserable conditions from 1929 onwards, but even leaving that aside temporarily, any statistical social classification of a mass organisation such as the SA clearly must simplify and generalise substantially, or attain levels of complexity bordering on the meaningless. In fact, the statistics alone cannot do all the work. The shades of meaning attaching to the relatively simplified tabular presentations and the devastating social impact of the depression will, therefore, be examined in a wider discussion of the SA and its members. To that extent the statistical analysis of the SA's membership serves as a prerequisite for interpretation. That said, even the relatively formal process of classifying by occupational category in tabular form raises problems. For instance, occupational descriptions reserved for formally trained skilled workers sometimes lost their meaning when skilled men were transferred to semi-skilled work. Other occupational descriptions not requiring a formal training were used by men of greatly varying degrees of skill. These and similar difficulties recommend use of the German census's largely formalistic approach which classified individuals basically according to their relationship to the means of production.[33]

Even this method must recognise that the depression disrupted German socio-economic life so massively as to complicate a basic tabular presentation. The official census grouped individuals according to the job held at the time of survey, which doubtless worked well enough during periods of economic stability. The principle could be extended to allow classification of SA members either according to the job held when their membership files were compiled, or to the last job held before each became unemployed. However, this brushes over the problems of interpretation produced by men working, or having last worked, in short-term jobs which fell well below their reasonable expectations.

This delicate problem was recognised by the SA's own membership lists and files, which tended to describe stormtroopers according to the job for which they had trained or in which they had last worked on a steady basis – a practice usually repreated by the stormtroopers in their own writings. As the depression made the very notion of a steady occupation a fiction for most stormtroopers, and blurred the distinction between skilled and semi-skilled labour in particular,[34] this approach probably reflects more accurately the social origins of the SA's membership. This more interpretative procedure has been adopted, while retaining the basic social categories used by the census, albeit in the knowledge that the stormtroopers' occupational status will be somewhat exaggerated in the process, and that the SA was more 'proletarianised' than results will suggest.

Any social analysis set in the German interwar era is shot through with linguistic pitfalls for the English-speaking reader. The translation of some terms literally from German into English has created considerable misunderstandings where perception of the terms differ greatly in the two languages. The most spectacular example of this occurs with the word *Handwerker* which, translated literally, means artisan or handicraftsman. To the English-speaking reader the word artisan produces an image rooted in pre-industrial times of the independent craftsman working at his trade in his own workshop. In interwar Germany, as suggested earlier, things were different. Certainly the word *Handwerker* could apply in this way, but it pertained equally in the case of skilled employees, working in firms of all descriptions, providing they had qualified as journeymen (*Gesellen*). The word journeyman also suggests a throwback to a bygone age in the English language, but in Germany the attainment of a skill – and often a craft skill – was more usual within the non-agricultural working class than it was to remain unskilled. Thus in Düsseldorf the workers on the city transport department's pay-roll were classified as 'leading artisans', 'artisans', and 'non-artisans'. More generally, of workers in industry and crafts, 71 per cent exercised a formal trade skill in 1925 and, even in 1933 in the depths of the depression and after eight years of rapid rationalisation, 56·6 per cent of employed workers continued to do so.[35] Of the remainder, a very high proportion were in semi-skilled work and sometimes possessed a journeyman's ticket none the less. Independent fitters, plumbers, painters, carpenters and the like could be identified in German by the suffix '-master' (*Meister*) after their occupation. In the case of storm-troopers, *curricula vitae* were available in thousands of instances and only on one or two occasions did an independent artisan omit to describe himself as a master or make his independent status perfectly clear in some other way in his formal job description; for instance, by using the word proprietor (*Inhaber*).

If the interpretation of source material raises problems, its selection is no less difficult. SA regulations demanded that stormtroopers belong simultaneously to the NSDAP and, had this procedure been observed, examination of the younger members in the relatively detailed and complete party membership records would have said much about the SA's social composition.[36] In fact, SA records indicate that before January 1933 only about half of stormtroopers belonged to the party,[37] while during 1933 and 1934 the SA recruited massively at a time when the party barred new members. By early 1934 perhaps only a quarter of stormtroopers belonged to the NSDAP.[38] This suggests both that an examination of party records alone is an insufficient basis for analysing the SA's membership and – while remembering that the party itself ceased recruitment in May 1933 – that the SA was possibly attracting elements of the population who found membership of the NSDAP uninteresting.

SA membership records were kept less systematically than the party's until 1934 and the subsequent loss and destruction of much material has not helped matters. None the less, a sufficient range and variety of sources, from areas contrasting greatly in socio-economic structure and cultural background, survive to provide a fair indication of the SA's social structure nationally.

Some sources are more helpful than others. Most informative are the regimental records compiled from 1934 which consist of a personal file for each stormtrooper. These contain a detailed membership record form containing biographical information as well as each SA member's service record. The files also frequently included a *curriculum vitae* and a short political essay written by recruits on joining the SA, and correspondence between the SA and external bodies, including employers, about the stormtrooper in question. With such detailed information many of the ambiguities surrounding the issue of social background can be resolved and similar types of records compiled by the Berlin Document Center and Gestapo offices are equally informative. Unfortunately, sources of this calibre are in limited supply, even for the years 1934 and 1935, and records compiled during the closing years of the Weimar Republic never meet these high standards. Nevertheless, the membership lists compiled by SA units at most levels in the chain of command which list storm-troopers individually by name, occupation, usually age, and sometimes both place of residence and date of entry into (and departure from) the SA are very helpful. When taken in conjunction with other information contained in the routine correspondence of the unit concerned, a reason-ably clear picture of that unit's social composition emerges.[39] The combination of such sources to produce a national picture obviously falls short of the techniques of stratified random sampling employed by the contemporary political scientist, but the cumulative impact of many individual sources which, with a few notable exceptions, tell a similar story, provides revealing evidence of the SA's social background during the early 1930s.

Some police and court records are equally detailed and have been included in this analysis.[40] Others, such as a batch from the far east of prewar Germany, are often less informative. Therefore only one such source has been presented, that from the District of Allenstein in East Prussia which, like the other sources in the batch,[41] suggests that in parts of north-eastern Germany the SA assumed distinctive characteristics.[42] Allenstein was, admittedly, an unusual district, for it contained a large, non-German minority. The 1925 census admitted to a Polish and Masurian (a Polish dialect) population of over 110,000, the majority of whom spoke little or no German, within a total population of under 550,000.[43] If this minority were concentrated within any particular social group (and many were farm labourers), then it is reasonable to assume that the group would be represented thinly in the chauvinist and racialist SA, irrespective of the SA's attractiveness to that social group elsewhere.

Before examining the SA's membership records, it is worth considering some of the comments of its contemporaries. The Australian historian, Roberts, who visited Germany during the mid-1930s noted that, 'The SA were a mixed body, mostly workers or students or lower-middle-class tradesmen; whereas the SS, from the outset, were more definitely bourgeois'.[44] Roberts does not quantify the relative strengths of these three social groups, but reports from provincial SA leaders, and party officials, in many districts of Germany agree broadly with Roberts, while stressing, in particular, the SA's attraction for the working classes. In 1929 the NSDAP in Elbing, East Prussia, noted that workers predominated among its recruits: 'Our SA numbers over seventy men; we are winning recruits daily, above all from the working class.'[45] SA leaders in Petersdorf, eastern Brandenburg, reported in April 1930 that their units contained '80 per cent manual workers',[46] while in mid-1930 the Berlin SA wrote of the 'pleasingly large numbers of proletarians in our ranks'.[47] The commander of the Upper Silesian SA painted a similar picture in 1932, reporting that recruitment was 'from the working class and the poorest sections of the population'.[48] The same picture prevailed after the Nazi takeover. For instance, when writing to SA headquarters in late 1934, the leader of the Rheinhessen SA stressed the predominance of workers in his units, although his assessment of working-class political sentiment appears over-optimistic:

> The Führer has succeeded in winning over the German worker as his truest follower. This is confirmed by the fact that the SA is composed largely of manual workers, who loyally and selflessly stand at the ready.'[49]

The SA's opponents, among them the KPD, were also interested in its social composition. The KPD was sufficiently concerned about the SA's penetration of the unemployed working classes to direct an energetic propaganda campaign at the SA's working-class members, which reinforces the plausibility of SA leaders' claims. Typical of this campaign was a leaflet produced in the second half of 1932:

> Proletarians of the SA and SS Companies . . . Break with Hitler! Come to us! . . . We'll win anyway, with or against you! Proletarians, consider where you belong! Workers as poor as yourself are speaking to you. Red Front![50]

However, while intriguing, these and similar reports are impressionistic and, sometimes, biased by their authors' motives. The recent historical debate has, therefore, centred justifiably on an evaluation of primary SA membership data which provides the fullest and most easily verifiable picture of the SA's social composition now available.

Notes

1 *Statistisches Jahrbuch für das deutsche Reich, 1934* (Berlin, 1934), Vol. I: *Gebietsein-teilung und Bevölkerung*, p. 19, table 14b.
2 L. Preller, *Sozialpolitik in der Weimarer Republik* (Düsseldorf, 1978), pp. 93–4.
3 Preller, *Sozialpolitik*, p. 96.
4 D. Blackbourn, *Class, Religion and Local Politics in Wilhelmine Germany. The Centre Party in Württemberg before 1914* (New Haven, Conn. and London, 1980); G. Eley, 'The Wilhelmine right', in R. J. Evans (ed.), *Society and Politics in Wilhelmine Germany* (London, 1978); R. Gellately, *The Politics of Economic Despair. Shopkeepers and German Politics 1890–1914* (London, 1974).
5 K. D. Bracher, *The German Dictatorship* (London, 1973), pp. 195–204; H. A. Winkler, *Mittelstand, Demokratie und Nationalsozialismus. Die politische Entwicklung von Handwerk und Kleinhandel in der Weimarer Republik* (Cologne, 1972).
6 Preller, *Sozialpolitik*, pp. 99–100.
7 ibid., p. 100.
8 ibid., p. 97.
9 ibid., p. 101.
10 ibid., p. 100.
11 ibid., p. 95.
12 *Statistisches Jahrbuch*, Vol. 1, p. 19, table 14b.
13 ibid., p. 23, table 20.
14 Preller, *Sozialpolitik*, pp. 106–11.
15 *Statistisches Jahrbuch*, Vol. 1, p. 23, table 20.
16 ibid.
17 ibid., p. 19, table 14c.
18 ibid.
19 ibid., p. 23, table 20.
20 ibid., p. 21, table 17.
21 ibid., p. 20, table 16c.
22 ibid., p. 24, table 21.
23 Preller, *Sozialpolitik*, pp. 115, 133–4.
24 ibid.
25 T. Childers, 'The social bases of the National Socialist vote,' *Journal of Contemporary History*, vol. 11, no. 4 (1976), p. 30; Eley, 'Wilhelmine right', pp. 122–3; R. N. Hunt, *German Social Democracy, 1918–1933* (Chicago, 1970), pp. 99–105, 128–30.
26 D. Mühlberger, 'The sociology of the NSDAP', *Journal of Contemporary History*, vol. 15, no. 3 (1980), p. 504.
27 For instance, T. W. Mason, 'The coming of the Nazis', *Times Literary Supplement*, no. 3,752, 1 February, 1974, p. 95. Cf. J. Wickham, 'The Working Class Movement in Frankfurt-am-Main during the Weimar Republic' (D.Phil., University of Sussex, 1979), ch. 1, where Wickham argues that the working-class movement cannot be equated with loyalty to particular parties.
28 Preller, *Sozialpolitik*, pp. 125–33.
29 T. Geiger, *Die Klassengesellschaft im Schmelztiegel* (Cologne and Hagen, 1949), pp. 57–73, 168–76.
30 M. H. Kater, 'Zur Soziographie der frühen NSDAP', *Vierteljahreshefte für Zeitgeschichte*, vol. 19, no. 2 (1971), pp. 132–7.
31 M. H. Kater, 'Zum gegenseitigen Verhältnis von SA und SS in der Sozialgeschichte des Nationalsozialismus von 1925 bis 1939', *Vierteljahresschrift für Sozial- und Wirtschaftsgeschichte*, vol. 62, no. 3 (1975), p. 356, n. 74.
32 J. Kuczynski, *A Short History of Labour Conditions under Industrial Capitalism. Vol. 3, Part 1: Germany 1800 to the Present Day* (London, 1945), pp. 222–54, esp. p. 229.

33 For an example of this process see *Statistisches Jahrbuch*, Vol. 1, p. 19, table 14c. The tables in ch. 3 of this book depicting the SA's social background either subdivide the basic categories of the official census or, when direct comparison is made with official figures, employ the basic categories themselves.

34 Even before the depression many skilled men, although still classified as skilled in labour statistics, had begun to take on semi-skilled tasks. This makes distinguishing between skilled and semi-skilled difficult, and when the depression joined forces with rationalisation to necessitate some trading down of skills by workers, the problem became still greater. Preller, *Sozialpolitik*, pp. 118–20.

35 Preller, *Sozialpolitik*, p. 118.

36 A number of historians have, in fact, assumed that this regulation was upheld: Kater, 'Soziographie', pp. 154–5; Mühlberger, 'Sociology', p. 510, n. 53.

37 For instance: of Hamburg stormtroopers attending Tinsdahl training camp during summer 1932, less than half were party members. Figures available for 8 out of 12 courses. 109 participants were party members, 183 were not (BA, NS23/402. SA der NSDAP, Hamburg. SA Ausbildungslager Tinsdahl). In 1932, Companies 1L, 3L and 4L of the Munich SA recorded party membership numbers in SA membership lists. 229 stormtroopers were in the party, 212 not so (Bayrisches Hauptstaatsarchiv München (BHStA), Abteilung I (Abt. I), Sonderabgabe I (So. I)/1549). Membership lists of above companies. See also M. Jamin, 'Zur Rolle der SA im nationalsozialistischen Herrschaftssystem', in G. Hirschfeld and L. Kettenacker (eds), *The 'Führer State'* (Stuttgart, 1981), p. 333.

38 Jamin, 'Rolle der SA', p. 333, n. 25. Although the figures apply to 1 January 1935 it seems unlikely that there were significantly more party members in the SA in early 1934.

39 These sources are utilised and identified in Chapter 3.

40 See Chapter 3, note 19.

41 All the sources are used in R. J. Bessel, 'The SA in the Eastern Regions of Germany, 1925 to 1934' (D. Phil., Oxford University, 1980), pp. 80–7. They are the most extensive material pertaining to the pre-1933 SA available for the particular area considered by Bessel, which explains his use of them, but they raise substantial problems. They do not identify SA members individually by name and occupation, imparting their information instead in tabular form under classifications which sometimes reflect social class, but in other cases within the same table identify economic sectors. The problems created hardly require elaboration and, unfortunately, too little of the groundwork from which the tables were compiled survives to allow any reassessment of the results. Even as it stands one of the tables fails to identify the district which it covers, leaving the hapless historian to guess its origin as best he may.

42 See Chapter 3, Table 3.2 and note 27.

43 *Statistisches Jahrbuch*, Vol. 1, p. 18, table 13.

44 S. H. Roberts, *The House that Hitler Built*, 12th edn (London, 1945), p. 107.

45 Staatliches Archivlager in Göttingen, Staatsarchiv Königsberg (Archivbestände Preussischer Kulturbesitz) – henceforward SAG – Rep. 240/C80a. Ortsgruppe Elbing, 11.8.1929.

46 BA, NSDAP Hauptarchiv (NS26)/214. Bericht über den SA-Aufmarsch am 5./6. IV in Stentsch und Schwiebus. Petersdorf, den 7. April 1930. gez. Friedrich u. Lindemann.

47 BA, NS26/133. Anonymous testimonial concerning Berlin SA (73 pp., undated), p. 63.

48 BA, NS23/474. SA der NSDAP. Bezug 2580/32. An Chef des Stabes, Ernst Röhm, München. Oppeln, den 22. September 1932.

49 BA, NS26/262. SA der NSDAP. Führer der Brigade 150, Rheinhessen. Lagebericht für das 4. Vierteljahr 1934. Mainz, den 19. Dezember 1934.

50 BA, Sammlung Schumacher (Sch)/330. Achtung! Lesen! Proleten der SA- und SS-Stürme. Die Kommune spricht zu Euch [6 November 1932]. See also H. Weber, *Völker hört die Signale. Der deutsche Kommunismus, 1916–1966* (Munich, 1967), pp. 39–44, 65–6, 108–10, 130.

3 *The SA's Social Composition*

The Occupational Background of the Active SA's Rank and File, 1929–35

During the final years of Weimar, the effects of the depression and a mistrust of, or disenchantment with, the republic's institutions combined to provide a fertile breeding ground for activist groups such as the SA. Between 1929 and January 1933 its membership expanded from under 50,000 to almost half a million.[1]

The rank-and-file SA was evidently a socially differentiated body during this period (Table 3.1), but certain occupational categories predominated. Particularly large numbers of stormtroopers worked, or before becoming unemployed had worked, as semi-skilled and skilled workers. Most remaining stormtroopers worked, or had worked, as unskilled workers or salaried staff and taking all workers and salaried staff, four-fifths of the stormtroopers in Table 3.1 are included. Of the remaining fifth, many were university students. Therefore, it seems that very few ordinary stormtroopers were men of independent means, with most middle-class stormtroopers being salaried employees. Furthermore, middle-class stormtroopers were outnumbered decisively by the working-class membership.

Columns 1 to 5 of Table 3.1 subdivide the data according to provenance, thereby revealing both similarities and differences between sources. The Eutin SA (column 1) was based in a small country town, albeit with a grander past as a grand-ducal residence, in eastern Holstein surrounded by an agricultural district containing some large estates.[2] Its membership included a rather high proportion of unskilled workers and relatively few skilled workers, a feature which apparently characterised SA units outside the larger towns and cities. Its middle-class membership evidently was not in the main independent, consisting instead predominantly of white-collar and salaried manual employees. In his study of the Eutin NSDAP, Stokes confirms this impression of the local SA, writing:

> Nearly two out of every five brownshirts in 1929 were either unskilled or trained workers, compared with only 17% in this category among those party members who had joined the *Ortsgruppe* before December 1929 and still belonged to it in May 1932. If to these are added the handicraftsmen (who in almost every case were probably too young to own their own shop), a clear majority of the SA was 'proletarian' whereas no more than 34% of the party membership at the end of 1929 could be so described. White-collar employees, along

Table 3.1 *Occupational Background of Stormtroopers, Active SA Rank and File, 1929–30 1 1933.*

Numbers Occupational Groups			Sources			Totals
	1	2	3	4	5	
Unskilled workers	11	23	54	45	43	176
(Semi-) skilled workers	20	14	349	84	108	575
Salaried manual	3	1	52	5	10	71
Salaried white-collar	13	4	148	20	34	219
Civil servants	0	4	11	4	1	20
Master craftsmen	0	0	4	3	2	9
Independent proprietors	4	8	12	3	4	31
Farmers	4	4	3	18	16	45
Assisting family members	0	0	0	0	1	1
Professions, independents	0	2	33	1	1	37
University students	0	1	93	6	5	105
Miscellaneous	0	0	14	3	6	23
Totals	55	61	773	192	231	1,312

Percentages Occupational Groups			Sources			Totals
	1	2	3	4	5	
Unskilled workers	20·0	37·7	7·0	23·4	18·6	13·4
(Semi-) skilled workers	36·4	23·0	45·1	43·8	46·8	43·8
Salaried manual	5·5	1·6	6·7	2·6	4·3	5·4
Salaried white-collar	23·6	6·6	19·1	10·4	14·7	16·7
Civil servants	0·0	6·6	1·4	2·1	0·4	1·5
Master craftsmen	0·0	0·0	0·5	1·6	0·9	0·7
Independent proprietors	7·3	13·1	1·6	1·6	1·7	2·4
Farmers	7·3	6·6	0·4	9·4	6·9	3·4
Assisting family members	0·0	0·0	0·0	0·0	0·4	0·1
Professions, independents	0·0	3·3	4·3	0·5	0·4	2·8
University students	0·0	1·6	12·0	3·1	2·2	8·0
Miscellaneous	0·0	0·0	1·8	1·6	2·6	1·8
Totals*	100·0	100·0	100·0	100·0	100·0	100·0

* Percentage totals not exact due to rounding.

Notes: Civil Servants – lower and middle grades only.

Proprietors – traders, independent salesmen, shopkeepers, small businessmen.

Assisting family members – family members working full-time on farms and in small firms.

Professions, independents – professions, senior civil servants, industrialists, landowners.

Sources: 1 Eutin, summer 1929.

2 Hessen-Nassau, 1929.

3 Munich, late summer 1932.

4 Small sources from throughout Germany, 1929–30 1 1933.

5 Police and courts records of stormtroopers.

with all but the two merchants and businessmen who were independent ... made up an additional 30% of the troop. The latter pair, a
pensioned non-commissioned officer, five farmers (some of whom
may actually have been agricultural workers on nearby estates), a
doctor and a lawyer ... – together 15% – rounded off the unit. In all
likelihood, hardly more than a half-dozen Eutin SA members
enjoyed a middle- class existence.[3]

In 1937 the *Gau* chronicler of Hessen-Nassau collected brief autobiog-
raphies from the 839 bearers of the Nazi Golden Medal of Honour
(*Goldenes Ehrenzeichen*) in his *Gau*.[4] Seventy-two of these were
identifiable as ordinary stormtroopers in the Active SA during 1929,
although the true figure is doubtless somewhat higher. Sixty-one
divulged their 1929 occupation or, if unemployed, their former occupation.

These stormtroopers (column 2) lived in a Prussian province which
stretched along the east bank of the Rhine and the north bank of the
Main from opposite Koblenz in the north to beyond Frankfurt-am-
Main in the east. It included much farmland and forest, but also towns
and industrial cities, notably Frankfurt itself. Confessionally Hessen-
Nassau was mixed, although with Protestants predominating. It seems
that in 1929 many stormtroopers from Hessen-Nassau were town and
city dwellers.[5] Of the unskilled workers only two certainly worked in
agriculture whilst eight worked or had worked in factories. Among the
remaining thirteen, whose precise type of work is unclear, ten were city
dwellers and therefore probably factory or workshop employees. The
skilled workers, too, were largely town or city dwellers, employed in
factories or, more often, workshops. These workshop-employed stormtroopers reflected Hessen-Nassau's economic structure with few large
factories outside the cities of the Rhine–Main basin and with many
small businesses even within Frankfurt.[6] The relatively high proportion of middle-class independents contrasted with the smaller numbers
of salaried employees, a situation which had probably reversed by 1932
in the Frankfurt SA at least and had certainly altered there by 1934.[7]
However, the small middle-class representation in the Hessen-Nassau
source precludes any further analysis.

The Munich SA (column 3) developed in an overwhelmingly urban
environment which contained a host population quite distinct from that
in Eutin and somewhat unlike that in Hessen-Nassau.[8] Urban Germany
contained high concentrations of white-collar staff and civil servants
and, unlike rural Germany, a largely skilled manual labour force. Rural
Germany certainly possessed skilled workers in the crafts sector, but
also featured a large, unskilled agricultural labour force. Munich was
no exception to the urban pattern and the dominance of semi-skilled
and skilled labour and of salaried staff among the stormtroopers seems

to reflect this aspect of Munich's social composition. However, the Munich SA was singularly unsuccessful in recruiting members of the independent *Mittelstand*, doing much better among another basically middle-class group, university students.

This said, the results in column 3 must be treated with caution. Munich's SA was organised within Regiment L which was subdivided into around twenty-seven companies.[9] Membership lists for nine companies and a battalion's motor troop have survived which means that perhaps a third of the Munich SA is present in Table 3.1. Eight of these nine companies belonged to Battalion I/L which was based in north and north-west Munich, covering areas of contrasting social background.[10] SA companies were usually based on a particular locality and, understandably, reflected that locality's social composition to some degree. Thus Company 3/L, based in south and central Schwabing around the university contained only 25·8 per cent workers, but 38·3 per cent salaried staff and 22·5 per cent students.[11] By contrast, Company 6/L from the more working-class district of Neuhausen-South was 63·5 per cent working class and 27 per cent salaried staff,[12] while Company 5/L from the working-class Borstei district was 72·3 per cent working class and, predictably, contained no students.[13] One company (16/L) belonged to Battalion II/L which was based in the working-class districts surrounding the Ostbahnhof. This particular company from Haidhausen and the streets north and west of the Ostbahnhof was 76·5 per cent working class and only contained 14·7 per cent salaried staff.[14] Most other units in Battalion II/L were probably similar in character. Battalion III/L was concentrated around Laim and the Westend, south of the main railway and west of the River Isar. In 1930 Laim already had a flourishing and predominantly working-class SA.[15]

Therefore, there were probably fewer students, relatively speaking, in the Munich SA than the surviving membership lists suggest. Were the lists from Battalion III/L and the remaining lists from Battalion II/L available they would probably reveal that this drop in the proportion of students was made up for largely by workers.

The small sources (column 4) include eleven complete SA units and part of a twelfth.[16] Of the 192 stormtroopers represented, 50 belonged to urban units, 8 to a town-based unit and 134 to small-town and rural units from many parts of Germany. Therefore, the small sources provide, admittedly in a rough-and-ready fashion, some indication of the SA's composition nationally. The presence of some rural units affects the result in several ways: the proportion of unskilled labour is higher than average, the representation of salaried staff is depressed and farmers are better represented. None the less, the dominance of workers and salaried employees remains unchallenged overall. Taking the eight small-town and rural sources alone, the workers generally outnumbered the middle-class group by a factor of three to one, with unskilled workers strongly represented. The middle class was represented more by independents, especially farmers, and less by salaried staff than average. One village deviated strikingly from this pattern. The SA in the agricultural village of Halvestorf, Lower Saxony, comprised 62·5 per cent farmers and 31·3 per cent workers in 1931. However, these farmers were extremely young and it is plausible that some were either farmers' sons anticipating their future status (if, indeed, they were to inherit the farm) or farm labourers exaggerating their social position.[17] In any case, the figure of 31·3 per cent workers was probably not appreciably different from the overall representation of workers in the local population – such a figure was typical for rural Germany. Perhaps more remarkable was the absence of any middle-class groups other than farmers. The town-based source from Allenstein, East Prussia, is unexceptional, as are two Munich-based sources (1930) from Laim and Neuhausen. The Frankfurt-am-Main unit, Company 17/81, by contrast, was only 51·9 per cent working class, with a powerful lower-middle-class representation (37 per cent). Of the ten lower-middle-class stormtroopers, eight were salaried employees. The remaining 11·1 per cent of the source were students.[18] Whether this small source is representative of the city's SA in 1932 is impossible to say, but the recurrence of a high proportion of salaried staff in a late Weimar urban source should be noted.

Not all stormtroopers were as committed to the SA as their leaders would have liked. Some attended musters and functions very irregularly, but others, often housed in SA hostels and frequently unemployed, devoted a great deal of energy to SA life. The SA's violence against political rivals, the authorities and property tended to involve these activists who, understandably, were thereby often at odds with the law. The police and court source (column 5) provides an impression of these activists' social background; of the seventeen sources, sixteen involved arrested stormtroopers and one a group under police surveillance.[19]

In fact, the activists do not differ greatly from the average in terms of occupational profile if all sources are considered together. Within the individual sources, some from East Prussia contain markedly fewer workers than average. In five sources stormtroopers had clashed with KPD or Reichsbanner formations which were presumably predominantly working class. The groups of stormtoopers involved in these fights were more working class than average which suggests that street fights between stormtroopers and the left's paramilitary formations did not represent violence between different classes but, rather, violence within a class.[20] Indeed, the KPD maintained that the SA in fighting the Communists were fighting their class brothers.[21]

Not all statistical evidence concerning the SA's occupational background points so unequivocally towards a strongly working-class SA. Police surveys from the far east of Germany appear to give a rather different picture although, as mentioned, these sources are problematical. The contents of the report from the County of Allenstein, East Prussia, regarding occupation are presented as found in the original document.

Table 3.2   *The SA, County of Allenstein, June 1931.*[22]

44.9%	farmers, farmers' sons, salaried agricultural staff.
33.5%	craftsmen and apprentices.
10.8%	white-collar staff and trainees.
7.7%	agricultural labourers.
3.1%	retired civil servants and public salaried staff.

Table 3.2 combines SA leaders and men which precludes any direct comparison with results for the rank and file alone, for leaders were markedly more middle class than their following.[23] That said, the Allenstein SA evidently recruited heavily from the farming population. As 84·6 per cent of these SA members were younger than 30,[24] most of these recruits were probably farmers' sons, although not necessarily heirs. The poor showing among agricultural labour was quite possibly due to the nationality problem in Allenstein discussed earlier. The figure of 33·5 per cent for craftsmen and apprentices is remarkably high as only 13·9 per cent of the working population in highly rural Allenstein were occupied in industry and crafts.[25] The youthfulness of the local SA indicates that few craftsmen were independents and as wage-earners they would have appeared in the census as workers, who comprised a third of the working population in Allenstein.[26] This conclusion is reinforced by a more detailed, but incomplete, police survey of the Allenstein leadership which indicates that even in this substantially older body, most craftsmen were employees rather than masters.[27] Therefore, in the Protestant border regions of eastern Germany the SA was evidently especially attractive to farmers' sons before 1933. However, it still won its fair share of workers – perhaps 40 per cent of the Allenstein SA where the host population contained only around 33 per cent workers – even if these (understandably!) came from the German-speaking towns rather than from the Masurian or Polish-speaking rural labour force.[28]

How did the stormtroopers' occupational profile compare with that of the male working population? The 1925 census distinguished subtly between different occupational groups, but also established a broader, more interpretative profile of the working population. This latter profile classified the population into five groups which reflected the main types of relationship to the means of production.[29] Wage-earners – described as workers – formed the largest group. All those enjoying an independent income, however spectacular or modest, and also the

Table 3.3 *Occupational Background of Stormtroopers, Active SA Rank and File, 1929–30 January 1933. Comparison with Census Returns for Male Working Population.*

Social Groups	SA Data		Census (%)	
	No.	*%*	*Nation*[31]	*Age Group*[32] *20–30*
Workers	751	63·4	53·2	62·9
Salaried staff, civil servants	310	26·2	18·7	20·1
Independents	122	10·3	21·7	7·3
Assisting family members	1	0·1	6·3	10·0
Salaried domestic servants	0	0·0	0·1	0·1
Totals	1,184	100·0	100·0	100·0*

* Total not exact due to rounding.

professions, comprised the next largest group: the independents. Salaried employees and civil servants at lower and middle grades (the senior civil servants being classified as independents) formed a further sizeable group. Family members who worked full-time in their family's business without a regular wage were classified as assisting family members, while domestic servants formed a further, minute, proportion of the male working population.

Table 3.3 reclassifies the 'late Weimar' data of Table 3.1 according to these official categories, which involves excluding stormtroopers such as students and schoolboys who counted as dependants of their parents' occupational groups in the census. Therefore, the overall total in Table 3.3 is slightly lower than in Table 3.1. The former emphasises that the working class were dominant among the stormtroopers, but also suggests that in relation to the age group 20 to 30,[30] from which the SA predominantly recruited, workers are well-represented rather than over-represented. In comparison, the salaried staff and civil servants are heavily over-represented. This over-representation is due almost entirely to the presence of many salaried staff in the SA. Civil servants, who comprised 30 per cent of the group in the census,[33] were scarcely represented in the SA. The relationship between results for independents and assisting family members appears odd and readjustment between these two categories will presently be invited by a closer examination of the SA's age structure.

Therefore, the different presentation of the results in Tables 3.1 and 3.3 point towards the same conclusion. The SA's ordinary membership was largely working class during the early 1930s, albeit with a sizeable lower-middle-class minority among whom salaried staff were predominant. The SA was, therefore, virtually a mirror image of the Nazi Party

with its large lower-middle-class component among whom independents were powerfully represented.

In mid-January 1933 the SA had 427,538 members and was in
decline,[34] but Hitler's appointment as Chancellor on 30 January transformed its fortunes literally overnight. It had an estimated 700,000
members by 31 January[35] and by May, before the absorption of rival
right-wing *Verbände* had commenced, there were 2 million stormtroopers.[36] By January 1934 the SA contained almost 3 million members[37] at
which level it more or less stabilised until, in the aftermath of the Röhm
purge, the organisation was reduced in size.

This period of explosive growth might conceivably have altered the
Active SA's social profile, but Table 3.4 indicates that changes were
relatively slight. There was an increase in working-class representation
at the cost of most middle-class groups, but the differing provenances
of Tables 3.1 and 3.4 preclude any precise comparison.[38] There are two
exceptions. The broader-based data in Table 3.4 eliminates the inflated
representation of students introduced into Table 3.1 by the 1932
Munich source, while the change of regime apparently increased the
proportion of civil servants in the SA.

Table 3.4 is subdivided into columns 1 to 7 according to provenance,
each of which is now discussed in turn. The small sources (column 1)
derive largely from small and medium towns[39] which possibly accounts
for the poor representation of salaried staff. However, middle-class
groups as a whole are thinly represented and the working-class representation of 75·2 per cent within the small sources is very high indeed.

The Berlin Document Center (BDC) has compiled individual files on
about 260,000 stormtroopers.[40] These vary in scope, but are often
remarkably informative, thereby giving a detailed social profile of many
stormtroopers. This certainly makes the BDC an invaluable source
regarding the SA's social composition, although it was founded by the
American authorities after the war to facilitate the tracing of former
Nazis and to provide as full a record as possible of their activities. The
SA files were arranged in alphabetical order as part of this exercise, and
not to provide a nationally representative sample of the SA for future
academic use! As it happens, about two-thirds of the files are Bavarian,
reflecting the rapid American advance into Bavaria and the consequent
capture of large amounts of undestroyed documentary evidence. Many
of the non-Bavarian records may have derived from a central cache of
Nazi records discovered in Thuringia but this, too, evidently contained
a haphazard selection of information.

The source from the BDC's SA files (column 2)[41] therefore reflects
the archive's contents rather than the membership of particular SA
units, but while unusual in this respect, its contents remain useful. As
intimated, the Bavarian SA is over-represented (source from BDC 63·6

Table 3.4 *Occupational Background of Stormtroopers, Active SA Rank and File, 30 January 1933–30 June 1934.*

Numbers

Occupational Groups	Sources							Totals
	1	2	3	4	5	6	7	
Unskilled workers	46	204	135	155	49	16	53	658
(Semi-) skilled workers	133	334	914	433	103	32	57	2,006
Salaried manual	9	23	80	45	12	0	2	171
Salaried white-collar	17	84	335	109	25	1	10	581
Civil servants	6	24	39	31	10	0	0	110
Master craftsmen	1	21	21	1	1	1	0	46
Independent proprietors	4	11	9	11	4	0	0	39
Farmers	6	59	0	9	1	5	0	80
Assisting family members	1	16	0	0	2	0	0	19
Professions, independents	5	37	47	2	8	3	0	102
University students	3	26	61	1	5	1	0	97
Miscellaneous	7	15	9	0	3	1	3	38
Totals	238	854	1,650	797	223	60	125	3,947

Percentages

Occupational Groups	Sources							Totals
	1	2	3	4	5	6	7	
Unskilled workers	19·3	23·9	8·2	19·4	22·2	26·7	42·2	16·7
(Semi-) skilled workers	55·9	39·1	55·4	54·3	46·2	53·3	45·6	50·8
Salaried manual	3·8	2·7	4·8	5·6	5·4	0·0	1·6	4·3
Salaried white-collar	7·1	9·8	20·3	13·7	11·2	1·7	8·0	14·7
Civil servants	2·5	2·8	2·4	3·9	4·5	0·0	0·0	2·8
Master craftsmen	0·4	2·5	1·3	0·1	0·4	1·7	0·0	1·2
Independent proprietors	1·7	1·3	0·5	1·4	1·8	0·0	0·0	1·0
Farmers	2·5	6·9	0·0	1·1	0·4	8·3	0·0	2·0
Assisting family members	0·4	1·9	0·0	0·0	0·9	0·0	0·0	0·5
Professions, independents	2·1	4·3	2·8	0·3	3·6	5·0	0·0	2·6
University students	1·3	3·0	3·7	0·1	2·2	1·7	0·0	2·5
Miscellaneous	2·9	1·8	0·5	0·0	1·3	1·7	2·4	1·0
Totals*	100·0	100·0	100·0	100·0	100·0	100·0	100·0	100·0

* Percentage totals not exact due to rounding.
Notes: Occupational categories as for Table 3.1
Sources: 1 Small sources from throughout Germany 30 1 1933–30 6 1934.
2 Berlin Document Center.
3 Frankfurt-am-Main, 30 6 1934.
4 Kurpfalz, June 1934.
5 North Rhineland 1933–4.
6 New recruits, December 1933.
7 Unemployed, early 1934.

per cent Bavarian, SA in March 1934 11·2 per cent Bavarian)[42] and the source also has a rural and small-town bias.[43] This arguably explains the under-representation of white-collar staff, the rather high proportion of unskilled labour and the presence of some farmers in the source. However, it appears that either the Bavarian SA failed to attract farmers as successfully as the SA on Germany's north-eastern border[44] or (rather less plausibly) that a mass exodus of farmers hit the Bavarian SA after Hitler's takeover. Since the strongly rural Hessian SA is also over-represented in the BDC source,[45] it, too, was presumably not especially attractive to farmers. Working-class representation is slightly below average in the BDC source, but the working class formed a smaller proportion of the economically active population in Bavaria than in Germany as a whole[46] and, in any case, workers still outnumbered middle-class stormtroopers by roughly two to one.

The source from the industrial, manufacturing and commercial centre of Frankfurt-am-Main (column 3)[47] is larger and more broadly based geographically than the 1932 Munich source.[48] That being said, the Frankfurt results are not so very different with 88·7 per cent of the source being either workers or salaried staff, while the independent middle classes are again virtually absent. However, the proportion of university students is much lower in Frankfurt while semi- skilled and skilled workers are more strongly represented, leading to a higher proportion of workers overall.

The SA's pioneer companies were intended to perform a similar role to the Reichswehr's pioneer units and ideally either sought Reichswehr pioneer veterans or trained their own pioneers. However, the Kurpfalz pioneer companies (column 4)[49] contained few ex-Reichswehr pioneers while only providing pioneer training for a fraction of the membership.[50] Furthermore, technical ability apparently played little part in selection for the pioneer units, as indicated by the large proportion of white-collar staff recruited. The units concerned came from both urban–industrial and more rural locations on the left bank of the Rhine between Speyer and Bingen and therefore their social composition probably reflected broadly the background of the SA as a whole in the central Rhine basin. Wage-earners are clearly dominant.

Table 3.5 includes the remaining pioneer units from Kurpfalz whose occupations were described by the SA in a fashion precluding their consideration in the main analysis. These units also came from both industrial and rural areas, including wine-growing areas and here, too, workers dominated with salaried staff also well-represented. Unless farmers were explicitly excluded from pioneer companies (and there is no record of this being so) their absence from these companies suggests that they were thinly represented in the Kurpfalz SA. This impression is strengthened by a report written later in 1934 by the

Table 3.5 *SA Pioneer Companies from Mainz, Worms, Bingen and Nierstein. June 1934.*[51]

Occupational Groups	No.	%
Unskilled workers	317	23·0
(Semi-) skilled workers	624	45·2
Salaried manual	113	8·2
Salaried white-collar, civil servants	284	20·6
Students, doctors	43	3·1
Totals	1,381	100.0*

* Total not exact due to rounding.
Note: The salaried white-collar, civil servants group was described by the SA as 'salesmen, civil servants and jurists'.

SA's commander in the district which commented on the predominance of manual workers within his units.[52]

The North Rhineland source (Table 3.4, column 5),[53] most of which consists of town and city dwellers,[54] stems from the Rhine valley and its hinterland from Cologne northwards. It derives from files compiled by Gestapo District Headquarters in Düsseldorf which include storm-troopers who had come under Gestapo scrutiny. This involved the routine surveillance of prospective civil servants, crime both petty and serious, contravention of SA regulations, sexual offences and political offences, with no single category predominating. Seventy-seven of the 223 stormtroopers in the group had a non-Nazi political past, but this was often incidental to the case in hand. Of the 152 working-class members, only 28 either belonged, or had belonged, to a left-wing organisation.[55] These varied reasons for inclusion in the Gestapo files provide a relatively broadly based source. It conforms largely to the norm in Table 3.4, although unskilled workers are strongly represented for a largely urban source whilst white-collar staff are less well represented. Routine Gestapo screening of candidates for appointment to, or promotion within, the public service explains the relatively strong representation of civil servants and members of the professions but, by the same token, the presence despite this of only eighteen such storm-troopers in the Rhineland source suggests that their actual strength in the working-class-dominated local SA must have been weak.

Therefore in the northern Rhineland where the KPD had enjoyed great electoral success, the paramilitary expression of fascism – sometimes considered as a lower-middle-class reaction to the dangers of 'Bolshevism' and proletarianisation – was largely working class and certainly lacked any substantial membership from the independent *Mittelstand*.[56]

The SA in the small market towns of Altötting (Upper Bavaria) and Eberbach (north Baden) recorded the recruitment of new members during late 1933 (Table 3.4, column 6).[57] By any standards, these new recruits were massively working class with only farmers and, surprisingly, members of the professions scoring at all well among middle-class groups. This result, although from small, localised sources, suggests that the proportion of workers in the Active SA may have been increasing during 1933 and 1934.

The unemployed stormtroopers from Baden and Upper Bavaria (Table 3.4, column 7)[58] resembled the majority of their comrades in being jobless during the early 1930s. However the exclusion of stormtroopers with jobs apparently diminishes the representation of middle-class groups, while unskilled workers are heavily represented.[59] This narrowly based source might be unrepresentative, but as the SA attracted many unregistered unemployed (for instance, about 40 per cent of the Hamburg SA in mid-1932)[60] and as many of the unregistered unemployed were unskilled workers the result is, arguably, not surprising.

Table 3.6 reclassifies the stormtroopers presented in Table 3.4 according to the official census's categories which again entails excluding those stormtroopers with dependant status. The result confirms that the expanding SA maintained and possibly even enhanced its working-class character after Hitler's accession to power, apparently at the expense of both the employed and the independent middle classes. However, it would be mistaken to argue that Hitler's takeover and the subsequent expansion of the SA resulted nationally in a body socially distinct from the pre-1933 organisation. The SA had always contained many workers.

Table 3.6 *Occupational Background of Stormtroopers, Active SA Rank and File, 30 January 1933–30 June 1934. Comparison with Census Returns for Male Working Population.*

| Social Groups | SA Data | | Census (%) | |
	No.	%	Nation[61]	Age Group[62] 20–30
Workers	2,664	69·9	53·2	62·9
Salaried staff, civil servants	863	22·6	18·7	20·1
Independents	267	7·0	21·7	7·3
Assisting family members	18	0·5	6·3	10·0
Salaried domestic servants	0	0·0	0·1	0·1
Totals	3,812	100·0	100·0	100·0*

* Total not exact due to rounding.

The wealth of detail in the BDC, North Rhineland and Frankfurt sources permits a closer examination of the SA's occupational background. A bare description such as 'unskilled worker' or 'salaried white-collar' is given additional substance both by considering the economic sectors and even individual work places in which stormtroopers were, or had been, employed, and by establishing their parental background.

Predictably, substantial regional variations in the economic structure of interwar Germany affected the SA. The essentially non-urban and strongly Bavarian BDC source[63] contains a substantial farming element, while the town- and city-based North Rhineland source[64] is conspicuously dominated by the industry and crafts sector. Looking at the distribution of stormtroopers within the economy in more detail (where their type of work could be determined); of 353 individuals in the BDC source, 124 worked in agriculture, 115 in industry and crafts, 60 in communications and commerce, and 54 in health, administration and the professions. By contrast, in the North Rhineland source, of 90 stormtroopers 3 worked in agriculture, 61 in industry and crafts, 13 in communications and commerce, and 13 in health, administration and the professions. As the 1934 SA had recruited heavily in rural, town and urban environments, there is therefore no reason to suppose that it had a particular appeal to any individual economic sector, but given the SA's size it could equally be said that it had substantial support from all economic sectors.

The uneven distribution of the sources within their district of origin makes comparison with official statistics difficult and, in any case, the results are affected somewhat by occupational terminology. The name or nature of work places sometimes featured in individual case files, but often the type of work place was gathered from a declared occupation, such as factory worker, farm labourer, miner, railway clerk or shop assistant. However, while white-collar employees described as bank clerks or shop assistants were placed in the commercial sector, those salaried employees describing themselves by the vague term *kaufmännischer Angestellte* could have worked either in industrial or commercial undertakings and therefore remained unclassified. Although industry-employed salaried staff did usually describe themselves in this way, their exclusion from the analysis due to lack of certainty has probably disadvantaged the representation of the industrial sector in both sources. In the North Rhineland source occupational terminology among manual workers probably further disadvantaged the industrial sector. Occupations such as furnacemen or stoker sound apt for the steel industry of the area but, for want of positive proof, a number of stormtroopers with such occupations are excluded from the analysis. On the other hand, the relative strength of the agricultural sector in the BDC source is probably exaggerated as the work place of every independent farmer could be unhesitatingly classified.

The original function of many documents comprising the sources probably exaggerates the strength of the health, administration and professions group. Some BDC records and all North Rhineland files were compiled during surveillance operations. The only occupational sectors particularly liable to undergo surveillance were the civil service and members of the professions in public service whose surveillance upon appointment or promotion was a matter of course.

Therefore the SA's appeal to the industry and crafts sector was possibly stronger than the initial results suggest but, even so, the SA clearly appealed to some degree to members of all economic sectors.

Looking at the stormtroopers' social composition within each sector, workers dominated within industry and crafts, the agricultural and the communications and commerce sectors were socially heterogeneous, and, understandably, the health, administration and professions sector was decidedly middle class.[65]

Of unskilled workers in the BDC source, about half (53 out of 117) were employed on farms, 3 in forestry, 1 by a master craftsman, 2 in quarries, 25 in factories and 13 in industrial or craft concerns of indeterminate size and character. Nine of the remaining 20 were railwaymen, 8 being engaged in track maintenance or in workshops. Of 75 semi-skilled and skilled workers, 5 were employed on farms, 12 by master craftsmen, 4 in mines and 40 in a variety of firms including Bosch, I.G. Farben and Siemens. Eight of the remaining 14 were railwaymen (6 employed on track maintenance or in workshops). Salaried employees worked in a range of concerns, while of the 24 civil servants 8 were teachers. Of those in the professions at least a third were starting their careers, occupying junior university, legal or upper-grade civil service posts. Within the farming sector many of the fifty-nine farms appear to have been small.[66]

Of the 16 unskilled workers in the North Rhineland source, 13 were factory employees while 3 worked in the building industry. Of 43 semi-skilled and skilled workers, 17 were coal miners, 15 were factory workers (with all their work places identifiable), 3 worked for master craftsmen, 1 in a small workshop, 1 in the building trade, 2 on the railways, 1 on a barge, 2 on farms and 1 as a waiter. The 31 middle-class stormtroopers worked for a variety of employers and in a variety of occupations with no clear pattern emerging. Clerical workers in industry (3), a shop assistant, civil servants, technical staff and assisting family members are all represented in the source.[67]

Therefore, the SA recruited from backgrounds ranging from farms and artisan enterprises to commerce and heavy industry. However, although a minority of stormtroopers – perhaps a third in some units – pursued regular everyday occupations, for most a steady job was merely a memory or a faint hope for the future. SA unemployment will presently be examined, but it is essential to remember that the SA's social profile was massively distorted by the effects of the Great Depression.

Vocational expectations often remain unfulfilled during times of economic crisis. In the early 1930s this was especially true for Germany, with registered unemployment among wage-earners and salaried staff of about 33 per cent.[68] German society also witnessed downward social mobility as people sought any work available to keep them off the dole queue. Were the SA's members so affected, then many stormtroopers would have held jobs lower down the social scale than they might normally have expected.

The occupations held, or formerly held, by stormtroopers suggest otherwise, for most were trained, either in blue- or white-collar occupations. An apprenticeship, which normally lasted three years in Weimar Germany, could prove financially burdensome to a trainee's family. Apprentices were poorly paid and some stormtroopers who had remained unapprenticed attributed this to their families' poverty. Thus, by virtue of receiving training, it appears that around 70 per cent of stormtroopers had entered that occupation envisaged when they left school.[69] Their social trauma had consequently more probably resulted from the loss of jobs for which they and their families had made sacrifices and not from resentment over their occupations as such.

None the less, many more stormtroopers' parents were apparently middle class than were the stormtroopers themselves. Whether this constituted unexpected or unusual downward mobility is another

Table 3.7 *Parental Backgrounds of Stormtroopers. Active SA Rank and File. 30 January 1933–30 June 1934. Effect of Age on Occupational Background.* (%)

| Social Groups | SA Data[70] | | Nation,[71] aged | |
	SA Men	Parents	20–30	40–60
Workers	67·69	44·65	62·93	42·20
Salaried employees, Civil servants	21·23	23·69	20·09	19·96
Independents	8·96	31·66	7·26	36·80
Assisting family members	2·12	0·00	9·95	0·97
Salaried domestic servants	0·00	0·00	0·07	0·07
Totals	100·00	100·00	100·00*	100·00

* Total not exact due to rounding.

Notes: 1 National figures apply to the male working population.

2 Figures are from the 1925 census which, admittedly, plays down the social distortions created by economic deflation.

3 SA data from BDC and Frankfurt SA, June 1934. Numbers; BDC 181, Frankfurt 264.

matter and Table 3.7 suggests not. The SA's social structure appears broadly comparable with that of relevant age groups in the male working population, although the relationship between independents and assisting family members is probably distorted and, as noted, consideration of the SA's age structure invites its reassessment. If anything, fewer stormtroopers than expected possessed independent family backgrounds while the SA did not, apparently, contain inordinately large numbers of workers who normally would have anticipated dramatic social advancement later in working life. In the BDC source with its rural and small-town bias, workers were, as seen, not restricted to craft enterprises where advancement to the level of master craftsmen might have been possible while, in addition, only seven labourers out of thirty-eight were farmers' sons and none of these mentioned that they were heirs.

This broad picture passes over the complexity of social change between generations. Some stormtroopers were upwardly mobile and others experienced changes in social position and prospects which the broad categories of Table 3.7 cannot depict. It was possible to establish the parental backgrounds of 181 stormtroopers in the BDC source. Thirty-eight subjects were unskilled workers and while 23 came from working-class families, the parents of 14 were skilled workers. The fathers (or, occasionally, working mothers) of the remaining 15 were mainly small independents (7 farmers and 3 master craftsmen) with a handful from other backgrounds. Some of these unskilled stormtroopers completed an apprenticeship, but then found no suitable work. Mathias Falterer of Poing in Upper Bavaria wrote:

> Nine months after the end of my apprenticeship I was given my cards because of the lack of work. I was jobless for one and a half years and am now employed as a farm worker.[72]

Other unskilled workers had suffered similarly and in better times would have been in skilled jobs.[73] A minority had received no training because of family circumstances and, for them, the depression was simply an additional burden. Such was the labourer Max Färber. After an unstable childhood he began training as a tailor, initially under his father, but the war intervened:

> I was barely out of school when my father died in action as a lieutenant in the war and things became increasingly difficult. I couldn't go on training as a tailor because no one could pay the apprenticeship fees, and I had to go out and earn a living to support my mother.[74]

The seven unskilled workers from farming backgrounds sometimes lost little in material terms, but the drop in status from farmer's son or even farmer to labourer probably rankled. One farmer had actually abandoned his small farm to become a quarry worker,[75] while a farmer's son explained that his parents' farm was very small, forcing him to seek work elsewhere.[76] A third, Christian Fluhrer of Erlbach in Franconia, was unfortunate to be a second son and consequently had to work as a farm hand outside his native village of Diebach.[77]

Of the 73 semi-skilled and skilled workers, most in fact being skilled, less need be said, for they worked, or had last worked, in their chosen occupation. About half came from working-class families and 12, whose fathers were unskilled workers, had advanced socially. Of the 36 from middle-class families, 12 were master craftsmen's sons, but had often learnt a different skill from their fathers' and therefore, presumably, did not expect to inherit the family business. Similarly, the 11 farmers' sons were often younger children and therefore unlikely to inherit. Thus both these groups had, until they lost their jobs, probably seen their careers develop as planned while even the five civil servants' sons had not fared badly. The drop from civil servant to skilled worker was, and is, not necessarily so dramatic in Germany where many more public employees enjoy civil service status than in Britain. Indeed, of the 5 civil service fathers involved, 2 were in manual occupations and 2 in low-grade clerical positions.[78] The numbers of middle-class stormtroopers who were socially mobile were too small to warrant a detailed analysis, but upward and downward mobility was most apparent among white-collar staff and civil servants.

Among the 264 subjects from Frankfurt-am-Main social mobility also follows a complex pattern, but the impression of downward mobility is less marked. Of 32 unskilled workers, 20 were from working-class families and only 6 from independent families. Ninety-nine out of 144 semi-skilled and skilled workers were from working-class backgrounds and only 26 from independent families, while of 50 white-collar staff, 15 were from working-class families. The source's urban provenance may explain this, for much of the apparent downward mobility in the BDC source involved the agricultural sector.

Therefore, the social experiences of stormtroopers before the depression struck appear as largely unremarkable and, as they were no doubt common enough outside the SA's membership, cannot be regarded as a defining characteristic of its social composition. Far from these changes in occupational background between generations blighting their lives, mass unemployment, which is considered presently, resulted in father and son alike losing their livings and often facing destitution. This destitution rather than petty social resentment was so prominent in the SA of the early 1930s.

In mid-1934 Hitler's conservative allies, in particular the army, and much of the Nazi movement pressed him to quash the SA's undisciplined and excessive activism. Accordingly, he sanctioned a purge of the SA's senior leadership, beginning on 30 June, which saw the execution of Röhm and many senior SA commanders.[79] Public opinion approved of Hitler's action[80] and a cowed SA found itself isolated. In the autumn a new, compliant SA Command initiated a systematic screening of the leadership which resulted in many further dismissals or invitations to resign. Ordinary stormtroopers also left in substantial numbers. Some perceived that the SA's political emasculation made the possibility of a commensurate reward for their time-consuming SA duties remote. Others were released from service or dismissed as the new leadership began to scale down the SA. Exiled left-wing anti-Nazis had previously despised the SA, but now some maintained that the Röhm purge and the subsequent cutbacks in SA strength marked the end of the proletarian SA.[81]

However, Table 3.8 suggests that the SA was not greatly altered socially by the purge and cutbacks. Working-class members remained predominant, salaried staff well represented and the independent *Mittelstand*, if anything, shows more weakly than ever. As in the pre-1933 period (Table 3.1), a single source boosts student representation.

The Munich source (column 1) consists of stormtroopers who volunteered for military service.[82] All but a 16-year-old were aged between 18 and 25, which, despite the marked youthfulness of the Munich SA, produces a distorted age distribution and, consequently, some distortion of the source's occupational composition. Schoolboys (classified under miscellaneous), assisting family members, and students would be strongly favoured and workers slightly favoured, while independents would be strongly disadvantaged and salaried staff and civil servants slightly disadvantaged. With the important exception of its favouring the student quotient, the 1932 Munich source had broadly the opposite effects. Therefore, the apparent rise in working-class representation is probably overstated and the apparent near absence of the independent middle classes somewhat overstated. In essence, little had probably changed.

The source from the manufacturing town of Offenbach in the Main valley (column 2) includes stormtroopers chosen for specialist military training within the SA[83] and in this respect resembles the Kurpfalz source in Table 3.4. Its strongly working-class profile and the large proportion of salaried staff are particularly marked.

The 1935 Frankfurt source (column 3)[84] is an especially useful guide to social trends within the SA as it is directly comparable with the 1934 Frankfurt source. A decline in independent lower-middle-class groups is again apparent, but here the lower-middle-class salaried groups benefited. However, despite a slight decline in the proportion of unskilled workers, working-class members remain preponderant in Frankfurt's Active SA.

Table 3.8 *Occupational Background of Stormtroopers, Active SA Rank and File, 1 July 1934–March 1936.*

Numbers

Occupational Groups	1	2	Sources 3	4	5	Totals
Unskilled workers	8	5	48	228	8	297
(Semi-) skilled workers	98	36	430	185	38	787
Salaried manual	10	4	45	22	6	87
Salaried white-collar	29	13	179	27	13	261
Civil servants	2	0	26	10	1	39
Master craftsmen	0	0	6	3	1	10
Independent proprietors	1	0	3	0	0	4
Farmers	1	0	0	7	2	10
Professions, independents	0	0	11	5	1	17
University students	27	0	28	103	0	158
Miscellaneous	4	1	3	5	1	14
Totals	180	59	779	595	71	1,684

Percentages

Occupational Groups	1	2	Sources 3	4	5	Totals
Unskilled workers	4·4	8·5	6·2	38·3	11·3	17·6
(Semi-) skilled workers	54·4	61·0	55·2	31·1	53·3	46·7
Salaried manual	5·6	6·8	5·8	3·7	8·5	5·2
Salaried white-collar	16·1	22·0	23·0	4·4	18·3	15·5
Civil servants	1·1	0·0	3·3	1·7	1·4	2·3
Master craftsmen	0·0	0·0	0·8	0·5	1·4	0·6
Independent proprietors	0·6	0·0	0·4	0·0	0·0	0·2
Farmers	0·6	0·0	0·0	1·2	2·8	0·6
Professions, independents	0·0	0·0	1·4	0·8	1·4	1·0
University students	15·0	0·0	3·6	17·3	0·0	9·4
Miscellaneous	2·2	1·7	0·4	0·8	1·4	0·8
Totals*	100·0	100·0	100·0	100·0	100·0	100·0

* Percentage totals not exact due to rounding.
Notes: Occupational categories as for Table 3.1.
Sources: 1 Munich, late 1934.
2 Offenbach, 20 12 1934.
3 Frankfurt-am-Main, 1 7 1935.
4 Upper Bavaria, July 1934–March 1936.
5 Small sources, Hochtaunus, Neckargerach.

The Upper Bavarian source (column 4) includes five SA companies, one from Burghausen and four from the Freising district.[85] All stem from similar economic backgrounds; a mixture of small towns and countryside in solidly Roman Catholic areas. The Burghausen company was strongly working-class. Of the Freising companies, two raise no problems. One was largely working class (63·4 per cent) while the other's rank and file consisted solely of ninety-eight students. The remaining two companies do raise problems concerning occupational classification. According to the occupations given in the membership lists, these units contained many farmers (43·1 per cent and 74·5 per cent) giving a figure of 27·4 per cent farmers in the Upper Bavarian source as a whole. However, doubts of varying importance arise. The first, relatively minor peculiarity lies in the minimal proportion of independent *Mittelständler* other than farmers in these two companies (0 per cent and 0·7 per cent). Since master craftsmen and small tradesmen were, socially speaking, closely connected with farmers in rural areas of Bavaria and elsewhere (Kater),[86] their virtual absence is puzzling. Similarly, the absence of farmers' sons is peculiar. A more compelling doubt is raised by the income of these farmers. The SA listed the members of these particular units to record payment of membership dues and therefore noted each stormtrooper's monthly income. The records of one unit, Company 8/2, which contained two-thirds of the problematical farmers are detailed and complete. They reveal that all but 5 of the 105 farmers earned RM 20 per month, with the other 5 receiving between RM 10 and RM 40 monthly. Not only is the homogeneity of income among these apparently independent farmers striking, but more so its exact correlation with the going rate for farm labourers which the SA reported as varying between RM 5 and RM 10 per week.[87] Therefore if the 105 'farmers' were really independent, it must be accepted that they earned no more than miserably paid farm labourers whose standard of living scandalised at least one provincial SA commander.[88] Furthermore, they would have earned less to a man than any other occupational group in the Freising area. The nine unskilled workers (none listed as farm workers) in Company 8/2 earned between RM 50 and RM 100 per month, while skilled workers received between RM 60 and RM 130. Unfortunately the lists omit the men's ages, but the general youthfulness of the Active SA is a further factor making unlikely the large-scale presence of any type of independent. Finally, the Nazi Party in Bavaria failed to recruit substantially among the devoutly Roman Catholic peasantry of Upper Bavaria who had remained largely loyal to the Catholic Bavarian People's Party until 1933.[89] Their sons were frequently members of the Catholic youth organisation which, far from collaborating with the SA, remained its bitter rival into the mid-1930s. Therefore the 'farmers' in the Freising companies were probably largely farm labourers and the description of farm workers as farmers has been noted in other sources.

The small sources (column 5) consist of two SA units, one from the Hochtaunus district north of Frankfurt-am-Main and one from Neckargerach, a small town in northern Baden.[90] Ten of the white-collar staff belonged to the Hochtaunus unit and lived in the outer suburbs of Frankfurt. Other than that, the preponderance of workers is clear.

Therefore, the individual sources are basically in accord and certainly the social polarisation between party and SA which, as will be seen, contributed to the crisis of mid-1934, was not resolved by a selective purge of stormtroopers from the working classes. In fact, Table 3.9 suggests that, if anything, the proportion of workers in the SA may have increased very slightly and the proportion of salaried staff and civil servants more significantly, but the independent *Mittelstand* appears virtually to have faded from sight.

Table 3.9 *Occupational Background of Stormtroopers, Active SA Rank and File, 1 July 1934–March 1936. Comparison with Census Returns for the Male Working Population.*

| Social Groups | SA Data | | Census (%) | |
	No.	%	Nation[91]	Age Group[92] 20–30
Workers	1,084	71·5	53·2	62·9
Salaried staff, civil servants	387	25·5	18·7	20·1
Independents	41	2·7	21·7	7·3
Assisting family members	0	0·0	6·3	10·0
Salaried domestic servants	1	0·1	0·1	0·1
Totals*	1,513	100·0	100·0	100·0

* Percentage totals not exact due to rounding.

Unemployment Levels within the SA, 1929–35

Any analysis of the SA's occupational background is incomplete without consideration of the unemployment question. Most stormtroopers, significantly, received a formal or an on-the-job training upon leaving school and many subsequently worked in their chosen occupation, but only a minority had retained or found new full-time jobs during the early 1930s.

The stormtroopers were victims of an economic crisis of unprecedented proportions which hit Germany particularly severely. By 1932 the German index of production stood at 60 per cent of its 1929 level, compared with 84·5 per cent in Britain and just below 70 per cent in France.[93] Profits in German industry and trade halved between 1929 and 1933.[94] Agriculture faced a structural crisis before 1929, but the depression brought a further decline in fortunes.[95] The 5 million small proprietors, including 3 million outside agriculture, who provided decisive support for the NSDAP, suffered their second great economic reverse since 1918.[96] However, this time employees, who comprised so large a part of the SA, also suffered badly. Those who kept their jobs saw hours worked fall by 10 per cent with a subsequent loss of earnings.[97] More seriously, of the 17·5 million jobs provided by the German economy in 1929, only 12·5 million remained in December 1932. Unemployment rose accordingly. From under 2 million in 1929, it rose with seasonal variations to over 3 million in 1930, 4·5 million in 1931 and 5·5 million in 1932.[98] By January 1933, 6·01 million – a third of wage-earning and salaried employees were registered as jobless.[99] Unemployment threatened to become the norm rather than the lot of an unfortunate minority. However, the first signs of an economic revival appeared during 1932. During the following years the new Nazi government in part witnessed and in part stimulated a slow recovery, but despite this improvement unemployment did not disappear overnight. In December 1935 2·51 million Germans were still jobless[100] and this continuing high unemployment rate influenced both the SA's social profile and its politics.

SA membership lists seldom detail unemployment, possibly because each individual's fortunes altered too rapidly for written records to remain up-to-date. None the less, SA commanders were deeply conscious of, and frequently reported on, the problem of unemployment. Using such sources and one membership list which does quantify joblessness, Kater assesses the SA's overall unemployment rate at between 60 and 70 per cent.[101] Further evidence suggests a rate approaching the top of this scale. Even in 1929 most of the Wiesbaden SA was jobless[102] and the rate was also high outside the cities. In 1930 the Widminnen SA, East Prussia, 'was composed largely of unemployed, [who] could barely pay the membership dues'.[103] In January 1931 the National Socialist leadership in Tilsit, also East Prussia, wrote: 'The difficulties confronting our unemployed party members and SA comrades ... are especially severe this winter, a large number receiving no unemployment benefit whatsoever.'[104] In Hessen-Nassau most of the Giessen SA was reported jobless in 1931,[105] while Eberstadt had little better to report between 1929 and 1933.[106]

In February 1931 the commander of the SA Group East, Captain Stennes, grew tired of Hitler's preoccupation with winning elections as he felt that this 'legalist policy' neglected the material well-being of his jobless men. He wrote bitterly to Röhm that rather than indulging in electioneering:

It is much more important to undertake measures to relieve the economic position of the SA. In Berlin there are Regiments containing 67 per cent unemployed. In Breslau a Company could not turn out for inspection – in frost and snow – because it completely lacked footware.[107]

There was no improvement during 1932 in town or country. In January the police reported that Company 24 of Munich 'contained about eighty SA members; most being unemployed'.[108] With the opening of an SA hostel in Eglharting, Upper Bavaria, in the same month it was taken for granted that the local SA was largely unemployed.[109] In September the SA commander in Breslau, Silesia, informed Munich headquarters that '60 per cent of SA men are long-term unemployed and it would not conform with the facts if I were to report that morale is especially good'.[110] The *Gau* chronicler of Hessen-Nassau summarised conditions in the SA nationwide during 1932 thus: '[It] had Companies which were composed solely of unemployed. For these men in particular, the creation of SA hostels was especially fortuitous. For many . . . , these hostels became their real home.'[111] By late 1932 the SA represented in the public eye unemployment, destitution and extreme violence. In September an article in the *Augsburger Postzeitung* illustrated this strikingly, if somewhat melodramatically, when contemplating the consequences of a Nazi electoral setback in the approaching general election:

Not only will 6th November fail to deliver the goods, it will result in a net loss of seats, whether this is thirty or fifty being irrelevant. Its glorious advance will be crushed . . . and millions will be robbed of their hopes for a Third Reich. We must prepare for this. There are almost a million vagrants loose on the highways of Germany, alienated from work.

THE DISBANDMENT OF THE UNSUPPORTABLE SA CONFRONTS THE NATION'S LEADERSHIP WITH ALMOST GREATER TASKS THAN DEMOBILISATION DURING THE FRIGHTFUL WINTER OF 1918–1919.

. . . Empty-handed, despairing in the SA Command's policies, faith in the Third Reich lost, homeless and penniless bands of starving elements will, like the peasants of the Thirty Years' War, roam the countryside. The impoverished villages and farms can no more help these people than can the remote central authorities. Has the authoritarian Reich government taken precautions? There is one which Bavaria, with its picturesque villages and patriotism can take: the strengthening of the Bayernwacht to a degree at which is can prevent robbery and arson. For behind the despairing SA men grins the MASK OF MOSCOW![112]

Clearly, for middle-class, rural Bavaria, the SA represented an alien, highly threatening, and potentially left-wing force.

The economic recovery and the Nazi accession to power might have improved employment prospects within the rapidly expanding SA after January 1933, but the general picture did not alter significantly. Eventually there were bitter recriminations. On 1 February 1933 the Hamburg SA reported a 75 per cent long-term unemployment rate[113] and during 1933 throughout Germany, improvements were both slight and local, usually reflecting the acquisition of seasonal work by stormtroopers. In late 1933, according to the Reich Finance Ministry, the SA (excluding its newly acquired members from the Stahlhelm) contained about a million utterly impoverished members who had been jobless for years.[114] By early 1934 there were more substantial improvements locally with some Bavarian SA units seeing their unemployment rates fall to around 25 per cent.[115] This was exceptionally good, for in the Rhine–Main basin and in much of central and northern Germany unemployment remained stubbornly high.[116]

The Röhm purge may have brought the SA into line politically, but much of its membership remained jobless. The picture was not uniform with some units, particularly in Bavaria, reporting very low unemployment levels by early 1935.[117] Even here, some work was apparently temporary or seasonal[118] and in many other parts of Germany 1935 proved a very bad year for the SA. Baden, Hessen, Hamburg and Silesia were among areas which reported high SA unemployment levels[119] and the commander of the Offenbach SA was speaking for most units when remarking: 'Naturally, discord still arises among the SA men, who are repeatedly promised work. They are registered regularly each month, but despite this still receive no jobs.'[120]

By mid-1935 the problem may have been relative rather than absolute. The SA was contracting steadily by then with many stormtroopers transferring to the army, or leaving the SA upon finding civilian jobs. None the less for those remaining in the SA joblessness was still commonplace. The SA's rapid growth during 1933 led to its becoming a reservoir for many of Germany's unemployed with perhaps 2 million or more jobless stormtroopers by early 1934. Its proletarian character compounded the problem, for the Nazi state disposed of jobs principally in administrative and similar areas. Nazi supporters did receive such jobs, but as Kater shows, the SS's occupational background left it far better suited than the SA for this form of official patronage after January 1933.[121]

The Age of the Active SA's Rank and File, 1929–35

The Active SA developed as a young, relatively fit body whose members, often because of joblessness, were able to dedicate a fair measure of time to the Nazi cause. Initially no maximum age limit was fixed, but older, less fit stormtroopers were organised in the less demanding Reserve SA. The Active SA always had a lower age limit of 18, although this was occasionally waived. In November 1933 it introduced an upper age limit of 35[122] which, in practice, sharply reduced rather than eliminated the proportion of older members. Therefore, although not rigorously enforced, SA regulations in themselves influenced the SA's age profile.

Table 3.10 *Age of Stormtroopers. Active SA Rank and File, 1929–30 June 1934.*

Age	1929–30 January 1933[123]		30 January 1933–30 June 1934[124]	
	No.	%	No.	%
19 minus	57	17·3	251	8·7
20–24	136	41·2	1,099	38·2
25–29	63	19·1	782	27·2
30–34	32	9·7	465	16·1
35–39	14	4·2	159	5·5
40–44	9	2·7	76	2·6
45 plus	19	5·8	48	1·7
Totals	330	100·0	2,880	100·0

Regulations apart, Table 3.10 indicates that the Active SA appealed decisively to the young, for while male Germans up to the age of 35 were free to join, most stormtroopers were younger than 30 and, until 1933, younger than 25. The SA apparently aged slightly as a body after January 1933, and as fresh recruits soon outnumbered veterans by four to one, their influence on the SA's age profile must have been decisive. Therefore, with Hitler's accession to power, the SA apparently recruited from a broader and consequently more socially representative age range than before. The limited sources from the period after Röhm's death suggest that the SA's contraction during late 1934 and 1935 affected all age groups equally.[125] The organisation aged very slightly, but the passage of time alone accounts for this.

Unemployed stormtroopers were probably even younger than the membership[126] as a whole and the same applied to activists.[127] Of stormtroopers listed in the pre-1933 police and court records, arguably activists *par excellence*, almost two-thirds were younger than 25. Thus if the 'ideal type' stormtrooper was a young worker, then activist as well as unemployed stormtroopers conformed more closely to this ideal type both in terms of age and occupational background than did the Active SA as a whole.

The SA's youth serves to confirm that the organisation contained few members of the independent *Mittelstand*. The crux of the matter lies in the fact that only around 394,000 male independents in the population were aged under 30 and hence within the age group from which the SA largely recruited.[128] Common sense suggests that before 1933 when the SA grew to number around 450,000 it could not have contained very many independents. By 1934 when the Active SA boasted 2·5 million members,[129] with 2 million younger than 30,[130] its dominance by the independent *Mittelstand* became a mathematical impossibility.

The stormtroopers' youth suggests that the occupational analyses are distorted in one respect. Of the independents, the farmers in particular were very young indeed. Half the farmers from the pre-1933[131] sources and 60·3 per cent from the 1933 to June 1934 sources were younger than 25,[132] while only 1·1 per cent of German farmers were so young.[133] By 1933 the apparent representation of farmers in the SA also becomes a mathematical impossibility, for Table 3.4 indicates that around 2 per cent, or 50,000, of Active stormtroopers were farmers during 1933/4. Therefore the SA would have contained around 30,000 farmers younger than 25, but this figure greatly exceeds the 21,400 male farmers of this age then working in Germany![134] Doubtless many 'farmers' were either farmers' sons (assisting family members) anticipating their future occupation, possibly factory workers or other employees who also occupied a parcel of land, or farm workers exaggerating their position. Thus the SA probably contained fewer independents, but more assisting family members, than the occupational analyses suggested.

Assisting family members, of whom there were about 657,500 males aged under 30,[135] provided the SA with a further source of recruitment from within the traditional *Mittelstand*. However, only 55,000 worked outside agriculture[136] which allows a reaffirmation that the non-agricultural SA must have consisted largely of workers and salaried staff by virtue of its age alone. Of the 602,300 young male assisting family members working in agriculture many were Catholics and, as rural, lower-middle-class Catholics, within a group which was relatively unattracted by Nazism. Protestant farmers' sons do appear in the SA's membership lists, even if sometimes described as 'farmers', but clearly they did not dominate the SA nationally.

The Marital Status of the Active SA's Rank and File, 1929–35

In the politically and economically troubled interwar years male Germans left marriage late. The 1925 census showed few marrying before

21, most still single at 25 and almost 30 per cent unmarried on their thirtieth birthday.[137] The depression compelled people to delay marriage still further,[138] which suggests that few stormtroopers would have been married. Indeed of its young, largely unemployed membership, only around a quarter were married in the late Weimar years.[139] In addition to stormtroopers' economic difficulties, the time-consuming and sometimes dangerous nature of SA service must have discouraged married recruits before 1933. Hitler's takeover saw the SA's membership age slightly, SA duties become decidedly safer and general economic conditions improve even if only gradually for stormtroopers. These factors arguably explain a rise in the proportion of married stormtroopers to around 35 per cent in the period 1933 to June 1934[140] and almost 50 per cent by mid-1935.[141]

Therefore, all in all, the SA attracted unmarried men and the 'ideal type' stormtrooper emerges not only as young, unemployed and working class, but also a bachelor. This economically deprived section of the population, bearing few of the responsibilities of older, married men and men of property were precisely the type of men the SA leadership required to act as political wreckers during the early 1930s.

Education, Religion and Politics in the Active SA

The connection between particular forms of education and career prospects was marked in the Weimar Republic.[142] All children entered primary school (*Volksschule*) when 6 and most remained there until their fourteenth birthday. The education received was one of questionable merit and attracted much criticism. As one commentator remarked: '[*Volksschule*] education does not plague the teacher alone in classes of sixty, seventy, eighty or more pupils'.[143] These eight years of formal education comprised the minimum statutory requirement, but all *Volksschule* pupils were obliged to attend part-time continuation school (*Fortbildungsschule*) until their eighteenth birthday. Here they received vocational training. A quarter attended general continuation school (*Allgemeine Fortbildungsschule*) which taught a range of general practical skills without qualifying its students for a particular trade. However, almost 57 per cent attended trade school (*Berufsschule*) and over 16 per cent technical school (*Technische Schule*) where they trained for a formal qualification in a particular trade or occupation.[144] In normal economic circumstances successful trade and technical school students expected to obtain relatively secure and well-paid jobs when 18.

A minority of pupils proceeded to a secondary education, leaving *Volksschule* when 10. Some attended middle school (*Mittelschule*) which, if still vocationally oriented, devoted rather more time to academic subjects than *Volksschulen* and were generally deemed to provide a higher quality of education. Although a few middle school pupils proceeded to more advanced schools, most saw the middle school's final examination, the *Mittlere Reife* (O-grade or O-level) as their goal. They left school when 16 and formed 'the basis of the technical professions and the middle-ranking civil service'.[145] The nine remaining types of secondary education, with attendance to the nineteenth birthday, can be categorised roughly as *Gymnasien* (grammar schools) and *Realschulen* (modern high schools). All provided access to further education, but the majority of university students came from the more prestigious *Gymnasien* with their largely classical education.

The middle schools were attacked during the Weimar period as bastions of privilege which creamed off better *Volksschule* pupils,[146] but the higher secondary schools were made more accessible and expanded. The numbers attending these higher schools, which took pupils on to *Abitur* (Highers or A-level), rose from 392,679 in 1911 to 475,047 in 1921/2 and 551,588 in 1926/7.[147] The numbers passing the *Abitur* also rose steeply; from 20,683 in 1926 to 40,227 in 1931.[148]

Just as these educational reforms produced many more well-educated Germans, the depression greatly reduced the scope of available employment. Further education provided a reprieve for the highly qualified, but this appeared temporary. By 1932 miserable economic prospects were driving students into the Nazi movement, causing the German Interior Minister to warn of 'the growth of an intellectual proletariat, a number of highly-educated young people unabsorbable within the economy, posing an enormous danger to the state'.[149]

Some evidently found their way into the SA, the membership of which was concentrated at the two extremes of the educational spectrum. Three quarters or more of stormtroopers had received a *Volksschule* education alone, but around 15 per cent had received a tertiary education – more than half of them at university. Therefore only around 8 per cent of stormtroopers concluded their education at middle school or higher secondary schools, this possibly signifying the enhanced employment prospects provided by these schools.[150] The large numbers of *Volksschüler* mainly reflect the predominance of workers in the SA, but most lower-middle-class stormtroopers shared this educational background, suggesting that most would have had limited prospects even without the depression. The stormtroopers with a tertiary education presumably either joined the SA from ideological conviction, or because the job crisis had left them extraordinarily embittered. The 8 per cent of stormtroopers who had graduated from secondary school were certainly embittered. A third were forced to become wage-earners and even some salaried employees

were disappointed, such as Heinrich R. of Würselen who took a probationary technical post at the Gouley open-cast coal mine. He commented:

> Although this job has absolutely nothing to do with my education, I
> am happy to be able to support my parents. My father is still
> unemployed and my brother only found work again a couple of
> weeks ago. How my career will develop and how I shall be able to use
> my education in any way whatsoever is still unclear to me.[151]

This frustration was matched at the lower end of the educational
spectrum. Skilled blue- and white-collar employees' *curricula vitae* indicate that most regarded their unemployment as completely undeserved
given their successful completion of a training. Under the circumstances their anger often assumed the dimensions of outright moral
outrage.

The Catholic political parties (Centre and BVP) remained largely un-
shaken by the massive electoral realignment of the early 1930s. Even in
March 1933 when the NSDAP did exceptionally well their decline was
relative, largely reflecting a failure to win new support in a higher poll
rather than a loss of existing support.[152] As a corollary, the NSDAP
fared best electorally in Protestant Germany with markedly weaker
performances in Catholic areas. The Catholic Church's open hostility to
Nazism before 1933 conceivably contributed to this result, but it need
not follow that the SA's appeal to Catholics was seriously affected.
First, little more than half of the Catholic population voted Centre or
BVP[153] and as working-class Catholics were those least attracted by
political catholicism the SA's task was, as a largely working-class body,
not hopeless. Furthermore, the SA might have recruited among
Catholics who were not otherwise especially attracted to Nazism.
    All else being equal, the SA's growth rates in Protestant and Catholic
areas respectively could indicate its relative attractiveness to each
denomination. These suggest that the SA attracted both denominations
more or less equally, for while it grew more rapidly in Protestant areas
during 1931,[154] the reverse occurred in 1932.[155] In absolute terms the
SA did remain weak in some Catholic areas, but in others it thrived.[156]
Its relative attractiveness to Protestants and Catholics can be tested
further by examining its denominational composition in areas of mixed
confession. The Bavarian element within the BDC source is best suited
for this.[157] The Bavarian population was 70 per cent Catholic and 28·8
per cent Protestant[158] while the Bavarian stormtroopers were 66·7 per
cent Catholic and 32·9 per cent Protestant (the Catholics being more
strongly working class) which suggests that in Bavaria, at least, the SA
had no particular attraction for Protestants. Presumably the SA's young

jobless recruits decided that their immediate plight overrode any denominational scruples some might have had.

The Weimar Republic was greeted with suspicion and animosity in many circles. Radical socialists regarded the establishment of a parliamentary democracy as an inadequate end, since they believed that the defeat and collapse of the empire presented the opportunity for a thoroughgoing social revolution. More crucially, many middle-class Germans feared the opposite. However restrained the 1918 revolution may have been, it appeared to release forces which threatened the position of the upper and lower middle classes alike. The First World War provided both the left- and right-wing anti-parliamentarian camps with a generation of Germans accustomed to military life and armed combat from which to recruit paramilitary forces, while providing the republican parties with potential recruits to take counter-measures in kind.

This environment spawned the NSDAP and, in 1921, the SA. War veterans did not comprise the SA's entire early membership, but it did recruit heavily among ex-soldiers who were organised on military lines by former army or Freikorps officers, some of the latter bringing Freikorps units intact into the SA.[159] Hitler eschewed the strategy of a direct assault on the state following the failure of the Munich putsch in November 1923, but this reduced temporarily rather than eliminated the SA's role within the Nazi movement. It continued to be of value as an instrument of propaganda, and of terror and coercion, in which guise its services again became indispensable during the early 1930s. However, despite this element of continuity in its role, the SA's unprecedented growth after 1929 need not have involved a fresh wave of war veterans.

The SA's age suggests that most recruits from 1929 onwards were not war veterans. Any stormtrooper born after October 1900 could not have seen active service, which means that less than a quarter of pre-1933 recruits and less than a tenth of post-January 1933 recruits could have fought in the war. Since some male adult Germans were exempted from military service, age merely sets a maximum limit to the possible proportion of war veterans. Sources from the years 1934 and 1935 provide details of war experience which indicate that war veterans were exceptional within the post-takeover SA. In 1934 only 7·3 per cent of stormtroopers had seen active service,[160] with a figure of 7·6 per cent for the 1935 SA.[161]

This is not to say that the war was irrelevant to stormtroopers. During their childhood or youth many experienced rationing and other shortfalls on the home front, factors which affected the working class particularly severely.[162] Moreover, many of their fathers and older male relatives were conscripted and some subsequently killed or wounded, all of which disrupted normal family life.[163] Following defeat, the effects of economic dislocation and, for some stormtroopers, foreign occupation or even annexation would have intensified further the relevance of the war. The street battles of the early 1920s formed a further part of their childhood experiences and therefore, while most stormtroopers lacked direct personal military experience, military activities had impinged on their lives. The relevance and effectiveness of party and trade union politics probably appeared questionable to say the least. The politics of the gun had decided Germany's fate in the First World War, or so it seemed, and helped shape the postwar political order.

In September 1930 the NSDAP achieved a spectacular electoral breakthrough as the depression tightened its grip on Germany. It attracted former right-wing voters, but did especially well among former abstainers and newly registered voters who turned out in their millions.[164] In July 1932 the NSDAP redoubled its vote, again attracting the lion's share of first-time voters, although also attracting several million former right-wing votes.[165] The SA's rapid growth coincided with the party's electoral success and one might ask whether the SA's recruits were converts from rival organisations or whether it, too, attracted many of the previously unaffiliated.

The information available does not provide a complete picture. Some forms of political activity, such as former membership of trade unions or sporting associations which often had political loyalties, were not recorded systematically by the SA, but it noted its members' former attachment to rival political parties, youth groups or paramilitary bodies with some care. In this respect, a reasonably complete profile of the Active SA's political background can be established – at least in as far as stormtroopers admitted to their political pasts, or the SA was able to discover them. Admittedly, most Germans did not belong to political parties before 1933 (for every SPD party member, for instance, there were nine voters),[166] but none the less an examination of the issue indicates how many stormtroopers had once committed themselves formally to a rival political cause.

The immediate impression given by three 1934 sources – BDC, North Rhineland and Frankfurt-am-Main[167] – is that few stormtroopers had previously belonged elsewhere. Of the 2,560 stormtroopers in these sources only 284 – around 11 per cent – had belonged to a total of 302 political organisations. Therefore, just as the NSDAP was singularly effective in mobilising the support of previous non-voters, the SA effectively recruited the formerly unaffiliated to its ranks, although given the organisation's youth this is not wholly surprising. Table 3.11[168] indicates that the minority of politically experienced stormtroopers had usually belonged to activist groups rather than political

Table 3.11 *Previous Political Affiliations. Active SA Rank and File,
1934.*

Political Parties	No.	%
Communist Party	44	48·9
Socialist Workers' Party	1	1·1
Social Democratic Party	29	32·2
German Democratic Party	1	1·1
Centre Party	6	6·7
Bavarian People's Party	2	2·2
German People's Party	1	1·1
National People's Party	6	6·7
Totals	90	100.0
Activist Groups	No.	%
Revolutionary trade union opposition	3	1·4
Left-wing activists	6	2·8
Reichsbanner	12	5·7
Iron Front	4	1·9
Catholic Youth	2	0·9
Bayernwacht	3	1·4
Stahlhelm	131	61·8
Bavarian Einwohnerwehr	2	0·9
Right-wing *Verbände*	8	3·8
Freikorps	39	18·4
French Foreign Legion	2	0·9
Totals	212	100·0*

* Total not exact due to rounding.
Note: The figures above were drawn from a base of 2,560 stormtroopers. See note 167
for sources.

parties. This tendency is enhanced if an organisational peculiarity of the
KPD is noted. In May 1929 the KPD's paramilitary wing, the Red
Front, was banned following a violent clash in Berlin between the
police and Red Front demonstrators.[169] It maintained an illegal,
shadowy existence, but its membership withered away whilst the KPD
itself expanded considerably.[170] The party had always been activist, but
now functional distinctions between it and the Red Front became
blurred with the KPD assuming most of the Red Front's functions.[171]

Ex-Stahlhelmer formed the largest single group among the activists
and overall. Some Stahlhelmer had been attracted to the SA individually,
but most joined in late 1933 when, for a variety of reasons, the conservative, monarchist Stahlhelm was partially absorbed by the SA. Older
Stahlhelm members, including many of the war veterans who formed
the organisation's original membership,[172] retained their separate iden-
tity. On 1 November 1933 Stahlhelmer aged between 36 and 45 were
formed into special SA Reserve units, designated SAR-I, [173] which

were later merged with the SA Reserve itself.[174] Many younger Stahlhelmer, aged under 36, were integrated within the Active SA, but a minority were permitted to join the SS and others were exempted from SA or SS membership.[175] The 131 of these largely involuntary recruits to the Active SA in Table 3.11 comprise 5.1 per cent of the base of 2,560 stormtroopers. If this ratio is projected on to the Active SA as a whole as it stood in early 1934, then around 127,500 stormtroopers would have been ex-Stahlhelmer.[176]

Most stormtroopers with political pasts had avoided such deals between institutions. Their decision to switch loyalties had been personal and therefore their presence in the SA indicates its relative attractiveness to individuals from different political backgrounds. With the exception of former Freikorps members who formed the original base of the SA, most converts were from the left, with ex-Communists prominent. The 99 former left-wingers comprise 3·9 per cent of the base of 2,560 individuals which, if projected on to the Active SA as a whole as it stood in early 1934, would amount to approximately 97,500 members.

Looking at social background, former left-wingers were, predictably, usually workers. More former Communists than ex-socialists were unskilled, while a minority of socialists, in particular, were salaried staff, and a Communist and socialist respectively were independent.[177] Former right-wingers, too, were, perhaps surprisingly, not particularly middle class. Of the ex-Stahlhelmer 58 per cent were working class and 26 per cent salaried employees, a result barely at odds with the SA's overall social profile.[178] The smaller body of ex-Freikorps members was 51·3 per cent working class and 35·9 per cent salaried staff, which would have made equally little impact on the Active SA's social profile.[179] Perhaps many middle-class Stahlhelmer avoided the largely working-class SA, taking the opportunity to join the more socially prestigious SS, if they joined a Nazi organisation at all. By 1935, after all, the army provided an alternative and less politically compromising choice.

The results presented in Table 3.11 require some modification. The collapse of left-wing parties and organisations in early 1933 and the integration of many Stahlhelmer later in the year produced SA units which consisted largely, or even entirely, of erstwhile rivals, but no such units are included in Table 3.11. In Frankfurt-am-Main one regiment, dissolved in April 1935, consisted principally of former Stahlhelmer[180] and the existence of similar units elsewhere probably boosted the proportion of Stahlhelmer in the Active SA above the 5·1 per cent mooted above. Units consisting of former left-wingers also existed, as illustrated by Diels's description of developments in Berlin during 1933:

Between January and November 1933 the SA [in Berlin] grew from 60,000 to 110,000 men. Easily 70 per cent of the new recruits were former communists. It spoke for the self-assurance of the SA that whole Companies along with their fife and drum bands consisted of former Red Front members.[181]

Diels possibly exaggerated but, even so, many thousands of Communists evidently transferred to the SA in Berlin alone. Similar transfers occurred in the north Rhine valley, for instance in Opladen[182] and Benrath,[183] while even in some rural areas the SA absorbed former Communists *en masse*. In Kruglinnen, East Prussia, the Nazi takeover transformed the SA dramatically, according to the local party history:

> In November 1932 there were still forty-five communists and over a hundred SPD men in Kruglinnen. After the takeover almost all these communists became SA men and the farmers' sons who were formerly in the SA were terrorised out by them.[184]

Therefore, while the results in Table 3.11 provide a broad guideline, some SA units evidently contained many political converts, which must have raised their representation overall. None the less, most stormtroopers evidently entered the SA politically inexperienced and, no doubt, often politically naïve.

The preceding results give some indication of stormtroopers' former voting records. Between 1930 and 1933 four general elections, a presidential election and state elections saw massive turnouts and while many stormtroopers were doubtless Nazi voters from the outset – and a minority still under voting age in 1933 – others presumably once voted for rival parties. With the ratio of SPD voters to party members at nine to one[185] and about 1·1 per cent of stormtroopers being ex-SPD members, many more stormtroopers than this had probably once voted SPD. Similarly, many stormtroopers probably once voted KPD, although any precise calculation is impossible.[186] Therefore, in terms of voting at least, many stormtroopers probably did have some very limited political experience, no doubt on the right as well as the left.

Leaders and Reservists

The stormtroopers belonged to a hierarchical organisation where guidance and control rested firmly with the leadership. A relatively brief, comparative survey of the leadership's social composition reveals marked differences between its background and that of the rank and file, and these differences facilitate an understanding of the SA's internal dynamics. The Reserve SA was much smaller than, and organisationally and functionally distinct from, the Active SA. It stood very much in the background, but an awareness of its social profile is none the less helpful. Had it been socially distinct from the Active SA, then it might have provided a counter-weight of sorts to the strongly working-class Active formations. Naturally, a strongly middle-class Reserve would also modify the SA's overall social profile. Consideration of the leaders and reservists also helps explain discrepancies between this book's findings and some earlier work where unrepresentatively large numbers of leaders or reservists were included in quantitative surveys of the SA's membership.[187]

Promotion within the SA was common, but few working-class stormtroopers rose beyond the rank of *Scharführer*.[188] The *Scharführer* (sergeant) who controlled the smallest unit, the *Schar*, with between 4 and 12 men,[189] comprised the majority of SA leaders. The next, and highest junior or non-commissioned rank, was that of *Truppführer* (sergeant-major) with command of a unit containing 20 to 50 men.[190] The lowest 'middle' rank, the *Sturmführer* (lieutenant) led between 70 and 200 men. Above him came the *Sturmbannführer* (major) leading 250 to 600 men, the *Standartenführer* (colonel) with 1,000 to 3,000 men and then the *Oberführer* and *Gruppenführer* who commanded the largest units.[191]

The *Scharführer* and also the *Truppführer* worked closely with their men and were expected to know them personally. The *Sturmführer* were expected at least to visit each subordinate in his home,[192] but from this rank upwards, despite the SA's aversion to bureaucratisation,[193] relations between leaders and men inevitably became more remote. Symbolic of this was the SA Intelligence Service which conducted surveillance of the stormtroopers for the senior leadership.

There is very little evidence concerning *Scharführer* during the late Weimar period. An undated survey by the Hanover police of SA leaders in Group North (roughly equivalent to present day Lower Saxony in area) included fifteen *Scharführer* of whom 60 per cent were working class, most of the rest being farmers (26·7 per cent).[194] Material was more forthcoming for the period after Hitler's takeover. Of 185 *Scharführer* in the BDC and North Rhineland sources, 51·9 per cent were working class and 31·9 per cent salaried employees or civil servants.[195] Therefore the *Scharführer*, who usually rose from the ranks, probably largely resembled the ordinary stormtroopers in their occupations, although their social profile appears slightly more middle class.

The *Truppführer* contrasted more markedly with their men. Most of the twelve men in the Hanover police survey were not workers,[196] while in the BDC/North Rhineland source the *Truppführer* were largely lower middle class. Of 127 only 28·3 per cent were workers, while 42·5 per cent were salaried employees or civil servants and 26·7 per cent independents.[197]

The more senior leaders from *Sturmführer* upwards who often only served briefly in the ranks, if at all, were usually middle class. The independents predominated in most cases, followed by salaried employees and civil servants with relatively few workers in evidence. This conclusion accords, in essence, with that of a larger, more systematic survey of the SA's middle and senior leadership presently underway.[198]

Of sources predating Hitler's takeover the largest was compiled in January 1933 by SA Group Nordmark (Schleswig-Holstein). This survey of more senior leaders contained 57·6 per cent independents and 27·9 per cent salaried staff and civil servants among its 593 members, but only 14·5 per cent workers.[199] The Hanover police survey's results for senior leaders contrasted less sharply with those for the rank and file, but even so, of its eighty-five subjects, 27·1 per cent were independents, 36·5 per cent salaried staff and civil servants, and only 24·7 per cent workers.[200] This variation in results probably reflected differing promotion policies within the SA or chronological differences, for the population structures of Schleswig-Holstein and Hanover were fairly similar.[201]

The post-takeover source (BDC/North Rhineland) is also predominantly middle class, containing 43·4 per cent independents and 34·9 per cent salaried staff and civil servants. In contrast with the pre-takeover sources many of the independents were professional people (29·6 per cent of the total source) – frequently SA doctors who usually held commissioned ranks. Comprising only 15·4 per cent of the source, the workers evidently remained a minority in the SA's leadership after Hitler's takeover. However, the component elements of the source differ, the North Rhineland element of thirty-four men being 35·2 per cent working class compared with the BDC figure of only 10·3 per cent.[202] Since the entire Nazi movement in the Ruhr District, leaders included,[203] was distinctly more working class than average, this is understandable. In early 1933, when the NSDAP nationally was 31·5 per cent working class,[204] the proportion of workers in the Ruhr NSDAP ranged from 37·5 per cent in *Gau* Westfalen-Nord, through 39·6 per cent in *Gau* Essen to 43·8 per cent in *Gau* Westfalen-Süd.[205]

Therefore the SA possessed a middle-class command whose socially determined attitudes and aspirations would have differed from those of its following. Indeed, the political standpoint of the senior leadership, the most middle-class section of the SA, contrasted markedly with their following's position and this contributed significantly to the SA's political weakness during the crisis of early 1934.[206] Even so, the gradation of contrast, with *Scharführer* largely resembling the ordinary stormtroopers in terms of occupational background probably lessened any resulting open antagonism, of which there is in fact comparatively little evidence.

The leadership was, not surprisingly, older than the ordinary stormtroopers and age rose with rank. Like their men, most *Scharführer* (65·5 per cent) were younger than 30 and only 0·6 per cent were 50 or above,[207] but the *Truppführer* were older, with only 37·6 per cent aged below 30 and 1·6 per cent aged 50 or more.[208] The process continued at the rank of *Sturmführer* and above, where in the BDC/North Rhineland source 26·3 per cent were younger than 30 and 4·4 per cent aged 50 or more.[209] In the pre-takeover Nordmark source, 24·0 per cent were 30 or younger and 16·5 per cent 45 or older.[210] This rise in age possibly reflected partly the rise in occupational status at higher ranks, for age and occupational status tend to rise together. However, stormtroopers in comparable occupations to their superiors were still generally younger which suggests that seniority in itself counted for something.

The more prestigious occupations of senior SA leaders helps explain the superiority of their education in comparison with ordinary stormtroopers. Educational attainment also rose with rank. In the 1934 BDC source 74·9 per cent of stormtroopers received a *Volksschule* education alone, but the proportion fell to 64·9 per cent for *Scharführer*, 42·2 per cent for *Truppführer* and 31·1 per cent for *Sturmführer* and above. As might be expected, the proportion of leaders with a tertiary education rose with rank. Thus 20·8 per cent of *Scharführer*, 32·9 per cent of *Truppführer* and 47·6 per cent of *Sturmführer* and above had received a tertiary education, compared with 16·1 per cent of stormtroopers.[211]

Education in itself was valued by the SA which associated a working-class background with a limited education and consequently with limited administrative competence. This is illustrated by an entry in the file of Obertruppführer Hans Fey of Hamburg who apparently was the exception which proved the rule: 'Fey is a lathe operator by occupation, but is none the less entrusted with paperwork.'[212] Similarly Rohe notes that the Reichsbanner's lower- and middle-ranking leaders were usually lower middle class, arguing that manual workers were considered over-stretched by the administrative tasks which accompanied promotion, presumably because of their educational background.[213] The SA rank of *Scharführer* placed relatively light administrative demands on an SA member, but the increasing volume of administrative work at progressively higher ranks was marked by the declining proportion of workers and *Volksschüler*. *Truppführer* and more senior leaders who had only attended *Volksschule* were generally in clerical, sales, administrative or independent occupations where their vocational training and occupation would have bestowed on them a higher level of administrative competence than their working-class counterparts possessed.

The military ethos pervading the SA's organisation and activities largely emanated from the body's more senior leadership. Therefore, most senior leaders were, predictably, war veterans, unlike ordinary stormtroopers, with the contrast once again gradated according to rank. While only 6·1 per cent of stormtroopers in the BDC source had seen war service the proportions for leaders were: *Scharführer* 14·6 per cent, *Truppführer* 43·7 per cent and *Sturmführer* and above 50·4 per cent.[214] Since the recording of military service in the BDC files is probably incomplete, these figures are possibly something of an underestimate of war experience and certainly the Nordmark survey points to a higher proportion of war veterans at *Sturmführer* and above, namely 73·7 per cent.[215] At the most senior levels almost all leaders had served in the armed forces (86·5 per cent) and 73·5 per cent had fought in the war.[216] Even so, most SA leaders had not risen particularly high in the armed forces.[217] The SA's Nordmark survey was partly intended to prove how few of Schleswig-Holstein's (and by implication Germany's) SA leaders were ex-officers. Only 10·7 per cent of the 437 ex-servicemen in the survey were former officers, while 51·9 per cent had served in the ranks and 37·5 per cent had been non-commissioned officers.[218] In the BDC source SA leaders of comparable rank with those in the Nordmark survey (*Sturmführer* and above) had enjoyed slightly more auspicious military careers. Only 27·9 per cent had served in the ranks while 41·2 per cent had been NCOs and 30·9 per cent officers. Predictably, the more junior SA leaders in this source had usually held lower ranks. However, of the thirty ex-officers among the BDC leaders, only four – other than certain medical officers – had risen above the rank of lieutenant.[219]

Experience of armed combat and familiarity with military techniques of organisation evidently assisted promotion within the SA, along with a superior pattern of education and a more prestigious occupational background than those possessed by most ordinary stormtroopers.[220] The preference for war veterans must also explain the age structure of the SA's leadership to some degree. Young men had not experienced army life, even in peacetime, for Weimar's peacetime army was restricted to 100,000 long-serving members under the terms of the Treaty of Versailles.

Nazism's fundamentally hostile stance towards the political left was manifested vehemently in the violent suppression of left-wing organisations after Hitler's takeover. The SA featured prominently in this process, despite the similarity in social background between stormtroopers and members of left-wing bodies. The SA's leaders, however, not only differed socially, but had political backgrounds well suited to the task in hand. In addition, many more leaders than stormtroopers had previous political experience; within the BDC source 6 per cent of stormtroopers, 9 per cent of *Scharführer* and 33·3 per cent of ranks from *Truppführer* upwards had once been active outside the Nazi movement. With two exceptions among 107 cases this past was extreme right-wing. Forty-five instances involved the Freikorps and these SA leaders doubtless relived the anti-Communist battles of the early 1920s as they smashed the organised left in early 1933 – this time revolutionary or otherwise. A further twenty-eight instances involved the Stahlhelm while the remainder had usually belonged to various right-wing *Ver-*

bände and splinter parties. Only six former DNVP members (all *Sturm-führer* or higher) were present, emphasising the SA's links with the paramilitary right rather than the right in Parliament and the board-room.[221]

Therefore, the SA's leaders and men differed in political background as in much else. Despite the SA's strengths, it lacked the unity of purpose which greater social or political homogeneity could have imparted. The lack of any coherent, positive Nazi ideology combined with the distinctions between leaders and men to keep the SA's political be-haviour largely reactive and negative.

The Reserve SA was founded on 28 March 1929 as a second string to the Active SA, which bore the brunt of the organisation's responsibilities and duties. It organised individuals who were incapable physically of meeting the demands of service in the Active SA, or whose working lives precluded full commitment to the cause. A weekly three-hour inspection and a fortnightly three-hour military exercise comprised the reservists' formal SA duties.[222] The minimum age for membership was 40, although until November 1933 stormtroopers over 40 could remain in the Active SA.[223] In November 1933, as the Stahlhelm was integrated with the SA, reforms placed stormtroopers aged between 36 and 45 in the SA Reserve I (along with many ex-Stahlhelmer) and those of 46 or older in the SA Reserve II which later became the SA Landsturm.[224] However, these limits were loosely observed and at their upper bounds were applied (without great rigour) to rank-and-file members only. The Reserve was small. In November 1931 it comprised 21·1 per cent of the SA's total membership,[225] but the proportion fell to 15·5 per cent by early 1934.[226] Here it remained for the rest of 1934, but during 1935 it rose steeply. Many Active SA members left the organisation, often for transfer to the armed forces, while the Reserve's numerical strength remained almost unchanged. Presumably with the SA's functions reduced to parades and the like, the mostly quiescent Reserve member-ship was as useful and less politically embarrassing than the Active SA and by November the Reserve constituted 29·5 per cent of the SA's membership.[227]

Wage-earners and salaried staff dominated the Reserve's occupational profile, as they did the Active SA. None the less, Table 3.12 indicates that the proportion of workers was lower in the Reserve, after Hitler's takeover at least, while the number of independents and especially civil servants was higher. Many civil servants joined Nazi organisations after Hitler's takeover to secure their jobs,[228] having no illusions over security of tenure under a Nazi regime, and for those lukewarm towards Nazism the Reserve SA was a relatively innocuous choice which also made few demands on their time. In some areas relatively large numbers of civil servants joined the Reserve SA simultaneously in early 1933.

Table 3.12   *Reserve SA Rank-and-File Members. Occupational Background. 30 January 1933 to 30 June 1934.*[229]

Occupational Groups	No.	%
Unskilled workers	175	14·5
(Semi-) skilled workers	476	39·6
Salaried manual	101	8·4
Salaried white-collar	148	12·3
Civil servants	126	10·5
Master craftsmen	45	3·7
Independent proprietors	34	2·8
Farmers	39	3·2
Assisting family members	1	0·1
Servants	3	0·2
Professions, independents	45	3·7
Students	4	0·3
Miscellaneous	6	0·5
Totals	1,203	100·0*

* Total not exact due to rounding.
Note: Occupational categories as for Table 3.1.

The four sources comprising Table 3.12 show variations in their occupational profiles, some arising from their geographical provenance. Thus farmers comprise 15·1 per cent of the largely rural BDC source, while the urban Frankfurt-am-Main source predictably contained no farmers. There were other reasons for these variations. Some Reserve units apparently organised young recruits whose occupational commitments prevented time-consuming service in the Active SA. The component source of this type, from Regiment R97 of Frankfurt-am-Main, was 68·9 per cent working class, while in the other three sources workers were a minority (Burghausen 47 per cent, Nuremberg 45·3 per cent and BDC 38·6 per cent). The Reserve SA consisted largely of these older units and therefore the 54·1 per cent working-class representation in Table 3.12 is probably an overestimate. Even so, the working-class presence in the Reserve SA was large and if, for the sake of argument, the SA's Reserve and Active rank and file were regarded as a whole, the SA would retain its strongly working-class character.

The Reserve SA suffered unemployment and older jobless reservists found it especially hard to obtain new work.[230] This said, unemployment was apparently lower than in the Active SA, perhaps partly because occupational commitments sometimes diverted recruits into the Reserve. Thus Battalion RI/15 of Nuremberg had 35·8 per cent of its members unemployed in mid-1933.[231] The comparable figure for

Nuremberg's Active SA is unavailable,[232] but the level is almost half that for the Active SA generally. Working-class reservists, like their Active counterparts, were more frequently unemployed than middle-class stormtroopers.[233] Therefore, while unemployment was less severe in the Reserve, its relatively high quota of jobless confirms that the SA overall attracted many unemployed recruits during the early 1930s.

While the Reserve was older than the Active SA, it still contained members below its minimum regulation age. Perhaps a quarter of members were younger than 30 while half were younger than 35 – the Reserve's minimum age limit. Variations between component sources are large; the proportion under 35 ranging between 18·5 per cent (BDC), 38·7 per cent (Nuremberg), 43·6 per cent (Burghausen) and 72·9 per cent (Frankfurt-am-Main).[234] Some younger Stahlhelmer apparently preferred the less demanding Reserve while, as mentioned, occupational commitments led others to the Reserve.

Reservists were usually married, the younger members included.[235] Age alone explains the higher marriage rates among the older reservists, but younger married stormtroopers were apparently reluctant to face the risks inherent in Active SA membership or to sacrifice time with their families. Indeed, the few reservists who left the SA after mid-1934 were almost always married.

Although the Reserve SA was more middle class than the Active SA, its members were no better educated. In the BDC source 80·8 per cent of reservists were ex-*Volksschüler* compared with 74·9 per cent of Active stormtroopers.[236] White-collar reservists and those from the civil service were usually well educated, but other middle-class reservists were not. None of the lower-middle-class independents had gone beyond *Volksschule* and therefore rather than redeeming the SA's intellectual image, the Reserve stormtroopers do the opposite.[237]

The Active SA, if anything, tended slightly towards Protestantism but, in Bavaria at least, the Reserve was slightly more Catholic[238] than the population at large. The Bavarian element in the BDC source was 75·9 per cent Catholic compared with a figure for Bavaria itself of 70 per cent[239] and a figure for the Active SA of 66·7 per cent.[240] Once again, the relative innocuousness of the Reserve SA may have contributed to this. Just as civil servants apparently favoured the Reserve, so Catholics who reluctantly felt obliged to join a Nazi formation after Hitler's takeover possibly regarded the Reserve SA as a fairly harmless choice.

There were relatively more war veterans in the Reserve SA, this being explained by its generally older membership. Even the relatively young Regiment R97 of Frankfurt-am-Main contained 23·8 per cent war veterans,[241] but the figure was higher on the whole. In the sources included in Table 3.12, 39·8 per cent of stormtroopers had seen war service[242] (Active SA 7·3 per cent) while in sources from the period July

1934 to the end of 1935, 54·4 per cent of stormtroopers were war veterans[243] (Active SA 7·6 per cent). Furthermore, unlike the Active SA, the Reserve contained many ex-NCOs and even a few former lieutenants and reserve lieutenants at rank-and-file level.[244]

Relatively few Reserve stormtroopers were politically experienced, but more reservists (15 to 20 per cent) than Active stormtroopers (11 per cent) did have a political past.[245] In most Reserve units these were usually right-wingers, over half being ex-Stahlhelmer and a good many others ex-Freikorps members.[246] In Regiment R97 the picture was reversed with former left-wingers, and among them Social Democrats, dominating.[247] The predominance of working-class storm-troopers in R97 probably accounts for this, but even so R97 contrasts with working-class Active units where the KPD was stronger than the SPD. This tendency to attract ex-Social Democrats probably partly reflects the low unemployment rates in R97. The SPD had maintained its following among the employed while the Active SA, like the KPD, recruited primarily from the unemployed.[248] Furthermore, Frankfurt-am-Main, where R97 was based, was an SPD stronghold and this doubtless depressed further the Communist representation in the unit.

While former Stahlhelmer were relatively numerous in the Reserve SA, only 13·8 per cent of reservists (excluding members of R97) left evidence of former Stahlhelm membership. If this percentage is extra-polated to cover the whole Reserve the organisation would have con-tained barely 60,000 Stahlhelmer even in its heyday in early 1934. Combined with an estimate for Stahlhelmer in the Active SA, it seems at first sight that perhaps no more than 200,000 Stahlhelmer joined the SA as a whole. This relatively meagre result compares unfavour-ably with Berghahn's estimate that a million Stahlhelmer transferred to the SA in November 1933[249] and Jamin's estimate of around 800,000.[250] The figure of 200,000 was therefore presumably supple-mented by units such as the 25th Regiment of Frankfurt-am-Main which consisted almost entirely of Stahlhelmer, but none the less it appears that many Stahlhelmer either avoided SA membership, or escaped full integration by joining the SA Reserve II.[251]

Therefore the Reserve's rank and file was, socially speaking, rather more heterogeneous than that of the Active SA. Politically, it had a more explicitly right-wing background than the Active SA's mem-bership, particularly as former members of right-wing *Verbände* had joined the Reserve rather than the Active SA in 1933. This develop-ment possibly suited the SA's leaders who thereby gained some political control over the members of the more conservative *Verbände* without their membership swamping the Active SA units. However, if the Reserve SA thereby conformed somewhat more closely to the social and political profile of the Nazi Party than did the Active SA, its social composition deviated from that of the Active SA rather than contrasting with it.

The contrasts between the composition of the SA's leaders and the ordinary stormtroopers highlight the problems of some earlier studies of the SA where leaders occupy a disproportionate numerical share of the material considered. Similarly, but less critically, the inclusion of disproportionate numbers of reservists could also contribute to a misleading result. Merkl's conclusion that the SA, although markedly more working class than the Nazi Party, was over half middle class may therefore have been affected by the predominance of leaders within his study, although his data's pre-1930 bias and the inclusion of SS members within the material prevent any clear conclusion.[252] A study by Reiche, however, which concludes that only 36·9 per cent of SA members joining between 1925 and 1934 in Nuremberg were working class, cannot be considered representative of the Active SA's rank and file who comprised the mass of the organisation.[253] His group of 265 stormtroopers included 100 who held middle or higher ranks[254] and, given their age, many more in the group were probably reservists.[255]

Until 1929 the SA had been among the smaller paramilitary groupings in Germany, numbering a few thousand men. Literature on the early SA cannot but leave one with the impression that it attracted cranks and misfits in the first instance.[256] The onset of the depression evidently changed the situation, not least because it produced several million jobless young Germans who had still to develop an established social and political routine. Most had worked, or had at least trained to work, but for insufficiently long to become involved in conventional politics, either within a trade union or a party. Neither had many attained the degree of economic security commensurate with marriage or the establishment of their own household. The SA attracted several hundred thousand such recruits before 1933 and 2 million or more after Hitler's takeover, as well as a minority of stormtroopers from different, or partially different, backgrounds. That most stormtroopers were workers was perhaps largely because so many young Germans and so many unemployed Germans were workers, but none the less it seems clear that the NSDAP had developed a paramilitary wing which contrasted socially with the parent party. The independent *Mittelstand* who provided the party with almost a third of its membership were largely absent among the rank-and-file stormtroopers.[257]

In the short term, the SA's success in recruiting so many jobless workers was undoubtedly advantageous for the Nazi movement. It gave the NSDAP an effective and an organised presence in the working-class areas of towns and cities where the party itself could make little headway while depriving the KPD, in particular, of many potential members. However, in the longer term Hitler's accession to power not only made the SA superfluous – the street-fighting days were soon over – but also a positive embarrassment to a party which had no constructive social policy for the very groups which characterised the SA's membership. The fuller implications of these issues will be discussed presently and it is equally important to establish why so many unemployed workers joined part of a movement which was bitterly opposed to the very parties which stood for, and had fought most strongly for, working-class emancipation.

Notes

1 See pp. 5–6.
2 I am very much indebted to Dr L. D. Stokes of Dalhousie University, Nova Scotia, for allowing me use of a membership list for the SA in Eutin, Holstein, 1929.
3 L. D. Stokes, 'The social composition of the Nazi Party in Eutin, 1925–32', *International Review of Social History*, vol. 23, pt 1 (1978), pp. 27–8.
4 BA, NS26/528–533. SA veterans (Active SA, rank and file) from Hessen-Nassau, 1929. The *Goldenes Ehrenzeichen* was given to Nazis who had joined the NSDAP, or an associated body, before 1930. In compiling this list of seventy-two storm-troopers it was ensured that they joined the SA (and not just the NSDAP) before 1930 and that they did not become leaders before January 1930.
5 Some of the veterans lived in Mainz and Giessen, which lay just outside Hessen-Nassau, when they came to write their recollections, but none the less they had belonged to the Hessen-Nassau SA.
6 J. Wickham, 'The Working Class Movement in Frankfurt-am-Main during the Weimar Republic' (D. Phil., University of Sussex, 1979), pp. 38–40.
7 See pp. 28–9, 34.
8 BHStA, Abt. I, So. I/1549. Companies from the Munich SA, 1932.
9 BHStA, Abt. I, So. I/1549. Stellenbesetzungs-Liste der Gruppe Hochland, pp. 1–3. Nineteen Active SA companies from Munich are named. The existing organisational framework at the time (October 1930) allowed provision for at least ten existing companies. The SA grew substantially between 1930 and 1932 and one would expect that existing companies grew, within limits, and that new companies were formed. The figure of twenty-seven companies assumes (conservatively) that nine new companies were created.
10 Addresses given in the membership lists indicate that the area was bounded by the main railway line and present-day inner-ring road to the south, the River Isar to the east, a line from the Nordfriedhof to the Westfriedhof to the north (with a few members from further north) and from the Westfriedhof due south to the Friedenheimer Bridge to the west.
11 BHStA, Abt. I, So. I/1549. Sturm 3, Schlageter June 1932, updated September 1932.
12 BHStA, Abt. I, So. I/1549. Sturm 6, September 1932.
13 BHStA, Abt. I, So. I/1549. Sturm 5 (Borstei), October 1932.
14 BHStA, Abt. I, So. I/1549. Sturmbann II/L – Sturm 16, April 1932.
15 See note 16 below. Laim SA 73·9 per cent working class.

16 BHStA, Abt. I, So. I/1549. Mannschaftsliste für Trupp Laim, Sturm 4 der NSDAP; BHStA, Abt. I, So. I/1870. Verzeichnis der Mitglieder der SA des Sturmes 5 (Neuhausen); BHStA, Abt. I, So. I/1870. Abschrift. Dienststelle, Trupp Weilheim Stu. 55. Stärkebericht für den Monat Dezember 1930; Hessisches Hauptstaatsarchiv Wiesbaden (henceforward HHW), NSDAP Gauleitung Hessen-Nassau (henceforward Abt. 483)/NSDAP 1053. Sturm 17/81. Namensverzeichnis [Frankfurt-am-Main, 1932]; HHW, Abt. 483/NSDAP 6348. Sturmbann IV/115, Auerbach/Hessen, 1931; Niedersächsisches Hauptstaatsarchiv (henceforward NHStA), Hann. 310 I E1. SA in Anderten, 1930–3; NHStA, Landratsamt Hameln-Pyrmont, Aktenstück A4[1]. SA Gruppe in Halvestorf, 1931; SAG, Rep. 240/C39d. Ortsgruppe Allenstein (SA); SAG, Rep. 240/C40c. Ortsgruppe Possessern. Geschichte. SAG, Rep. 240/C47e. SA Abteilung, Ortsgruppe Kiauten; SAG, Rep. 240/C61b(1). Ortsgruppe Widminnen. Geschichte, pp. 20–1; BHStA – Staatsarchiv München (henceforward SM), NSDAP 803. SA Sturmbann II/4. Neuötting/Burghausen, 1932.

17 Of the ten farmers, three were teenagers and a further six were in their twenties. NHStA, Landratsamt Hameln-Pyrmont, Aktenstück A4[1]. SA Gruppe in Halvestorf, 1931. See also note 257.

18 HHW, Abt. 483/NSDAP 1053. Sturm 17/81. Namensverzeichnis [Frankfurt-am-Main, 1932]. The relatively high incidence of students combined with a large block of workers resembled the situation in at least some Austrian cities where the SA was similarly comprised. See F. L. Carsten, *Fascist Movements in Austria: From Schönerer to Hitler* (London, 1977), p. 198.

19 BHStA, Abt. I, So. I/1551. Auszug aus dem Bericht des Polizeipräsidenten in Berlin vom 19. September 1930, Tgb. 439. IA 7/1929 Anlage 2. Verhaftete SA-Mitglieder; BHStA, Abt. I, So. I/1554. Namensverzeichnis der 23 Berliner SA-Leute die sich vom 20. Mai bis 2. Juni in München aufhielten; BA, NS26/522. Alfeld/Leine. Kriminalpolizei, Juli 1932; BA, NS26/523,527. Miscellaneous police sources, 1930–2; BA, NS26/596. Prussia. Stormtroopers arrested for possession of firearms, September 1930–August 1931; BA, NS26/513. Schurgerichtsache München, 14. Dezember 1932. Anklageschrift des Staatsanwaltes bei dem Landgerichte München I; BA, NS26/522. Deutsch Eylau. Kriminalpolizei, 14. März u. 15. April 1932; Institut für Zeitgeschichte (henceforward IfZ), MA 616/21,474344,45/46 (SA III – Ausschreitungen). Der Oberstaatsanwalt als Leiter der Anklagebehörde bei dem Sondergericht Görlitz, 28. Nov. 1932; IfZ, MA 616/21, 4353–4661 (SA III – Ausschreitungen). SA men in Luetgebrune papers, Nov.–Dec. 1932; IfZ, MA 616/20, 2954 (SA III – Ausschreitungen). SA men in Luetgebrune papers, Görlitz area, Sept. 1932; SAG, Rep. 37–5. Haffke u. Gen. Tannenwalde, Aug. 1930–Mar. 1931. SA men involved; SAG, Rep. 37–5. SA men charged with arson. Königsberg, August 1932; SAG, Rep. 37–14. SA men in fight with KPD. Königsberg, July 1932; SAG, Rep. 37–15. Ortsgruppe Metgethen, attack on Reichsbanner. Königsberg, November 1930; SAG, Rep. 18–14. Court proceedings. Lyck, 15 March 1931; SAG, Rep. 240/C67b. Der Oberstaatsanwalt als Leiter der Anklagebehörde beim Sondergericht, Anklageschrift. Allenstein, 30. August 1932; SAG, Rep. 240/ C67b. Court proceedings. Ortelsburg, 21 September 1931.

20 This observation demands that parts of the working class be located outside the established labour movement – as it was. See, for instance, Wickham, 'Working class', pp. 12–20.

21 See pp. 21, 159, 169.

22 SAG, Rep. 18–13. Staatl. Kriminalkommissariat. Betr.: SA der NSDAP. Allenstein, 19.6.1931.

23 See pp. 58, 60.

24 See note 22.

25 R. J. Bessel, 'The SA in the Eastern Regions of Germany, 1925 to 1934' (D. Phil., Oxford University, 1980), p. 84.

26 ibid., p. 83.
27 SAG, Rep. 18–13. Zusammenstellung über die im Regierungsbezirk Allenstein vorhandene SA der NSDAP nach dem Stande vom 10.6.1931.
28 See p. 20. Note 257 below suggests that the presence of so many farmers in the SA might have been primarily a north-east German phenomenon. However, the comparison of pre- and post-takeover sources invites caution.
29 *Statistisches Jahrbuch für das deutsche Reich, 1934* (Berlin, 1934), Vol. 1, p. 20, table 16c.
30 ibid., p. 24, table 21.
31 See note 29.
32 See note 30.
33 *Statistisches Jahrbuch*, Vol. 1, p. 19, table 14c, note 5.
34 BA, NS23/337. SA der NSDAP. OSAF Führungsamt. München, 3.9.1935.
35 A. Werner, 'SA und NSDAP' (Dissertation, Friedrich Alexander Universität zu Erlangen, 1964), p. 552. Werner is unaware of the decline in SA membership during late 1932. His figure of 700,000 has been repeated widely. Since the SA's own much lower figure for January was compiled from returns made during the month, the flood of additional recruits must have followed Hitler's takeover. Werner gives no source for his figure.
36 M. Broszat, *Der Staat Hitlers* (Munich, 1969), p. 256.
37 BA, NS23/127. OSAF, F. Nr. 4513. München, 27. März 1934.
38 The provenances overlap, but the post-January 1933 data contains little East Prussian material and rather more from western Germany.
39 SM, NSDAP 833. Sturm 24/25, Burghausen, 1934; SM, NSDAP 728. Sturm 1/10, Ingolstadt. Namensliste 1933–4; BA, NS23/8,11. Small, miscellaneous Prussian sources; BA, NS23/398. Stormtroopers from Hamburg, 1933–4; Nordrhein-Westfälisches Hauptstaatsarchiv (henceforward NWHStA), RW 23. SA Standarte J8, Würselen, 1933/4; NWHStA, RW 23. SA Standarte 25, Aachen, 1. Juli 1934. This source falls outside the period by a day, but the returns would have been compiled during June 1934.

Location of Sources	Size	% working class	% lower middle class	% salaried staff
Aachen	30	70·0	23·3	10·0
Burghausen	8	87·5	12·5	0·0
Hamburg	10	50·0	50·0	20·0
Ingolstadt	108	77·8	17·6	7·4
Prussia (mixed)	52	78·8	19·2	13·5
Würselen	30	70·0	26·7	23·3

The percentage of salaried staff is also counted in the lower-middle-class percentage. Both are percentages of the overall total. The very high working-class percentages in the Bavarian towns of Burghausen and Ingolstadt are repeated in neighbouring Austria. See Carsten, *Fascist Movements*, p. 198.

40 Berlin Document Center (henceforward BDC), SA Archive (SA). The intention was to examine all files with surnames beginning with 'F'. Lack of time restricted the survey to surnames with the initial letters FA to FM.
41 BDC, SA 774–878.
42 For source: BDC, SA 774–878; for SA: BA, NS23/127. OSAF, F. Nr. 4513. München, 27. März 1934.

43 Place of residence established in 819 cases.

Towns, population	BDC source	Reich
10,000 or less	62.5%	52.0%
10,000–50,000	11.7%	13.2%
50,000–100,000	6.8%	5.2%
100,000 or more	18.9%	29.6%

44 Religion no doubt played a part here. The Catholic middle classes were slow to turn to Nazism during the early 1930s, if they did so at all. See E. Fröhlich, 'Die Partei auf lokaler Ebene', in G. Hirschfeld and L. Kettenacker (eds), *The 'Fuhrer State'* (Stuttgart, 1981), pp. 255–60, where the miserable performance of the NSDAP among Bavarian farmers before 1933 and the localised nature of Nazi success in rural, Catholic Bavaria after 1933 is made clear.
45 BDC source, 8·3 per cent Hessian; SA in March 1934, 4·7 per cent Hessian. Sources as for note 42.
46 Reich, 45·1 per cent working class; Bavaria, 36·7 per cent working class. *Statistisches Jahrbuch*, Vol. 1., p. 21, table 17.
47 HHW, Abt. 483/NSDAP 1381, 1382, 2522–2524 (Standarte 25); HHW, Abt. 483/NSDAP 1346–1362, 2100–2213 (Standarte 81); HHW, Abt. 483/NSDAP 1368–1379, 2214–2284 (Standarte 99). Results for 30 June 1934 obtained by combining results for 1 July 1935 with those stormtroopers who left the SA in the preceding year, during which time new recruitment was minimal.
48 The three regiments examined came from the industrial suburbs of Höchst and Griesheim; the commercial, residential and academic Westend and central Frankfurt; poor inner-city areas such as Bockenheim, and some outlying residential suburbs. Even so, the 1,650 men included did not constitute the entire Frankfurt SA, which numbered 18,176 leaders and men even in October 1934 after cutbacks in size had begun. BA, Sch 415. Stärke der SA Gruppen und Brigaden am 1. Oktober 1934.
49 BA, NS23/306. Sturmbann II/2, Pionierstürme 11/2, 12/2, 13/2, Standort Speyer, 26. Juni 1934; Standarte 31, Pioniersturm 14/31, Ludwigshafen, 19. Jun, 1934; Standarte 22, Pioniersturm 9/22, Zweibrücken, 21. Juni 1934; Standarte 8, Pioniersturm 16/8, Wolfstein, 22. Juni 1934; SA Gruppe Kurpfalz, Pioniersturm 16/17, Maximiliansau, 21. Juni 1934.
50 Sturm 16/8: 4·5 per cent in war as pioneers, 6·0 per cent with SA training. Of additional units included in Table 3.5:
Stürme 1/25–7/25: 4·8% in war as pioneers, 1·1% SA-trained.
Sturm 15/21 : 5·5% in war as pioneers, 5·5% SA-trained.
Sturm 18/27 : 9·2% in war as pioneers, 0·8% SA-trained.
Sturm 6/118 : 1·4% in war as pioneers, 1·9% SA-trained.
51 BA, NS26/306. Die Pionierstürme der Brigade 150, Rheinhessen; Stürme 1–7, Mainz, Juni 1934; Sturm 6/118, Worms, Juni 1934; Sturm 18/27, Bingen, Juni 1934; Sturm 15/21, Nierstein, Juni 1934.
52 BA, NS23/262. SA der NSDAP. Führer der Brigade 150, Rheinhessen. Lagebericht für das 4. Vierteljahr 1934. Mainz, den 19. Dezember 1934. This report does note that some sons of small farmers had joined the local SA.
53 NWHStA, Gestapo(leit)stelle Düsseldorf (henceforward Ge).
54 The source is: 84·1 per cent urban; 0·9 per cent towns 50,000–100,000; 3·1 per cent towns 20,000–50,000; 2·7 per cent towns 10,000–20,000; 9·3 per cent small town and rural.
55 NWHStA, Ge.
56 The party also did remarkably well in recruiting workers in the northern Rhine-

land. D. Mühlberger, 'The sociology of the NSDAP'. *Journal of Contemporary History*, vol. 15, no. 3 (1980), pp. 499–502.

57   SM, NSDAP 803. SA der NSDAP, Sturm 22/25. Probweise Aufnahme von SA–Anwäretern vom 1. bis zum 5.12.1933. Altötting; Generallandesarchiv Karlsruhe (henceforward GLAK), Abt. 465d/1307. SA der NSDAP, Sturm 16/469, Eberbach, 13.12.1933. (a) Verzeichnis der in der Zeit 1. – 5. November neu angemeldeten SA–Anwärter. (b) Verzeichnis der in der Zeit v. 1. – 5. November neu angemeldeten u. auswärts wohnenden SA–Anwärter.
58   SM, NSDAP 658. Verzeichnis der Arbeitslosen des Sturmes 5/10, Ingolstadt, 1934; SM, NSDAP 971. Sturm 5/J5, Isen. Freiplätze aus der Hitlerspende; GLAK, Abt. 465d/1303. Folgende SAM sind arbeitslos in Zug 6 1/112. Neckargerach, 4.1.1934; GLAK, Abt. 465d/1303. SA der NSDAP, Sturm 1/112, Eberbach a.N. SAM Arbeitslosenmeldung für den Monat Februar 1934, 28.2.1934. (No duplication of names between this and the previous source.)
59   The unskilled workers derive principally from the Ingolstadt source.
60   BA, NS23/398. Untergruppe Hamburg. Tagesbefehl. 10.8.1932.
61   *Statistisches Jahrbuch*, Vol. 1, p. 20, table 16c.
62   ibid., p. 24, table 21.
63   BDC, SA 774–878.
64   NWHStA, Ge.
65   Industry: 176, of whom 150 were workers. Agriculture: 127, of whom 63 were workers and 60 independents. Communications and commerce: 73, of whom 34 were workers, 21 were salaried staff, 6 civil servants and 12 were independents or members of their families.
66   Evidence from BDC files, SA 774–878.
67   Evidence from NWHStA, Ge. Files containing personal details on stormtroopers.
68   *Statistisches Jahrbuch*, Vol. 1, p. 19, table 14c; Vol. 9, p. 307, table 11.
69   Skilled workers, salaried manual, salaried white-collar. Civil servants and master craftsmen could also be included.
70   BDC, SA 774–878; HHW, Abt. 483/NSDAP 2100–2213. Standarte 81, Frankfurt-am-Main. Stormtroopers leaving the regiment between 1 July 1934 and 30 June 1935. This small, exploratory sample resembled closely the wider Frankfurt source. For instance, Standarte 81 (as above): 64·3 per cent working class. Wider Frankfurt source, 63·6 per cent working class.
71   *Statistisches Jahrbuch*, Vol. 1, p. 24, table 21.
72   BDC SA 784. Mathias Falterer, Poing, den 5.11.33.
73   For instance: BDC, SA 794. Christian Fehr, born 4.5.1910; BDC, SA 791. Karl Federholzer, no date of birth given; BDC, SA 829. Ernst Finkbeiner, born 19.12.1914.
74   BDC, SA 777. Max Färber, born 8.6.1900.
75   BDC, SA 781. Friedrich Falk, born 11.1.1914.
76   BDC, SA 809. Ludwig Fenzl, born 10.8.1913.
77   BDC, SA 878. Christian Fluhrer, born 31.1.1914.
78   BDC, SA 800. Michael Feistenauer, born 16.6.1910; BDC, SA 790. Emil Fauter, born 5.5.1915; BDC, SA 843. Georg Fischer, born 15.12.1912; BDC, SA 871. Johann Fleischmann, born 6.5.1911.
79   Bennecke lists 83 executions, which he acknowledges to be incomplete. 50 individuals on the list are SA leaders. Bloch estimates the total number of executions at between 150 and 200. See H. Bennecke, 'Die Reichswehr und der "Röhm Putsch"', Beiheft 2, *Politische Studien* (Munich, 1964), Anlage 5; C. Bloch, *Die SA und die Krise des NS-Regimes 1934* (Frankfurt-am-Main, 1970),p. 104; K. Gossweiler, 'Der Übergang von der Weltwirtschaftskrise zur Rüstungskonjunktur', *Jahrbuch für Wirtschaftsgeschichte*, vol. 2 (1968), pp. 98–116.
80   I. Kershaw, 'The Führer image and political integration: the popular conception of Hitler in Bavaria during the Third Reich', in G. Hirschfeld and L. Kettenacker

(eds) *The 'Führer State': Myth and Reality. Studies on the Structure and Politics of the Third Reich* (Stuttgart, 1981), p. 143.
81 *Weissbuch über die Erschiessungen des 30. Juni 1934* (Paris, 1935), pp. 46–50; K. Bredow, *Hitlerrast* (Saarbrücken, 1935), pp. 34–5.
82 SM, NSDAP 977. Meldungen zum Eintritt in den Heeresdienst.
83 BA, NS23/298. SA–Gruppe Kurpfalz. Geh. 111/34. Stellung von SAM. Mannheim, 20. Dezember 1934.
84 HHW, Abt. 483/NSDAP 1381, 1382 (Standarte 25); HHW, Abt. 483/NSDAP 1346–1362 (Standarte 81); HHW, Abt. 483/NSDAP 1368–1379 (Standarte 99).
85 SM, NSDAP 792. SA der NSDAP, Sturm 14/J5, Trupp III, Burghausen. Namentliche Liste mit Berufseinteilung; SM, NSDAP 878. SA Gruppe Hochland, Brigade 85 (Obb.), SA Standarte 2, Stürme 5/2, 6/2, 7/2, 8/2. Nachweisung der ausgegebenen Quittungskarten . . . , 1. April 1935 mit 31. März 1936. Sources from a largely Protestant area in north-west Germany suggest that, even there, independent farmers, or their sons, were scarce in the SA at least after 1933. See note 257.
86 M. Kater, 'Sozialer Wandel in der NSDAP im Zuge der nationalsozialistischen Machtergreifung', in W. Schieder (ed.), *Faschismus als soziale Bewegung* (Hamburg, 1976), p. 33.
87 BA, NS23/262. SA der NSDAP. Führer der Brigade 150, Rheinhessen. Lagebericht für das 4. Vierteljahr 1934. Mainz, den 19. Dezember 1934. (c) Landhelfer.
88 ibid.
89 Fröhlich demonstrates that the NSDAP did make political advances after 1933 in some Catholic rural areas ('Partei', pp. 261–8), but none the less the numbers and proportion of farmers in the Upper Bavarian NSDAP remained very low (Reichorganisationsleiter der NSDAP (ed.), *Parteistatistik* (Munich, 1935), pp. 112–13, 150).
90 HHW, Abt. 483/NSDAP 1380. SA Standarte 166, Hochtaunus; GLAK, Abt. 465d/1302. SA Trupp, Neckargerach, 1934. Standarte 112.
91 *Statistisches Jahrbuch*, Vol. 1, p. 20, table 16c.
92 ibid., p. 24, table 21.
93 T. Balogh, 'The national economy of Germany', *Economic Journal* (September 1938), p. 462, table 1.
94 ibid., p. 471, table 7.
95 ibid.
96 The first being the post-1WW inflation which peaked in 1923.
97 Balogh, 'Economy', p. 461, table 1. Real wage rates only declined slightly during the depression, the fall in output being reflected instead in rapidly rising unemployment: D. Abraham, *The Collapse of the Weimar Republic – Political Economy and Crisis* (Princeton, NJ, 1981), pp. 247–9.
98 Balogh, 'Economy', p. 461, table 1.
99 *Statistisches Jahrbuch*, Vol. 9, p. 307, table 11. Of these, 4·9 million were male and, therefore, potential SA recruits.
100 Balogh, 'Economy', p. 463, table 2.
101 M. H. Kater, 'Zum gegenseitigen Verhältnis von SA und SS in der Sozialgeschichte des Nationalsozialismus von 1925 bis 1939', *Vierteljahresschrift für Sozial – und Wirtschaftsgeschichte*, vol. 62, no. 3 (1975), pp. 361–2. Buchloh notes a figure of 50 per cent for the Duisburg SA in 1931 which, probably, was fairly low for an urban formation. I. Buchloh *Die nationalsozialistische Machtergreifung in Duisburg* (Duisburg, 1980), p. 53.
102 BA, NS26/530. Georg Weiss, Personal Recollections. 19 December 1936.
103 SAG, Rep. 240/C61b(1). Ortsgruppe Widminnen. Parteigeschichte. Here, it refers to the period before the September 1930 general election.
104 SAG, Rep. 240/C33d2. Bezirk Tilsit der NSDAP. An alle Ortsgruppen des Bezirks Tilsit. Tilsit, den 8. Januar 1931.
105 BA, NS26/528. Adolf Treser, Personal Recollections. Giessen, 28 December 1936.
106 BA, NS26/529. Adolf Weber, Personal Recollections. Eberstadt, 5 January 1937.

107 BA, NS26/325. Abschrift 1161/31 St/v.B. gez. Stennes.
108 BHStA, Abt. I, So. I/1552. PND Nr. 764. Appell des SA-Sturms 24 ... am 21. Januar 1932 ...
109 BHStA, Abt. I, So. I/1870. 'Ein neues SA-Heim in Eglharting', *Die Front*, 30 January 1932.
110 BA, NS23/474. SA der NSDAP, Standarte 11. Stimmungsbericht. Breslau, den 22. September 1932.
111 A. Gimbel, *So kämpften wir* (Frankfurt-am-Main, 1941), p. 175.
112 BHStA, Abt. I, So. I/1774. 'Und die SA?', *Regensburger Anzeiger*, no. 270, 30 September 1932, p. 2, quoted from the *Augsburger Postzeitung*.
113 BA, NS23/399. Gau Hamburg, den 1. Februar 1933. gez. Wilhelm Grundlach.
114 BA, Reichsfinanzministerium (R2)/18740a. Abschrift. Der Reichsminister der Finanzen J 7750–78. Berlin, 17. November 1933. p. 1.
115 SM, NSDAP 977. SA der NSDAP, Jägerstandarte 3, Sturmbann III/J3. Versorgungsstelle. Reichenhall, den 5. April 1934. (SA members who had joined before 30 January 1933 were regarded as veterans. Party veterans had to have joined before 1930.); SM, NSDAP 678. SA der NSDAP. Der Führer des Sturms 21/25. Geldverwaltung, Neuötting, den 7. November 1934. This report only applied to non-party members, who did form the majority of the unit.
116 BA, NS23/266. SA der NSDAP, Standarte 13, Gross Gerau. Vierteljahresbericht, den 14. Juli 1934; BA, NS23/266. SA der NSDAP, Standarte 80, Wiesbaden. Vierteljahresbericht, den 26. Juni 1934; BA, NS23/266. SA der NSDAP, Standarte 61, Buchschlag in Hessen. Vierteljahresbericht, den 27. Juni 1934; BA, NS23/266. SA der NSDAP, Standarte 168, Offenbach/Main. Vierteljahresbericht, den 27. Juni 1934.
117 SM, NSDAP 689. SA der NSDAP. Beiträge. München, den 25. Oktober 1934. This list showed 146 men in a Munich company to be in work, and 5 to be jobless in October; SM, NSDAP 791. SA der NSDAP, Sturm 5/J5. An den Führer des Sturmbanns I/J5, Erding. Unterbringung von erwerbslosen SA-Männern, den 11. März 1935.
118 SM, NSDAP 678. As note 115. gez. R., Sturmmann.
119 SM, NSDAP 792. SA der NSDAP, Sturmbann I/25, Garching a/Alz., den 28. Februar 1935. An die Standarte 25, Garching. Betr.: Fürsorge. gez. Der Führer des Sturmbanns I/25; BA, NS23/265. SA Brigade 250. Vierteljahresbericht, Offenbach Main, 9. 1. 1935; BA, NS23/265. SA der NSDAP. Der Führer der Standarte R 8. An die SA–Brigade, 151 Westpfalz. Kaiserslautern, den 9.1.1935. The age of the unit's remaining 600 unemployed proved a hindrance to their receiving work; BA, NS23/265. SA der NSDAP, Standarte 31, Ludwigshafen, den 3. Januar 1935. An Brigade 51, Neustadt an der Haardt. Vierteljahresbericht; BA, NS23/353. SA der NSDAP, Brigade 12 (Hamburg), den 3. Mai 1935. Auszug aus dem Rundschreiben der Obersten SA-Führung v. 15. April 1935, Abt. F., Nr. 19995. Betr.: Richtlinien für die Ausbildung, Unterkunft usw. in den SA Hilfswerklagern, p. 1; BA, NS23/349. SA der NSDAP. Der Führer der Gruppe Hansa, Hamburg, den 2. Oktober 1935. Gruppenbefehl Nr. 66. gez. Fust; BA, NS23/128. Der Oberste SA- Führer Nr. 27132. Betrifft: SA-Hilfswerklager. München, den 16. Mai 1935. gez. Lutze.
120 GLAK, Abt. 465d/1356. SA der NSDAP, Sturm 1/250, Bruchsal, den 17. September 1934. An Sturmbann I/250. Betr.: Vierteljahresbericht der SA. gez. Walter E., Sturmführer, p. 2.
121 Kater, 'Verhältnis', pp. 361–4, 372–4.
122 BA, Sch 404. Der OSAF, Ch. Nr. 1634/33. Betreff: Gliederung der gesamten SA. München, den 6. November 1933. gez. Röhm.
123 BHStA, Abt. I, So. I/1549. Mannschaftsliste für Trupp Laim, Sturm 4 der NSDAP; BHStA, Abt. I, So. I/1549. SA München, Trupp M/1L, Stürme 2/L, 5/ L, 7/L, 8/L; NHStA, Landratsamt Hameln-Pyrmont, Aktenstück A4¹. SA Gruppe in Halvestorf, 1931. The Allenstein police survey also indicates that the SA was

very youthful: SAG, Rep. 18–13. Staatl. Kriminalkommissariat. Betr.: SA der NSDAP. Allenstein, 19.6.1931.
124 BDC, SA 774–878; HHW, Abt. 483/NSDAP 1381, 1382, 2522–2524 (Standarte 25); HHW, Abt. 483/NSDAP 1368–1379, 2214–2284 (Standarte 99); SM, NSDAP 728. Sturm 1/10, Ingolstadt. Namensliste, 1933–4; SM, NSDAP 803. SA der NSDAP, Sturm 22/25, Altötting; SM, NSDAP 658. Verzeichnis der Arbeitslosen des Sturmes 5/10, Ingolstadt, 1934; NWHStA, Ge; NWHStA, RW 23. SA Standarte J8, Würselen, 1933/4; NWHStA, RW 23. SA Standarte 25, Aachen, 1. Juli 1934; GLAK, Abt. 465d/1307. SA der NSDAP, Sturm 16/469, Eberbach, 13.12.1933.
125 Frankfurt: HHW, Abt. 483/NSDAP 1381, 1382, 1346–1362, 1368–1379. Standarten 25, 81, 99; Munich: SM, NSDAP 972. Brigade 86, Leibstandarte, den 25.10.1934. This source was not part of the occupational analysis.
126 SM, NSDAP 971. Sturm 8/J5. Liste der bei Sturm 8/J5 vorhandenen Arbeitslosen. Betr.: Feststellung der arbeitslosen SA Angehörigen. An den Stuba. I/J5 Erding. den 19.11.34; GLAK, Abt. 465d/1303. Arbeitslose im Sturm 1/112 Zug 6, den 4.1.1934; GLAK, Abt. 465d/1303. Sturm 1/112. Arbeitslosenmeldung, den 23.2.1934. No overlap with source above; BA, NS23/298. As note 83.
127 For sources see note 19, material listed under file headings: BHStA, Abt. I, So. I/1551, 1554; BA, NS26/596, 513; IfZ, MA 616/20, 616/21; SAG, Rep. 37–5, 37–14; SAG, Rep. 240/C67b. See also, BA, NS23/8,11. Police papers, 1933–4.
128 *Statistisches Jahrbuch*, Vol. 1., p. 24, table 21.
129 New Year 1934: 445,611 in SAR; 2,500,000 in Active SA. BA, Sch 407. Der OSAF. München, den 19. Februar 1934.
130 If 75 per cent of the Active SA are taken to be younger than 30, the figure would be just below 1,900,000.
131 There were fourteen farmers in the sources listed under note 123 of whom seven were younger than 25.
132 There were sixty-three farmers in the sources listed under note 124 of whom thirty-eight were younger than 25.
133 *Statistisches Jahrbuch*, Vol. 1., p. 24, table 21.
134 ibid.
135 ibid.
136 ibid.
137 ibid., p. 16, table 10.
138 Statistisches Jahrbuch, Vol. 2., p. 27, table 1.
139 (i) Halvestorf, 1931: no. 16; married 12·5%, single 87·5%; (ii) Munich, 1932: no. 91; married 22·0%, single 78·0%; (iii) Görlitz, 1932: no. 27; married 37·0%, single 63·0%; (iv) Königsberg, 1932: no. 8; married 25·0%, single 75·0%. Sources: (i) NHStA, Landratsamt Hameln-Pyrmont, Aktenstück A4[1]. SA Gruppe in Halvestorf, 1931; (ii) BHStA, Abt. I, So. I/1549. Namensverzeichnis, M/1L, Stand v. 20. September 1932. Namensverzeichnis, Sturm 7/L, September 1932; (iii) IfZ, MA 616/20, 2954. MA 616/21, 4353–4661 (SA III – Ausschreitungen). SA men listed from Görlitz area, Luetgebrune papers, autumn 1932; (iv) SAG, Rep. 37–5. SA men charged with arson. Königsberg, August 1932.
140 Berlin Document Center, 1934: no. 638; 30·3% married, 69·7% single; North Rhineland, 1933/4: no. 170; 52·9% married, 47·1% single; Aachen, 1934: no. 29; 41·4% married, 58·6% single. Sources: BDC, SA 774–878; NWHStA, Ge; NWHStA, RW 23. SA Standarte 25, Aachen, 1. Juli 1934.
141 Frankfurt-am-Main, 1.7.1935: no. 764; 47·4% married, 52·6% single. HHW, Abt. 483/NSDAP 1381, 1382, 1346–1362, 1368–1379. The different provenances of sources in the three periods makes anything more than a rough-and-ready comparison between periods inadvisable.
142 O. Boelitz, *Der Aufbau des preussischen Bildungswesens nach der Staatsumwälzung* (Leipzig, 1925), pp. 22, 47.
143 ibid., p. 37.

76 Stormtroopers

C. Führ, *Zur Schulpolitik in der Weimarer Republik. Die Zusammenarbeit von Reich und Ländern im Reichsschulausschuss (1919–1923), und im Ausschuss für das Unterrichtswesen (1924–1933)* (Weinheim, Berlin and Basle, 1970), p. 343.

Boelitz, *Aufbau*, p. 47.

Führ, *Schulpolitik*, pp. 43–4, 58.

BDC, SA 774–878; NWHStA, Ge; NWHStA, RW 23. SA Standarte 25, Aachen, 1. Juli 1934; NWHStA, RW 23. SA Standarte J8, Würselen, 1933–4. All sources provided similar results.

NWHStA, RW 23. SA Standarte J8, Würselen, 1933–4. Membership file of Heinrich R., born 14.5.1910. Curriculum vitae.

A. Milatz, *Wähler und Wahlen in der Weimarer Republik* (Bonn, 1968), p. 151. But cf. Fröhlich, 'Partei', pp. 261–3.

Neumann cites a figure of 60 per cent. S. Neumann, *Die Parteien der Weimarer Republik* (Stuttgart, Berlin, Cologne and Mainz, 1965), p. 44.

BA, Sch 415. Darstellung des Anwachsens der SA in % vom 1.1.–1.4.1931. München, den 18. Mai 1931.

BA, Sch 415. Der OSAF. Betr.: Stärke der SA im Juli 1932. München, 1.9.1932. gez. v. Krausser. (Comparison made with June figures.)

BDC, SA 774–878. Those files containing Bavarian Active SA rank-and-file members.

Statistisches Jahrbuch, Vol. 1, p. 18, table 12.

K. D. Bracher, *The German Dictatorship* (London, 1971), pp. 127–8.

BDC: no. 854; 6% war veterans (3·5% privates, 2·5% NCOs). BDC, SA 774–878; North Rhineland: no. 223; 7·6% war veterans. NWHStA, Ge; Frankfurt-am-Main: no. 1,650; 8% war veterans. HHW, Abt. 483/NSDAP 1381–1382, 2522–2524, 1346–1362, 2100–2213, 1368–1379, 2214–2284.

HHW, Abt. 483/NSDAP 1381–1382, 1346–1362, 2214–2284, no. 779.

A. Rosenberg, *Imperial Germany. The Birth of the German Republic, 1871–1918*, trans. I. F. D. Morrow (Oxford, 1970), p. 110.

21·1 per cent of the 1934 Frankfurt source had lost their fathers in childhood, the majority because of the war.

A. Milatz, *Wähler und Wahlen in der Weimarer Republik* (Bonn, 1968), p. 151.

L. Bergsträsser, *Geschichte der politischen Parteien in Deutschland* (Munich and Vienna, 1965), p. 25.

BDC, SA 774–878; NWHStA, Ge; HHW, Abt. 483/NSDAP 1381–1382, 2522–2524, 1346–1362, 2100–2213, 1368–1379, 2214–2284.

Neumann, *Parteien*, p. 137; W. Tormin, *Geschichte der deutschen Parteien seit 1848* (Stuttgart, Berlin, Cologne and Mainz, 1968), p. 182.

Membership figures: January 1930, 133,000; December 1930, 176,000; February 1931, 200,000; January 1933, 300,000. Tormin, *Parteien*, p. 210. This growth of membership fails to demonstrate how many people passed through the KPD, for membership of the KPD was generally a short-term affair. Of around 180,000 KPD members at the end of 1930, 'only 20·5 per cent had more than a year's standing; 143,000 had entered the party during the year, but 95,000 had left it'. R. N. Hunt, *German Social Democracy, 1918–1933* (Chicago, 1970), pp. 101–2.

O. K. Flechtheim, *Die KPD in der Weimarer Republik* (Frankfurt-am-Main, 1976), ch. 2.

V. R. Berghahn, *Der Stahlhelm, Bund der Frontsoldaten 1918–1935* (Düsseldorf, 1966), pp. 13, 14, 27–8, 34–5, 39, 52, 156–7.

173 BA, Sch 404. As in note 122.
174 BA, Sch 470. Obergruppe III. Gruppe Berlin-Brandenburg, Berlin, den 28.5.1934.
175 BA, NS26/308. Der Oberste SA-Führer, Ch. Nr. 1540/33. Betreff: Stahlhelm. München, 26.9.33.
176 Active SA had 2·5 million members in early 1934. BA, Sch 407. As note 129.
177 KPD: 43·2% unskilled workers, 40·9% (semi-)skilled workers, 11·4% white-collar staff, 2·3% professions, 2·3% invalids. SPD: 13·8% unskilled workers, 58·6% (semi-)skilled workers, 3·4% salaried manual, 20·7% salaried white-collar, 3·4% small independents.
178 Stahlhelm: 20·6% unskilled workers, 37·4% (semi-)skilled workers, 4·6% salaried manual, 21·4% salaried white-collar, 0·8% civil servants, 1·5% master craftsmen, 0·8% small independents, 3·1% farmers, 6·9% professions, 0·8% schoolboys, 1·5% students, 0·8% miscellaneous.
179 Freikorps: 7·7% unskilled workers, 43·6% (semi-)skilled workers, 12·8% salaried manual, 23·1% salaried white-collar, 5·1% civil servants, 2·6% master craftsmen, 5·1% professions.
180 HHW, Abt. 483/NSDAP 1381–1382.
181 R. Diels, *Lucifer ante Portas* (Zurich, 1949), p. 153. See also pp. 334–5.
182 BA, NS23/9. Meldung von 1011. An V99. Opladen, den 11. Juli 1933. gez. N1101.
183 BA, NS23/8. Br. B. Nr. 380/34. Stimmungsbericht (Benrath), den 11. Juni 1934, pp. 1–2. Betr.: SA und Stahlhelm. Here it is noted that the Stahlhelm had complained that the SA was full of Communists. The report does not challenge the Stahlhelm allegations. Rather, it finds the Stahlhelm complaint itself obnoxious.
184 SAG, Rep. 240/C61a. Ortsgruppe Upalten. Parteigeschichte, p. 3.
185 Bergsträsser, *Parteien*, p. 25. Hunt, *Social Democracy*, p. 102, cites a ratio of 1:10.
186 Flechtheim, *KPD*, does not venture a ratio of KPD members to voters. However, Hunt notes that the SPD's ratio of 1:10 was the best member:voter ratio in Weimar Germany. Therefore, presumably, the 1·72% of ex-KPD members in the SA were complemented by a sizeable tally of former KPD voters.
187 E. G. Reiche, 'The Development of the SA in Nuremberg, 1922–1934' (Dissertation, University of Delaware, 1972), ch. 7. P. H. Merkl, *Political Violence under the Swastika* (Princeton, NJ, 1975), pp. 582 FD–65, 590, 593 FD–66. Merkl also combines SA with SS members in his analysis, both here, and in his *The Making of a Stormtrooper* (Princeton, NJ, 1980).
188 Below *Scharführer* were the ranks of *SA–Anwärter* (SA probationer), *SA–Mann* (SA man), *Sturmmann* (lance-corporal), and *Rottenführer* (corporal).
189 Werner, 'SA und NSDAP', p. 536. Leaders below the commensurate rank for the command of any unit were sometimes none the less entrusted with such a command. See BDC, SA 774–878 for numerous examples of this. In this work, leaders acting in a more senior capacity than their rank suggested are classified at the more senior level.
190 Strictly speaking there was an intermediate rank between *Scharführer* and *Truppführer*, the *Oberscharführer*. The same occurred at higher levels, e.g. *Obertruppführer*. In terms of additional responsibilities, these ranks had little significance.
191 Werner, 'SA und NSDAP', p. 536.
192 BHStA, Abt. I, So. I/1871. Polizeidirektion, München. Bericht des Preussischen Minister des Innern über die Entwicklung der NSDAP, 1931. See also Werner, 'SA und NSDAP', p. 536, n. 33.
193 Werner, 'SA und NSDAP', pp. 518–19, 543. See also 'Säuberung des Reiches und der Länder', *Der SA-Mann*, year 2, no. 7 (18 February 1933), p. 1.
194 Unskilled workers 33·3 per cent, (semi-)skilled workers 26·7 per cent, salaried white-collar 6·7 per cent, farmers 26·7 per cent, assisting family members 6·7 per

cent. NHStA, Hann. 80, Hann. II, Nr. 793. Der Polizeipräsident Hannover. Landeskriminalpolizeistelle 143 06/40.

195   Unskilled workers 21·1 per cent, (semi-)skilled workers 30·8 per cent, salaried manual 4·9 per cent, salaried white-collar 20·0 per cent, civil service 7·0 per cent, master craftsmen 2·8 per cent, small independents 2·2 per cent, farmers 3·8 per cent, assisting family members 1·1 per cent, professions independents 5·4 per cent, others 1·5 per cent. BDC, SA 774–878; NWHStA, Ge. Ranks here and in all subsequent BDC and NWHStA data taken for 30 June 1934.

196   Unskilled workers 8·3 per cent, (semi-)skilled workers 33·3 per cent, salaried white-collar 8·3 per cent, master craftsmen 16·7 per cent, farmers 25 per cent, jobless ex-soldiers 8·3 per cent. Source as in note 194.

197   Unskilled workers 9·4 per cent, (semi-)skilled workers 18·9 per cent, salaried manual 7·1 per cent, salaried white-collar 24·4 per cent, civil service 11·0 per cent, master craftsmen 5·5 per cent, small independents 7·9 per cent, farmers 3·1 per cent, professions, independents 10·2 per cent, others 2·4 per cent. Sources as for note 195.

198   M. Jamin, 'Zur Rolle der SA im nationalsozialistischen Herrschaftssystem', in G. Hirschfeld and L. Kettenacker (eds), *The 'Führer State'* (Stuttgart, 1981), p. 329. M. Jamin's dissertation, 'Zwischen den Klassen. Eine quantitative Untersuchung zur Sozialstruktur der SA-Führerschaft' (Dissertation, Rühr-Universität-Bochum, 1982) was passed after the completion of this book.

199   Manual workers 14·5 per cent, salaried staff 19·4 per cent, master craftsmen, traders, salesmen, etc. 25·5 per cent, independent farmers 21·0 per cent, professions 11·1 per cent. Figures from: 'Woher kommen unsere SA-Führer?', *Völkischer Beobachter* no. 30 (30 January 1933). In files of Polizeidirektion, München, 2.II,1933. BHStA, Abt. I, So. I/1554B.

200   Unskilled workers 5·9 per cent, (semi-)skilled workers 18·8 per cent, salaried manual 3·5 per cent, salaried white-collar 27·1 per cent, civil service 5·9 per cent, master craftsmen 3·5 per cent, small independents 8·2 per cent, farmers 11·8 per cent, assisting family members 1·2 per cent, professions 2·4 per cent, landowners 1·2 per cent, retired officers 4·7 per cent, students 3·5 per cent, others 2·4 per cent. For source, see note 194.

201   What differences there were would have worked the other way. *Statistisches Jahrbuch*, Vol. 1, p. 21, table 17.

202   Unskilled workers 2·4 per cent, (semi-)skilled workers 13·0 per cent, salaried manual 7·1 per cent, salaried white-collar 21·3 per cent, civil service 6·5 per cent, master craftsmen 3·6 per cent, small independents 7·1 per cent, farmers 3·0 per cent, professions, independents 29·6 per cent, others 6·5 per cent. For sources, see note 195.

203   Böhnke estimates that 15–20 per cent of Nazi leaders in the Ruhr were workers. W. Böhnke, *Die NSDAP im Ruhrgebiet, 1920–1933* (Bonn–Bad Godesberg, 1974), pp. 200–1.

204   Reichsorganisationsleiter der NSDAP (ed.), *Parteistatistik*, p. 70.

205   Böhnke, *NSDAP*, p. 199.

206   See pp. 166–9, 217–8.

207   *Scharführer*: no. 171. 19 minus 4·7%; 20–24, 34.5%; 25–29, 26·3%; 30–34, 18·7%; 35–39, 8·2%; 40–44, 4·7%; 45–49, 2·3%; 50–54, 0·6%. BDC, SA 774–878; NWHStA, Ge.

208   *Truppführer*: no. 125. 19 minus 0·8%; 20–24, 17·6%; 25–29, 19·2%; 30–34, 20·8%; 35–39, 23·2%; 40–44, 13·6%; 45–49, 3·2%; 50 plus 1·6%. BDC, SA 774–878; NWHStA, Ge.

209   *Sturmführer* and above: no. 160. 20–24, 12·5%; 25–29, 13·8%; 30–34, 22·5%; 35–39, 26·9%; 40–44, 16·3%; 45–49, 3·8%, 50–54, 3·1%; 55–59, 1·3%. BDC, SA 774–878; NWHStA, Ge.

210   No. 593. 25 minus, 8·0%; 25–30, 16·0%; 30–35, 24·0%; 35–45, 35·5%; 45 plus, 16·5%. Source as for note 199.

211 BDC, SA 774–878. Furthermore, the proportion of *Truppführer* and *Sturmführer* and above who completed their education after secondary school was also markedly higher than that for SA men.

212 BDC, SA 795. Hans Fey, no date of birth given.

213 K. Rohe, *Das Reichsbanner Schwarz Rot Gold. Ein Beitrag zur Geschichte und Struktur der politischen Kampfverbände zur Zeit der Weimarer Republik* (Stuttgart, 1965), p. 272.

214 BDC, SA 774–878.

215 See note 199 for source.

216 BA, NS23/125. OSAF II Nr. 1290/33. Übersicht über die Zusammensetzung des SA–Führerkorps bei den Gruppen. München, 19.6.33. gez. Schmid.

217 See Reiche, 'SA in Nuremberg', pp. 265–6.

218 'Our political opponents have repeatedly asserted that the leadership of our movement and particularly of our SA consists almost entirely of former, battle-weary officers ... With unadulterated figures, we can vanquish all the slanders and accusations of our opponents. And what applies to the Group Nordmark applies, broadly speaking, to the whole movement ...' (Source as for note 199).

219 BDC, SA 774–878.

220 Military experience, especially war service, was officially declared to be an advantage in seeking promotion when Röhm declared in February 1933 that the names of all SA personnel suitable for promotion to middle and higher positions in the leadership be forwarded to him so as to obviate the need to recruit SA leaders from outside the organisation as it continued to expand rapidly. 'In the main, these will be former war veterans of all ranks with qualities of leadership': BA, NS23/124. Der Oberste SA-Führer, Ch/II Nr. 555/33. Verfügung. München, den 20. Februar 1933. gez. Röhm. Andreas Leicht of Alzey/Framersheim noted that a similar preference for war veterans as leaders existed in 1930: BA, NS26/533. Andreas Leicht, Personal Recollections. Alzey (Framersheim), 18 November 1936.

221 BDC, SA 774–878.

222 BA, Sch 403. OSAF, SABE SA Reserve (SAR). München, den 28. März 1929. At this stage the SAR was prohibited explicitly from taking recruits younger than 40, but by the end of 1931 the recruitment of younger members had begun: BA, NS26/1404. Berichte der Staatspolizei Württembergs zur politischen Lage. 20.12.31. For SA duties see BA, NS23/419. SAR Sturmbann I/15, Nürnberg. Bericht über den Appell der Truppführer und Scharführer am 12. September 1933. gez. Korn.

223 BA, Sch 403. As in note 222.

224 BA, Sch 404. As in note 122.

225 BHStA, Abt. I, So. I/1871. As in note 192. p. 130 of document.

226 Reserve strength, 445,611. cf. overall SA strength, 2,950,000 on 1 January 1934. BA, Sch 407. Der OSAF. München, den 19. Februar 1934.

227 BA, NS23/337. Vergleichende Übersicht über die Stärkebewegung der SA im Monat November 1935. Stärkenachweis nach Altersklassen und Parteizugehörigkeit (Stand am 20.11.35), Anlage 4. For transfer to armed forces, see Anlage 2. Between October and November 1935 the SA suffered a net loss of 48,020 members of whom 23,235 went into the armed forces.

228 In the case of Company 24/25 of Burghausen the membership list was drawn up as people joined. On one occasion in early 1933, nine civil servants joined simultaneously. SM, NSDAP 797. SA Reserve, Burghausen, Sturm 24/25, 1933/4.

229 Sources as follows: Sturmbann RI/15, Nuremberg 1933. No. 139: BA, NS23/419. Erlasse und Befehle, Sturmbann RI/15; Sturm 24/25, Burghausen, 1933/4. No. 317: SM, NSDAP 797. As note 228; Berlin Document Center, Reserve SA rank and file, 30 June 1934. No. 251: BDC, SA 774–878; Standarte R97, Frankfurt-

am-Main, 30.6.1934. No. 496: HHW, Abt. 483/NSDAP 2525–2540, 1363–1367.

230 For instance, see BA, NS23/265. SA der NSDAP. Der Führer der Standarte R8. An die SA–Brigade 151, Westpfalz. Kaiserslautern, den 9.1.1935.

231 BA, NS23/419. Sturmbann RI/15. Erlasse und Befehle.

232 Reiche argues that the depression and resulting unemployment helped bring younger men into the SA between 1929 and 1932 ('SA in Nuremberg', p. 254), but otherwise omits discussion of unemployment from his examination of the Nuremberg SA's social profile.

233 For the Active SA see Table 3.4, column 7 and p. 36. In the Nuremberg source 62·8 per cent of the unemployed were workers or, alternatively, 50 per cent of the workers in the source were unemployed compared with an average of 35·8 per cent overall. See also M. H. Kater, 'Ansätze zu einer Soziologie der SA bis zur Röhm Krise', in U. Engelhardt *et al.* (eds), *Industrielle Welt, Sonderband, Soziale Bewegung und politische Verfassung* (Stuttgart, 1976), p. 811.

234 Age profile of Reservists (no. 1189): 19 minus, 0·8%; 20–24, 6·4%; 25–29, 18·8%; 30–34, 23·9%; 35–39, 18·8%; 40–44, 12·5%; 45–49, 7·9%; 50–54, 5·5%; 55–59, 3·3%; 60 plus, 2·0%

235 For example, in the relatively young Standarte R97, 75·4 per cent of those who left the SA between July 1934 and June 1935 were married. Of those who remained on 1 July 1935, 64·3 per cent were married.

236 BDC, SA 774–878, no. 104: *Volksschule*: 80·8 per cent; *Mittelschule*: 1·9 per cent; *Realschule*: 4·8 per cent; *Gymnasium*: 1·0 per cent; tertiary: 7·7 per cent; university: 3·8 per cent.

237 See Reiche, 'SA in Nuremberg', pp. 263–4.

238 BDC, SA 774–878. Those reservists from Bavaria.

239 *Statistisches Jahrbuch*, Vol. 1., p. 18, table 12.

240 See pp. 53–4.

241 HHW, Abt. 483/NSDAP 2525–2540, 1363–1347. No. 496.

242 Individual sources: Nuremberg, no. 139, war 63·3 per cent; Burghausen/BDC, no. 568, war 48·1 per cent; Frankfurt-am-Main, no. 496, war 23·8 per cent. Sources as in note 229.

243 Frankfurt-am-Main, Standarten R63, R99, in war, 54·4 per cent. HHW, Abt. 483/NSDAP 1329–1345, 1368–1379.

244 In the Nuremberg/BDC data, privates 28·7 per cent, NCOs 17·1 per cent, officers 2·3 per cent of total. Remainder not ex-military.

245 BDC material: no. 251, 16·7 per cent; Frankfurt R63, R99 (1935): no. 351, 25·1 per cent.

246 BDC: SPD 4, USPD 1, DNVP 1, Stahlhelm 30, Freikorps 6, Einwohnerwehr 2, Reichsbanner 1, right-wing youth groups 1; Frankfurt, R63, R99: SPD 8, DNVP 3, Zentrum 1, Stahlhelm 53, Freikorps 21, Reichsbanner 3.

247 Frankfurt R97: SPD 22, KPD 3, Zentrum 1, Freikorps 11, Reichsbanner 9, Iron Front 4, RGO 4, Stahlhelm 4.

248 Flechtheim, *KPD*, pp. 316–17; Tormin, *Parteien*, p. 210.

249 Berghahn, *Stahlhelm*, pp. 266, 286.

250 Jamin, 'Rolle der SA', pp. 333–4. However, cf. J. M. Diehl, *Paramilitary Politics in Weimar Germany* (Bloomington, Ind. and London, 1977), p. 294 where he cites a membership total of 340,000 for the Stahlhelm in 1932 which spurted to 750,000 by May 1933 as some of the previously uncommitted and some members of banned left-wing organisations joined up.

251 There is a certain ambiguity here. SA sources never quote a membership figure above 3 million, but Werner, 'SA und NSDAP', p. 592, and Bloch, *SA*, p. 87, quote a figure of 4·5 million. This figure, based on sources in Potsdam, may conceivably point to the existence of Stahlhelm units and other right-wing *Verbände* which, although nominally under SA command, were never integrated into the SA's organisation.

252 Merkl, *Political Violence*, pp. 581–99. Similar figures are reproduced in Merkl, *Stormtrooper*, p. 99, table II–3 and p. 155, table III–3 which again appear to combine SA and SS.
253 Reiche, 'SA in Nuremberg', p. 256.
254 For middle and higher leaders, ibid., p. 270. There are also many lower-ranking leaders present in Reiche's sample, ibid., pp. 269–70, leaving the rank and file in the minority.
255 ibid., pp. 255, 256, table 3.
256 Merkl, *Political Violence*, pp. 581–99.
257 In July 1982, some SA lists from north-west Germany came to light among unsorted material in the Staatsarchiv Bremen (Staatsarchiv Bremen [SB], 7, 1066/62–1. [D 52]). They concern 485 stormtroopers from Group Nordsee who were drafted into SA welfare camps in late 1934/early 1935. Most were working class. Thus:

Brigade 61 (Hanover.)	25 men – 4 unskilled workers, 20 (semi-)skilled workers, 1 salaried manual.
Brigade 62 (Lower Weser).	149 men – 32 unskilled workers, 80 (semi-)skilled workers, 4 salaried manual, 29 salaried white-collar, 3 farmers, 1 student.
Brigade 63 (Oldenburg/ East Friesland).	108 men – 33 unskilled workers, 47 (semi-)skilled workers, 1 salaried manual, 8 salaried white-collar, 2 farmers, 17 miscellaneous or unknown.
Brigade 64 (Osnabrück).	97 men – 21 unskilled workers, 56 (semi-)skilled workers, 1 salaried manual, 10 salaried white-collar, 1 master craftsman, 4 farmers, 1 farmer's son, 3 miscellaneous.
Marine-Brigade 2 (North Sea, based in Bremen).	68 men – 18 unskilled workers, 43 (semi)skilled workers, 2 salaried white-collar, 1 civil servant, 1 professional, 1 student, 2 miscellaneous.
Regiment 427 (Wunstorf).	49 men – 5 unskilled workers, 40 (semi-)skilled workers, 1 salaried manual, 1 salaried white-collar, 2 miscellaneous.

These stormtroopers originated from much larger units and all, as draftees to welfare camps, were presumably unemployed. This would have excluded most self-employed stormtroopers, including farmers, but had the latter's sons joined the north-west German SA in large numbers, then it is surprising that only one appears in these lists. The SA in north-west Germany was, therefore, probably strongly working class, at least after January 1933.

The stormtroopers were predominantly very young; either in their late teens or early twenties.

4 The SA and the Employment Question

The Reich Ministry of Finance reported that in November 1933 the SA, excluding the Stahlhelmer who were then being transferred to it, contained about 'one million men who are to be considered destitute; they have been jobless for years'.[1] This estimate presumably excluded stormtroopers who had lost their jobs for shorter periods, those who had re-entered employment by November 1933, and those who had been forced to take poorly paid casual or part-time work. Some historians suggest a connection between this material deprivation and the SA's growth, while others add that not only did poverty drive individuals into the SA, but that stormtroopers sought and received practical benefits from the organisation. These assertions are not surprising, but much remains to be said on the form and extent of the aid to stormtroopers and on the degree to which SA membership contributed to the ultimate resolution of their destitution through the acquisition of work.

Furthermore, the evident coincidence of SA membership and poverty or joblessness might obscure rather different motives which led recruits to join the SA. Clearly, recruits joined so large an organisation for a variety of motives, but consideration of the views of stormtroopers themselves and an examination of their leaders' response to the issue do confirm that poverty and, above all, the unemployment which had created this poverty were indeed issues of prime importance. Most stormtroopers were only able to explain the causes of the economic crisis in a rudimentary and sometimes patently inaccurate manner, but most regarded SA membership as a function of their poverty. Many also regarded the SA, idealistically or cynically, as the means to resolve their personal misery, or even unemployment nationally. Most written evidence from ordinary stormtroopers derives from biographical accounts compiled on joining the SA, or from short essays written at the same time entitled 'Why I joined the SA'. This evidence stems largely from the period after Hitler's takeover when the SA began keeping more systematic membership records, but fragmentary evidence concerning the late Weimar years tells a similar story, even if many accounts were only written in the mid-1930s.[2] All these writings must be taken with a pinch of salt. Their authors had an interest in pleasing their superiors by saying what was expected of them, while accounts drafted in the mid-1930s often seem to reflect propaganda absorbed by the authors over half a decade or more. None the less, if these problems are noted, the accounts of individual stormtroopers often remain very revealing. Mention of specific political issues emphasised by Nazi propaganda, such as the Treaty of Versailles, the divisiveness of party politics or, surprisingly, even the Jewish question do not feature particularly frequently in their writings, but the issue of unemployment crops up repeatedly. Working-class stormtroopers, in particular, concentrated on providing largely biographical accounts (in contrast to the sometimes articulate and often right-wing political comment of lower-middle-class stormtroopers), but none the less they described the advent of unemployment with an evident sense of shock or even outrage. It seems to have provided the decisive impetus which led them into paramilitary politics and the SA.[3]

Thus Emil Sauer was partly attracted to the SA and Nazism in 1928 by the SA's activism in itself, but more specifically because he regarded action as the answer to economic misery; a motive he also attributed to other recruits.[4] For some stormtroopers the SA's ethos was related axiomatically to material deprivation, as a letter written in June 1931 by Paul Maikowski from prison in Berlin to his better-known brother Hans illustrates. He perceived a direct correlation between socialism and poverty, concluding, 'we SA men are certainly all socialists because things are going badly for us'. By the same token, he resented the acceptance of Schacht and Prince August Wilhelm, the crown prince, as members by the NSDAP: 'Have you ever seen a man with plenty of money and property, but nonetheless an honest socialist? I haven't!'[5] Everyday life in the SA reflected this poverty. The diaries of SA hostels reveal a greater concern for material survival than for political adventure. The Augsburg SA Hostel's diary for the winter of 1931–2, for example, contains extensive information on the collection of food, especially potatoes, from the surrounding countryside with which to survive the winter.[6]

Many stormtroopers who joined after 1933 also associated their entry into the SA with personal experience of unemployment. Heinrich Maul, an electrical fitter from Frankfurt-am-Main, lost his father when 10 and his mother when 17, but the collapse of his working life was the final blow which drove him into the SA: 'Work was out of the question because the Marxist government did not understand how to provide the people with work and bread.'[7] The last words, underlined by an SA official in the original document, occur frequently in biographical material. These sentiments were echoed by the shop assistant Rudolf Jung whose career was in ruins. Nine months after successfully completing his training he lost his original job in 1928. He soon found employment as a postal worker, but was subsequently jobless from 1931 until his placement by the SA as a railway worker in June 1934. Upon joining the SA in December 1933, he remarked that, 'A life without work and obligations is no kind of life and therefore I am ready to join the fighters' ranks.'[8] Even stormtroopers who had escaped personal economic disaster none the less often perceived the SA's purpose as the eradication of unemployment. These luckier stormtroopers were apparently frequently those salaried employees better able to express themselves than the average SA man.[9] The white-collar employee Wilhelm Keller, who was only jobless for three weeks, none the less joined the SA because of his 'wish to participate in that organisation which guarantees the unity of the German people and provides the German worker with the means of reintegration within the productive process'.[10] Similarly, the salesman Wilhelm Reisser spoke largely of the economic collapse when explaining carefully his motives for joining the SA in February 1934 in an essay which also substantially reflected Nazi propaganda:

> Unemployment has been combated with great success, hunger and want greatly reduced and some countrymen saved from despair. . . . We must, in addition to Adolf Hitler, thank his SA men. Only because of the dedication and discipline of his Brown Guard was our Leader able to achieve such success.
>
> Personally I feel constrained to contribute at least a fragment to the rebuilding of my homeland and believe, that by joining the SA, in order to fight alongside my brothers and sisters [!] for a better future, I can best achieve this.[11]

However, these articulate, often politicised SA recruits contrast with the generally less well-educated, working-class recruit whose command of German in itself often precluded theorising of any sort. Many such recruits were at least partly attracted to the SA through opportunism or even cynicism and while most made an effort to hide this, others, deliberately or inadvertently, let their true motives be known. For instance, the Gestapo noted the boast of a 25-year-old foundry worker in Essen:

> The government isn't going to last long. The main thing for me is that I've got work through the SA. I played along up till then, now the SA can go to blazes. The SA will be dissolved sooner or later anyway.[12]

This type of opportunism did not lure recruits into the SA alone, as illustrated by the case of a 33-year-old coal miner from Essen who joined the NSDAP in October 1929, but after losing his job in 1932 switched to the KPD for two months to obtain work through a Communist town councillor. He subsequently joined the SA, but faced expulsion in September 1935 under suspicion of firearms, fraud, and political offences.[13]

The SA's leaders recognised the importance of unemployment and poverty to many of their recruits, regardless of whether the latter had joined the SA for cynical or idealistic reasons. The leaders themselves had contributed to this situation by regarding the jobless as their special constituency[14] and accordingly gearing recruitment propaganda to the issue of economic decline.[15] Thus the SA Inspector General wrote in December 1931 that 'many stormtroopers and leaders believe that with the commencement of NSDAP government they will become paid officers and NCOs',[16] while many more evidently hoped for any kind of work. Similarly, when discussing the related issue of welfare provision, the commander of Sub-Group Leine illustrated its political importance, reporting in September 1932 that the SA's 'better social welfare' in itself had attracted temporarily a few recruits from the left.[17] In the same month the threat of financial collapse threatened the very existence of the Upper Bavarian SA as its commanders doubted both their own and their men's prospects for seeing through the coming winter.[18]

Until January 1933 the SA's leaders enjoyed the comparative luxury of being able to criticise the Weimar authorities, but with Hitler's takeover the rapid solution of the unemployment problem became the cornerstone of their domestic politics. Time seemed relatively short. Even in February 1933, only days after the Nazi takeover, the KPD perceived and tried to play on mounting impatience among the stormtroopers by depicting the Nazi government's social policies as a failure. A poster designed for the March elections stressed this theme, declaring:

SA worker awake! What has the Third Reich brought? Instead of bread and work, fraternal murder. But the hunger goes on. The Red Aid appeals to you: you too belong in our ranks! Fight in the united front army. Vote list three – the KPD![19]

The appeal came too early. The surge in SA recruitment continued throughout 1933, before the SA leadership's inability to provide enough work, either by using official channels or by sweeping the same channels away, became apparent. None the less, SA leaders made the right noises. In August 1933 Röhm declared the 'first aim of the National Socialist movement is to create work for every German countryman',[20] a theme he frequently repeated in public addresses to SA units.[21] The SA's weekly journal, *Der SA-Mann*, included regular features on unemployment rates both in Germany and within the SA itself.[22] However, when these early hopes were insufficiently fulfilled and unemployment levels within the SA remained relatively high, the SA leadership took an aggressive stand on the issue. On 17 February 1934 the *SA-Mann* published an article which called for both state and private aid for the SA's unemployed:

(1) The provision of a job for all veterans, if necessary in the private sector.

(2)   The preferential allocation to veterans of posts in public concerns and public administration.

(3)   No mere allocation of work, but of the best positions ...

An excellent ideological awareness, love of the people and homeland,
and the test of fighting for our Third Reich must be more highly
valued than technical know-how.[23]

The publication of such articles doubtless met with approval from
jobless stormtroopers, but in taking this line the SA's leaders revealed
possible desperation over the persistently high unemployment levels.
Their stand defied Hitler's declaration that 'only ability can be of
importance in the economy',[24] and agreements to the same effect
reached between the government and employers.[25]

The State, Public Institutions and SA Employment

Despite the SA's claim that it had fared so badly, there is still considerable disagreement among historians on the question of job allocation.
Mason regards the Nazi government's efforts to provide its own supporters with jobs as successful, writing that by October 1933 'in no
district were fewer than 40 per cent of the jobless "members of the
Nationalist paramilitary organisations" found new work, and in some
as many as 70 per cent'.[26] These organisations included the SA, but
writing of 1935 and 1936 Kater paints a bleak picture of job prospects
for stormtroopers. He remarks that the SA contained 'in comparison
with the national population, the NSDAP and SS ... by far the greatest
proportion of socially weak, socio-economically disadvantaged, and in
particular, jobless'.[27]

No doubt the SA would have agreed with Kater, but reference to
central government and other official sources helps clarify what had
happened and why. On assuming power, Hitler's government recognised that the 6 million unemployed constituted an explosive political
and social problem which required a speedy resolution. Although the
economy was beginning to recover, the free market was not left to deal
alone with the problem. Special schemes were mooted to occupy a
proportion of the jobless until the recovery gave them more permanent
work and, in addition, certain groups received favoured treatment in
job allocation.

The Reich Ministry of Labour established a scheme in spring 1933 to
create between 470,000 and 700,000 jobs for a year at a cost of RM 1 to
1·5 billion and some stormtroopers certainly benefited from this.[28] In
late June German Railways committed RM 560 million to employing
250,000 workers for a year on construction projects,[29] while in August

the Post Office announced a similar scheme.[30] The SA benefited to some extent, but less dramatically than it might have hoped. Recruitment for the schemes was entrusted to the public services themselves and applications were to proceed via the unemployment offices. Certain applicants were to be favoured, the veteran members of all right-wing paramilitary organisations among them, but only if their former employment suited them for the jobs available, if they were long-term unemployed and, in the Post Office's case, if they were heads of households.[31] Therefore, the SA had no direct say in placing its members in these schemes while, at best, a fifth of the stormtroopers qualified as veterans in any case.

With regard to long-term jobs, the government identified two groups for special treatment. Applicants younger than 25 were to be favoured by unemployment offices on social grounds, irrespective of their past or present political loyalties.[32] Therefore, while many stormtroopers were sufficiently young to benefit, their membership of the SA was completely irrelevant to the acquisition of work in this way. The government also acknowledged its political debt to its longer-standing supporters who were to be allocated jobs on a favoured basis through the unemployment offices, a scheme dubbed the Special Action (Sonderaktion). Those eligible were SA, SS, and Stahlhelm members who had joined up before 30 January 1933, NSDAP members with membership numbers 1 to 300,000, and party office bearers who had held their posts for at least a year.[33] Since the SA had only numbered around 425,000 in January 1933, relatively few of its greatly enlarged post-takeover membership were eligible for favoured treatment within the terms of the Special Action.

The Special Action was evidently intended to place around half a million people in work as quickly as possible.[34] Since unemployment fell by over 2 million between January and November 1933 the task was not impossible,[35] yet by then little more than half the paramilitary veterans had been found work at a time when unemployment had fallen by a third in any case. In October the Reich Institute for Job Allocation and Unemployment Insurance circulated a report to unemployment offices assessing the success of the Special Action in placing paramilitary veterans in jobs. Mason's observation that 40 to 70 per cent of paramilitary members had been found work is taken from this report and therefore applies to veterans only.[36] Even here problems were arising, with the Reich Institute commenting that 'reports also show in considerable detail the difficulties which have arisen during the execution of the Special Action'.[37] Indeed just a month earlier the president of the Reich Institute had written to the SA Command warning that the press was painting too optimistic a picture regarding the Special Action. He continued: 'I therefore consider it desirable that all parties exercise some restraint in publications concerning the Action, to prevent a deep-rooted discontent taking hold among the jobless members of the paramilitary formations, and instead that they try harder actually to attain our goal.'[38]

By April 1935 the Special Action had still not found work for all veterans. In Baden and Württemberg 947 were still seeking placement, of whom 636 remained completely unemployed. Of these 636 over two-thirds were in the SA and SS.[39] Nationwide various difficulties had arisen which the central authorities were unable to overcome entirely. Industry had neglected to notify vacancies to the Special Action, which consequently found relatively few jobs in the private sector.[40] Not all civil servants in the unemployment offices were keen to administer the Special Action in the spirit intended.[41] The SA itself had not helped by trying to place members directly in jobs rather than observing official procedures, with chaotic results,[42] while SA officials who had been placed as liaison officers within individual unemployment offices often aggravated rather than assisted matters.[43]

Therefore, while stormtroopers certainly found work after Hitler's takeover, their membership of the SA was often irrelevant to their good fortune. The SA believed with increasing bitterness that, as an organisation, it had been let down and there is evidence to support Kater's observation that the SA fared worse than other institutions when jobs were handed around. In early 1934 it pressed to obtain public white-collar and civil service posts as they became vacant, but without much success. Although half the available white-collar posts were to be reserved for veteran stormtroopers, these same men should long since have found work through the Special Action.[44] In June 1935 Hitler reserved a tenth of civil service vacancies for Nazi veterans, including stormtroopers, but again these were the very people whom the Special Action had sought to place for two years.[45] Only in late 1935 were stormtroopers who had belonged to the SA for a year included among those favoured for employment in the public sector.[46]

In February 1933 the government created an auxiliary police force of 100,000 or more men,[47] ostensibly to prevent the left instigating politically motivated disorder, but in reality to allow the NSDAP to break up the political organisations of the left, including the trade unions, in a distinctly disorderly yet quasi-legal manner. These police units were composed of SA, SS and Stahlhelm members and therefore provided some jobless stormtroopers with maintenance and work of a sort. However, some districts preferred stormtroopers in work,[48] while in the Rhine Province and Westphalia, at least, it was planned that stormtroopers should comprise only a fifth of the auxiliary police's membership. Individuals and not whole formations were to be recruited and were to be carefully selected.[49] In practice, almost half the auxiliary police in these two provinces were stormtroopers[50] and quite probably workers in the main,[51] while in Bavaria the proportion of stormtroopers was higher still.[52] This dubious role as the guardians of 'law and order' proved short-lived for the SA, however, as the auxiliary police was disbanded in late 1933.

If the SA received relatively few state sector jobs, the Voluntary Labour Service (VLS) provided a potential alternative. The scheme was introduced by the Weimar authorities in 1931 to mitigate the effects of unemployment, although some quarters had pressed for a compulsory scheme to eradicate joblessness altogether.[53]

At this stage the NSDAP, which planned to introduce its own comprehensive compulsory labour service following a Nazi takeover, ignored the scheme, even if some individual leaders such as Gregor Strasser advocated participation or even the establishment of Nazi-run camps.[54] Only in late 1932 did a few of the latter appear.[55] The SA's leaders were even less enthusiastic, perceiving anybody's camps as a threat to the SA's integrity[56] and the appointment of party (rather than SA) officials to arrange possible transfers of stormtroopers to the VLS hardly reassured them.[57] Few stormtroopers were forwarded to either the VLS or to Nazi camps. In late 1932 Lutze, then commander of Obergruppe II, typified the SA's mood when writing that only the dire material circumstances of his men had induced him to allow a few into the VLS 'in organised formations under SA leaders for a specified period'.[58]

Little changed after the Nazi takeover. In December 1933 Böckenhauer, commander of Sub-Group Hamburg, objected to releasing men to the VLS ostensibly because an official request was poorly formulated and had not been confirmed by the SA. However, his real grounds for objecting were betrayed when he concluded: 'Present knowledge is that SA leaders are instructed to hinder a transfer of SA members to the VLS to avoid weakening unnecessarily the SA.'[59] His allusion to a higher authority suggests that the SA Command had encouraged his and similar stands. Feelings were probably mixed on this score, for while the senior commanders understood perfectly well the importance of re-employment, they must have shared local leaders' fears that a rapid return to work or transfer to labour camps would reduce the SA's size and influence. A similar attitude had possibly cost stormtroopers jobs in the state and private sectors. In March 1933 German Railways notified the SA of 90,000 vacancies for manual workers, but at least some SA commanders ignored the opening.[60] Similarly, in early 1934 SA leaders encouraged men offered heavy farm work to refuse it, thereby keeping their formations intact while simultaneously allowing their men to avoid this uncongenial form of work.[61] However, when it came to permanent jobs rather than places on labour schemes the SA High Command condemned this form of backsliding in no uncertain terms.[62]

None the less, economic misery again prevented the SA from ignoring the VLS entirely. Thus Böckenhauer released some 200 men from his Hamburg units to the VLS in December 1933, remarking:

It should be added that with persistent unemployment, the need to experience a 'regular routine' once more: daily routine, meals, dressing etc., through temporary membership of a Labour Service camp is growing. This applies especially to the urban SA which is suffering appallingly.[63]

If extreme necessity motivated transfers to the VLS until mid-1934 the Röhm purge changed attitudes dramatically and on 9 August the alternatives of military service or VLS were proposed for stormtroopers.[64] The new High Command's political convictions played little part in this, for regional commanders who had opposed the VLS now sat at headquarters in Munich, but the SA's political emasculation proved quite persuasive enough. Attitudes in the regions adjusted quickly to the changed circumstances with commanders even encouraging stormtroopers to volunteer for the VLS.[65] Ironically, the effects of transfers to the VLS on the SA's size were relatively small. The 'cleaning up' measures announced by the SA on 17 August 1934[66] and a drift of members from the SA as they finally found long-term jobs made a far greater impact. Thus in Frankfurt-am-Main only a tenth of those leaving the SA in the year after the Röhm purge were joining the VLS.[67]

Conditions on Nazi labour schemes were harsh and possibly discouraged SA volunteers anyway. The motorway projects were no exception, with the SA Central Office remarking in June 1934 that 'wages on the national motorways are being described as starvation wages and this is being exploited by agitators'.[68] The following year saw little change, leading an outraged SA regimental commander in Baden to remark: 'It will not be surprising if workers still estranged from the Third Reich are thereby educated as Bolshevists rather than National Socialists; they are treated like slaves.'[69] In fact, the same report noted the reluctance of private contractors carrying out the work to employ stormtroopers anyway: '[They] favour those not belonging to an NS organisation because they can do what they wish with such workers, whilst they fear the SA and SS men.'[70]

In the end Hitler's initial preparations for war allowed the state to contribute decisively to the solution of the SA's unemployment problem, although immediately after the Nazi takeover this seemed a distant prospect. Relations between the SA and army ranged from uneasy to hostile and this tension was eventually to contribute to the Röhm purge of mid-1934. In March 1933 the SA sought to flood the armed forces with stormtroopers, but the military, recognising the danger this scheme posed to their political independence, blocked the SA's move by declaring most of its applicants physically or medically unfit.[71] The SA demanded government intervention[72] but, as is well known, Hitler supported the army's stance, not least because of the unfavourable international implications inherent in any transgression of the Versailles Treaty by expanding the army beyond 100,000 men at this stage. Transfers from the SA to the army usually remained small-scale and specialised until mid-1934. None the less, there were local exceptions and by April 1934 a transfer of stormtroopers to the army in north Baden was sufficiently large to account partly for a contraction of the SA there.[73]

Shortly after the Röhm purge the SA Command, envisaging developments on a grander scale, established procedures for transfer to the military. Stormtroopers were to relinquish party and SA membership but, if discharged honourably from the armed forces, could rejoin party and SA under their original number with their membership regarded as unbroken.[74] By October 1934 the Chief of the Army Command, von Fritsch, regarded the SA as a means of circumventing recruitment restrictions and made arrangements with the new SA chief, Lutze, to recruit stormtroopers for two-month army training courses from 1 January 1935.[75] In fact, in the year following the Röhm purge, 6 per cent of those leaving the Frankfurt-am-Main SA were entering the army which, repeated nationally, would total 60,000 men.[76] However, the real increase in transfers only followed the reintroduction of conscription on 16 March 1935. On 25 March it was planned to draft 20,000 stormtroopers into the Luftwaffe Reserve for anti-aircraft defence,[77] while by autumn transfers to the military had assumed far greater proportions with a total of 26,004 between October and November alone. The overall net decline in SA strength during this month was 48,000.[78] How far these transfers involved jobless stormtroopers is not immediately clear, but those in long-term jobs were probably not drafted ahead of their jobless counterparts. Whatever the case, the army's recruitment of stormtroopers would have shortened the queue of jobless directly or indirectly. If employed stormtroopers did join up, the resulting job vacancy might have fallen to a jobless comrade.

The public sector further influenced stormtroopers' employment prospects through the state unemployment offices which were responsible for job allocation generally and for some state-run vocational training schemes. Before 1933 employment offices operated under statutes which forbade any discrimination on political or religious grounds,[79] although some individual officials did allow their personal politics to influence their treatment of job applicants. This did not disadvantage stormtroopers alone, but Fritz Wenderoth of Giessen was typical in complaining that in 1930 'the party boss (Reichsbanner) Meier was employed at the labour exchange, and he gave no work to National Socialists'.[80]

After January 1933 the position became more complex precisely because the staff in the employment offices were expected to exercise systematic political discrimination which was not necessarily to their liking. Their only formal obligation towards the SA involved favouring the SA veterans who registered with them under the Special Action. Other jobless stormtroopers were to be treated as routine clients.[81] This arrangement worked relatively smoothly in much of Germany and in June 1934 a senior SA official noted that 'Employment Offices make a special effort to assist stormtroopers when allocating jobs'.[82]

In south-western Germany, however, the employment office officials reacted negatively to the Special Action and got on pretty badly with the SA in general.[83] The SA in *Gau* Odernheim, Baden, complained in April 1934 that 'the Employment Exchanges are making little effort to place SA men',[84] while Brigade 51, Bavarian Palatinate, reported in the same month that 'among the officials here, and indeed, among the employers, the necessary sympathy and often, even goodwill are badly lacking'.[85] The Röhm purge failed to improve matters with Battalion III/250 Odenheim reporting in September 1934:

> Morale in the SA (principally in veteran units) has been depressed severely by the Röhm revolt, and [units] consider themselves disadvantaged in job allocation in particular.
>
> Morale can only be raised if the SA High Command for its part exerts strong pressure and the Employment Exchanges responsible are so tightly controlled that at last, all veteran SA men receive the employment they deserve.[86]

The 70th Regiment, Saarbrücken, made a similar complaint over a year later,[87] while in August 1935 Group Kurpfalz accused the employment offices of politically motivated sabotage.[88]

The SA's anger was possibly exaggerated and it had not acted blamelessly itself. Its liaison officers in the employment offices had often exceeded their brief,[89] some SA units had tried to slip newer recruits into the Special Action[90] while others had tried to by-pass the employment offices altogether by placing stormtroopers directly in work.[91] Even so, the NSDAP itself complained in March 1935 that the attitude of officials in the Baden employment offices left much to be desired and urged the same officials to set aside personal doubts concerning the Special Action.[92] The Prussian government, too, was concerned in April 1934 that the civil service was not supporting the Special Action sufficiently and that Nazi veterans of any kind in public service were receiving the cold shoulder from longer-standing employees.[93] Clearly the Nazification of the civil service was no easy task where the civil servants themselves were ill-disposed towards the process.

The Private Sector and SA Employment

If the public sector failed to favour the SA to any great degree, the private sector provided an alternative. Of course, firms were shedding labour until 1933 rather than recruiting many new workers, but stormtroopers might have retained jobs longer than other employees. The revival of the private sector during 1933 coupled with falls in both relative and absolute unemployment levels in the SA by mid-1934 suggest that after the Nazi takeover stormtroopers benefited in some measure. However, the significant issue, as in the public sector, is whether SA membership itself clinched jobs or whether this membership proved either irrelevant or disadvantageous.

The politics of most employers understandably influenced their attitude towards the SA and agriculture was no exception to this pattern. The Catholic farmers of Germany were among the staunchest supporters of the Centre Party and the Bavarian People's Party (BVP), which arguably explains the dearth of evidence indicating any widespread favoured treatment of stormtroopers in rural Catholic Germany, either before or after the takeover.

In Protestant Germany the picture was more complex. Looking at the late Weimar years, Fetscher writes that the big landowners of northern Germany greatly assisted the advance of Nazism during 1932,[94] but a favourable attitude to the Nazi Party need not have rubbed off on the SA. Certainly, some landowners joined the SA as well as the NSDAP and they often occupied leading positions within the SA.[95] On these men's estates stormtroopers were presumably favoured before and after Hitler's takeover. Most big landowners were not Nazis, however, belonging to or supporting the German National People's Party (DNVP). Relations between these landowners and local Nazi organisations were often poor, as illustrated particularly colourfully by the local NSDAP history of the Reichensee district, East Prussia. Of the early 1930s it wrote:

> The reactionaries, the ruling classes who dominated working men, much rather supported the Reichsbanner and the KPD than the Nazis. The estate owner von Quassowski once actually said during an election campaign: 'I prefer to have communists as workers on my estate rather than these bloody Nazis.' Another estate owner (Iwan Jagodnen) said [of us]: 'workers' party, how can the likes of us associate with the workers? There's too strong a stench of sweat there.'[96]

Taking a broader perspective, relations between the DNVP's paramilitary confederate, the Stahlhelm, and the SA provide an indication of how stormtroopers fared on the large estates of northern Germany. By mid-1932 relations were almost universally poor, typical being the comment from Mecklenburg that 'the SA rejects any link whatsoever with the reactionary Stahlhelm'.[97] The Stahlhelm responded bitterly to this antagonism and, in rural mid-Silesia at least, this cost some stormtroopers their jobs. SA Sub-Group Middle Silesia explained that:

> Relations with the Stahlhelm, which were more than good and comradely before, have cooled markedly after the recent developments. This affects particularly SA men in purely rural areas, many of whom have been sacked by their employers who belong to the Stahlhelm.[98]

In East Prussia the Stahlhelm and DNVP became opposed to the whole Nazi movement and by the time of the 1933 local elections (if not sooner) workers on estates owned by DNVP members were pressurised to vote DNVP.[99] Therefore, on many estates stormtroopers were probably not favoured as employees and possibly were disadvantaged. The Nationalists' retention of political influence in the months after the Nazi takeover probably prevented any great change in the overall position.

The smaller farmers of Protestant Germany often regarded the SA differently. Many were themselves Nazi adherents and some were stormtroopers.[100] Furthermore, grass-roots SA activity often helped these longer-standing adherents of Nazism, as in Schleswig-Holstein where the SA sabotaged the auctioning of bankrupt farms by the authorities: 'Bombs and hand-grenades were used as defence against state finance offices which drove remorselessly our fellow countrymen from house and farm.'[101] In return, the farmers contributed to SA welfare collections[102] and, therefore, where small Protestant farmers employed outside labour at all stormtroopers were presumably well placed. Unfortunately for the SA's members, insufficient numbers of small, Protestant farmers were able to employ them and in June 1934 the SA attacked agriculture overall for preferring labourers outside the SA.

The relationship between big business – particularly heavy industry – and Nazism during the early 1930s has stimulated substantial historical controversy. A number of writers have argued that Hitler and the Nazi movement were, more or less, brought to power by big business and that the Nazi movement basically reflected the interests of monopoly capitalism.[103] Other historians, notably Turner and Hentschel, have argued that the evidence for so direct a community of interests is very thin, and that big business contributed rather to the weakening of the institutions and functioning of the Weimar Republic – thereby indirectly assisting Nazism.[104] Whatever the outcome of this debate, direct evidence concerning the ordinary stormtroopers is absent from this examination of high politics. Furthermore, a sizeable proportion of labour was employed in medium and small firms whose political and economic outlook could differ sharply from that of big business and, according to many analysts, provided the basis for the NSDAP's brand of anti-capitalism.[105] Their distinctive attitude may have had consequences for stormtroopers' employment prospects.

SA records themselves indicate that the private sector, in general, did little to provide the stormtroopers with work. Some SA members asserted in their personal reminiscences that their politics led to their dismissal from jobs, but while they presented themselves retrospectively as political martyrs, their ill-fortune possibly arose for more mundane reasons. In other cases stormtroopers explained precisely why their politics had created difficulties for them. Writing of the years 1929 to 1931 Paul Krause of Wiesbaden commented, 'I made every effort to get honest work ..., but as soon as people knew I was an SA man, I was driven from my workplace.'[106] How often anti-Nazi workforces could pressurise employers into dismissing Nazis from their workforce at the height of the depression is debatable, but some employers were unwilling to risk confrontation with the trade unions and therefore complied with union wishes, whatever their own political sympathies. Fritz Walper of Mainz wrote:

> In 1929 I got work at the waterworks. ... When the trade union official Bauer turned up, the workers urged him to kick me out. He answered: 'If you showed solidarity, the Nazi would have long since gone.' I went to that illustrious gentleman, the boss, and told him of this. He none the less dismissed me from his office and I was sacked.[107]

At other times the employer and workforce shared an antipathy towards Nazism although their politics differed,[108] while sometimes the employer's politics alone could result in a sacking.[109]

The SA's persistently high unemployment rates suggest that these accounts (which could be repeated almost indefinitely) were representative, but it seems that by 1932 the NSDAP was sufficiently well established in some factories and firms to make SA membership less risky.[110] Furthermore, there were cases where employers did favour stormtroopers, although these instances do stand out as exceptions. In March 1931 the *Münchner Post* published an article describing a deal between the NSDAP and the Hessian industrialists Dyckerhoff, Schindler and Jung who were reportedly Nazi Party members. Hitler had apparently written to the *Gauleiter* of Hessen-Nassau, commenting that not only was money from these sources important, but that these employers had helped SA men obtain work – and could do so again to attract workers to National Socialism. The accuracy of this newspaper report could not be checked, but the Munich police took it sufficiently seriously to place it on file.[111]

The post-takeover period failed to produce better prospects for the SA's jobless members. The SA High Command had expected that Nazi control of government would permit it to solve its socio-economic problems in its own way, and similar beliefs were expressed at local level. The SA and other Nazi organisations began to interfere directly in firms' affairs, partly in an attempt to expedite the allocation of jobs to their own members.[112] In mid-1933 the NSDAP leadership, the president of the Reich Institute for Job Allocation and Unemployment Insurance and the Confederation of German Employers' Associations met in Berlin to regulate the situation. The employers agreed to co-operate with the Special Action, but refused to relinquish control of their own labour recruitment. The meeting agreed that 'the existence of genuine vacancies and the professional and personal suitability [of applicants] must remain decisive, despite the guidelines [concerning the Special Action]', while firms retained the right to re-employ former longstanding employees in the first instance. In return for these grudging concessions, which the employers sometimes disregarded in any case, the SA and other Nazi formations were ordered to stop interfering in industry forthwith.[113]

As the SA High Command realised that its membership, some veterans included, would not receive jobs quickly, gloom and even bitterness mounted. By September 1933 it complained publicly:

> The allocation of vacant jobs to our SA, SS and Stallhelm men is not occurring to the extent desired by the SA High Command.
> Although it must be considered a moral duty to provide the National Socialist Revolution's fighters with work and bread, there are very many employers – both in private- and state-owned concerns – who still distance themselves somewhat from National Socialism. Instead of drawing on our fighters to fill vacancies, as should be their duty, they actually appoint members of disbanded parties and organisations on a preferential basis.[114]

By 1934 things were little better and the ordinary stormtroopers were growing impatient. Faced with this mounting pressure the SA Central Office lashed out at employers on 20 June:

> Recriminations concerning employers' egoistic and anti-social attitude. Veterans are complaining about bad pay and the employers'

scanty awareness of National Socialism, which includes little inclination to employ SA veterans ... Farmers prefer labourers who do not belong to the SA because they do not have to attend musters and exercises.[115]

The Central Office also cast a jaundiced eye on other institutions and the news media, as a summary of reports and assessments on SA affairs which it published on 14 June 1934 illustrates. Entitled 'Fight against the SA', it lashed out at its enemies: 'intolerable relations with the P.O. ... , VLS receives preferential economic treatment, ... Stahlhelm, a reactionary melting pot, ... provocative diocesan letters and proclamations by German bishops'.[116] However, the Central Office devoted most attention to foreign press reports, which it believed received their information from the SA's 'opponents of every [political] colouring within Germany'.[117] These sources describe a fundamental split between Röhm as leader of the impoverished, radical SA, and the conservative members of Hitler's Cabinet – an interpretation the Central Office reproduced without comment:

> The Chief of Staff [Röhm] reportedly the leader of the anti-capitalist movement and the opponent of Schmitt and Göring. His secret order to the SA, which, because of the social situation cannot stand idly by any longer, has resulted in great unease on the part of Schmitt and Seldte.
>
> Their complaints to Hitler have provoked a counter-attack by Röhm, who is demanding the removal of Schmitt, Schacht and Seldte.
>
> Hitler is avoiding a decision by taking refuge in the mountains.
>
> The ministers Graf Schwerin-Krosigk and Seldte have chaired Cabinet meetings concerning the ending of state subsidies to the SA. Its functions could be better performed by the MORE AFFLUENT [sic] SS and Stahlhelm members, and would then cost almost nothing at all.
>
> Comment by the Chief of Staff: That would drive the SA into the arms of Bolshevism.
>
> Compromise proposal by the Leader [Hitler]: subsidies should be raised by means of collections; step by step cutback in the SA's size for reasons of foreign policy. Strengthening of the SS, the military value of which is greater than the SA's, by way of compensation to 350,000 men. The SA to be compensated by greater consideration in the allocation of work.[118]

The Reich Chancellory papers omit any mention of such Cabinet meetings, but it seems likely that less formal discussions did occur. Whatever the case, the SA's leaders clearly felt saddled with a social problem which was beyond their power to solve, while they received little support from elsewhere.

Local developments usually justified the bleak picture painted by the SA Command. Of course, there were exceptions. Some firms, including I. G. Farben, did provide jobs,[119] but even some of these quickly changed their tune and in most cases there was no room for optimism.[120] Even after the Röhm purge had cowed the SA politically, relations with industry remained poor. Battalion III/250 of Odenheim complained in September 1934 that the disfavouring of stormtroopers by employers had made them the mockery of their political opponents:

> Veteran SA men are still being mocked and ridiculed by former Centre Party members and Socialists who hold good positions. They have every justification for doing so. The SA man does his duty, pays his subscriptions and uses up his time whilst the others quietly earn their living and thus have every reason to ridicule a stupid SA man who, up to this day, has no work.[121]

In Darmstadt the disadvantages of SA membership were so apparent that stormtroopers were urged by their families to quit the SA 'because they will then have more time and money for themselves'.[122] In January 1935 Brigade 250, Offenbach, complained that 'the attitude of employers and entrepreneurs to the employment of jobless SA men is patchy and still repeatedly provides grounds for complaints',[123] while Brigade 153, Heidelberg, accused employers of explicit prejudice against stormtroopers with crippling effects on SA morale:

> Sometimes discharged SA men mock their former comrades' devotion to duty because the former are in no way disadvantaged by their discharge. Indeed, it is actually true that some employers give preference to employees who do not belong to the SA at the cost of SA men.[124]

Similarly, the SA noted that by mid-1935 employers were often swift to lay off stormtroopers 'at every opportunity',[125] and Group South-West noted more generally that 'the veterans' poor economic circumstances ... have a devastating effect on overall SA morale'.[126] Such reports may have exaggerated the SA's problems and SA leaders, embittered by their rapidly dwindling relevance in public life, possibly complained at every opportunity. However, the reports cited were directed to their own High Command in Munich rather than constituting any public appeal and, in effect, local SA commanders were having to admit to their superiors that morale in their units was at rock-bottom and that their membership, including some veterans, still remained without work over two years after Hitler's takeover. Of course, they were reluctant to allocate themselves any share of the blame but the extent of the SA's social problem is clear enough.

Under the circumstances stormtroopers understandably put the acquisition or retention of work before their devotion to SA duties and even casual labourers who presumably were best able to arrange their working lives to fit in with other commitments put work first.[127] During 1934 and 1935 the problem intensified as stormtroopers drifted away in growing numbers upon realising that the SA was unable to find its members work. In desperation SA leaders attempted to attach the acquisition or retention of a job to continued SA membership. Individual stormtroopers were warned that neglect of SA duties might lead to expulsion and the recommendation that they forfeit their jobs.[128] In December 1934 Group Ostmark requested the High Command to ensure 'that men expelled from the SA should also lose their jobs'.[129] However, the SA Command was slow to lay down general principles, if it was in a position to do so. In April 1935 a labour court in Bielefeld dismissed a clerical worker from a public enterprise because of his expulsion from the SA,[130] but the SA itself only responded to this verdict in September. On 9 September Böckenhauer, chief of the SA's Justice Office, wrote to Hess that the SA considered the 'Bielefeld verdict as a special case' and continued that the SA would take no clear stand on the issue. However, he then distinguished between public and private concerns remarking that those expelled 'from the party or one of its formations ... are no longer suited to retain employment in state or other public concerns'.[131] Even so, it appears that the SA either failed to act on this before the end of 1935 or was still unable to do so.

The evident reluctance of employers throughout the private sector to take on stormtroopers cannot be explained by the SA's formal political stance, for the SA Command lacked any general policy regarding the ownership or control of productive assets. Furthermore, employers were far more concerned about labour organisations of the left until 1933 and, whatever political disagreements there were between the SA and employers after Hitler's takeover, the former was ultimately answerable to Hitler, and he certainly wished to maintain amicable relations with business and commercial circles.

Part of the explanation lay in the SA's everyday behaviour. In general it was composed of losers who were not only deeply embittered, but also chronically incapable of adapting adequately to an everyday routine. Life had, to a greater or lesser degree, consisted of struggle, violence and disruption, none of which ideally had a place in the factory, on the farm or in an office. Not surprisingly, employers shied away from using such labour. After Hitler's takeover matters were particularly bad as SA units combined with other sections of the Nazi movement to attack and even occupy factories, offices and commercial premises.[132] The authorities were able to bring the worst of these excesses under control by mid-1933, but even in 1935 stormtroopers were creating problems within the factories. While some SA groups, such as Hansa, complained that stormtroopers 'resist the instructions of management, or prefer to posture as "advocates of SA ideology"'[133] in early 1935, other groups sided with their men. For instance, in July 1935 Group South-West remarked that:

> Industry rejects SA men as workers with few exceptions. The veteran SA man is an uncomfortable colleague for the gentlemen employers. These gentlemen are completely unprepared to hear the truth from SA men once in a while in an SA-style, open manner.[134]

The problem did not end with verbal outbursts of this sort, for local SA leaders sometimes intervened directly in firms' affairs to protect their members' interests. Some incidents were relatively trivial, as when an SA unit near Regensburg tried unsuccessfully to take a bank manager into protective custody in September 1933 after he had dismissed a stormtrooper from his staff.[135] Other cases were more serious. SA Battalion RII/10 of Eichstätt, Upper Bavaria, intervened after the Konstein Glassworks laid off a number of stormtroopers in April 1934. Its commander wrote:

> The SAR men Andreas Herrle of Konstein, Norbert Eger of Wellheim and Anton Biber of Konstein who have been employed in your works for more than thirty years have asked the battalion for work placement, since they have been made redundant by your firm's cutbacks.
> Might I kindly have the *particular* reasons the works had for laying off these three SAR men, while in fact 100 workers are still employed in your works.
> Equally, I would be obliged if you would agree to give back the above-mentioned SA men regular work. As SAR men and long-serving members of your firm, they certainly possess the right to permanent employment.[136]

The firm felt obliged to take the complaint seriously and, in its detailed reply, pointed out that Herrle had already been re-employed. It asserted that Biber had voluntarily retired because of poor eyesight and since the SA, in turn, accepted this explanation, their original intervention appears to have been overzealous. Eger was considered 'unsuited' for any available jobs, and the firm took care to stress that even non-vacant, potentially suitable jobs were all occupied by stormtroopers.[137] The SA accepted the reply as a whole, but urged the firm to re-employ all remaining stormtroopers, presumably laid off at an earlier date, as soon as possible.

The Röhm purge did not end this sort of action. In January 1935 Brigade 250 of Offenbach reported to Munich (thereby indicating that SA headquarters at least condoned this type of activity) that it had intervened successfully in the affairs of a large automobile producer:

> The firm Adam Opel of Rüsselsheim laid off a large number of SA men in the second half of 1934. Therefore a campaign was launched in conjunction with Brigade 50 (Starkenburg) of Darmstadt against the firm Adam Opel. This was in fact successful, and a number of SA men recovered their jobs.[138]

No doubt it occurred to Opel that without stormtroopers on its pay-roll this problem could have been avoided and neighbouring firms presumably came to the same conclusions.

Therefore the widespread reluctance of employers to recruit stormtroopers is not surprising. SA members may have been welcomed initially as a means of circumventing the power of the established trade unions. However, any such favouritism apparently faded as the left lost its ability to organise openly, and former Social Democrats, KPD members – and Centrists – who remained outside the Nazi movement became, ironically, the equivalent of unorganised labour. In contrast, unlike the harmless corporatist DAF,[139] the SA and, for a time, the NSBO, could and did defend their members' interests.

This fundamental problem was complemented by the routine demands of SA membership which called full-time employees away from their jobs with irksome frequency. Röhm urged SA units to arrange musters and exercises outside working hours as early as August 1933,[140] but exactly two years later employers remained reluctant to employ stormtroopers for this reason. Group Kurpfalz complained:

> Widespread accusations are being made of entrepreneurs being unwilling to employ SA men. The justification is that SA duty makes excessive demands on the men, and thereby makes them insufficiently productive.[141]

Group South-West made similar complaints while unwittingly demonstrating that employers had every reason to avoid hiring stormtroopers even had their behaviour within the factories been beyond reproach:

> Factory management has no sympathy for the execution of SA service. For this reason alone they reject SA men if at all possible, on the grounds that they must be able to exercise control over everyone in a factory, especially when overtime is being worked. SA duties often make it impossible for SA men to work overtime. From this one can

appreciate clearly the attitude of the bosses to purely idealistic considerations.[142]

Therefore the unorganised worker – and after 1933 that effectively included all non-Nazi workers – was potentially more productive and benefited accordingly.

The SA's Own Measures

The SA's own efforts to intervene directly in job allocation only had limited success. Its liaison officers within the employment offices could, as we have seen, cause as many problems as they solved and, similarly, the SA's rather amateurish efforts to provide labour directly to employers simply often made matters worse.[143] Some stormtroopers, particularly leaders, were themselves employers and in these circumstances both leaders and men could be pleased with the results. The leaders recognised that jobs so provided actually increased their following's dependence on the SA, while the men found themselves (for once) directly and unreservedly favoured. Typical was the case of a local Bavarian commander who, in January 1932, promised to 'provide every SA man in his regiment with shoes, and employ some of the men in his factory (the Inselmühle Iceworks) in the summer'.[144] Of course, only a small part of the labour market was controlled by the SA in so direct a fashion. The captains of industry, commerce, and agriculture were seldom SA members, which made this particular form of relief at best a palliative. After 1933 some foremen who belonged to the SA were able to obtain jobs for their comrades, but again the scale of such relief was dwarfed by the problem it sought to combat.[145]

So, whatever the expectations of stormtroopers when they joined the SA, the organisation's record in job provision was not particularly good. The SA's leaders understood very well how crucial this issue was, but for a variety of reasons were often unable or sometimes unwilling to remedy the problem. Above all, the SA was the victim of its own success. Röhm had consciously set out in the early 1930s to recruit the unemployed of Germany into the SA and thereby prevent their mobilisation by the Communist Party. Until Hitler's takeover this battle was not finally won, but after January 1933 the younger male unemployed of Germany flocked to the SA. The sheer scale of this problem, the effects of prolonged unemployment on many stormtroopers, and a range of political considerations combined to thwart stormtroopers' hopes of finding work by virtue of their SA membership. Of course, most eventually found gainful employment of some kind, but success arguably came more often irrespective of, rather than because of, SA membership.

Notes

1 BA, R2/18740a. Abschrift. Der Reichsminister der Finanzen, J 7750–78. Berlin, 17. November 1933, p. 1.
2 P. H. Merkl, *The Making of a Stormtrooper* (Princeton, NJ, 1980), contains further informative biographical detail, but most of his subjects joined the SA before the depression while it remained a small organisation. Unemployment, therefore, features less strongly in his findings. Merkl, in fact, comments in *Political Violence Under the Swastika* (Princeton, NJ, 1975), p. 12, which uses the same sample material as *Stormtrooper*, that the 'sample is representative mostly of the pre-1930 party when it was still clearly an extremist fringe group of a mere 130,000, and not of the landslide popular movement of 1933'.
3 B. Moore, Jr, *Injustice* (London, 1978), ch. 12, argues similarly. Merkl, *Stormtrooper*, pp. 190–4, argues that joblessness was not so vital, but given the provenance of his material (note 2 above) this is hardly surprising.
4 BA, NS26/530. Emil Sauer, Personal Recollections, p. 1. Sommersonnenwende, 1928.
5 BA, NS26/323. Letter dated 25 June 1931, written by Paul Maikowski, Company 33, Berlin, to his brother Hans.
6 BA, NS26/327. Tagebuch des SA Heims in Augsburg, 26.10.1931–9.2.1932.
7 HHW, Abt. 483/NSDAP 2250. Heinrich Maul, born 2 September 1899.
8 HHW, Abt. 483/NSDAP 2238. Rudolf Jung, born 23 January 1908.
9 The correlation of white-collar status and economic good fortune is observed in Table 3.4 (p. 33). See also Merkl, *Political Violence*, pp. 581–93.
10 HHW, Abt. 483/NSDAP 2146. Wilhelm Keller, born 8 July 1912.
11 HHW, Abt. 483/NSDAP 2262. Wilhelm Reisser, no date of birth given.
12 NWHStA, Ge 49,130. Release of name forbidden.
13 NWHStA, Ge 31,035. Release of name forbidden.
14 M. Weissbecker, 'Nationalsozialistische Deutsche Arbeiterpartei (NSDAP) 1919–1945', in D. Fricke *et al.* (eds), *Die bürgerlichen Parteien in Deutschland* (Leipzig, 1970), p. 403.
15 BHStA, Abt. I, So. I/1554B. Mobilmachung!
16 BHStA, Abt. I, So. I/1533. Der Generalinspekteur. B.B. Nr. 453/31. Stabschef. I. Stimmung in der SA. Abschrift. Kassel, den 17.12.31.
17 BA, NS23/474. NSDAP. Der Führer der SA-Untergruppe Leine. Abt. IIb. Briefb. Nr. 756/32. Betrifft: Stimmungsbericht. Hameln, den 22. September 1932. (1) Stimmung in der SA.
18 BA, NS23/474. SA der NSDAP. Der Gruppenführer Hochland. München, den 26.9.1932.
19 SAG, Rep. 18–26. 'SA-Arbeiter aufgewacht!'. KPD election leaflet, February 1933.
20 BA, Sch 414. Der OSAF. Verfügung. München, den 10.8.1933. gez. Röhm.
21 For instance, see the report of Röhm's speech to the Saxon SA rally of April 1934 in *SA-Mann*, year 3, no. 15, 14 April 1934.
22 'Der innerpolitische Kampf', *Der SA-Mann*, year 2, no. 33, 19 August 1933, p. 2. See also *Der SA-Mann*, year 3, no. 34, 26 August 1933, p. 2.
23 'Die SA als Garant der Zukunft', *Der SA-Mann*, year 3, no. 7, 17 February 1934, p. 1.

24 Quoted in C. Bloch, *Die SA und die Krise des NS-Regimes 1934* (Frankfurt-am-Main,) 1970, pp. 51–2.
25 GLAK, Arbeitsämter (460)/42(B). Arbeitgeberverband Badischer Gemeinden. Einstellung arbeitsloser Angehöriger der SA, SS und des Stahlhelms. Karlsruhe, den 15. Juli 1933.
26 T. W. Mason, *Arbeiterklasse und Volksgemeinschaft. Dokumente und Materialien zur deutschen Arbeiterpolitik 1936–1939* (Opladen, 1975), p. 53.
27 M. H. Kater, 'Zum gegenseitigen Verhältnis von SA und SS in der Sozialgeschichte des Nationalsozialismus von 1925 bis 1939', *Vierteljahresschrift für Sozial- und Wirtschaftsgeschichte* vol. 62, no. 3 (1975), p. 371.
28 BA, Reichskanzlei (R43II)/536. Reichskanzlei. Gegenstand: Arbeitsbeschaffung. Berlin, den 4. Mai 1933.
29 BA, R43II/536. Zu Rk 8016. Berlin, den 27. Juni 1933.
30 GLAK, Abt. 460/102(K). Der Präsident der Reichsanstalt für Arbeitsvermittlung und Arbeitslosenversicherung. II 5055/93. Betr.: Zusätzliches Arbeitsbeschaffungsprogramm der Deutschen Reichspost für 1933. Abschrift zu II 5055/93. Berlin-Charlottenburg, den 18. August 1933.
31 As note 30, and GLAK, Abt. 460/42(B). Der Präsident der Reichsanstalt für Arbeitsvermittlung und Arbeitslosenversicherung. Betr.: Sonderaktion zur Vermittlung arbeitsloser Mitglieder der nationalen Wehrverbände zur deutschen Reichsbahn-Gesellschaft. Berlin-Charlottenburg, den 26. August 1933.
32 BA, Deutscher Gemeindetag (R36)/1511. Deutscher Gemeindetag. Landesdienststelle Baden. Tgb. Nr. 1138/35. Rundschreiben B. Nr. 17/35. Karlsruhe, den 14. März 1935.
33 GLAK, Abt. 460/42(B). Der Präsident der Reichsanstalt für Arbeitsvermittlung und Arbeitslosenversicherung. II 5380/74. Betrifft: Unterbringung arbeitsloser Angehöriger der nationalen Verbände. Berlin-Charlottenburg, den 18. Oktober 1933.
34 This assumes a fair degree of double membership between organisations (which was indeed the case) and a fair quota of veterans either having work in 1933, or finding it themselves.
35 *Statistisches Jahrbuch*, Vol. 9, p. 307, table 11.
36 See note 33.
37 ibid.
38 GLAK, Abt. 460/42(B). Abschrift. Der Präsident der Reichsanstalt für Arbeitsvermittlung und Arbeitslosenversicherung. II 5380/51. Betrifft: Vermittlung von Mitgliedern der nationalen Wehrverbände. Berlin-Charlottenburg, den 18. September 1933.
39 GLAK, Abt. 460/42(B). Landesarbeitsamt Südwestdeutschland. Die Arbeitssuchenden und Arbeitslosen aus dem Personenkreis der Sonderaktion. Ende April 1935.
40 GLAK, Abt. 460/42(B). II 5380. Auf den Erlass vom 22.7.1933 – II 5380/1310. Sonderaktion zur Vermittlung arbeitsloser Mitglieder der nationalen Wehrverbände. 24. Juli 1933.
41 BA, R36/1511. An die Geschäftsführer der Arbeitsbeschaffungsausschüsse in Baden. Betrifft: Sonderaktion. Karlsruhe, den 9. März 1935. NWHStA, BR 1021–168. Unterbringung der alten Kämpfer der nationalsozialistischen Bewegung. Rd. Erl. d. FM zgl. i. R. d. M.Präs. u. aller St.M. v. 11.4.1934 Lo. 222II (Pr. Bef. Bl. S166).
42 GLAK, Abt. 460/42(B). Der Oberste SA-Führer IV Nr. 535/34. Betrifft: Aufhebung nicht amtlicher Arbeitsvermittlungsstellen. München, den 12. Januar 1934.
43 GLAK, Abt. 460/42(B). Der Präsident des Landesarbeitsamts Südwestdeutschland. II 5380/1200. Betrifft: Sonderaktion. Stuttgart, den 29. Mai 1934.
44 BA, NS23/1. Der Oberste SA-Führer. Verwaltungsamt Nr. 11950. Betrifft: Unter-

bringung von bewährten Kämpfern für die nationale Erhebung. München, den 24. Mai 1934.

45 BA, NS23/128. Der Oberste SA-Führer. Führungsamt F5 Nr. 34411. Betrifft: Unterbringung arbeitsloser SA-Angehöriger. gez. Lasch.
46 BA, R43II/552. Der Reichsminister der Finanzen. P2120–12718 IB. Berlin, 25. November 1935. This circular concerned apprenticeships in public administration and factories.
47 F. L. Carsten, *The Rise of Fascism* (London, 1976), p. 153; J. Klenner, *Verhältnis von Partei und Staat 1933–1945. Dargestellt am Beispiel Bayerns* (Munich, 1974), pp. 78–9.
48 BA, NS23/399. Untergruppe Hamburg. An die SA-Gruppe Nordsee, Bremen. Hamburg, den 4. Juli 1933.
49 NWHStA, Regierung Aachen/22757. Bericht über die am 21.2.1933 in Düsseldorf stattgefundene Besprechung des Höheren Polizeiführers im Westen mit den Vertretern der Regierungen ... Aachen, den 22. Februar 1933.
50 NWHStA, Regierung Aachen/22757, s. 49. Hilfspolizei. Gesamtstärke im Regierungsbezirk. Aachen, den 3. März 1933. gez. Freiherr von Langermann.
51 NWHStA, Regierung Aachen/22758. Der Höhere Polizeiführer im Westen. Hilfspolizei zur Verwendung durch den Herrn Regierungs-Präsidenten aus dem Kreise Monschau. Recklinghausen, den 17.5.1933.
52 Klenner, *Verhältnis*, pp. 78–9.
53 W. Benz, 'Vom freiwilligen Arbeitsdienst zur Arbeitsdienstpflicht', *Vierteljahreshefte für Zeitgeschichte*, year 16, no. 4 (1968), pp. 317–46.
54 ibid., pp. 329–31. In fact, in late 1931 a close associate of Gregor Strasser, Paul Schulz, wrote to Röhm on the need to organise the SA for labour service after a Nazi takeover – a proposal Röhm evidently ignored. BHStA, Abt. I, So. I/1545. Abschrift. Oberstleutnant a.D. Schulz, an Herrn Oberstleutnant Röhm. Trossingen, den 21.11.31.
55 These were in Lower Silesia, Bochum, Danzig and Pomerania. Benz, 'Arbeitsdienst', p. 331.
56 ibid.
57 BA, NS23/399. Abschrift. Richtlinien für die Zusammenarbeit der Abt. Arbeitsdienst mit der SA. München, den 5. Dezember 1932.
58 BA, NS23/399. NSDAP, SA-Obergruppe II. An die Untergruppe Hamburg. Betr.: Freiwilliger Arbeitsdienst. Hannover, den 22. Dezember 1933. gez. Lutze.
59 BA, NS23/399. Untergruppe Hamburg, der SA-Gruppe Nordsee. Hannover, den 22. Dezember 1933. gez. Böckenhauer.
60 BA, NS23/124. Der Oberste SA-Führer, Chef Nr. 726. Betrifft: Einstellungen bei der Reichsbahn. München, den 16. März 1933. gez. v. Krausser.
61 GLAK, Abt. 460/42(B). Abschrift. Der Oberste SA-Führer. Betrifft: Vermittlung arbeitsloser SA-Angehöriger. München, den 18. Januar 1934.
62 ibid.
63 See note 59.
64 BA, NS23/306. Die Fragen des Aufbaus der SA. den 9.8.1934. IV, p. 4.
65 BA, NS23/371. SA der NSDAP. Der Führer der Gruppe Hansa. Besondere Anordnung! Hamburg, den 20.8.1934. gez. Fust.
66 BA, NS23/265. OSAF. Verf. vom 17. August 1934. Ch. Nr. 21053. Cited in: Brigade 250. Vierteljahresbericht. An der SA Gr. Kurpfalz, Mannheim. Offenbach/Main, den 9. Januar 1935. In fact, such a 'clean-up' was mooted almost immediately after the Röhm purge.
67 HHW, Abt. 483/NSDAP 2100–2213, 2525–2540, 2214–2284. Stormtroopers leaving SA. Of 1,103 cases where the reason for leaving could be identified and where members definitely left during this period, 114 or 10·3% joined the VLS. Lowest quote (Regiment R 97) 1·5%. Highest quote (Regiment 99) 16·9%.
68 BA, NS23/1. Der Oberste SA-Führer, Zentralamt. Bericht Nr. 4. Der SA-Mann

und sein Arbeitsamt. München, den 20. Juni 1934. p. 2.

69 BA, NS23/265. SA-Brigade 153 (Unterbaden). Oberführer v. Haldenwang. Betr.: Vierteljahresbericht, Reichsautobahn. Heidelberg, den 19. Juli 1935. pp. 1–2.

70 ibid., p. 2.

71 BA, NS23/399. RW und Reichsmarine Einstellungen. Der SA Gruppe Nordsee. Abt. Ia/IIa. Hannover, 10.3.33. gez. Böckenhauer; BA, NS23/399. Marine Sturmbann. Betr.: Einstellung von Angehörigen des Sturmbanns I/1 in die Reichsmarine. Hamburg, den 25.3.1933. gez. Bultz.

72 BA, NS23/399. Marine Sturmbann – as note 71.

73 GLAK, Abt. 465d/1356. SA der NSDAP, Sturmbann III/250, Odenheim. Betr.: Vierteljahresbericht. Odenheim, den 5. April 1934.

74 BA, Sch 378. SA der NSDAP. Der OSAF, P Nr. 24951. München, den 26. September 1934. gez. Lutze.

75 BA, Sch 407. Der Chef der Heeresleitung. T.A. Nr. 5450/34 geh. Kdos T2 III. Berlin, den 17. Oktober 1934. An den Chef des Stabes der SA, Herrn Lutze. gez. Frhr. v. Fritsch.

76 Here, the Active SA, where most of the members were of suitable age to enter the armed forces. In a group of 825 (compiled under the same constraints as in note 67), 49 or 5·94% joined the armed forces. Sources as in note 67.

77 BA, Sch 407. Der Reichsminister der Luftfahrt. Betr.: Überführung von SA-Angehörigern in die Luftwaffenreserve. Berlin, 25.III.1935.

78 BA, NS23/337. Vergleichende Übersicht über die Stärkebewegung der SA im Monat November 1935.

79 BA, R36/1528. Entwurf. Richtlinien für die Durchführung der Arbeitsvermittlung in den Arbeitsämtern. pp. 48–9.

80 BA, NS26/528. Fritz Wenderoth, Personal Recollections. Giessen, 5 January 1937.

81 GLAK, Abt. 460/42(B). As note 33. p. 2 of document.

82 BA, NS23/1. Der Oberste SA-Führer, Zentralamt. Bericht Nr. 4; Der SA-Mann und sein Arbeitsamt. München, den 20. Juni 1934. gez. Seydel.

83 GLAK, Abt. 460/42(B). Der Präsident des Landesarbeitsamts Südwestdeutschland. II 5380/1200. Betrifft: Sonderaktion. Stuttgart, den 29. Mai 1934.

84 GLAK, Abt. 465d/1282. SA der NSDAP, Gau-Odernheim, den 9. April 1934. Betr.: Vierteljahresbericht. Br. B. Nr. 930/34. VIII. Verhältnis zu anderen Gliederungen. C. Zu staatlichen Behörden.

85 GLAK, Abt. 465d/1282. SA der NSDAP, Brigade 51 (Pfalz-Saar). Vierteljahresbericht. VII. Kameradschaftsdienst. Neustadt an der Haardt, 19. April 1934. gez. Schwitzgebel.

86 GLAK, Abt. 465d/1356. SA der NSDAP, Sturmbann III/250, Odenheim. Betr.: Vierteljahresbericht der SA. Bezug: OSAF 13628/II. Odenheim, den 18. September 1934.

87 BA, NS23/250. SA der NSDAP, Standarte 70. Saarbrücken, den 25. Juni 1935.

88 BA, NS23/250. SA der NSDAP, Gruppe Kurpfalz. Vierteljahresbericht (2. Vierteljahr 1935). Mannheim, den 27. August 1935.

89 GLAK, Abt. 460/42(B). Der Präsident des Landesarbeitsamts Südwestdeutschland. II 5380/1200. Betrifft: Sonderaktion. Stuttgart, den 29. Mai 1934.

90 GLAK, Abt. 460/42(B). Der Präsident des Landesarbeitsamts Südwestdeutschland. Betrifft: Sonderaktion. Stuttgart, den 11. Juli 1934.

91 GLAK, Abt. 460/42(B). As note 25; GLAK, Abt. 460/42(B). SA Gruppe Südwest. Betrifft: Fürsorgereferat und Sonderaktion. Stuttgart, 4.10.1934.

92 BA, R36/1511. Gau Baden der NSDAP. Referat für Arbeitsbeschaffung. Betrifft: Sonderaktion. Karlsruhe, den 9. März 1935.

93 NWHStA, BR 1021–168. Unterbringung der alten Kämpfer der nationalsozialistischen Bewegung. Rd. Erl. d. FM zgl. i. R.d.M.Präs. u. aller St.M. v. 11.4.1934. Lo. 222II (Pr. Bef. Bl. S166).

94 I. Fetscher, 'Faschismus und Nationalsozialismus', *Politische Jahresschrift*, Vol. 3 (1962), pp. 42 ff.
95 SAG, Rep. 18–13. Zusammenstellung über die im Regierungsbezirk Allenstein vorhandene SA der NSDAP nach dem Stande vom 10.6.1931. Even so, as many workers as landowners commanded SA units at local level in Allenstein.
96 SAG, Rep. 240/C59e. Ortsgruppe Reichensee.
97 BA, NS23/474. Der Führer der Untergruppe Mecklenburg. Stimmungsbericht. Verhältnis zum Stahlhelm. Rostock, den 26. September 1932. Reports of a similar tenor from much of northern Germany are found in BA, NS23/474.
98 BA, NS23/474. SA der NSDAP, Untergruppe Mittelschlesien-Süd. 9. Verhältnis zum Stahlhelm. Reichenbach, den 26. September 1932. This source suggests that in mid-Silesia, at least, many stormtroopers were farm labourers and not farmers in 1932.
99 SAG, Rep. 240/C43a. Kreis Darkehmen. Tätigkeitsbericht für den Monat Feb./ März '33. Darkehmen, den 15.3.1933.
100 See pp. 28, 29–30.
101 SAG, Rep. 240/B31c. 'Wie kam es nun zum 1. August 1932?'
102 See pp. 118, 118–9, 121–2.
103 E. Czichon, *Wer Verhalf Hitler zur Macht? Zum Anteil der deutschen Industrie an der Zerstörung der Weimarer Republik* (Cologne, 1967); G. Hallgarten, and J. Radkau, *Deutsche Industrie und Politik von Bismarck bis heute* (Frankfurt-am-Main, 1974); D. Stegmann, *Die Erben Bismarcks* (Cologne, 1970).
104 V. Hentschel, *Weimars letzte Monate. Hitler und der Untergang der Republik* (Düsseldorf, 1978), pp. 102–38; H. A. Turner, *Faschismus und Kapitalismus in Deutschland. Studien zum Verhältnis zwischen Nationalsozialismus und Wirtschaft* (Göttingen, 1972). Turner has replied to more recent criticism of his work in H. A. Turner, 'Grossunternehmertum und Nationalsozialismus 1930–1933. Kritisches und Ergänzendes zu zwei neuen Forschungsbeiträgen', *Historische Zeitschrift*, Vol. 221. no. 1 (August 1975), pp. 18–68.
105 K. D. Bracher, *The German Dictatorship* (London, 1973), pp. 187–8; A. Schweitzer, *Big Business in the Third Reich* (London, 1964), pp. 75–6, 113–19, 200.
106 BA, NS26/530. Paul Krause, Personal Recollections. Wiesbaden, 29 December 1936.
107 BA, NS26/529. Fritz Walper, Personal Recollections. Mainz, February 1937.
108 BA, NS26/533. August Eckhart, Personal Recollections. Steinbach, 20 April 1937.
109 BA, NS26/529. Willy Fach, Personal Recollections. Mainz, 26 December 1936.
110 The National Socialist Factory Cell Organisation (NSBO) constituted a sizeable presence in some firms by 1932. Its membership contained both salaried staff and workers. It expanded as follows:

1931: March	4,131	1932: January	43,793
April	4,898	February	57,320
May	7,100	March	78,134
June	10,994	April	87,716
July	14,014	May	106,158
August	18,116		
September	22,014	1933: January	400,000
October	25,480		
November	31,256		
December	39,316		

Source: G. Starke, *NSBO und Deutsche Arbeitsfront* (Berlin, 1934), p. 40.
111 BHStA, Abt. I, So. I/1507. From the *Münchner Post*, no. 68, 24 March 1931. Filed in Polizei Nachrichtendienst records in Munich.

112   See M. Jamin, 'Zur Rolle der SA im nationalsozialistischen Herrschaftssystem', in
      G. Hirschfeld and L. Kettenacker (eds), *The 'Fuhrer State'* (Stuttgart, 1981), pp.
      335–8, where she argues that the interference represented 'primarily vague, anti-
      capitalist resentment deriving from a middle class standpoint', but none the less
      notes that industry did regard the same interference within the factories as class
      struggle of a much more dangerous kind.

113   GLAK, Abt. 460/42(B). As note 25.

114   BA, NS23/126. Der Oberste SA-Führer. Betr.: Unterbringung von arbeitslosen
      SA, SS, und Sta. Angehörigen. München, den 23. September 1933. p. 1. The
      mention of the SS here and elsewhere reflects the SA's attempt to maintain their
      theoretical control over the SS, which was not reflected in reality.

115   BA, NS23/1. Der Oberste SA-Führer, Zentralamt. Bericht Nr. 4. Der SA-Mann
      und sein Arbeitsamt. München, den 20. Juni 1934.

116   BA, NS23/1. Der Oberste SA-Führer, Zentralamt. 'Kampf gegen die SA': Auszüge
      aus eingelaufenen Berichten und Presseveröffentlichungen. pp. 1–2.

117   ibid., p. 3.

118   ibid., pp. 3–4. Bloch, *SA*, pp. 137–50, is partly in accord with this interpretation,
      although he believes that the SA had friends as well as enemies in industry.

119   BA, NS23/126. OSAF IV Nr. 535/34. München, den 12. Januar 1934; GLAK,
      Abt. 465d/1282. SA der NSDAP, Brigade 51 (Pfalz-Saar). Vierteljahresbericht.
      VII. Kameradschaftsdienst. Neustadt an der Haardt, den 19. April 1934.

120   BA, NS23/262. Gruppe Südwest. Bericht über die wirtschaftliche und soziale
      Verhältnisse der SA Männern im Bereich der SA-Gruppe Südwest, den 13. Juli
      1935. 5. Klagen gegen sonstige Betriebe. (a) Industrie, p. 6.

121   GLAK, Abt. 465d/1356. SA der NSDAP, Sturmbann III/250, Odenheim. Betr.:
      Vierteljahresbericht der SA. Bezug: OSAF 13628/II. Odenheim, den 18. Septem-
      ber 1934.

122   BA, NS23/262. SA der NSDAP, Brigade 50 (Starkenburg). Lagebericht: Berich-
      tszeit, 15. August bis 15. Dezember 1934. Darmstadt, 17.12.1934.

123   BA, NS23/265. SA der NSDAP, Brigade 250 (Offenbach). Vierteljahresbericht.
      VII. Kameradschaftsdienst. Offenbach/Main, den 9. Januar 1935.

124   BA, NS23/265. SA Brigade 153. Vierteljahresbericht. Heidelberg, den 18. Januar
      1935. gez. v. Haldenwang.

125   BA, NS23/262. As in note 120.

126   ibid., IV.

127   GLAK, Abt. 465d/1291. SA der NSDAP, Sturm 1/112, Trupp I. An Truf. Herm.
      Rockenau, 27.10.34. gez. Otto Schmelzer, SA Mann; GLAK, Abt. 465d/1291. SA
      der NSDAP, 1/112. An Truf. Herm. Rockenau. Entschuldigung. Rockenau,
      27.10.34. gez. Wilhelm Nebel.

128   For instance: HHW, Abt. 483/NSDAP 2272. SA der NSDAP, Sturm 39/99. An SA
      Mann Walter Schnell, Fechenheim. Ffm.-Fechenheim, den 17. Februar 1934.

129   BA, NS23/199. SA der NSDAP. Der Führer der Gruppe Ostmark, Abtg. P 1 Nr.
      6708 (Q). An die OSAF. Betrifft: Beschäftigung ausgeschlossener SA-Männer.
      Frankfurt (Oder), den 15. Dezember 1934.

130   BA, NS23/199. Cutting from *Münchner Beobachter*, no. 230, 18 August 1935.

131   BA, NS23/199. Hauptabteilung G1 403/35. An den Stellvertreter des Führers.
      Zusätzliche Bestrafung von SA-Angehörigen durch Entlassung aus ihrer Arbeits-
      stelle. den 9. September 1935. gez. Böckenhauer.

132   Jamin, 'Rolle der SA', pp. 335–8.

133   BA, NS23/374. SA der NSDAP. Der Führer der Gruppe Hansa. An die Brigade
      12, Hamburg. Hamburg, den 28. Januar 1935.

134   BA, NS23/262. As in note 120.

135   Geheimes Staatsarchiv München (GStAM), Reichsstatthalter (R) 276/1. Halbmo-
      natsbericht des Regierungspräsidiums von Niederbayern und der Oberpfalz. Nr.
      1063. Regensburg, 19.9.1933.

136 SM, NSDAP 979. SA der NSDAP, Stuba. RII/10. Betr.: Arbeitsfürsorge. An die Glashütten A.G. Konstein. Eichstätt, den 22. April 1934. gez. Kleinknecht.
137 SM, NSDAP 979. Abschrift. Bayer. Glashütten-Aktien-Gesellschaft Konstein. An die SA der NSDAP, Sturmbann RII/10. Eichstätt. den 26. Juni 1934.
138 BA, NS23/265. SA der NSDAP, Brigade 250 (Offenbach). Vierteljahresbericht, VII. Kameradschaftsdienst. Offenbach/Main, den 9. Januar 1935.
139 At least in south-western Germany the SA found that the German Labour Front (DAF) regarded it with hostility. See note 134 for source.
140 BA, Sch 414. Der OSAF. Verfügung. München, den 10. August 1933.
141 BA, NS23/265. SA der NSDAP, Gruppe Kurpfalz. Vierteljahresbericht (2. Vierteljahr 1935). Mannheim, den 27. August 1935.
142 BA, NS23/262. As in note 120.
143 See pp. 88, 96 and GLAK, Abt. 460/42(B). As in note 42. For a more general discussion of the SA's penetration of the state's institutions, at least in Bavaria where this process was most extensive, see O. Domröse, *Der NS-Staat in Bayern von der Machtergreifung bis zum Röhm Putsch* (Munich, 1974), ch. 3.
144 BHStA, Abt. I, So. I/1552. PND Nr. 764. Appell des SA-Sturmes 2 (Dachau) am 26.1.1932 im Gasthaus Hupfloher in Augustenfeld bei Dachau.
145 GLAK, Abt. 460/42(B). SA Gruppe Südwest. Betrifft: Fürsorgereferat und Sonderaktion. Stuttgart, den 4.10.1934.

5   The SA and its Sources of Financial and Welfare Assistance

The SA was unable to produce many jobs, but it managed to provide tangible relief of other kinds. This varied enormously in form and scope: from clothing and food, to accommodation, health care and even vocational training schemes. The effort was often piecemeal, as with job provision, but while efforts to provide employment were dissipated, the variety of welfare measures had something of a cumulative effect. State welfare provision and financial assistance under Hitler's regime were important to the SA, although less so than might have been expected. Private sources also played a limited part. The Nazi movement's own finance and welfare-generating activities were much more significant well before Hitler's takeover and remained so after January 1933, while the SA did a considerable amount to help itself.

Financial Assistance and Welfare Provision from the State

The Nazi takeover transformed the state into a potential benefactor of the SA and this is precisely what the stormtroopers expected. Of course, some unemployed SA members already received various state welfare benefits, but Weimar's welfare system was unequal to the economic crisis and consequently many stormtroopers received no public assistance at all. In any case, benefits were reduced by the Papen government in an attempt to balance national and local government budgets and the Nazi government did nothing to remedy this.[1] All in all, the stormtroopers regarded public welfare as scant reward for the services they had rendered to Nazism and they found that the Nazi government was not particularly generous to the SA. The wave of new recruits who joined after Hitler's takeover may have contributed little to the Nazi victory, but were no less impatient when the expected benefits of SA membership failed to materialise.

At first sight, the state's contributions to the SA might appear generous after all. In the financial year 1933/4 it provided the SA with RM 72 million[2] and in the following year RM 66 million.[3] Of the RM 72 million, which came from a total state budget of RM 5,900 million, the Ministry of the Interior provided RM 44·9 million with payments beginning in May 1933 and increasing up until March 1934 at the end of the financial year.[4] This RM 44·9 million, or less than RM 20 per stormtrooper, served primarily to cover the SA's administrative costs. Each group received RM 9,000 monthly and the smaller units progressively less with each step down the chain of command. Companies received RM 170 monthly,[5] but since there were 24,000 such units, they absorbed the greater part of the SA's total administrative costs of over RM 33 million annually.[6] Of the remaining money from the Ministry of the Interior, over RM 4·5 million covered the initial cost of establishing SA welfare camps and just under RM 4 million bought boots, shirts and underwear for 150,000 needy stormtroopers.[7] The Ministry of Finance provided the remaining RM 28 million during 1933/4 to purchase winter clothing for the German SA, the Austrian SA (who received RM 4 million) and the SS, who received RM 1·4 million, and to provide medical equipment for the SA (RM 1 million).[8]

By April 1934 when the Finance Ministry assumed responsibility for all state funding, the chief of SA Administration, von Schreyer, estimated its monthly financial requirements at RM 10 million,[9] towards which Röhm asked the state to contribute RM 8 million.[10] The Finance Ministry agreed to do so for two months, but stipulated a progressive reduction of the subvention by RM 1 million at two-monthly intervals, leaving the SA with a state funding of RM 3 million by February 1935 and hence RM 66 million for the financial year 1934/5.[11]

The impact of this squeeze was devastating. A discussion between Finance Ministry and SA officials in March 1934 revealed both the SA's dependence on state funds and the inadequacy of these even for efficient administration. State income had reached its peak of RM 8 million monthly by March, in addition to which the SA received around RM 1 million in membership dues and about RM 1 million monthly from party sources, the latter sum being paid into a central contingency fund.[12] Any other donations, including those from local government, were inconsequential[13] and while marginal savings in SA administrative costs were agreed upon,[14] the cuts in state subventions from June 1934 quickly led to howls of protest from individual units. Rural units, in particular, found it almost impossible to run their affairs. The 253rd Regiment, although based in Wiesbaden, operated over a substantial area around the city and in June reported to Munich that it could not supplement the inadequate state grants because of the appalling economic climate which had left 'three-quarters of the regiment's territory [as] an economic disaster area'.[15] The unit's commander continued:

A regiment spread over a large area fares decidedly worse than a purely urban regiment. The same applies to subordinate units. The huge commitments of a rural regiment such as vehicle maintenance, petrol costs, telephone and postal charges are escaped by urban regiments and can be diverted to equipping these formations. Problems in the material sector are mirrored by personal ones.[16]

However, the urban formations also had their problems, and by 1935, with state finance greatly reduced, their finances were woefully inadequate. The difficulties reported by the 70th Regiment of Saar-brücken's commander to Munich in June were typical:

> The present financial position is bad. The regiment cannot carry on administration forever on a budget of RM 1,000, far less a battalion with a mere RM 600, or a company with RM 70. . .
>
> It is desperately important to hold leadership courses, but the means for this are lacking. Nothing more may be raised from within the SA. The extremely poor SA men are burdened with payments for uniforms; this will not be settled before the autumn.[17]

If the state failed to cover adequately the SA's administrative costs, it did little better in the social field. Apart from the one-off payment from the Ministry of the Interior, the RM 22·5 million provided by the Ministry of Finance for clothing during 1933/4 would have given most, but not all, of the SA's 1 million utterly destitute members a coat and nothing else were the coats all obtainable at the minimum rate of RM 26·80 rather than the higher rate of RM 45·45.[18] Further, smaller sums were earmarked for SA welfare in the financial year 1934/5, but the paucity of this aid is shown by reports from provincial SA units. In June 1934 the 80th Regiment of Wiesbaden noted that only half its members possessed coats of any kind and that only 30 per cent were fully equipped.[19] In Offenbach Brigade 250 reported in January 1935 that most of its members lacked coats and boots: 'this makes itself especially and unpleasantly apparent in this cold season, often arousing discontent among the poverty-stricken SA men'.[20] The commander of Brigade 150 in Mainz was similarly concerned about conditions in his area, writing on 22 January that:

> Because of prolonged unemployment . . . and because of limited earnings, only a strictly limited proportion of SA men can afford SA service coats . . . Only 25 per cent of SA members presently possess coats. SA members who continually stand on duty and freeze must sometimes reflect that every member of the Voluntary Labour Service already has a coat.[21]

In Bavaria, too, where unemployment was not so severe a problem, equipment was absent in many units. The leader of Company 22/25 in Altötting, Upper Bavaria, appealed for some very basic items from the 1934/5 Winter Relief Scheme: 8 pairs of boots, 15 pairs of underpants, 15 pairs of socks, 6 pullovers, 8 pairs of SA trousers, 6 SA coats, 20 pairs of gloves and 20 food coupons.[22] Company 21/25 of nearby Neuötting managed to issue clothing by 1935 on its own initiative, but the equipment lent to members was very basic and included relatively little clothing specifically required for SA service, consisting largely of socks, underpants, civilian shirts and the like.[23]

Therefore the National Socialist state reluctantly provided relief for its own paramilitary wing. In general, it advanced rather too little finance to satisfy the stormtroopers' basic material needs and behind the façade of triumphant processions of uniformed, disciplined and enthusiastic stormtroopers whom many regarded as a concrete manifestation of the Nazi state, there existed the reality of impoverished, demoralised SA units. Even so, without help from the state, the SA could not conceivably have expanded from 425,000 members in January 1933 to about 3 million in January 1934. It provided the SA with just sufficient sums to allow this expansion during the politically critical months after Hitler's takeover, but once the SA's usefulness to the fledgling state was exhausted, it was left to get by as best it could.

Assistance from Private Sources

Private sources assisted the Nazi movement in various ways, and the debate over relations between big business and Nazism has, as mentioned, proved especially controversial. It now seems that business circles provided relatively little direct financial aid,[24] and certainly there is little evidence that the SA received substantial private funds either before or after Hitler's takeover. The individual accounts of SA units seldom reveal any support from private sources before 1933. A typical unit, Brigade I of *Gausturm* Munich/Upper Bavaria, enjoyed an income of RM 1,240 during January and February 1931 combined, all of which derived from regular SA membership subscriptions and adoption fees paid by new recruits.[25] Sauer notes that after the Nazi takeover Röhm requested RM 12 million from industry, but is unable to establish either how much of this sum was paid to the SA or for what purpose it was required.[26] According to testimony at the Nuremberg Trials, the SA received payments from an unspecified source within I. G. Farben, but the amounts concerned were small, totalling RM 44,528 between April and December 1933, RM 74,224 during 1934 and RM 29,446 during 1935. Doubtless the gesture was appreciated, but it is unclear for what purposes the money was used. Since the above are not round figures they were probably intended for specific purposes rather than constituting a block grant of some kind.[27] No comparable records of such links with other firms before the Röhm purge have emerged and personal connections between the SA and I. G. Farben, through a Dr Gattineau, possibly accounted for this one.[28] More often help was sought by individual units from firms within their locality. Typical was the request of the 21st Regiment of Zinten, East Prussia, for RM 80,000 for equipment from the Co-operative Dairy in Heiligenbeil which resulted in a donation of RM 100.[29] After the Röhm purge the position apparently improved somewhat. In August 1934 the donations from industry to the Hitler Appeal in the Ruhr District were channelled directly into the SA,[30] but the severe financial difficulties experienced by the SA even in this period suggest that any such help was restricted.

Firms did sometimes provide assistance in kind or provide the SA with goods or services at discount rates. In June 1932 the firm of Bernard Schmeding gave the Hamburg SA an unspecified amount towards the expenses of a summer camp at Tinsdahl, but ten firms, rather than give cash, either donated items for this camp or sold them at reduced prices.[31] Similarly, the firm Nippel & Köhler of Hagen provided the SA with a motor vehicle free of charge for a week in August 1931.[32] In September 1932 the haulier Otto Rauenbusch of Weissenburg, Bavaria, gave the SA preferential treatment even though he 'could have carried out other journeys which were already booked'. His services were more preferential than he had intended, since the SA subsequently refused payment of his bill.[33] A few national arrangements of this kind existed; from late 1933, for instance, the whole SA enjoyed a free boot-soling service courtesy of the German Shoemakers' Guild.[34]

Larger firms made mutually beneficial agreements with the SA, for by 1932 the stormtroopers and their close relatives comprised a sizeable, if impoverished, market. An order from the commander of *Gausturm* Hessen-Nassau-Nord reveals an appeal to this market by the firm Deutsches Margarine Kontor which offered the SA RM 1 for every 50 kg of margarine bought:

> Each 'Kampf-Margarine' packet produced by Deutsches Margarine Kontor carries a seal of guarantee which SA men should collect from their wives. SA men are to hand these to company leaders who receive payment in cash for them. The seals are not vouchers and private collectors cannot benefit from them. Only company leaders or other SA officials who send them to the firm Deutsches Margarine Kontor . . . receive payment.
>
> Regiments will inform me along with their monthly membership report how much money has been raised in this way.[35]

While replies from this district remain undiscovered, the same arrangement was worth RM 50 a month to the Berlin SA.[36]

The Nazi takeover and the expansion of the SA coupled with the proliferation of SA camps of various kinds allowed firms which concluded agreements with the SA for the supply of goods at discount prices to reap substantial benefits. Such deals were common and sometimes the SA combined its own financial interests with social considerations when choosing suppliers. This was the case with the Bavarian firm

Konservenfabrik Kötzing GmbH in August 1933 which, the SA noted, 'employs a significant number of workers, including in particular some of the poorest inhabitants of the [Czech] border zone, the mushroom and fruit gatherers'.[37] However, whatever thoughts the SA might have had for such groups, the main beneficiaries of the cheap supplies delivered to the SA were the stormtroopers themselves.[38]

Assistance from the Nazi Movement

If sources outside the Nazi movement provided a motley patchwork of assistance, there were substantial resources within the expanding, socially heterogeneous Nazi movement which were mobilised to the SA's benefit. The indispensability of the impoverished SA during the Nazi drive for, and consolidation of, power, undoubtedly helped the stormtroopers to attract assistance from a range of Nazi institutions, including the party itself.

The 'SA Insurance Scheme', which was largely intended to assist wounded or injured stormtroopers was one means of transferring party resources to the SA. A voluntary subscription of 20 Pf was raised primarily from the stormtroopers themselves until April 1930, but subsequently the amount was increased to 30 Pf and demanded from all party members.[39] Some party officials strove to raise the subscriptions, as in Sorau district, Niederlausitz, where the deputy district leader, Kasche, demanded the 'fastest and smoothest possible resolution' of the matter.[40] However, the Prussian police estimated that less than half the NSDAP's German membership, or 117,028 individuals, were paying up by 1 September 1930. None the less, this performance represented a payment of RM 35,108·40 monthly into the fund.[41] In November 1931 the scheme's director, Martin Bormann, broadened its scope, declaring that it should benefit all National Socialists and renaming it the 'assistance fund' (*Hilfskasse*).[42] This was possibly to encourage non-contributors and, whatever Bormann's success, the growth of both party and SA membership must have increased the level of payments with time. Since most injured or wounded Nazis were stormtroopers, they undoubtedly remained the chief beneficiaries.[43]

Until mid-1930 every party member saw 10 Pf of his monthly party dues transferred to the SA and following unrest over finances in the Berlin SA a 20 Pf monthly surcharge was paid from autumn 1930 by party members.[44] This money reached SA units via the Munich Command, but regional (*Gau*) and local party offices also made regular payments to the SA.[45] These seldom satisfied the recipients. Problems were not necessarily created by ungenerosity, for regional party formations received no financial help from headquarters[46] and had to manage affairs on limited budgets.[47] The financial misery of both local SA and party formations none the less frequently led to friction, notably before and during the Stennes Revolt of April 1931. The situation varied from area to area, but 1931, as a whole, generally witnessed poor relations between the SA and party. In December the SA Inspector General described the overall mood when writing to Röhm that:

> The withholding of money designated for the SA by the party leaders in many *Gaue* always clouds the SA's high morale. The bitterness in the *Gaue* concerned is immediately evident, from the group commanders right down to the last SA man when conversation turns to the question of money.[48]

During 1932 the position grew especially grim as the political tide turned against Nazism. In September the Sub-Group Lower Franconia reported that 'the most primitive essentials are lacking' because of its failing finances,[49] while the Upper Bavarian SA doubted in the same month whether it would survive the winter financially.[50] Despite these problems, at least some SA commanders felt that the party had done its best. The leader of Group West, based in Koblenz, wrote on 21 September that 'the financing of the SA is inadequate because of the *Gaue*'s weak financial position, but the *Gaue* none the less give willingly what they can'.[51] However, these generous sentiments were unusual and Hitler's takeover did nothing to improve matters. The issue remained unresolved for the duration of SA financial autonomy which ceased on 1 April 1935.[52]

The party also frequently assisted the SA on a hand-to-mouth basis, usually with some specific purpose in mind – a process which illustrates the mutual dependence of party and SA. For instance, the Berlin SA sold copies of Goebbels' newspaper, *Der Angriff*, during 1930 and in return retained some of the sales revenue.[53] The party constantly required SA protection at various functions and with relations between the two bodies frequently strained, it possibly felt compelled to offer the stormtroopers material inducements in return for their assistance. Thus when the SA was ordered to attend a rally in Drossen, Niederlausitz, on 25 May 1930 Kasche hastened to assure it that the party was providing what funds it could. However, he also promised to cover travel costs, provide a lunch for 20 Pf, a free supper, and free accommodation for the stormtroopers, albeit with some terse criticism of further SA demands.[54] In East Prussia, too, SA–party relations were soured by financial difficulties. In spite of, or perhaps because of, this the party leader in Treuburg promised the SA midday meals in return for attendance at a recruiting drive on 20 and 21 June 1931.[55] The stormtroopers attending the National Socialist German Day held in Rosenberg, West Prussia, in August 1931 were even better provided for:

From 12.30 to 13.30, a communal lunch for all guests in the Hotel Lehmann (peas, bacon, smoked sausage and bread roll). SA members receive lunch free (up to three helpings) on showing their entrance ticket which costs 30 Pf for SA members. Party members pay 30 Pf per helping. The entrance ticket, only available for SA men, entitles them to free admission to the meeting and concert as well as to lunch and, possibly, supper.[56]

Help from the party was not always meant to be so immediate an inducement. Some of the SA hostels which provided many young, jobless stormtroopers with bed and keep – often at no cost to themselves – were maintained or founded by local party bodies. A report from the *Gau* of East Prussia of May 1931 illustrated this when asserting that the SA hostel in Johannisburg was the party's responsibility.[57] Similarly, the party in Kreuzburg, East Prussia, launched a local SA hostel in November 1931. The party leader reported: 'We have succeeded in acquiring a suitable room for an SA hostel above a storeroom in Kirchenstrasse 65; the unemployed SA men are occupied in fitting it out comfortably.'[58]

The stormtroopers also benefited from the party's commemoration of religious festivals and similar occasions. On 20 December 1931 the party branch in Gumbinnen, East Prussia, held a very successful Christmas celebration where 'SA, Hitler Youth, German Girls' League and the Children's Group were given presents and treated to coffee and cakes'.[59]

This type of assistance continued after Hitler's takeover. In December 1933 the party in Saxony met an urgent plea from the 18th Regiment for RM 87 with a payment of RM 67, leaving the local party organisation to make up the remaining RM 20.[60] In the same month the party in Heiligenbeil, East Prussia, provided the 21st Regiment in Zinten with RM 10,000 for equipment; 'RM 5,000 to be paid immediately, the rest in the next financial year'.[61]

Such a patchwork of help would normally have played a minor part in the construction of a mass movement, but the swelling wave of unemployment and hunger sweeping Germany made even a hot meal noteworthy for many stormtroopers and potential recruits. SA members attached great importance to such gestures and unrest could follow whenever they were lacking. Commenting on developments in Franconia during autumn 1932 the newspaper *Münchner Post* wrote: 'The proletarian SA is starving and there have been hostile incidents more than once owing to the wretched food slopped out to SA guards at the [Nuremberg] Hitler House.'[62] The paper added that all SA companies around Nuremberg were in debt – a picture of widespread misery confirmed by Reiche's work on the Nuremberg SA.[63] In these circumstances, the importance even of individual charitable acts for the SA's morale is illustrated by another incident reported by the *Münchner Post* in late 1932:

> Farmers in the Bamberg area offered a large quantity of asparagus for a feast to be held for SA men as a reward for their effort in the election campaign. There was indeed a feast of asparagus, in fact with sausages – for the party leaders and their families; the SA proletarians received nothing. This bit of fun cost the Nuremberg Nazi Party 250 [SA] resignations.[64]

Such blatant provocation was undoubtedly exceptional and it seems that where possible the party did enough to sustain the SA which, politically, was decidedly in its interests until Hitler was firmly installed as Chancellor. After that, a small proportion of the SA's financial needs were met by the party, but the sums involved were equalled by the stormtroopers' own membership dues and were eclipsed by state subventions.[65]

The NSDAP developed a range of auxiliary formations during the early 1930s which gave the SA invaluable material assistance. They sometimes co-operated with the party itself when providing help for the SA, but also played crucial independent roles, with the women's groups being most prominent.[66] The German Women's Order, based in Berlin, sought financial support from wealthy citizens which was channelled into the SA and other Nazi formations. In February 1930 the Prussian police observed that:

> The German Women's Order has formed recently a charitable circle, which has so far attracted 100 people of both sexes. They are well-to-do people who are to support the Nazi movement as a whole through donations. The members of the charitable circle need not necessarily belong to the NSDAP.[67]

Like other Nazi organisations, the Order suffered its own financial difficulties and consequently had to move into more modest premises in spring 1931. None the less it remained useful to the SA, providing facilities for injured SA men in its new headquarters and continuing its charitable work.[68] It frequently helped the SA outside Berlin, such as in August 1931 when its Munich branch 'distributed sandwiches and beer' at a muster of SA Company 18.[69]

Other women's groups were equally busy. The Prussian police noted the operations of the NSDAP's Women's Action Committee (WAC) in Berlin during autumn 1930:

> During the election period food was collected energetically and distributed to stormtroopers whilst they were on duty. Hot food was

actually prepared in various SA pubs and given to the SA members. This provision was continued after the election for long-serving SA men in larger units. During the metal-workers' strike, the WAC distributed all food at its disposal to the striking party members, prepared hot food and fed the unmarried party members three times daily in their SA pubs.

Recently the WAC has switched to collecting more money than before in order to buy foodstuffs for the forseeable future. However, food is being collected in still greater amounts from the farmers in the countryside so that money can be used in the approaching winter to buy clothing. When collecting from tradespeople, a questionnaire entitled 'German Tradespeople' is presented for completion. In the main they wish to persuade the traders to give a donation immediately.[70]

This group was also active in the provinces, as in Königsberg, East Prussia, where it assisted with the running of an SA hostel despite being in financial difficulties itself.[71]

During 1931 the women's organisations continued to help the stormtroopers. The WAC's branch in Gumbinnen, East Prussia, was among the more active and mobilised a wide range of social groups, being 'composed of all sections of the population; senior, middle and lower grade civil servants' wives, tradesmen's wives and workers' wives, the last group comprising 50 per cent [of membership]'.[72] In Tilsit, where the Nazi community suffered great material hardship during the winter of 1930/1, the party leadership noted that the women's group had established an emergency kitchen in the town's SA hostel which was providing forty unemployed Nazis, many receiving no state benefit, with a hot midday meal.[73] The Steindamm (Königsberg) party branch also praised the achievements of their women's group during 1931 and the variety of help given was certainly impressive:

The twelve female party members of 1931 would not have been able to cope with the steadily growing volume of welfare work for jobless party members and SA men and their families, however much they had tried. However, it went without saying that the Nazi Women's Group included the wives and daughters of party members, even if the former were not themselves members. Thus the countless tasks; organising the SA hostel, food and clothing collections, Christmas gifts, care of the ill and the imprisoned, first aid duty at meetings etc. could always be mastered with a larger body of helpers.[74]

The mobilisation of the female relatives of party members in Steindamm was fairly typical of social work at branch level, which involved many more people than party membership figures alone might suggest.

In autumn 1931 Gregor Strasser laid down national guidelines for social work during the approaching winter. These envisaged a continuing, extensive role for the women's organisations, categorised as economic, medical, spiritual and educational work, and the SA was seen as a major potential recipient of assistance.[75] According to the SA Inspector General's report for 1931, these ambitious plans were bearing fruit, for the women's groups received special praise:

> Good relations appear to exist almost everywhere between the women's groups and the SA. The women's groups support the SA, SS and Hitler Youth as energetically as possible by means of welfare assistance. SA welfare is often left to the Women's League alone (which is not right). With regard to welfare, the women's groups are accorded nothing but recognition and high praise by the SA.[76]

These groups continued to help the SA up to and beyond the Nazi takeover. Some help was unspectacular, such as the two vests donated to SA man Arnecke of Hamburg Staff Troop,[77] but other assistance was substantial. Between January 1932 and March 1933 the Laak Women's Organisation in East Prussia collected RM 842·85 worth of food, RM 87·60 in cash and three pairs of shoes worth RM 10·50 for needy party members, the SA, and the National Socialist People's Welfare. As the group added: 'Not included with this are the Christmas collections of 1932/3, the 300 packages from the Hitler Birthday Appeal of April 1933, the baskets of sandwiches, the collections of old clothes, and other help given in emergencies by the Women's Organisation.' Since the Laak group claimed to belong to a 'very poor branch', this help was all the more impressive.[78] Thus, although relations between the SA and the women's groups were not invariably idyllic, as Stephenson shows,[79] the overall contribution by these groups to the SA's welfare cannot be overestimated.

Once the NSDAP had taken power, its auxiliary relief organisations operated more systematically and new bodies were founded. Of these the Winter Relief Scheme (WRS) or Winterhilfswerk provided the SA with substantial assistance. Many SA units acknowledged this help, such as the 250th Regiment of Bruchsal, Baden, which wrote in January 1934 that 'a large proportion of the needy SA men have been provided with articles of clothing and are still being given food, particularly by the WRS'.[80] Similarly, the 23rd Regiment of Kaiserslautern noted in April 1934 that 'the extreme destitution of SA members' was eased by the WRS as well as a local welfare organisation, the People's Socialist Self-Help.[81] The WRS continued to help the stormtroopers as the 1934/5 winter approached. In November the Hamburg SA reported that veteran stormtroopers were to receive a special welfare payment from the WRS. The money was paid quickly, but the restriction of the scheme to veterans indicates both the size of the SA's welfare problems almost two years after the takeover and the finite resources available to the WRS.[82] Indeed, the WRS could not always aid the SA directly. Instead, it could help the SA circumvent the effects of restrictions on autonomous SA fund-raising by providing it with WRS postcards, badges and similar articles to sell on a commission basis. The cash raised in this way by the SA was used for social purposes, as illustrated by the case of the rural Bavarian Battalion III/25 of Altötting:

> The WRS *Gau* Office Munich–Upper Bavaria has provided the SA with a large number of WRS sports postcards to sell. Each company will receive 450 of these cards for sale on a commission basis.
> ... The welfare officers must explain in conjunction with the company and troop leaders to SA men at musters the purpose and social ideal behind the sale of the cards. Indeed, many needy comrades can be helped with the proceeds. The SA will receive 10 Pf per card sold.[83]

These various Nazi auxiliary organisations were instrumental in staving off the total destitution which threatened so many stormtroopers. Like other assistance this was not a panacea for the SA's problems, but it added to the diverse effort which made SA membership materially advantageous.

A corollary of this aid was the willingness of individual Nazi sympathisers to donate cash or goods to the party or its auxiliary formations. Alternatively, the Nazi movement's ability to extract funds from less willing donors was often important. This latter point is illustrated by developments in Widminnen, East Prussia, where in 1932 the Nazi movement relied on donations from the townspeople to sustain both the autumn election campaign and its social work. When this support waned after the autumn election campaign, the NSDAP reacted swiftly to avert disaster – not least within the SA:

> Naturally collections were attempted; but after the elections the citizens of Widminnen believed that everything had been achieved – the donation lists looked pitiful. The SA, which was largely composed of unemployed, could barely pay subscriptions and so we launched an energetic campaign to squeeze funds from the populace.[84]

While the Nazi movement did sometimes have problems with its sympathisers and casual supporters, the volume of assistance received was often impressive. Within strongly Nazi rural districts, in particular, the painstaking collection of food, clothing and cash eventually represented a plausible response to the movement's social needs, including the SA's, in both rural and urban areas.[85]

A more detailed look at the activities of three rural branches illustrates both the variety and the extensiveness of local activity. The party branch in Bladiau, East Prussia, collected sizeable amounts of food and some clothing for the SA Winter Relief Scheme between 15 and 30 November 1931, providing: 1,750 kg of grain, 875 kg of potatoes, 300 kg of white cabbage, 50 kg of peas, rice and rye respectively, 250 kg of porridge oats and suet, 3 jackets, 2 storm-proof jackets, 3 pairs of trousers, a shirt, 2 pairs of socks, a pair of shoes and 3 hats.[86] In September 1932 the NSDAP in Alfeld, Lower Saxony, appealed for food of all kinds, specifying potatoes, lentils, meat, sausages, grain and eggs in particular.[87] Records of the response are unavailable, but in another Lower Saxon town, Wetteborn, a similar, successful, appeal yielded: RM 1 in cash, 2 cases of meat, 12 kg of bacon, 200 kg of potatoes, 30 cases of sausage, 2 kg of loose sausage, 3 individual sausages, 25 kg of wheat and 622·5 kg of rye.[88] The varying sizes and nature of these contributions suggest that rich and poor alike supported the collections, of which the SA was a major beneficiary. The generosity of individual party members and sympathisers also benefited the stormtroopers on specific occasions. Members gave gifts to forty stormtroopers in Domnau, East Prussia, at Christmas 1931,[89] while ten members of SA Company 5/J5 of Isen, Bavaria enjoyed holidays paid by contributions to the Adolf Hitler Spende in mid-1934.[90]

The violence of SA life also created problems which required a response. Before 1933 certain lawyers represented stormtroopers in court,[91] while fellow Nazis succoured SA members who had fled the locality of their crimes. For instance, in August 1932 stormtroopers from the Königsberg area unleashed a wave of arson and murder, subsequently fleeing to the Italian Tyrol. Here they lived from money and other help sent by fellow East Prussian Nazis.[92]

The Nazi movement, as a whole, therefore gave the SA significant help. This aid failed to satiate the stormtroopers' material despair, for the scale of their destitution was too great to permit its resolution through the means and methods available to the Nazi movement. However, there was enough help to convince many stormtroopers that in material terms SA membership was advantageous, at least until late 1934. The aid flowing to the SA came largely from and through a grass-roots, mass organisation which supplemented the inadequate welfare efforts of state institutions and established a rudimentary 'shadow welfare state' for Nazism's supporters.

The Provision of Assistance from within the SA

The SA did not depend entirely on external sources for material aid. Most stormtroopers were certainly very poor, but the minority of wealthier members (especially leaders) were a potential source of assistance. More significantly, the mass of stormtroopers represented a sizeable labour force which the leaders could exploit for the organisation. Attempts to utilise this range of potential resources met with varying success.

Those stormtroopers who belonged to the party helped provide the SA with a regular income through the payment of 80 Pf for the unemployed and RM 1 for others in party dues,[93] but much of this money was retained by the party, and non-party members frequently paid no dues at all. In March 1934 Röhm sought to obtain dues from all SA members to ameliorate the financial pressures confronting the SA, but anticipated that this might create as many problems as it solved.[94] Whatever benefits extra finance might provide, the initial payment of dues often involved great sacrifices. This problem was solved partly by a patron – often a wealthier SA member – paying a stormtrooper's dues, but this was always regarded as a palliative.[95] Despite these difficulties individual units certainly benefited discernibly from the receipt of dues. Non-party members were especially valuable if they could be induced to pay up since the party received none of their contributions. In April 1934 the 21st Regiment of *Gau* Odernheim, Baden, recognised this,[96] while a Munich formation reported in autumn 1934 that between January and October an average membership of 182·7 non-party members contributed RM 1,645 in dues to its funds, despite non-payment by some members.[97]

These regular monthly payments of RM 1 or less by individual stormtroopers were useful, but were unlikely to effect their material salvation, no matter how well the SA used the tenth of its income[98] so derived. It therefore developed a variety of *ad hoc* measures to supplement this regular source of income. Many local units adopted a savings stamp scheme which was used principally to enable poorer stormtroopers to buy a uniform, often after actually obtaining it from their unit.[99] Other local schemes raised cash within the units, such as the drive by the Berlin SA in May 1930 to collect funds to aid imprisoned and injured stormtroopers.[100] In late 1931 Battalion III/149 of the Prützenwalde Estate in Silesia raised money by holding concerts and by encouraging a redistribution of wealth within the unit: 'Social welfare is managed so that SA men suffering hardship are helped by the better-off, and by the utilisation of public assistance.'[101] Similar schemes existed in the post-takeover period when, for instance, Brigade 150 of Rheinhessen successfully created a social fund to combat poverty among its unemployed members.[102] Group South-West admitted in mid-1935 that hitherto it had failed to deal adequately with the pressing economic and social problems confronting its formations. A report detailing the socio-economic position of its members proposed to alleviate this unsatisfactory situation through the creation of an internal social support fund which would also maintain the confidence of storm-troopers in their leaders:

> The SA man does not seek help from the party, or from other offices; he wants to be helped exclusively by his SA leader. He seeks help here and has trust in the [leaders] alone. This trust must not be destroyed.[103]

Some commanders helped their men through personal acts of generosity. Party member Reuter of Gudwallen in East Prussia founded the local SA in autumn 1929 by providing four SA uniforms for its first members at his own expense.[104] In January 1932 the battalion leader, Mayer, promised his Dachau units that he would provide footwear at his own expense, a gesture doubtless appreciated in the depths of a Bavarian winter.[105] SA accounts indicate that relatively little help came in this way, but the symbolic value of such generosity must have been greater, consolidating stormtroopers' personal loyalty to their commanders and the SA in general.

After Hitler's takeover some SA leaders received a lucrative state position which placed them materially well above their men. Röhm felt these leaders had an obligation to their following and in December 1933 created a national Special Fund to channel some of their new-found wealth to the rank and file.[106] However, in May 1934 he complained that many leaders had ignored the fund:

> Although a considerable number of leaders have accorded with my wish, I must conclude that the receipts for the Special Fund have not been as successful as I might [originally] have hoped.
>
> A large proportion of our excellent SA leaders and men are in severe economic difficulty without being personally to blame. It is a matter of honour that all comrades who have secured incomes through the National Socialist revolution which have relieved them of economic worries give needy comrades the means to free themselves from financial burden through payment of a fixed monthly sum.[107]

The Röhm purge evidently ended any such concerted action and, in any case, the subsequent upheavals in the leadership were followed by moves to reduce considerably the SA's size. It continued with social measures, but the cutback in its size proved more effective in relieving the SA's social pressures.

With the SA deriving limited benefits from its internal fund raising, it sought to raise cash from the public at large. Its methods resembled those of the party and its welfare bodies, which of course helped the SA, but it hoped to reap the full benefit of collections by organising its own, and, in the process, to attain a measure of political independence. However, the party strove to retain control of fund-raising and was largely successful. Party officials feared that a plethora of autonomous Nazi collecting agencies could antagonise the public, but a power struggle between the party and SA lay at the heart of the matter. The Stennes Revolt illustrates this process dramatically, for the mutiny of eastern German leaders in April 1931 was strongly motivated by their resentment of the political leverage over the SA afforded to the party through control of finance.[108] The Bell Affair of 1932 arose from a similar desire by the SA Command to loosen the party's financial grip. Röhm hired Bell to:

Discover sources of aid from suitable interested parties and also to attempt to halt money flowing to the party and divert it directly to the SA. The aim thereby pursued by [Bell] was to build up the SA in such a fashion that it was well known at home and abroad and was organisationally and economically independent of [the NSDAP].[109]

Like the Stennes Revolt the attempt failed and curbs on independent fund-raising remained, although an SA newspaper, *Der SA-Mann* was established through Bell's efforts.[110]

By 1930, if not sooner, regional party officials had begun curbing autonomous SA collections at local level. In April 1930 *Gau* Ostmark issued a circular which, ostensibly with the SA's consent, prohibited SA collections.[111] Whatever the regional SA Command may have agreed under duress here, local SA units soon complained of the policy's implications, resenting their loss of independence:

The political leadership suppresses any independent SA organisation and activity. It forbids the sale of newspapers and the inception of any financial assistance for the SA.[112]

In Glogau, Silesia, the SA complained during late 1931 that a similar policy was creating social and administrative difficulties,[113] while in January 1932 Battalion VI of Liegnitz reported similar problems.[114] During 1932 SA units continued to complain about finance, with Sub-Group Brunswick resenting particularly bitterly in September the restrictions placed on its fund-raising activities by an all-powerful party organisation:

Any collections for the units *themselves* cannot possibly be arranged, because steps of this kind are at the party chief's mercy. Consequently they are invariably prohibited. The financial situation is utterly wretched![115]

The commander of the Hamburg SA argued that only by removing the party's financial monopoly could the situation be improved.[116] However, despite his protestations it appears that his units did collect money in their own right before 1933. Perhaps the party sometimes turned a blind eye, but its inability to apply legal sanctions before 1933 coupled with the stormtroopers' desperation would have made total containment of the SA very difficult. Thus in July 1931 the Hamburg SA learnt that Röhm was to hold an inspection some distance from the city. A good turnout was subsequently attributed partly to the stormtroopers' ability to collect money for their fares to the parade site 'by self-help in true National Socialist fashion'.[117] The Hamburg SA also collected publicly for their fares to the Brunswick Rally in autumn 1931. Stormtroopers received news of the rally on 24 September and were given until 17 October to raise RM 7·90 for their fares.[118] The rally itself was a convincing propaganda success for the NSDAP, but collecting the fare money was difficult, causing friction between the Hamburg and the neighbouring Altona SA which was collecting for fares in the same way: 'The Altona Battalion I/31 has accused [Hamburg] SA men of collecting for the Brunswick journey within Altona's town limits.'[119]

Sometimes tension between the SA and the public in Hamburg justified the party's reservations over autonomous SA collections, although these were not always sanctioned by the SA leadership. In July 1932 Böckenhauer, SA commander in Hamburg, protested:

Recently complaints have been received repeatedly about door-to-door collections taken within tenements in various parts of the city for the uniforming of the SA ... The sub-group expects SA leaders to intervene to prevent fraudulent collections. Judging from telephone calls and written complaints from the population this blackens our name very seriously, since it amounts to door-to-door begging.[120]

Some SA collections continued after Hitler's takeover with the party's blessing, but usually with an auxiliary welfare agency acting as an intermediary. Other collections, however, involved SA formations and individuals whose methods were uncontrolled and sometimes criminal.[121] Public resentment grew and the authorities became uneasy. In August 1933 the Bavarian government reported:

Complaints are being made about the uncontrollable activities of people in SA uniform in rural districts, who are conducting collections and commercial activities ... A mayor was forced to accept fifteen photographs of Hitler for which he had to pay RM 22·50, on the pretext that each mayor had to buy a fixed number of Hitler photographs in proportion to the population of his district.[122]

The authorities in Bavarian Swabia complained in October 1933 that the Augsburg stormtroopers were pressing the public to purchase the newspaper *Neue Nationale-Zeitung*, doubtless to enhance their finances,[123] and similar incidents abounded. In rural Franconia a junior SA leader was convicted of terrorising with his men a farmer who refused to contribute to an SA food-collection campaign during late 1933.[124] In summer 1934, after the Röhm purge the SA's command structure was sufficiently dislocated around Bayreuth to allow stormtroopers to turn to vagrancy. A government official warned: 'The town of Bayreuth has noticed wandering SA men passing through it recently. They travel around the countryside penniless. Naturally this is intolerable for the SA's reputation.'[125] The trouble continued. In September 1934 the Augsburg police reported that the zealousness of the local SA's collecting drives had alienated the public and that the SA was, in any case, ignoring a ban imposed on SA collections by Hitler after the Röhm purge.[126]

Taken as a whole, this collecting and even begging of money and other assets represented an attempt by impoverished men to get by. Their membership of the SA legitimised these activities, but the collectors and beggars had no clear political goals. An exception occurred in September 1933 when Ernst, commander of the Berlin and Brandenburg SA, issued an order which revealed his frustration with the miserable economic conditions both within the SA and society at large. He began uncontroversially, declaring that 'no countryman may starve or freeze this winter',[127] but the methods he proposed to achieve this were extremely radical:

Every SA leader and SA man [of the Berlin-Brandenburg Group] must be on immediate call:

(a)   To administer controls on food in big warehouses, to safeguard it, in order to prevent hoarding.
(b)   To register immediately all fuel depots and guard them.
(c)   To confiscate the products listed under (a) and (b) in mid-October and distribute them to needy countrymen.
(d)   To locate immediately all empty large houses. Lists are to be made of them, including the number of rooms, floorspace, address and owner. These lists will be submitted to the regiments by 8 October. The regiments shall pass these to the group via the brigades by 12 October.
(e)   To accommodate the unemployed and tenants with large families who live in dwellings unfit for human habitation in the large houses located, with the help of force.

> I demand of every SA man the conscientious, dutiful execution
> of the tasks allotted to him. Any one who contravenes these
> orders will be treated by me as a saboteur and dismissed from
> our ranks.[128]

Ernst claimed that Hitler supported these policies, but this seems
unlikely and, in any case, the plans came to nothing. Hitler could not
have contemplated a programme which would have lost him his invaluable conservative political allies and his potential allies in the military.
Furthermore, most SA leaders were disinclined to go as far as Ernst,
finding it difficult enough simply to raise sufficient funds to maintain
the SA.

While the SA was restrained from begging, it borrowed money
before and after the takeover. Bessel notes widespread borrowing in
eastern Germany before 1933, particularly in Pomerania.[129] In Franconia the practice was common in 1932[130] and in that summer the 138th
Regiment in Duisburg borrowed well beyond its means. An SA commander later recalled:

> In spite of my reservations, the then leader of the 138th Regiment,
> Born, drew up a contract with the firm Selbsthilfe so as to uniform
> the largely unemployed Duisburg, Hamborn and Meiderich SA with
> caps and shirts. As far as I can remember the purchase price was
> around RM 25,000.
>   About four weeks later, difficulties arose over the repayment of
> instalments of the loan.[131]

After the Nazi takeover, borrowing continued and in October 1934 the
SA Command questioned all SA groups on their indebtedness. Group
Kurpfalz, for one, admitted to RM 321,854·71 in covered debts and
RM 15,095·85 in uncovered debts,[132] but this sum was fairly modest,
amounting to only RM 2·58 for each member of the group.[133] With
borrowing generally on this scale, it served more as yet another financial
prop rather than as a cure-all.

Before 1933 the SA became involved in some Nazi-run enterprises,
such as the Nazi Outfitters. This operated, in principle, as a non-profit-
making concern, with 'any profits being credited back to the SA as a
commission on sales'.[134] The most significant benefits derived from the
SA-owned Sturm Cigarette Factory in Dresden, which paid a fixed
percentage of its turnover to the SA at group or sub-group level.[135] The
exact percentage paid cannot, unfortunately, be determined, but the
effects of the payments are clear enough. The 83rd Regiment, Kassel,
wrote in July 1932 that Sturm money was being used to maintain on SA
hostel.[136] By September most SA groups identified Sturm subventions
as an important source of finance in quarterly reports to Munich, even

if Sub-Group Brunswick reserved most praise for the quality of the cigarettes![137] Thus Group Thüringen found arrangements with Sturm satisfying in every respect[138] and Group West remarked: 'The payments from the Sturm Cigarette Factory have become a substantial part of SA revenue; the payments arrive promptly and are still growing'.[139] Within Group West, Sub-Group Koblenz-Trier provided figures which emphasise the significance of the Sturm payments:

SA Finance:
Monthly budget; around RM 500–600.
Contributions from Sturm turnover in August: RM 278·05.[140]

The impact of this small firm underlines the paucity of SA finances. Its internal funding operated in a complex, makeshift way which never satisfied its wants, but at least held out the prospect of their resolution. The very multiplicity of methods used, which often involved the individual stormtrooper, doubtless impressed on him that, unlike the anonymous and bureaucratic state welfare agencies, the SA cared and was doing its best. When results were disappointing the blame could easily and plausibly be placed elsewhere; perhaps with the party, or better still with Nazism's external foes.

The stormtroopers themselves formed a further asset, perhaps the SA's greatest asset, being available as an extremely cheap workforce standing at the organisation's disposal. There were exceptions, such as stormtroopers in regular work, those with irregular attendance records, and those whose demoralisation and loss of self-esteem made them unsuitable for most tasks. However, it appears that many stormtroopers were put to work by the SA. Some instances were trivial enough. In June 1930 the SA helped prepare lunch at a rally in Meseritz, Niederlausitz.[141] Other projects were less ephemeral, such as the establishment by the Munich–Upper Bavarian SA of its own VLS in July 1931 to mitigate the misery of unemployment.[142] Stormtroopers were often employed to fit out or even build their hostels, as in Eglharting, Upper Bavaria. The Nazi newspaper *Die Front* praised the hostel's completion in January 1932:

As the spectre of unemployment scoured the German countryside ever more horribly, as the red mob became ever cheekier on the streets, so grew the need of our jobless SA comrades to have a home they could call their own – a home in the truest sense of the word.

Now the Kirchseeon Troop of Company 15/2 has established a hostel. Company leader Denk took the initiative, Party member Dr Ebner gave valuable financial help, the SA did the actual work. Our SA members gladly used the limited means which they managed to earn from farmers during the summer to build their hostel. With united strength they set to work; soon the walls were built, the roof followed and then the furnishing went ahead. It stands neat and friendly and offers the jobless comrades rest and refreshment.[143]

This work continued after January 1933. In June 1934 the 80th Regiment in Wiesbaden proposed using 150 men to equip an SA welfare camp.[144] In addition to the practical benefits of these projects, their symbolic and ideological significance was certainly crucial. While idleness and hunger confronted millions of individuals, stormtroopers often had the opportunity of accomplishing a useful, tangible task.

Some stormtroopers doubtless contemplated a future of everlasting relief payments, welfare assistance and idleness, but the great majority evidently sought new work. The relative indifference of state-owned and private concerns towards the SA after Hitler's takeover spurred the SA into taking compensatory measures intended to make the employment of a stormtrooper a more attractive proposition. The SA Command founded the technical training companies (TTCs) and training workshops in late 1933, commenting in December:

> Jobless SA men who formerly had a trade, in other words are skilled workers, cannot find a new job in most cases because they have, sometimes long since, lost touch with their earlier occupation. They therefore cannot produce the skilled work which is required by the employer, and indeed must be required.[145]

While their primary task was to retrain the jobless, the TTCs also trained, as highly skilled workers, stormtroopers already in work thus providing them with the chance of advancement in their careers.[146]

The TTCs received recognition and some support from the state following negotiations between the SA High Command and the Reich Institute for Job Allocation and Unemployment Insurance in November 1933. The president of the institute instructed employment offices to pay 8 Pf per participant per hour of instruction to the TTCs, or RM 3·20 per participant per forty-hour week, with further assistance in some cases. In addition, the national director of the WRS empowered local WRS offices to pay a supplement of 20 Pf per head per day to the TTCs during the 1933/4 winter.[147]

In some respects the TTCs and training workshops were successful. In June 1934 the 80th Regiment, Wiesbaden, observed that they 'allow on the one hand the employment, nourishment and vocational training of a number of jobless and, on the other, the possibility of producing relatively cheaply all kinds of equipment for the formations'.[148] It is less clear how many stormtroopers found jobs after these courses. In any case, the TTCs were specialist institutions and the SA could not provide sufficient camps to deal even with those jobless stormtroopers who were skilled workers. It therefore established its own welfare camps (*Hilfswerklager*) in early 1934 in an attempt to cope with the unemployment problem more satisfactorily. Both the SA and the Reich Institute for Job Allocation recognised that the Special Action had met with difficulties because veteran Nazis had often been unemployed for so long 'that their reintegration into working life appears possible only after a thorough and gradual preparation and period of adjustment'.[149] Veteran stormtroopers accordingly comprised about a third of the camps' membership[150] which was intended initially to reach 36,000[151] but, in fact, probably never exceeded 20,000 and was generally between 15,000 and 16,000.[152]

In June 1934 the vocational aspects of the camps were still stressed by the SA Command, 'the jobless SA men are above all to be given the chance to re-learn their old trade or learn a new trade',[153] but after the Röhm purge the emphasis altered. The new SA leaders discovered a further rationale for the welfare camps which reflected the decisive shift in the balance of power within the Nazi movement towards the party. The SA commanders no longer spoke of revolution, instead exhibiting an overriding concern to remove the stormtroopers from the streets, the very place where they had been invaluable until mid-1933:

> The welfare camps were created through the SA's living socialism and are institutions for comradely assistance, to provide the uprooted SA man with ties, and strength to face life. The welfare camp [member] must become a useful member of society again through ideological education. He is thereby to be freed from the moral subversion of the street and simultaneously prepared for absorption in working life.[154]

However, a month later the High Command noted the stormtroopers' reluctance to enter the welfare camps. Perhaps 'moral subversion' had taken too firm a hold, or possibly the grim experiences of some SA volunteers for Labour Service dampened enthusiasm for the relatively new scheme. The High Command possibly suspected this, for they stressed that 'the welfare camps are *an SA social institution* intended to provide economic support for SA men for the duration of their unemployment' (italics in original). This order threatened coercion if persuasion failed, reminding unemployed stormtroopers that they could be drafted into the welfare camps.[155]

Each group exploited its welfare camps differently. The Berlin SA organised a training scheme at the Tegel Welfare Camp in October 1935 with specialist vocational objectives. It enabled jobless SA veterans from throughout Germany to spend six months' training for administrative jobs in local government, commerce and hospital administration.[156] In the same month, Hamburg instituted a general retraining scheme for its 1,000 remaining unemployed members in Wandsbek Welfare Camp. Attendance was compulsory, with all malingerers facing expulsion from the SA.[157]

At first, single stormtroopers aged between 20 and 25 were favoured for admission and young, single SA members remained the predominant group within the camps.[158] Married stormtroopers were admitted by late 1934 'when exceptional want and long-term unemployment pertained',[159] but only 600 married men were in the welfare camps in October.[160] The problem lay with their families who, until October, lost their public welfare benefit when the father entered a welfare camp. The SA succeeded in persuading the reluctant local authorities to pay unemployment and emergency benefits directly to the families at this stage, but only on the understanding that the number of such cases would remain very low.[161]

Like most SA undertakings the welfare camps faced financial difficulties and had to search around for cash. In the financial year 1933/4 the state provided the SA with slightly over RM 4·5 million for the establishment and operation of its welfare camps,[162] but in April 1934 the SA itself estimated that it required just over RM 1·25 million per month to run its fifty-one, fully established camps and a further RM 1·45 million to establish eleven further camps.[163] No doubt the SA allowed a generous margin of error when stating its needs, but the discrepancy is clear and the consequences were equally so. Occasionally local government provided assistance and in June 1934 the establishment of a camp in Mannheim was made conditional on local government aid:

> Contacts are to be established with local authorities willing to host an SA institution and ready to render assistance through the provision of buildings and exercise grounds. Naturally it is also desirable that they contribute to the fitting out [of welfare camps] since we can expect SA High Command resources to be limited, and the group has nothing at its disposal. The cost per camp can be estimated at RM 30,000 to 40,000.[164]

The national authorities occasionally, if reluctantly, helped financially during 1934 and in October the Wiesbaden SA persuaded the Finance Ministry to relax 'its fundamentally negative attitude' towards the establishment of welfare camps in its own case.[165] Finally, in January 1935, after protracted negotiations between the Reich Institute for Job Allocation, the Reich Labour Ministry and the Finance Ministry, a lump sum of RM 13 million was made over to the SA to cover part of the costs of the welfare camps.[166]

If the state was reluctant to contribute towards establishing and equipping welfare camps, it recognised that they were playing an important part in vocational retraining[167] and therefore paid for the maintenance of inmates through the Reich Institute for Job Allocation from 1 April 1934.[168] This money usually merely replaced the state welfare or unemployment benefits the stormtroopers would have received. Even so, by November 1934 the Reich Finance Minister estimated that the welfare camps would cost the Institute RM 6 million during the financial year 1934/5[169] and the actual cost eventually approached RM 12 million.[170] These mounting expenses as much as anything persuaded the authorities by October 1935 that stormtroopers in the camps should be found work through the institute as rapidly as possible.[171] Even by then RM 9 million had been allocated to cover the period April to December 1935,[172] by which time, it was hoped, most camp participants would be found work. A further sum would then tide over the rump of participants until 31 March 1936 when the camps would finally close.[173] In fact, some camps remained open longer into 1936.

Quite how many stormtroopers were assisted by the welfare camps is unclear. Camp training lasted between six weeks and fourteen months until April 1935 when stays were limited to six months to increase the turnover of personnel.[174] Depending on which type of course predominated, between 50,000 and 400,000 stormtroopers could have attended the camps.[175] How many participants found work through attendance is also unclear, but by 1935 they represented the hard core of the SA's unemployment problem. As the Ruhr SA noted in August 1935, most welfare camp participants were 'long-term, utterly destitute unemployed',[176] and, therefore, people whose problems might not have been solved by the welfare camps alone. During 1935 and 1936 the drafting of stormtroopers into the army probably provided many with an occupation of sorts.

In 1931 the SA channelled some of its limited resources into founding its own welfare service.[177] This developed steadily until, by the end of 1934, the welfare officers exercised a wide range of functions under the supervision of the High Command.[178] A reorganisation of its Welfare Office in November 1934 provides a picture of the service at this time. All units from the company upwards were to include a welfare officer, and those 'in regiments and brigades are whenever possible to be SA members who, through their civilian positions, have direct or indirect contact with an employment office, welfare department or social security department'.[179] This attempt to co-ordinate SA and public welfare activities, at least informally, was reinforced by the ruling that the all-important welfare officer be a candidate of above-average capacities. His range of duties was very wide, being designed to protect the SA man from whatever ills the outside world cared to inflict on him:

Priority for veteran SA men in job provision; support for post-January

1933 men in their search for work; the conduct of negotiations with public and private concerns to prevent lay-offs or to transform short-term contracts into permanent jobs; support for reinstatement after unjustified dismissal; backing for *justified* claims for productivity-linked wage increases; care of sick and convalescent SA members ... through the Hitler Fund, Lung Care, etc.; support for SA men in all matters connected with the NSDAP Benefit Fund and all other social insurance schemes; placement of stormtroopers' convalescent children; the placing of deserving SA men not helped by the public welfare department within the care of the NS People's Welfare or Winter Relief Programme; support for SA men in disputes with landlords and bailiffs; co-operation with SA accommodation officers; the informing of SA members [of job redeployment and retraining schemes] to enable them to play their full part in the movement and in working life.[180]

Limited resources and the lack of statutory powers restricted the effectiveness of the welfare officers. None the less, the SA set about providing its members with a partial, if rudimentary, substitute for the trade unions which it had helped to destroy less than two years before.

The SA also provided its members with a health service which, like its general welfare service, was founded well before the Nazi takeover.[181] This service suffered from shortages of personnel and resources until spring 1934 when reforms were undertaken. Brigade 150 of Rheinhessen reported in April:

Doctors and first-aid staff are available in adequate numbers. The health service, which was very deficient when the brigade was established, is already partly organised. Further developments are being undertaken with great energy. Provision of equipment is rapid, but still leaves much to be desired. In this area, too, the lack of funds is noticeable ...
... The general health inspection is in full swing, so that the release of unfit men can begin very shortly. The general state of health is good.[182]

Brigade 51 of the Pfalz-Saar reported similarly, adding that the absorption of the Stahlhelm had provided the SA with adequate numbers of doctors.[183] Since many Stahlhelmer remained outwith the mainstream SA, some Stahlhelm doctors were conceivably pressurised into joining the SA to expand its health service.

The SA's welfare effort allowed it to offer the stormtroopers advantages which complemented other material benefits of SA membership. None of these services was outstandingly efficient and none really had sufficient resources. Even so, they must have reinforced considerably the image of a 'caring' SA. More help came from outside and while it would be fruitless to seek a single, decisive source of assistance, the diverse range of aid accumulated sufficiently to maintain the SA. These resources were sometimes provided grudgingly, but none the less the SA became relatively more attractive to many jobless Germans than most other remedies on offer. Among the unemployed and the very poor, news of this kind of assistance must have spread rapidly and helped to attract new recruits to the SA. The success of this modest, makeshift system of self-help therefore indicates the helplessness of conventional social and political institutions during the early 1930s and, in particular, was a measure of the public authorities' inability to cope adequately with the material consequences of the Great Depression.

Notes

1 L. Preller, *Sozialpolitik in der Weimarer Republik* (Düsseldorf, 1978), pp. 448–51.
2 (i) BA, R2/11913a. Zu IB 370/34. Bericht über die Prüfung der Vereinnahmung der der Obersten SA-Führung (OSAF) vom Reichsministerium des Innern im Rechnungsjahr 1933 aus dem Ausgabekapitel V E 16 Titel 15 (SA–Hilfswerk) überwiesenen Reichsgelder und über die Prüfung der Verwendung dieser Gelder. Potsdam, den 8. Juni 1934. (ii) BA, R2/11913a. Zu IB 370/34. Bericht über die Prüfung der Vereinnahmung der der Obersten SA-Führung (OSAF) vom Reichsminister der Finanzen im Rechnungsjahr 1933 zur Beschaffung von Bekleidungsstücken und Schuhwerk für minderbemittelte SA-, SS- und Stahlhelm-Kameraden und zu sonstigen Sachbeschaffungen überwiesenen Reichsgelder und über die Prüfung der Verwendung dieser Gelder. Potsdam, den 8. Juni 1934.
3 BA, R2/31013. Abschrift. Der Reichsminister der Finanzen. An den Herrn Reichskanzler Berlin. Berlin, den 16. März 1934. gez. Graf Schwerin von Krosigk.
4 BA, R2/11913a. As in note 2(i). p. 2.
5 BA, R2/31013. Aussprache über SA-Angelegenheiten am 21. und 22. März 1934.
6 BA, R2/11913a. As in note 2(i). p. 4.
7 ibid.
8 BA, R2/11913a. As in note 2(ii). p. 3.
9 BA, R2/31013. Übersicht über den Geldbedarf der Obersten SA-Führung im April 1934. pp. 1–3.
10 BA, R2/31013. As in note 3.
11 ibid.
12 BA, R2/31013. As in note 5.
13 ibid.
14 ibid.
15 BA, NS23/266. SA der NSDAP, Standarte 253. Vierteljahresbericht. Geldlage und Geldversorgung. Wiesbaden, den 27. Juni 1934. gez. Maier.
16 ibid.
17 BA, NS23/265. SA Standarte 70. Vierteljahresbericht. II. Vierteljahr 1935. Saarbrücken, den 25. Juni 1935.
18 BA, R2/11913a. As in note 2(ii). p. 4.
19 BA, NS23/266. SA der NSDAP, Standarte 80. Vierteljahresbericht. Betr.:

Bekleidung und Ausrüstung. Wiesbaden, den 26. Juni 1934.

20 BA, NS23/265. SA der NSDAP, Brigade 250 (Offenbach). Vierteljahresbericht. V. Bekleidung und Ausrüstung. Offenbach/Main, den 9. Januar 1935. gez. Keller.

21 BA, NS23/265. SA der NSDAP. Der Führer der Brigade 150, Rheinhessen. V. Bekleidung und Ausrüstung. Vierteljahresbericht für das 4. Vierteljahr 1934. Mainz, den 22. Januar 1935. gez. Schönborn.

22 SM, NSDAP 803. SA der NSDAP, Sturm 22/25. An den Stuba III/25, Altötting. Betr.: SA-Strassensammlung für das Winterhilfswerk. Altötting, den 6. Januar 1935.

23 SM, NSDAP 679. SA Hochland, Sturm 21/25, Neuötting. Bekleidungs- und Ausrüstungsgegenstände 1934–5.

24 See also, R. J. Bessel, 'The SA in the Eastern Regions of Germany, 1925 to 1934' (D. Phil., Oxford University, 1980), pp. 122–3,where the paucity of external financial support for the NSDAP in eastern Germany is noted. I. Buchloh, (*Die nationalsozialistische Machtergreifung in Duisburg,* (Duisburg, 1980), p. 53, however, notes that jobless stormtroopers in Duisburg did receive support from local tradesmen.

25 BHStA, Abt. I, So. I/1565. Einnahmen und Ausgaben des Gausturms München/ Oberbayern (Brigade I) nach heutigem Stand unter Zugrundelegung der Ergebnisse der Monate Januar und Februar 1931.

26 W. Sauer, *Die Mobilmachung der Gewalt,* Vol. 3 of K. D. Bracher, G. Schulz and W. Sauer, *Die nationalsozialistische Machtergreifung* (Frankfurt-am-Main, Berlin and Vienna, 1974), p. 259. Sauer argues in his footnotes that I. G. Farben alone did pay RM 924,142 to the Adolf Hitler Spende, much of which went to the SA, but no figures are given and the purposes to which the SA put any money are not examined.

27 SAG, NI–8442. Office of Chief Council for War Crimes. Staff evidence analysis. By Heilbrunn. 30 May 1947.

28 BA, NS23/124. OSAF II/B 192/33. München, den 18. April 1933. gez. Röhm; C. Bloch, *Die SA und die Krise des NS-Regimes 1934* (Frankfurt-am-Main, 1970), p. 145.

29 SAG, Rep. 240/C49d. Der Kreisleiter, Heiligenbeil. An die Standarte 21, Zinten, den 8. März 1934.

30 SAG, NIK-9215. Abschrift. SA der NSDAP. Der OSAF. Der Stabschef. München, den 15. August 1934. gez. Lutze.

31 BA, NS23/402. F.P.A.-Gauführung. Betr.: Sommer-Zeltlager. 9. Juni 1932. gez. Böckenhauer.

32 BA, NS23/470. Der Polizeipräsident. Hagen, den 13. August 1931.

33 BA, NS23/474. Otto Rauenbusch, Weissenburg in Bayern: Spedition und Möbeltransport, den 8. September 1932. An Herrn Walter Tromsdorff, Motor Haupttruppführer der Standarte 13.

34 BA, NS23/126. OSAF IV Nr. 4628/33. München, 28.11.33. gez. Schreyer.

35 BA, NS23/474. NSDAP, SA Untergruppe Gausturm Hessen-Nassau-Nord. Kassel, den 1. September 1932. gez. Steinhof.

36 ibid.

37 BA, NS23/125. Der Oberste SA-Führer IV Nr. 1195/33. Betr.: SA-Schulungslager, hier Küchenwirtschaft. München, den 8. August 1933. gez. Schreyer.

38 BA, NS23/126. OSAF IV Nr. 4373/33. Betr. SA-Hilfswerklager, hier Küchenwirtschaft. München, den 15. November 1933; BA, NS23/126. Der Oberste SA-Führer IVb Nr. 170/33. Betr.: SA-Schulungslager, hier Küchenwirtschaft. gez. Schreyer.

39 SAG, Rep. 240/C33a. Nachrichtenblatt Nr. 4 des Bezirks Königsberg Pr. der NSDAP. Königsberg/Pr., den 1. Januar 1930; BA, NS26/214. Rundschreiben! Gau Ostmark, den 5. April 1930. gez. Veltjens, Kube; BA, NS26/207. NSDAP Gau Ostmark. Bez. Sorau N. L. April 1930. gez. Kasche.

40 BA, NS26/207. As note 39.

41 BHStA, Abt. I, So. I/1870. Auszug aus den Mitteilungen Nr. 21 des Polizeipräsidiums Landeskriminalpolizeiamt (IA) Berlin vom 1. November 1930. Stand der SA Versicherung.

42 BHStA, Abt. I, So. I/1870. Zur dringender Beachtung. München, den 17.11.1931. gez. Bormann.
43 Between 1928 and 31 August 1932, 142 Nazis were killed, of whom 118 were SA members. Of 7,718 injuries inflicted on Nazis by political opponents between 1 January and 31 August 1932, 5,122 were inflicted on SA members. IfZ, MA 616/20, 73794 (SA III – Ausschreitungen).
44 Bessel, 'SA', p. 125.
45 ibid.
46 BA, NS26/214. Siegfried Kasche. Sorau N. L.. z.Z. Friedrichshafen, den 28. April 1930. An den Oberführer des Gausturms BR., Herrn Pg. Veltjens, Berlin.
47 SAG, Rep. 240/C71b. Rechenschaftsbericht 1930 der Ortsgruppe Pr. Holland O. Pr.. Pr. Holland, den 8. März 1931. – Receipts for the year, RM 4,670·43; SAG, Rep. 240/C73b. NSDAP Ortsgruppe Bischofsburg. Ergebnis der Kassenprüfung vom 28. Februar 1931 der NSDAP. – Receipts Oct. to Dec. 1930, RM 536·68; NHStA, Hann. 310 I E24. Kassenbuch der Ortsgruppe Pyrmont 1930–2 – as examples: March 1931, receipts RM 117·75, March 1932, receipts RM 200·26; NHStA, Hann. 310 I E1. Jahresabrechnung, Anderten, den 7. Februar 1932 – Receipts, RM 1,549·40.
48 BHStA, Abt. I, So. I/1545. Abschrift. NSDAP. Der Oberste SA-Führer. Der Generalinspekteur, B.B. Nr. 284/31. Bericht über die Stimmung in der SA (hauptsächlich aus dem Westen und Süden). Kassel, den 22.7.31. gez. Ulrich. See also, P. Hüttenberger, *Die Gauleiter* (Stuttgart, 1969), pp. 69–71.
49 BA, NS23/474. Untergruppe 'Unterfranken'. Würzburg, den 21. September 1932.
50 BA, NS23/474. Der Gruppenführer Hochland. München, den 26. September 1932.
51 BA, NS23/474. SA der NSDAP. Der Gruppen-Führer West. Stimmungsbericht. Koblenz, den 21. September 1932.
52 BA, NS23/474. SA der NSDAP, Gruppe Hansa. Gruppenbefehl Nr. 34. Betr.: Verwaltung. Hamburg, den 9. April 1935. gez. Fust.
53 BA, NS26/133. Anonymous testimonial concerning Berlin SA (73pp., undated).
54 BHStA, Abt. I, So. I/1545. As note 48.
55 SAG, Rep. 240/C78b. Abschrift. NSDAP Ortsgruppe Treuburg. Betr.: Sturm-befehl für den Werbetag am 20. u. 21. Juni 1931. An den Sturmbannführer Pg. Jäger, Lyck. Treuburg, den 21.6.1931. gez Redottee, O.G.L.
56 SAG, Rep. 240/C81c. Deutscher Tag unter Hitlerfahnen in Rosenberg (Westpr.). Sonntag den 2. August 1931.
57 SAG, Rep. 240/C37e. An den Gaukommissar Pg. Dr. Knabe. Friedrichshof, den 15. Mai 1931.
58 SAG, Rep. 240/C70b. Monatsbericht der Ortsgruppe Kreuzburg. Monat November (1931). Kreuzburg, 3.XII.31. gez. Joachim von Kulckstein.
59 SAG, Rep. 240/C48b. Tätigkeitsbericht für Monat Dezember 1931 der Ortsgruppe Gumbinnen.
60 BA, NS26/214. NSDAP, Standarte XVIII, den 8. Dezember 1933.
61 SAG, Rep. 240/C49d. Der Kreisleiter. An die Standarte 21, Zinten. Heiligenbeil, den 19. Dezember 1933.
62 BHStA, Abt. I, So. I/1511. 'Der braune Pleitegeier in Nürnberg', *Münchner Post*, no. 237, 12 October 1932.
63 E. G. Reiche, 'The Development of the SA in Nuremberg, 1922 to 1934' (dissertation, University of Delaware, 1972), pp. 166–7.
64 See note 62.
65 BA, R2/31013. As in note 5. pp. 1–2.
66 For a fuller discussion of the role of NS women's groups, see J. Stephenson, *The Nazi Organisation of Women* (London, 1980).
67 SAG, Rep. 240/A5d. Aus den Mitteilungen des Landeskriminalpolizeiamtes (IA) vom 15.2.1930. Nr. 4. 2: 'Opferring des Deutschen Frauenordens'.
68 SAG, Rep. 240/A5d. Aus den Mitteilungen des Landeskriminalpolizeiamtes (IA).

Nr. 8. Berlin, vom 15. April 1931. In fact, the Order had become involved in a struggle for influence with the WAC. In Berlin, Goebbels favoured the WAC, this no doubt contributing to the Order's problems. Stephenson, *Nazi Organisation*, p. 39.

69   BHStA, Abt. I, So. I/1552. PND Nr. 747. Polizeidirektion München, den 17.9.1931. Appell des SA-Sturms 18 der NSDAP am 19.8.1931 im Wittelsbachergarten.

70   SAG, Rep. 240/A5d. Aus den Mitteilungen des Landeskriminalpolizeiamtes (IA). Berlin, vom 15. November 1930. (g) Frauenarbeitsgemeinschaft innerhalb der Nationalsozialistischen Deutschen Arbeiterpartei in Berlin.

71   SAG, Rep. 240/C33a. An sämtl. Ortsgruppenleiter des Bezirks Königsberg Stadt. Königsberg i./Pr., den 8. August 1930.

72   SAG, Rep. 240/C48b. Ortsgruppe Gumbinnen, den 7. März 1931. gez. Dettmer, O.G.L.

73   SAG, Rep. 240/C33d2. Bezirk Tilsit der NSDAP. An alle Ortsgruppen des Bezirks Tilsit. Tilsit, den 8. Januar 1931.

74   SAG, Rep. 240/C54b. Chronik der Ortsgruppe Steindamm (Königsberg).

75   SAG, Rep. 240/A5d. 'Auszug aus dem Verordnungsblatt der Reichsleitung der NSDAP', Folge 11. München, den 16. November 1931. Bekanntgabe, pp. 3–4.

76   BHStA, Abt. I, So I/1533. Abschrift. Der Generalinspekteur. B.B. Nr. 453/31. Stabschef. I. Stimmung in der SA. Kassel, den 17.12.31. pp. 3–4, (d).

77   BA, NS23/406. SA Untergruppe Hamburg (Stabstrupp). An die Frauenschaft der NSDAP, Hamburg. Hamburg, den 23. März 1932.

78   SAG, Rep. 240/C45b. Chronik der NS-Frauenschaft. Ortsgruppe Laak (Königsberg). Sammlung Januar 1932–März 1933.

79   Stephenson, *Nazi Organisation*, pp. 15, 31, 46–7, 49.

80   GLAK. Abt. 465d/1355. SA der NSDAP, Brigade 53, Baden Nord, Standarte 250. Betr.: Vierteljahresbericht. Bruchsal, den 13. Januar 1934. (6) Fürsorge.

81   GLAK, Abt. 465d/1282. Standarte 23, Kaiserslautern. Vierteljahresbericht, den 14. April 1934. VII. Fürsorge.

82   BA, NS23/371. SA der NSDAP, Gruppe Hansa, Fürsorgeamt. Hamburg, den 28. November 1934. gez. Fust.

83   SM, NSDAP 689. SA der NSDAP, Stuba. III/25. An alle Stürme des Stubas III/25. Betreff: WHW Postkartenverkauf. Altötting, den 27. März 1935.

84   SAG, Rep. 240/C61b(1). Ortsgruppe Widminnen.

85   The collections detailed below were intended mainly to succour the Nazi movement in towns and cities. See also pp. 118–9.

86   SAG, Rep. 240/C49e. NSDAP Ortsgruppe Bladiau, den 7.12.1931. Sonntag, den 15. bis Montag den 30. November – Sammlung für die SA-Winterhilfe.

87   NHStA, Hann. 310 I E36. Winterhilfe, NSDAP Kreisleitung, Alfeld/Leine, im September 1932.

88   NHStA, Hann. 310 I E36. NSDAP O. G. Wetteborn, den 3.12.1932. Abschrift der gesammelten Winterhilfe in der Ortsgruppe Wetteborn.

89   SAG, Rep. 240/C41b. NSDAP Gau Ostpreussen. Gaukommissariat Natangen. Domnau Ostpr., den 4. Januar 1932.

90   SM, NSDAP 971. SA der NSDAP. Der Führer des Sturmes 5/J5. Betreff: Freiplätze aus der Hitlerspende. Isen, den 16. Juni 1934.

91   For an account of the activities of one such lawyer, Luetgebrune, in 1932, see: IfZ, MA 616/20, 73794–73819 and 616/21, 74521–74523 (SA III – Ausschreitungen).

92   SAG, Rep. 240/B31c. 'Wie kam es nun zum 1. August 1932?'

93   BA, NS23/356. Der OSAF, Chef Nr. 5039/34. Betr.: Beitragszahlung. München, den 3. März 1934. gez. Röhm.

94   ibid.

95   ibid.

96   GLAK, Abt. 465d/1282. SA der NSDAP. Der Führer der Standarte 21. Vierteljahresbericht. VI. Geldlage und Geldversorgung. Gau Odernheim, den 9. April 1934.

97 SM, NSDAP 689. SA der NSDAP, München. Beiträge. München, den 25. Oktober 1934.
98 BA, R2/31013. As in note 5. pp. 1–2.
99 BHStA, Abt. I, So. I/1533. Abschrift. Vierteljahresbericht des Sturmbanns III/149. Gut Prützenwalde am 27.12.31; BA, NS23/265. SA Standarte 12. An Brigade 51 Ostpfalz, Neustadt/Haardt. Mussbach, den 5. Januar 1935.
100 BHStA, Abt. I, So. I/1553. Auszug aus Lagebericht Berlin v. 15.11.30. (Mitteilungen des Landeskriminalpolizeiamtes (IA) Berlin vom 15.11.30 Nr. 22.) (e) SA- Gefangenen- und Verwundetenhilfe.
101 BHStA, Abt. I, So. I/1533. Abschrift. Vierteljahresbericht des Sturmbanns III/149. Gut Prützenwalde am 27.12.31.
102 GLAK, Abt. 465d/1282. SA der NSDAP. Der Führer der Brigade 150, Rheinhessen. Vierteljahresbericht für das 1. Vierteljahr 1934. VII. Fürsorge, 'Kameradschaftsdienst'. Mainz, den 18. April 1934.
103 BA, NS23/262. Bericht über die wirtschaftlichen und sozialen Verhältnisse der SA-Männer im Bereich der SA-Gruppe Südwest, den 13. Juli 1935, p. 7. III. Anregungen und Vorschläge für eine Aenderung der derzeitigen Missstände. 1. SA-Dienstliches: Schaffung eines Unterstützungsfonds.
104 SAG, Rep. 240/C43a. Abschrift. Pg. Ehmke, Gudwallen. 'Der Weg zur Partei'. Gudwallen, den 10. Januar 1943.
105 BHStA, Abt. I, So. I/1552. PND Nr. 764. Appell des SA-Sturmes 2 (Dachau) am 26.1.32 im Gasthaus Hupfloher in Augustenfeld bei Dachau.
106 BA, NS23/271. Der Oberste SA-Führer, Chef Nr. 10167. Betr.: S-Fonds. München, den 4. Mai 1934. gez. Röhm.
107 ibid.
108 BHStA, Abt. I, So. I/1551. Zu IAN 2100 a 2, SH 1/13.5. Gründe und Auswirkungen des Zwistes Hitler-Stennes, pp. 1–2; BA, NS26/325. Abschrift 1161/31 St/ v.B. An die Oberste SA-Führung z. Hd. des Herrn Oberstleutnant Röhm, München. pp. 1,6. This is not to deny that political factors played a crucial role. See pp. 166, 193, 194, 207–8, and Reiche, SA in Nuremberg, pp. 180–204.
109 IfZ, Sp.-2 127–130, Du Moulin-Eckart, 3 (SA III – Verh. z. NSDAP). Spruchkammerverfahren Du Moulin-Eckart, München, den 23. Dezember 1932. VII A 487/32. An das Landgericht München I, 7. Zivilkammer. In Sachen Bell ./. Röhm, wegen Forderung.
110 ibid.
111 BA, NS26/214. Gau Ostmark. Rundschreiben. April 1930. gez. Kube. Veltjens, den 5.
112 BA, NS26/214. Bericht über den SA-Aufmarsch am 5/6. IV. in Stentsch und Schwiebus. Petersdorf, den 7.IV.1930. gez. Friedrich u. Lindemann.
113 BHStA, Abt. I, So. I/1545. SA der NSDAP. Vierteljahresbericht, p. 4. (f) Finanzierung. Glogau, Schlesien. Dez. 1931.
114 BHStA, Abt. I, So. I/1533. Abschrift. Sturmbann VI, Liegnitz. Vierteljahresbericht an die Gruppe Schlesien. Liegnitz, den 5. Januar 1932.
115 BA, NS23/474. NSDAP. Der Führer der SA-Untergruppe Braunschweig. 1a Briefb. Nr. 463/32. Braunschweig, den 22. Septbr. 1932.
116 BA, NS23/474. SA der NSDAP, Untergruppe Hamburg. Stimmungsbericht, Finanzierung der SA, pp. 4–5. Hamburg, den 23. Sept. 1932. gez. Böckenhauer.
117 BA, NS23/398. Untergruppe Hamburg. Tagesbefehl, den 8. Juli 1931. gez. Böckenhauer.
118 BA, NS23/398. Untergruppe Hamburg. Tagesbefehl, den 2. Okt. 1931. (4) Geldsammlung für Braunschweigfahrt.
119 ibid.
120 BA, NS23/398. Untergruppe Hamburg. Tagesbefehl, den 24. Juli 1932. gez. Böckenhauer.
121 See R. Diels, *Lucifer ante Portas* (Zurich, 1949), p. 152.

122 GStAM, R276/1. Nr. 2970. Halbmonatsbericht des Regierungs-Präsidiums (16. mit 31. Juli 1933) Politische Lage. München, den 5. August 1933.

123 GStAM, R276/1. Nr. 1839. Abdruck. Lagebericht (Halbmonatsbericht) des Regierungspräsidenten von Schwaben und Neuburg. Augsburg, den 21. Oktober 1933.

124 BHStA, Abt. I, M. Inn/71719. C1601/33. Der Oberstaatsanwalt bei dem Landgerichte Ansbach. Betreff: Strauss, Wilhelm, verh. Schmied in Degersheim wegen Amtsanmassung u.a. An den Herrn Generalstaatsanwalt bei dem Oberlandesgericht, Nürnberg. Ansbach, den 2. November 1933.

125 GStAM, R280/1. Nr. 1342. Lagebericht des Regierungspräsidiums von Oberfranken und Mittelfranken (Juli 1934), p. 8. Ansbach, den 9. August 1934.

126 GStAM, MA 106697. Polizeidirektion, Augsburg. Lagebericht. Augsburg, den 1. September 1934.

127 BA, NS26/322. SA-Gruppe Berlin-Brandenburg. Gruppenbefehl Nr. 68. Berlin, 25. September 1933. gez. Ernst.

128 ibid.

129 Bessel, 'SA', pp. 127–8.

130 Reiche, 'SA in Nuremberg', p. 186.

131 BA, NS23/295. Der Gruppenführer. Per. Angelegenheit Born, Stand. 138. Duisburg, den 8. März 1935.

132 BA, NS23/306. Der Gruppenführer (Kurpfalz). F. Geh. 132/34. Schulden von SA-Dienststellen. Die Oberste SA-Führung. München, den 24. Oktober 1934.

133 BA, Sch 415. Nachweis der Stärke der SA am 1. Oktober 1934.

134 BA, NS26/306. OSAF I Nr. 7367/31. München, den 8. Dez. 1931. (d). gez. Röhm.

135 BA, NS23/474. NSDAP, SA Standarte 83. An Stub. I. V/83. gez. Löwenstein.

136 ibid.

137 BA, NS23/474. NSDAP. Der Führer der Untergruppe Braunschweig, 1a Briefb. Nr. 463/32. Braunschweig, den 22. Septbr. 1932.

138 BA, NS23/474. SA der NSDAP. Der Führer der Gruppe Thüringen. Stimmungsbericht. Weimar, den 21. September 1932. gez. Zunkel.

139 BA, NS23/474. SA der NSDAP. Der Gruppenführer West. An Chef des Stabes, persönlich. Koblenz, den 21. September 1932.

140 BA, NS23/474. SA der NSDAP. Der Führer der Untergruppe Koblenz-Trier. Stimmungsbericht. Wissen-Sieg, den 23. Sept. 1932.

141 BA, NS26/207. NSDAP, Gau Ostmark. Plan der Veranstaltungen am Sonntag, den 1. Juni 1930 in Meseritz. Bez. Sorau N.L., den 8. Mai 1930.

142 SM, NSDAP 803. Sturm 19/II/3 M.O. Sturmbefehl Nr. 8/31. Garching Alz., den 29. Juli 1931. gez. Fichtl.

143 BHStA, Abt. I, So. I/1870. 'Ein neues SA-Heim in Eglharting', *Die Front*, 30 January 1932.

144 BA, NS23/266. SA der NSDAP, Standarte 80. Vierteljahresbericht. Wiesbaden, den 26. Juni 1934.

145 BA, NS23/356. Der Oberste SA-Führer I Nr. 1697/33. Betreff: SA-Hilfswerklager. München, den 1.12.1933. gez. v. Krausser.

146 BA, NS23/126. OSAF I Nr. 2283. Betreff: Technische Lehrstürme der SA. München, den 17. Februar 1934.

147 BA, NS23/126. Der Präsident der Reichsanstalt für Arbeitsvermittlung und Arbeitslosenversicherung, Gesch. Z. : II 5559/64. Betrifft: Berufliche Bildungsmassnahmen für Arbeitslose, hier: Technische Lehrstürme und Lehrwerkstätten der SA. An Herrn Präsidenten der Landesarbeitsämter. Berlin-Charlottenburg, den 30. Januar 1934.

148 BA, NS23/266. As in note 144.

149 BA, R2/18518. Der Präsident der Reichsanstalt für Arbeitsvermittlung und Arbeitslosenversicherung, Gesch. 2.: II 5559/75. Betrifft: Berufliche Bildungsmassnahmen für SA-Angehörige. An Herrn Reichsarbeitsminister. Berlin-Char-

lottenburg, den 2. März 1934. See also BA, NS23/1. SA, OSAF, Verwaltungsamt. Verw. Nr. 12871. Betr.: Hilfswerklager. München, den 1. Juni 1934.

150 BA, R2/18519. D.R.d.F. Ar. 3020–493I. Ref. Poer., Gs. Berlin, 19. Oktober 1935.
151 BA, R2/18518. Der Reichsminister der Finanzen. Ar. 3020–437 I. Betrifft: Alu. für Insassen von Hilfswerklagern. Berlin, 6.11.1934.
152 BA, R2/18519. As in note 150; and BA, R2/18518. Der Präsident der Reichsanstalt für Arbeitsvermittlung und Arbeitslosenversicherung, Gesch. Z: II 5559/148/153. Betrifft: Berufliche Bildungsmassnahmen (SA-Hilfswerklager). Berlin-Charlottenburg, den 23. Januar 1935.
153 BA, NS23/266. As in note 144.
154 BA, NS23/353. SA der NSDAP, Brigade 12 (Hamburg). Auszug aus dem Rundschreiben der Obersten SA-Führung v. 15. April 1935, Nr. 19995. Betrifft: Richtlinien für die Ausbildung, Unterkunft usw. in den SA-Hilfswerklagern. Hamburg, den 3. Mai 1935.
155 BA, NS23/128. Der Oberste SA-Führer. Betrifft: SA-Hilfswerklager. München, den 16. Mai 1935. gez. Lutze. This document also accused junior SA officials of failing to explain adequately to SA men the meaning and aims of the welfare camps.
156 Landesarchiv Speyer (LAS), H33/987. SA der NSDAP. Lehrgang für Gemeindedienst im SA-Hilfswerklager Tegel. Betreff: Umschulung alter Kämpfer für den Gemeindedienst. An die Herren Oberpräsidenten, die Herren Oberbürgermeister, die Herren Landräte. Berlin, den 30. Oktober 1935. gez. Dr Zeitler.
157 BA, NS23/349. SA der NSDAP. Der Führer der Gruppe Hansa. Gruppenbefehl, Nr. 66. Hamburg, den 2. Oktober 1935. gez. Fust.
158 BA, NS23/474. SA der NSDAP, Brigade 12 (Hamburg). B.B. Nr. G. 45/34. Betrifft: SA-Hilfswerklager Hansa in Schwerin. Hamburg, den 28. Juni 1934.
159 BA, NS23/127. Der Oberste SA-Führer. Abteilung Fürsorge III/2 5715. Betrifft: Hilfswerklager. Hier: Unterstützung der Angehörigen der Lagerinsassen. München, den 25. Oktober 1934. gez. Marxer.
160 BA, R36/1015. Deutscher Gemeindetag. III 4089/34. Unterstützung der Familienangehörigen der Insassen von Hilfswerklagern der SA. Berlin, den 3. Oktober 1934.
161 ibid. See also note 159.
162 BA, R2/11913a. Zu IB 370/34, as in note 2 (i). p. 4.
163 BA, R2/31013. Übersicht über den Geldbedarf der Obersten SA-Führung im April 1934, p. 3.
164 BA, NS23/298. SA der NSDAP, Gruppe Kurpfalz. Der Gruppenführer. Br. B. Nr. 51/34. Geheim. Betreff: SA Hilfswerklager. Mannheim, den 19. Juni 1934.
165 BA, NS23/298. Standarte 80. An die Gruppe Kurpfalz. Betr.: Hilfswerklager. Wiesbaden, den 17. Oktober 1934.
166 BA, R2/18518. Der Reichsminister der Finanzen. Betr.: SA-Hilfswerklager. Berlin, den 5. Januar 1935.
167 BA, R2/18518. Abschrift. Der Präsident der Reichsanstalt für Arbeitsvermittlung und Arbeitslosenversicherung, Gesch. 2.: II 5559/75. Betrifft: Berufliche Bildungsmassnahmen für SA-Angehörige. Berlin-Charlottenburg, den 2. März 1934.
168 ibid., Vermerk.
169 BA, R2/18518. As in note 151.
170 BA, R2/18518. Abschrift. Der Präsident der Reichsanstalt für Arbeitsvermittlung und Arbeitslosenversicherung, Gesch. 2: IB (2) 3810/1512. Betrifft: Berufliche Bildungsmassnahmen für SA-Angehörige. Berlin-Charlottenburg, den 5. Juni 1935.
171 BA, R2/18519. As in note 150.
172 BA, R2/18519. Der Reichs- und Preussische Arbeitsminister. IIc 7991/35. Betrifft: Arbeitslosenunterstützung für Insassen von Hilfswerklagern. Berlin, den 11. September 1935.

173 BA, R2/18519. D.R.d.F. Ar. 3020–493I. (2) An den Herrn Reichs- und Preussischen Arbeitsminister, Berlin. Betrifft: Arbeitslosenunterstützung für Insassen von Hilfswerklagern. Berlin, 19. Oktober 1935.

174 BA, NS23/353. SA der NSDAP, Brigade 12 (Hamburg). Auszug aus dem Rundschreiben der Obersten SA-Führung v. 15. April 1935. Hamburg, den 3. Mai 1935.

175 That is, assuming an average attendance of 15,000–16,000.

176 BA, NS23/207. Der Führer der Gruppe Niederrhein. Brief. Nr. G. 2887. Duisburg, den 1. August 1935.

177 A. Werner, 'SA und NSDAP' (Dissertation, Friedrich Alexander Universität zu Erlangen, 1964), Beilagen I, II – following p. 538.

178 BA, NS23/371. SA der NSDAP. Der Führer der Gruppe Hansa. Verfügung! Hamburg, den 15.12.1934.

179 ibid.

180 ibid.

181 Werner, 'SA und NSDAP', p. 505, and Beilagen I, II, III – following p. 538.

182 GLAK, Abt. 465d/1282. SA der NSDAP. Der Führer der Brigade 150, Rheinhessen. Vierteljahresbericht für das 1. Vierteljahr 1934. IV. Sanitätswesen. Mainz, den 18.4.34. gez. Schönborn.

183 GLAK, Abt. 465d/1282. SA der NSDAP, Brigade 51 (Pfalz-Saar). Vierteljahresbericht. IV. Sanitätswesen. Neustadt an der Haardt, den 19. April 1934. gez. Schwitzgebel.

6 Ideology and Politics of the SA

The Weimar Republic is sometimes portrayed as a polity doomed from the outset, and certainly a daunting historical legacy combined with immediate, pressing problems. None the less, in the middle years of its existence it fared reasonably well in both domestic and foreign policy, although without overcoming a basic hostility towards its existence on the right. The 1928 election seemed to confirm this improvement; the SPD's prominent position within the republic was reinforced, while the extreme right virtually disappeared from the Reichstag. Behind the scenes, however, the NSDAP had come to dominate the radical right and, although the movement's electoral performance was abysmal, the party and its affiliated organisations – the SA included – were being reshaped for an electoral assault on the republic. The NSDAP began to register local successes in north-western Germany in 1928 and 1929 through its exploitation of mounting difficulties in the agricultural community there. The economic crisis of 1929 provided the opportunity for a national resurgence as the bitter hostility of the traditional right to Weimar was reinforced and eventually outpaced by an upsurge of populist right-wing radicalism.

In fact, heightened political consciousness and radicalisation occurred across the board. More Germans turned out to vote. Participation in national elections rose from 74·6 per cent in May 1928 to 83·4 per cent in July 1932[1] with more voters opting for the largest radical parties: the KPD and NSDAP. While these parties polled 13·25 per cent of votes cast in May 1928, the figure rose to 31·38 per cent in September 1930 and 51·66 per cent in July 1932. Both parties gained votes, but the KPD's steady progress was eclipsed by the NSDAP's explosive growth which made it the largest party in the Reichstag by July 1932.[2]

The Nazi Party attracted floods of new members, but an equally telling indication of the progressive radicalisation of German political life was the growth in the numbers and size of paramilitary formations, including the SA, which sought to shape political life in the streets rather than through the lobby and debating chamber. Political relations between left and right were mediated partly through these formations' activities.[3] Therefore, whilst the SA's material attractions were undeniably vital in its growth and development, its history also demands an examination of the politics of the organisation within the context of political radicalisation.

The SA played its part in the high politics of the era. Historians have detailed its contribution to the Nazi seizure and consolidation of power, while noting its disagreements with the rest of the Nazi movement and the latter's political allies.[4] The rivalry between the SA's leaders and the Reichswehr's commanders featured prominently here, as Röhm sought to destroy the traditional military hierarchy and replace it with an SA- dominated, populist mass army. Although Röhm lacked well-developed, abstract political goals, his experience as a wartime officer (shared, of course, by many SA leaders) had provided him with a rough-and-ready ideology of sorts.[5] He declared his wish to create a state of workers, peasants and soldiers or, as he described this group, front-line soldiers.[6] This perception of civil society in military terms was elaborated in a speech to the Diplomatic Corps in Berlin in April 1934 where the comradeship of the front line was proposed as an organising principle in society. The identification of the Army Officer Corps with the old order discredited them in Röhm's eyes.[7] The common fate shared by the active participants during the war was certainly a positive lesson, but the war had its negative side. He believed it had been fought for the sectional interests of 'politicians, stock-exchange magnates, captains of industry, oil magnates . . .' whose 'personal cowardice' and the chaos which he accused the civilians of creating after 1918 led him to regard civilian society with deep contempt.[8] The Officer Corps would do nothing to eliminate civilian society, in place of which Röhm proposed to establish a front-soldierly egalitarianism where 'the old, divisive contradictions of estate, occupation, class and confession have been eliminated'.[9] As he commented to the Diplomatic Corps, 'we have not created a national, but a national socialist revolution, whereby we stress in particular the word "socialist"'[10] – although clearly his socialism contrasted with that of either the SPD or the KPD. The degree of abstraction in Röhm's political thought seldom went further. He consciously rejected democracy in the liberal sense of the word, seeing no role for the will of a majority of individuals in Nazi Germany – 'the National Socialist revolution means an inner break with the philosophy of the great French revolution of 1789' – [11] but a succinct definition of his standpoint was not forthcoming. This contrasted with the left of the Nazi movement, one of whose adherents, Ernst zu Reventlow, once defined his faction's position with illuminating precision: 'Just as we view national questions on the side of the German Nationalists, we view economic and social questions on the side of the Social Democrats and Communists.'[12] More typical of Röhm were blustering tirades which condemned much, but had little constructive to say. His enemies came from everywhere: Marxism, the bourgeoisie, the bureaucracy, the Army Officer Corps; all were suspect. As he declared: 'In the last resort, SA and SS leaders, you will decide whether Bolshevism will be given free rein through bourgeois half-measures and sterile reaction, or whether you are committed with me to give the [SA and SS] the order enabling them to achieve the one sacred task – Germany's freedom and honour.'[13] Röhm's more tangible proposals verged on the quaint while contradicting much of his rhetoric. He was apparently secretly a Bavarian monarchist who, in return for the restoration of the Wittelsbach dynasty, would have accepted the restoration of the Hohenzollern monarchy in Prussia.[14]

Historians have also considered the sentiment and activities of the SA as a mass movement. This approach at least opens the way to an examination of rank-and-file ideology, but simultaneously subsumes it into some form of wider 'SA ideology' which assumes common interests between leaders and men and, as often as not, a common social background. Schweitzer writes of a lower-middle-class style of anti-capitalism present within an SA composed of small shopkeepers, independent artisans and white-collar staff.[15] Allen, too, places the SA on the right and notes its extreme nationalism.[16] Bloch asserts that the lower middle class was especially strong in the SA and argues that this group expected implementation of the Nazi Twenty-Five Point Programme confining their concept of anti-capitalism to the boycotting of Jewish shops.[17] However, he later adds that the SA did inadvertently represent some working-class interests.[18] More recently, Bessel has regarded the SA's paramilitarism as vital: its formation into army-style units, the military chain of command, the uniforms – all descending from a relatively longstanding tradition of militarism in German society. He believes that the SA's ideology was rooted in the Freikorps campaigns during the civil-war-like conditions of the early 1920s, which certainly provided the SA with many of its leaders. In the renewed crisis of the early 1930s, he argues, the stormtroopers attracted a younger generation of predominantly lower-middle-class recruits drawn by its militarist stance.[19] However, these interpretations share the fundamental weakness of misunderstanding the SA's social composition, for all explicitly or implicitly relate the stormtroopers' ideology to the allegedly lower-middle-class character of the organisation. While this interpretation of social background holds true for the leaders, the same does not apply to the mass membership.

Fest speaks in more general terms of activism being the key organising principle behind SA ideology: 'The ideology of the SA was activity at any price',[20] and certainly its activism is not in doubt. However, he sets the SA apart from society as a whole to the point where it becomes a somewhat distasteful oddity operating virtually within its own world. Fest distinguishes between the SA's politics and those of 'the workers', arguing that it acted for material reasons at the expense of a rational political philosophy:

> Konrad Heiden coined the unforgettable phrase 'SA class' for those classes whose aim was a secure existence through state aid and who, instead of claiming the state for their own, as the

workers did at the time of their greatest self-confidence, were
content to make claims upon the state – desperadoes in search of a
pension.[21]

This desperation undoubtedly existed, although Fest (like others)
appears unaware that most stormtroopers were workers, but workers
facing a recession of unprecedented severity which precluded the development of conventional political loyalties. In social terms, the distinction between the jobless workers of the SA and KPD/Red Front, and
the employed within the SPD would seem more apposite than that
between the SA and 'the workers'.[22]

In fact, Fest notes the intimate relations between the SA and Red
Front which combined violent struggle with co-operation and a mobility of membership between the two organisations:

> Above all in the big cities a permanent underworld war was carried
> on between the SA and Red Front (RF), in which both sides made
> use of low taverns as bases, not without occasional tactical alliances
> and, following National Socialist reverses at the end of 1932, fre-
> quent desertions from the SA to RF, which in the spring of 1933
> were offset by whole units of the RF going over to the SA.[23]

Schüddekopf remarks that the growing volume of grass-roots links
between the SA and KPD caused problems for the Nazi leadership by
mid-1932, which confirms the picture painted by Fest.[24] However,
these glimpses of a world where Nazis and Communists could sometimes agree with each other do not explain the nature of that world, in
ideological or any other terms. Rosenhaft has examined the problem
from the point of view of young, Communist activists in Berlin during
the early 1930s and here the unemployment crisis and the common
socio-economic environment of Communists and stormtroopers come
out more strongly.[25]

Contemporary sources outside the Nazi movement tended to characterise the SA as a body out of step with Hitler and the Nazi Party and
certainly further to the left than most of the Nazi movement. When
discussing relations between the SA and the left, the former Chief of the
Gestapo, Diels, distinguishes sharply between the SA and the SPD/
Reichsbanner, regarding the Social Democratic movement as both
older and markedly less activist.[26] He asserts that the SA was socialist
and that the SPD failed to attract its membership precisely because of
the age factor and the Social Democrats' predilection for theoretical
politics: 'But Hitler promised these masses that he would make good
the social revolution which the Social Democratic leadership had let
slip.'[27] When comparing the SA and KPD, Diels stresses the similar-

ities rather than the distinctions between them, both in terms of social background and, partly as a consequence of this, political outlook.[28]

Verification of the factual content of Diels's outspoken work is difficult. His job doubtless left him well informed, but his book contains little documentation and this problem is common to much writing of the early 1930s and to personal reminiscences written at a later date. None the less, contemporary sources are not without interest. Left-wing opposition groups in exile were particularly interested in the Röhm purge and in this context examined the rank-and-file politics of the SA more closely than most recent works. At least one exiled group distinguished explicitly between the politics of the stormtroopers and those of their leaders.

The *White Book (Weissbuch)*, an anonymous left-wing resistance publication produced in Paris in 1935, attributed a rudimentary socialism to the stormtroopers:

> They may not have had any clear conception of socialism. However, they certainly included within it the end of the hated capitalist system and a conduct of the economy in the interests of the masses; to give them work and bread.[29]

It continued that the SA's social composition caused it to reflect the mood and, after Hitler's takeover, the discontent of the working population. Hitler, the *White Book* maintained, exploited this restlessness as a political weapon against left and right, while Röhm used the same discontent to pressurise Hitler into backing him against the Reichswehr's leadership – a bluff which Hitler called.[30] The *White Book* concluded that Röhm's own politics made his threat a hollow one; '[he] never contemplated unleashing the anti-capitalist forces of the SA in an uprising and thereby instituting a movement which would have far exceeded his military ambition'.[31] In fact, by mid-1934 Röhm was disturbed with what he saw; the SA and Stahlhelm were literally coming to blows[32] while SA verses such as 'We are the swastika army,/ Raise the red flag high,/We fight for German labour's freedom', symbolised rank-and-file impatience.[33]

Another opposition writer, using the name Bredow, published in the League of Nations sanctuary of Saarbrücken. He considered the SA possibly susceptible to Otto Strasser's brand of socialism,[34] but his description of a potentially explosive political dynamic within the SA is particularly striking:

> After the victory, Röhm had expanded the SA enormously, in an obsession for size, from its strength of 600,000 in early 1933. Now these [newcomers] were in part proletarians of the best order; workers, some of whom were disappointed with their former parties and

now expected fulfilment from Hitler – but none the less still fulfilment of their old, socialist ideals, ideals which had not changed in content through the change of name to Nazi. However, many proletarians consciously joined the SA to sabotage it, with the firm intention of remaining Communists or Social Democrats and of making the same out of former Nazis. They, too, may initially at least have been embraced by the new community. However, with time, the relationship between effect and reaction reversed: the ideology of the SA assumed ever more socialist content and, frequently enough, socialist form. Many SA companies are Communist or Social Democratic without any attempt at disguise. They are jokingly called beefsteaks – brown outside, red inside. There is a joke about two SA men, one of whom complained that there were 'so many Nazis' in his company. The other replies: 'In our company there are still three, but we'll soon chase them out too.' In fact this is more than a joke, for the SA itself distinguishes between SA members and Nazis; there are, after all, 3 million SA-members, but not even 2 million party members.[35]

The SA's social basis did not change so drastically in 1933 and, in fact, Bredow's interpretation virtually presupposes a continuity in social composition. A solidly lower-middle-class, reactionary SA would not have attracted many former socialists and Communists. Even if expediency alone had drawn them to the stormtroopers in 1933, they could not have achieved the results described without a certain empathy existing between them and the original stormtroopers.

Therefore a wide range of interpretations of the SA's politics and ideology exist, but these conflict with one another and, individually, face various problems. Some studies barely relate to the sociology of the SA, ascribing petit bourgeois motivation to jobless workers, while other studies are largely undocumented. Few examine political and ideological tensions within the SA, especially between leaders and men and, therefore, beyond the interesting work completed so far, a great deal concerning the stormtroopers' ideology remains to be substantiated, resolved, or even examined at a basic level.

Ideological Heterogeneity and Radical Activism within the SA

The stormtroopers' material deprivation made them enemies of Weimar by experience and this is reflected in their writings. However, these same writings (largely *curricula vitae* and short essays produced when joining the SA) reveal the stormtroopers' failure to develop any distinctive, abstracted political philosophy. Instead, a varied and often conflicting range of ideological standpoints emerges among SA veterans and post-takeover recruits.

Anti-Semitism might have been general among the stormtroopers, and explicit at that, but this was not entirely so. The limited volume of evidence left by veteran members reveals a measure of anti-Semitism, as did some stormtroopers' behaviour in the street, but many SA men were happy to buy uniforms or other equipment from Jewish firms.[36] When Lutze, as commander of SA Group North, complained that 'an SA man who buys from Jews demonstrates that he has not grasped the meaning of National Socialism',[37] he was possibly making more revealing an observation than he intended. After January 1933 many more stormtroopers put pen to paper, largely because the leadership now sought new recruits' views in writing, as well as information from some veteran members. Once again the picture was confused and the stormtroopers' behaviour also lacked consistency. On the one hand, the SA High Command forbade stormtroopers from patronising Jewish concerns in mid-1933, behaviour which ignored earlier orders.[38] Even this intervention from the top failed and the problem persisted in December 1934.[39] Some stormtroopers placed personal friendships with Jews above any ideological considerations,[40] while others appreciated the absurdity of Nazi dogma. A *Scharführer* from Krefeld called out during a broadcast by Goebbels which reviled the Jews: 'The poor Jews are people too, it's all lies!'.[41] On the other hand, many stormtroopers attacked Jews personally, their property, and even their cemeteries with such enthusiasm that the state and the SA's leaders felt obliged to restrain them, but only did so with difficulty.[42] In September 1935 the situation threatened to run completely out of control in north-western Germany, necessitating particularly vigorous intervention by Group Hansa's commander to stem the violence – if only for the sake of appearances.[43]

Right-wing nationalism featured in the SA, as illustrated by Sturm-mann Karl Stenger, a worker from Frankfurt-am-Main:

I have not belonged previously to any other party, other than the League of German Colonial Scouts for four years. In this league we always stood exclusively for the ideal of German homeland and that of the NSDAP ... In July 1932 I joined the NSBO and on 16 September 1932 the SA and NSDAP.[44]

Other right-wing nationalists elaborated further, often linking their nationalism with a rejection of left-wing politics. The SA probationer Wilhelm Schecker, an engineer and designer from Frankfurt-am-Main wrote:

In particular, however, I declare that I joined the SA to support my leader and Germany in the battle against communism and the SPD, those traitors to people and homeland, and to support the eradication of these parasites, to the very end, may it cost me my life![45]

The worker Fritz Kleinhenz made a similar case less virulently: 'I am in the SA because I was brought up as a nationalist from childhood, because my father [also a worker] had no time for the SPD or KPD.'[46] In other cases, racialist connotations prevailed, as with the worker, SA man Ludwig Schucherd of Frankfurt-am-Main who declared that he had 'not participated in political life, belonged to any party or any other movement – as an Aryan German it was beneath me to support this boss and Jew government'.[47]

Some nationalist stormtroopers had belonged previously to other paramilitary organisations or patriotic military associations – hardly a surprising discovery given the SA's origins. Thus the worker, SA man Hermann Feige of Oberröblingen in Bavaria had joined the Military League in 1925,[48] while the salaried employee, Truppführer Roman Fischer of Ansbach had fought in the Freikorps after the war and participated in the suppression of the Munich Soviet.[49] However, neither elaborated on their essentially factual accounts – a tendency typical of other individuals from this background. The farmer's son Christian Fehr of Wollrode in Hessen merely revealed that he had joined the Kyffhäuser Youth on 1 January 1933,[50] while most Stahlhelmer who were transferred to the SA during 1933 also refrained from elaborating on a bare factual statement to this effect, whatever their occupation or class, or from wherever they came.[51]

Since the Stahlhelm had been incorporated more or less compulsorily into the SA, some of its members had not abandoned their old beliefs, but accepted absorption into the SA out of expediency. While many did remain silent, some either revealed or betrayed their true feelings, such as the fitter J. H. of Essen. In 1935 H. was talking with a workmate at Krupps; also a fitter and also a stormtrooper. The workmate reported the conversation to the authorities, remarking that H. had declared: '"Yes indeed, something else will replace this system." He answered my question as to whether he meant a monarchy with "Yes".'[52]

Some SA members were refugees from the territories lost by Germany after the First World War and were nationalists for this reason, while others seem to have been more attracted by Hitler's personal stature. The SA probationer Hans Funken, an office clerk from Würselen near Aachen wrote: 'The new movement, the Leader Principle, aroused my interest long ago, since I was convinced by our leader's National Idea and appreciated the tremendous accomplishments.'[53]

However, while much of this evidence is colourful and consequently tempting material for the historian, it is untypical even of 'nationally minded' stormtroopers. More typical of stormtroopers' writings was the rather duller assertion of the worker Heinrich Vollberg: 'I am nationally minded, love the Fatherland and have not previously belonged to any political party.'[54]

Leaving aside the Stahlhelmer drafted into the SA, right-wing nationalists were probably outnumbered by recruits from the political left. Some SA units as a whole exhibited left-wing traits, such as the 76th Regiment of Hamburg whose members sang 'The Internationale' as a battle song in 1931 (with the words slightly altered!), to the Hamburg leadership's evident dismay.[55]

Stormtroopers from the left explained their past and their change of sympathies in various ways. Perhaps their writings should be treated with caution, given the political atmosphere of 1933 and 1934, but certain patterns of explanation are discernible and some former left-wingers had probably been genuinely converted to the Nazi cause. There had, after all, been transfers from the KPD and SPD to the SA before the Nazi triumph of 1933 made membership of a Nazi organisation, at least theoretically, especially attractive.

Recruits from the left were usually reluctant to discuss their political beliefs in detail, but some accounted briefly for their change of loyalties. The worker J. F. of Essen belonged to the KPD's Revolutionary Trade Union Opposition (RGO) from 1928 to 1929 'because I was unemployed', but on 1 December 1932 he joined the SA, achieving promotion to *Oberscharführer* by 1934. He merely explained that after leaving the RGO he 'became convinced that the NSDAP's aims were very probably the right ones'.[56] Another convert was the former Communist, joiner Georg Stegmaier of SA Company 62, Munich, who in July 1931 joined in an attack on a policeman. When arrested and questioned he declared:

> ... I have belonged to the NSDAP since January 1931. Before that I was in the KPD for about four years. I was also a member of the Red Front until it was banned. I was not a functionary. I left the KPD because I no longer perceived its aim as correct and because Germany's poverty was only worsened by this party. I joined the NSDAP from political conviction and not as a spy or provocateur.[57]

These statements illustrate a tendency of converts from the left to connect politics with their material circumstances, whilst Stegmaier, even as an ex-Communist, supported national rather than class interests. Unfortunately, the majority of pre-1933 accounts written by former left-wingers contain less detail than Stegmaier's, possibly because most resulted from police questioning and arrested SA men seemed reluctant to reveal more than necessary to their enemies, the police. The stormtrooper Reinhard Zinkl who was arrested in Munich in December 1931 for defying an official ban on SA uniforms merely declared:[58]

> I was a member of the KPD for about two years. I have belonged to the NSDAP for about three weeks. I will not say why I left the KPD. Sometimes things happen in the party which go against the grain. I believe that my aims are pursued by the NSDAP. I am in Company 62, Troop I of the SA.

Communists who joined the SA after Hitler's takeover – and Communists presumably had the most explaining to do – often said even less than earlier recruits. The former farmworker, SA man Josef Kinateder of Hessen-Nassau simply mentioned his membership of the KPD between January and May 1931. The SA accepted this reticence and Kinateder only left the SA in December 1934 because of a new, demanding job.[59] The worker and SA Rottenführer Franz Noth of Frankfurt-am-Main admitted to his earlier membership of the KPD, but when applying to join the SA, simply declared that he was entering 'to serve and obey the German people and government with all my strength and become an active fighter for the Third Reich'.[60] Some senior Communist officials also joined the SA for unspecified reasons (although some certainly intended to sabotage it). Thus Wilhelm Fessel of Würzburg, a former election candidate, an industrial group leader in the RGO, a member of the Red Front and of several other Communist organisations, joined the SA for a time after the Nazi takeover.[61]

Where Communists did explain their motivation fully, their accounts probably reassured the SA that former Communists were not necessarily particularly sophisticated, ideologically speaking. Given the extraordinarily high turnover in KPD membership during the early 1930s,[62] this is possibly not too surprising. The jobless factory mechanic Gustav Finkbeiner of Pforzheim, who joined the SA in November 1933, became unemployed at Christmas 1930 and remained so, despite trying unsuccessfully to establish his own bicycle repair business in 1933:

> In that era of political parties and confusion I too ended up in the KPD, luckily not for long because I was made out to be a Nazi and a saboteur, because the big words and slogans didn't mean anything to me, I got whipped up again and worked actively in the Rural Agitation in Tälmann [sic] Peasants' Aid Programme, was of course immediately caught by the law, because I was still honest and worked while the others laid low, that was in June 1930 ... The worst was that all this didn't tie in with my goals which I picked up in the Scouts and Wandervögel.[63]

The simplistic and confused tone of this passage rings true enough
and the factory-employed, building joiner Adolf Selig of Frankfurt-
am-Main gave a similarly simplistic account of his 'conversion':

> So far I have never been active politically, I have sympathised
> with the left-wing parties (KPD) after the leaders of this party
> (KPD) fled after the victorious NSDAP election campaign, they
> showed how dirty and cowardly they were, because if they had
> nothing to answer for and didn't feel guilty they didn't have to flee
> I saw through this swindle too late. I went to National Socialist
> meetings and events and realised my path was the wrong one and
> recognised Adolf Hitler as the liberator and saviour of Germany, I
> therefore joined the SA ...[64]

Perhaps Selig was one of the many former left-wingers who sought to
save their skins, but once again it appears that the SA need not have
overexerted itself with political reindoctrination to retain many
recruits who, although once members or supporters of rival organisations, had little grasp of the finer points of any group's ideology.

Some former Social Democrats claimed that closed shops had
forced them into the trade unions and subsequently into the SPD.
The fitter turned fireman Heinrich Weimann wrote in September
1933:

> I was taken on by the Adler Works in 1919. At that time I had to
> organise within the trades' union movement, and politically. I
> belonged to the SPD from April 1920 until March 1933 [!] and the
> Reichsbanner from September 1925 until June 1931.[65]

The worker Wilhelm Desheimer was more emphatic in denouncing
his old party, as well as Weimar society as he saw it:

> I have long since yearned for an ordered Germany, uninfested
> with Jews, and yearned for the day when the SPD's boss-rule
> would be abolished. In fact I would have joined the SA long ago if
> I hadn't been ashamed of having once been forced into the SPD.[66]

Other socialists admitted joining the SPD or Reichsbanner freely,
but either passed this off as a youthful foible, or claimed to have
seen the error of their ways. The apprentice August Wenzel of
Frankfurt-am-Main made light of his period in the Reichsbanner
between July 1930 and December 1932: 'As a young man I found
the marching fun.'[67] The electrical mounter Hermann Theisen,

employed by the firm Karl Diehl in Frankfurt-am-Main, wrote that he left the SPD because of its failure to tackle Germany's problems:

> I was politically active in the Iron Front (SPD) for about eighteen months. As I gradually became aware of the SPD's poor leadership and realised that their efforts couldn't help us, I resigned from the party. On the other hand, I am convinced that the new Germany, led by our People's Chancellor Adolf Hitler means advancement and awakening, and I wish to devote my entire strength to this.[68]

Theisen's perception of Hitler as the 'People's Chancellor' is notable. It appears that many recruits from the left, in particular, attributed to the Nazi movement populist emancipatory attributes which it hardly merited, given the eventual emergence of the élitist and brutally repressive SS state. In fact, the propensity for recruits from many ideological backgrounds to latch on to Hitler as the embodiment of their own aspirations was common. Perhaps stormtroopers were sometimes thereby able to reconcile their own beliefs with obvious contradictions, both within the SA and in the wider Nazi movement. Alternatively, stormtroopers may simply have repeated Nazi propaganda for the benefit of their leaders, for some eventually had doubts about Hitler's politics.[69]

However, while the SA contained recruits who had extremely diverse political backgrounds, the mass of stormtroopers' writings lacked any such political or ideological content. Virtually any ideological standpoint can be found within the SA, but ideological consciousness in the conventional sense was not especially common among the rank and file. The joiner Karl Fischer of Stockhausen, Hessen, simply stated that he joined the NSBO in July 1932 and the SA on 27 January 1933.[70] The worker, SA man Richard Hock of Frankfurt-am-Main commented:

> In fact I always wanted to belong to the SA or SS. Since I was in the Labour Service there was no point, because I couldn't have carried out my duties. When I left the Labour Service, my first concern was to join the SA.[71]

This ideological vacuum disrupted the SA in its own way. An Upper Bavarian unit complained in June 1934:

> Attendance rates in the troop have been extremely poor recently. This is only partly due to shift work. Many stay away because of indifference towards an SA man's duties.[72]

As the SA was reduced in size after the Röhm purge, further indications of ideological nonchalance arose. Most stormtroopers who left the SA, whether voluntarily or involuntarily, went with patent willingness.

Outright expulsions from the SA could, therefore, be reserved for more serious cases, but even here 'lack of interest', presumably in an extreme form, featured as grounds for dismissal. A group of Ruhr regiments reported thirty-one expulsions between August and December 1934, of which thirteen were for 'lack of interest',[73] and things were similar in Company 17/4 of Neuötting, Upper Bavaria.[74] Of 825 cases within the Frankfurt-am-Main SA where release or expulsion definitely occurred between July 1934 and June 1935 (in many more cases the date was unavailable) and where a reason for this step was provided, only 5 were linked directly to political unreliability or unacceptability. The most common single reason for leaving the SA was ill-health, but many stormtroopers evidently sought release on the most spurious of pretexts – and were allowed to go.[75]

From this it might appear that the mass of stormtroopers had no ideology which distinguished them as a collectivity, either of their own or appropriated from elsewhere. In this case, although the stormtroopers were, by their leaders' own admission anything but committed Nazis, it could seem that they had no 'counter-ideology' distinguishing them from the middle-class militarism of their leaders. Some historians certainly suggest that the economic crisis played so great a role in driving recruits into the SA that any ideological orientation was unnecessary. Böhnke writes of the Ruhr SA: 'These men didn't join the SA and NSDAP out of political conviction alone; instead many simply sought food and shelter in one of the many SA hostels built by 1932',[76] and Fest argues similarly for the entire SA.[77]

In fact there was more to SA ideology than this. Certainly the depression was vital in providing the SA with recruits, but not simply in the form of young men looking for beer, a bite to eat, and a good punch-up to relieve the monotony of unemployment. Although the stormtroopers' political distinctiveness only became apparent relatively late in the period, the diversity of political views – or lack of views – was reconciled or compensated for partly by loyalty to the Führer, but more especially by the radicalism common to most of the SA. Bearing in mind that the majority of stormtroopers were from the working class, and many of the rest clerical staff, the SA's radicalism is largely attributable to these groups' experiences during the depression years.

To recapitulate briefly, German workers had, traditionally, usually obtained a formal trade qualification and, therefore, the German working class was very highly skilled indeed. The largest proportion of unskilled labour was found in agriculture, some of the public services, and in one or two industrial sectors such as chemicals and quarrying. Many of these skilled workers were active in smaller firms and, of those in the larger firms, many had received their training in small firms run by master craftsmen. This created an intimate relationship between the industrial and so-called handicrafts sectors, and maintained a powerful crafts tradition in German industrial life.[78]

Thus by their eighteenth birthday most stormtroopers had passed through adolescence and, with the exception of the difficult years after the First World War, past working-class experience would have left them expecting a relatively well-paid and secure future, and even the prospect of advancement to foreman, supervisor or possibly master craftsman. Many did work for some years in their chosen occupations and almost all for a few months at least, but with the onset of the economic crisis the majority were deprived of their vocation and, soon afterwards, of any decent existence.

Not untypical was the case of the fitter Adolf Fischer of Frankfurt-am-Main/Niederrad, and the same depressing pattern was repeated, with variations, throughout Germany:

I was born on 23 June 1912 as the son of the worker Bartholomäus Fischer in Frankfurt/Niederrad. I entered the *Volksschule* in Nieder-rad (Goldstein School) on my sixth birthday and left the top class at Easter in 1926. Then I trained as a fitter with the firm F. L. Fries Engineering Works in Frankfurt, Schulstrasse. I completed my training in June 1929 and took my journeyman's examination with the result 'good'. I then worked in the firm F. L. Fries & Son as a journeyman until I was laid off in October 1929 due to a scarcity of work. Fourteen days later I began work as a storeman with the heating firm Käuffer & Co. of Feldbergstrasse, Frankfurt. I was laid off here in January 1930, also because of a scarcity of work. Since then I have been unemployed, working for four or five days a month as a casual worker with a furniture delivery firm.[79]

This sequence was repeated frequently. A period as a skilled worker or salaried employee was followed sometimes by a spell of semi-skilled or unskilled work and then, finally, by unemployment. Time and again words such as 'passed my craftsman's examinations' and the 'laid off due to a scarcity of work' crop up. The sacrifices made by countless individuals to acquire a skill, not to mention the sacrifices made on their behalf by their families, seemed to have come to nothing. A generation of young Germans was being thrown on the scrapheap. Not surprisingly many sought desperately for a radical solution to their problems, and for the guilty parties.

Any conventional political organisation or conventional ideological framework was ill-suited to this. German political parties, whether of the left or of the right were geared generally for operation within an economically successful society and their modes of operation – bureaucratic procedure, compromise and gradualism were products of national economic success. For the jobless workers and clerical staff of the early

1930s this was not acceptable, for while their original expectations had stemmed from an era of economic growth, their prospects by the early 1930s were grimly different. Most were convinced that as long as the Weimar Republic's political institutions survived, and as long as the socio-economic order remained the same, they would never work again. The 'system', as they described it, had to be destroyed.

Therefore the SA's radicalism was essentially negative. It was quick to identify enemies, but failed to develop a coherent, constructive programme for change such as that produced by the left in Weimar. The tendency to identify enemies rather than define positive aims resulted in the SA's radicalism being expressed on one level through frenetic activity and, often enough, violence – a phenomenon reinforced by the stormtroopers' material desperation and their paramilitary training.

Police reports frequently noted the SA's involvement in political violence and the police also attempted to quantify the level of political violence as a whole. Their reports seldom distinguished between the different wings of political movements, and SA violence was usually described as Nazi violence. None the less, a measure of the SA's involvement in violent incidents throughout Germany lies in the body's casualty figures which show that it undoubtedly bore the brunt of injuries and deaths suffered by Nazis while serving their cause.[80] This violence mushroomed from 1930 onwards. In 1928 the NSDAP still came a poor second to the KPD/Red Front, the former disrupting 60 political meetings in Prussia against the Communists' 200 or more.[81] In Saxony the authorities accused the Communists of initiating 41 fights and the NSDAP a mere 7.[82] Whether or not police reports in general were biased, they indicate that the relative level of Nazi violence subsequently increased sharply. The NSDAP was involved, for example, in 20 out of 24 incidents in the Prussian town of Wuppertal[83] and 21 out of 30 in Altona between 1930 and 1933.[84] During 1931 the NSDAP initiated 297 incidents out of 509 in Bavaria.[85]

In some ways this violent activism accorded closely with Williams's definition of paramilitary politics:

A paramilitary organisation must have a clearly recognisable political goal. Normally this goal was negative in the first instance and directed towards the elimination of the political system in which the organisation operated. All methods leading to the attainment of its goal are acceptable to such a group. . . . The political aims or convictions of a paramilitary organisation need not be clearly recognisable or even vaguely rational. A reservoir of theoretical ideas or a partial continual tradition of political behaviour (even if its merely borrowed) is equally unnecessary as a point of orientation for a future policy.[86]

Certainly, impatience within the SA grew when the immediate demise of Weimar appeared in doubt and ordinary stormtroopers could let their feelings be known on this. In February 1932 a Munich-based group of SA radicals expressed their disappointment that the NSDAP had not smashed finance capital and founded the Third Reich 'in the national revolutionary spirit and in the fastest way; that is by force of arms'.[87] Stresses mounted later in 1932 as prospects of a decisive Nazi victory faded further and by the autumn the SA faced a crisis of confidence which the KPD was quick to exploit. Focusing on Hitler's apparent failure to seize power by electoral means, Communist propaganda declared: 'The November 6 election result should have made clear to every SA man that the "legal takeover" with the desired 51 per cent [of Reichstag seats] is finished for good.'[88] The KPD continued that the Nazi Party's policy of fighting elections to win power had already driven many stormtroopers into the Communist ranks, now the rest should follow.[89]

The authorities, too, noted that radical activism had assumed extreme forms within the SA and feared that should the NSDAP lose the July 1932 election an SA uprising might follow. Before the elections the army made preparations accordingly: 'On Monday an order went out from the Army Command to the military districts; in certain circumstances local actions and some uprisings by the SA can be expected in connection with the election.'[90] The authorities in the Palatinate expressed similar fears before the election,[91] whilst the police elsewhere in Bavaria remained alert to the possibility of such an uprising several days after the election.[92] By October the danger appeared to have passed without serious incident, but the Bavarian police noted that the ordinary stormtroopers were not prepared to indulge in a long-term struggle for electoral success.[93]

Therefore, the SA's violence was not entirely mindless. The immediate political objective considered necessary by Williams was, in this case, the destruction of Weimar and the motivation for the stormtroopers' activism lay in the devastating economic slump for which the SA blamed Weimar.

Hitler's accession to power both provided sufficient short-term gratification for most veteran stormtroopers and attracted simultaneously a flood of new recruits. However, many stormtroopers, new and old, regarded the takeover as the prerequisite for the eradication of Weimar's visible institutional and socio-economic structure, even if they lacked any clear plan of action for this second revolution. Most gradually lost heart during 1933 as this revolution failed to materialise, but some radical fringe groups condemned Hitler's apparent compromise with the existing social and political system from the outset. They regarded this compromise as evidence enough that there was to be no 'second revolution' and as a Munich group wrote: 'Hitler and his supporters have been given the role of an anti-Communist dam by the capitalist exploitative system.'[94] The group continued that the duplicity of the Nazi leadership 'could not satisfy the working-class circles within the NSDAP' and that 'the impossibility of realising the heterogeneous Party Programme must, without doubt, revenge itself on the leadership'.[95] The use of left-wing terminology by some stormtroopers in this way reflected partly the presence of some former Communists in the SA, partly the presence of Communists hoping to subvert the SA, but also the realisation by parts of the SA that this terminology went some way towards expressing their grievances and even their interests.

However, as in the late Weimar era, action rather than political philosophising characterised the stormtroopers' way of expressing outrage with their poverty and the unemployment which had blighted their lives. This action was not always directed at targets within Germany. In border areas where territorial losses after the First World War or subsequent German territorial ambitions made the border contentious, SA violence or the threat of violence could occur. In eastern Germany the SA was, in any case, intimately involved in an official border protection scheme, the Grenzschutz,[96] and this seems to have encouraged autonomous SA measures against Poland. On 14 April 1933 the commander of the Silesian SA, Heines, hardly a pacifist in his own right, banned the carrying of weapons and the holding of marches within two kilometres of the Polish border because of SA attacks on Polish frontier patrols.[97] The Prussian government subsequently reinforced this measure on 26 April by banning the wearing of SA, SS or Stahlhelm uniforms within ten kilometres of the Polish border in East Prussia, Silesia and the Grenzmark Posen.[98] At the other end of the country, the Bavarian Political Police discovered plans in June 1933 by persons unknown to invade Austria. Although there was a mysterious absence of leaders, it was 'none the less certain that a large proportion of SA units in the foothills of the Alps became involved in the plan with the utmost enthusiasm'.[99]

The Response of the Leadership

The SA's leaders therefore faced a dual problem with their membership: ideological heterogeneity or indifference and an extreme form of radical activism which could serve the NSDAP well, but often threatened to run out of control. From early on SA leaders understood that the somewhat fluid membership of their expanding organisation was not being converted ideologically to Nazism or even the SA's brand of it. In August 1931 Röhm complained:

The SA is the activist wing of the National Socialist movement. Only those who are ideologically committed to a cause can fight unquestioningly for it. Therefore every SA man must understand the ideological foundations and the aims of our movement. This understanding is still widely lacking, as can be gathered from many observations.[100]

During the same summer, SA leaders tried to remedy the situation. In Prussia the police observed that recruits were undergoing careful screening in probationary units before joining the SA proper. However, the police believed that progress with ideological education was limited – perhaps the diverse and sometimes almost contradictory nature of Nazi ideology itself did little to help – and that existing SA units were deeply discontented, ideologically speaking.[101] During 1932 the SA suffered recurrent ideological crises which, combined with the stormtroopers' growing susceptibility to Communist influence,[102] left the leadership without an ideologically coherent SA before Hitler's takeover.

If the unstable and often expanding membership of the pre-1933 era added to the leadership's problems, the veritable flood of recruits from a wide range of social and political backgrounds after the takeover further destabilised matters. Although the SA possessed an intelligence service to observe developments, systematic control of personnel seldom extended beyond the appointment of leaders.[103] The subsequent execution of some of these in 1934, combined with the release or dismissal of others, suggests that not even this operation was an unqualified success.

This same purge provided the NSDAP and the SA's surviving leaders with an opportunity to remedy matters. On 6 July, while senior SA leaders were still being eliminated, the new SA Chief of Staff, Lutze, stressed in an interview with the *Frankfurter Oder-Zeitung* the importance of moulding the SA into 'a politically reliable instrument of the [NS] movement'.[104] This view was reinforced by one of his staff in *Der SA-Mann* on 17 October 1934:

> The growth of the movement after the takeover of power in 1933 brought men into the Brown Army who did not fulfil the requirements to fight for our Leader's Idea.
>
> Unacceptable conditions, created by a multiplicity of individual instances necessitated a clean-up, which indeed began on 1 August 1934.[105]

The implicit praise of the pre-1933 SA was, at best, generous but, in any case, from August 1934 the political re-education of the stormtroopers proceeded systematically. The orders initiating this process stressed, and thereby confirmed the existence of, past shortcomings. Battalion III/25 of Altötting, Upper Bavaria, wrote in November 1934:

> If we wish to achieve the tasks set by the Leader, very intensive political schooling is necessary. Therefore I request the *Sturmführer* to

make every effort to achieve this goal. Schooling may only be carried out by personnel who can be relied on to see that SA men do actually absorb something of National Socialism.[106]

Ideological education was moderately successful during 1935. In August tests carried out in units around Speyer revealed that over half the stormtroopers had attained an adequate or good ideological grounding.[107] Similarly, the Gestapo in Dortmund reported, in the same month, that the previously neglected ideological schooling of the SA had made great strides 'since the cleaning up of, and reduction in size of the SA'.[108] The report hoped that the SA would thereby 'again become an unreservedly reliable instrument in the Leader's hands',[109] although it neglected to name any period when this had been so!

Der SA-Mann was regarded as a vital medium for ideological training and every effort was made to increase its circulation within the SA. In April 1934 (before the Röhm purge) Brigade 155, Hohenlohe-Odenwald set a target of 25 to 30 per cent for subscriptions from its membership, at a time when subscription rates in its nine regiments averaged 10·44 per cent.[110] In October 1935 Group Hansa demanded that each *Schar* receive at least one copy of *Der SA-Mann*, and that 'every SA man who can afford it is to order the paper'.[111] Overall circulation figures for the paper, extending from January 1932 to beyond 1935, demonstrate the campaign's success. Circulation rose faster than membership until spring 1934 and went on to peak at 505,145 in March 1935 despite the decline in SA membership. The subsequent fall in circulation lagged behind the drop in membership, indicating the paper's continued growth in popularity.[112]

Thus only with the consolidation of the Nazi state and the massive cutbacks in the SA after the Röhm purge did the SA begin to resemble an ideologically reliable formation. Ironically, this achievement post-dated the period when the SA performed its critically important role within the Nazi movement. Consequently, when the SA was rendering its vital contribution to the success of Nazism through the destabilisation of Weimar and the physical elimination of left-wing and many Catholic organisations after the takeover, relatively few stormtroopers were convinced Nazis.

This ideologically inchoate body was very valuable to Nazism largely because its leaders harnessed the organisation's ideologically unifying strand – its radical activism, with which they had some sympathy. This was not an easy task, for the stormtroopers' radicalism arose from a very different social and political milieu from that of their leaders. Consequently, the danger always existed that the SA would simply fly apart. In July 1931 the SA's Inspector General warned that 'the grumbling of the activists about the persistent declarations of legality, which they either do not or will not understand', had greatly depressed morale.[113]

Provincial SA leaders also noted the radical pressure from below throughout the closing years of Weimar. For instance, the commander of Sub-Group Westfalen feared in August 1932 that anti-SA measures by the police would rile his impatient following. He warned that the police chiefs of Dortmund and Bochum were cracking down on the SA and that:

> Within the SA, so strong a fury has arisen because of these conditions that events could occur at any moment which are not in accordance with the movement's ideals. Everyone who understands the characteristics of the industrial-SA knows that even the toughest leader can do nothing against this.[114]

Similar reports of frustration, often coupled with reports of collapsing morale, were written by leaders all around Germany in the second half of 1932. Hitler's failure to win an absolute majority in the July Reichstag elections was decisive when, despite the apparently boundless energy and enthusiasm of both SA and party workers, the NSDAP won only around 37 per cent of the votes cast. The feeling grew both within and outside the Nazi movement that this was the high-tide mark. Despite the subsequent collapse of the Papen government and the announcement of a further election, many SA units were simply losing heart. The situation was especially serious in Franconia, where entire SA units and individual stormtroopers had borrowed heavily to assist in the final push for power in the mistaken belief that a Nazi victory would cover their debts.[115] Disappointment expressed itself partly through falling recruitment rates and rising desertion rates which, in Franconia, included an increase in 'transfers to the KPD from the ranks of the SA'.[116] Things were no better in Silesia, where the Upper Silesian SA had lost all faith in elections:

> The SA will work in the coming election campaign with the deepest misgivings. The SA is ready to march and the great majority is convinced that it would be a trifle to conquer the state.
> The Upper Silesian SA awaits the Leader's order to march.[117]

The overall mood was little better, with widespread antipathy to the conservative government threatening to erupt in violence. Many SA commanders only countered this by occupying their men with SA duties whenever possible.[118] Although most stormtroopers welcomed the collapse of negotiations between Hitler and Papen, in which Papen had proposed that he remain as Chancellor and that Hitler deliver his votes in the Reichstag as Vice-Chancellor,[119] and although many welcomed the further election subsequently announced,[120] this was insufficient compensation for their frustration. SA members both desperately wanted and felt they needed a decisive Nazi success.[121] Group South-West reported that 'the SA men ... are awaiting a decision of some sort',[122] a message repeated by many groups, including Thüringen.[123] The commander of Sub-Group Brunswick recognised the link between his members' wish for an activist solution to the political stalemate and their economic desperation.[124] Similarly the commander of Sub-Group Baden wrote:

> I have heard how, as a high-ranking leader said, 'We can wait quietly for everything', the SA men said among themselves: 'Yes, they can right enough, they've still got food to guzzle, but we've almost had enough of starving.'[125]

Only in Sub-Groups East Hanover and Göttingen was morale still virtually unaffected by the election result, and it is instructive that in both these areas the commanders ensured that their men were fully occupied. In Hanover energy was devoted to 'training and field tactics',[126] whilst in Göttingen confrontation with the 'bourgeois clique' and the Stahlhelm was absorbing excess energy.[127]

The leadership's fears were confirmed by sources outside the Nazi movement. The Communist activist Scheringer, himself a former Nazi, well understood that appeals to the stormtroopers' radical sentiment might win them for the Communist cause as early as 1931.[128] In November 1931 the SPD-oriented *Münchner Post* noted that the SA's leadership was simulating purposeful activity to dampen down discontent within the organisation:

> There is unrest in Hitler's private army. Thus Hitler's watchword to the SA; don't lose your nerve at the eleventh hour. Thus the extraordinary activity within the SA Command, so as to awaken the feeling among the Praetorians that the balloon will go up tomorrow, or the day after.[129]

In October 1932 reports by the same newspaper agreed with official circles that attempts to maintain SA morale were failing.[130] Röhm reportedly responded to the deteriorating situation by pursuing a more activist course and by urging Hitler to abandon his policy of legality.[131] As the *Münchner Post* remarked: 'He justified his swing to illegality on the grounds that the SA and SS could not be held intact any longer by the existing policies.'[132]

The leadership's reaction to this radicalism was never straightforward. They sought to avoid too violent an upsurge of radical activism from below which, before 1933, might have prejudiced the Nazi movement's fortunes, but they recognised that if harnessed and channelled in the right way, this radicalism and the accompanying sense of commitment was invaluable to the Nazi movement. Added to this, while most SA leaders were men of the right and did not share the stormtroopers' abject poverty, they, too, were radicals. Although their view of political developments was slightly more realistic than their men's, they were torn frequently between taking a purist radical stance and working within the constraints laid down by Hitler.

Before Hitler became Chancellor, SA leaders often were able to channel their men's radical zeal into the NSDAP's assault on the republic. The SA's organisation on military lines,[133] the training of SA members in combat techniques and the use of firearms,[134] their frequent deployment in violent situations,[135] both served to satisfy and actually reinforce the stormtroopers' radicalism. Rabble-rousing speeches and proclamations pandered to, and whipped up, radical sentiment still further: 'It is our duty to see that the "System" does not recover from this battle',[136] or, 'Should such a procession not be allowed in Bavaria ... , then the SA would have to take to the streets in uniform on its own account and thus initiate a trial of strength'[137] being typical.

However, the High Command and most provincial leaders largely respected Hitler's policy of legality, and during the early 1930s worked to contain their following's impatience. In July 1931 the Prussian police observed that in the SA 'almost all leadership positions are being filled with people who work completely in accordance with the new party line and remain loyal to Hitler',[138] while southern German SA leaders were similarly loyal to the party line.[139] Perhaps the shock of the Stennes Revolt had pulled loyal leaders more closely into line, but throughout 1932 they still sought to keep their following's activism within acceptable limits. For instance, stormtroopers and party members were warned in April to ignore left-wing provocation,[140] while in August a Munich SA company was warned that any violence would probably result in punishment by the state authorities.[141] As morale deteriorated in October, Röhm sought to restrain attacks on DNVP meetings, because of their counter-productiveness and because they risked provoking the authorities: 'For every German National meeting attacked, the Reich Commissioner for Prussia, Dr Bracht, intends to ban an NSDAP meeting in the same area.'[142]

Even so, the latent tension between the anti-parliamentarian SA leadership and the party during the final years of Weimar sometimes came into the open. Röhm himself declared revealingly on 4 August 1932 that 'too many parliamentarians are a curse'.[143] Some leaders' violently radical utterances may have been intended partly for the ears of their impatient membership. For instance, the SA leader von Killinger denounced the policy of legality and the misdemeanours of capitalism in Magdeburg in March 1932:

Hitler must finally become Reich President. If all else fails, this must be achieved by revolutionary means . . . The banks must be nationalised. Whoever speculates in shares will be executed. Once a dozen men hang from the lamp posts, the cheating will stop. Nazism means hate, and still more hate.[144]

Other leaders also spoke for themselves when making their loyalty to the policy of legality conditional upon its success. By autumn 1932 a combination of rank-and-file pressure and their own misgivings led this group openly to demand violent change. In October 1932 the Baden SA's commander, Ludin, reportedly demanded that the NSDAP 'finally put an end to the policy of legality', continuing that, 'the shaping of politics with the gun is certainly terrible, [but] if the hour arrives when we must take the illegal road in the national interest, the SA will grasp victory in Germany'.[145] Similarly, the deputy and SA leader Merker threatened the government at a Nazi meeting in Alt Reetz, East Prussia, on 4 November 1932, simultaneously expressing disdain for the Stahlhelmer present:

You are protecting the Papen/Schleicher government. I only hope you don't experience the same fate at Schleicher's hands as we did. We don't fear him any more. We are ready with a million rifles. We will see a revolution after 6 November [election day] which we shall launch together with the Communists.[146]

The willingness of some impatient radicals to make common cause with the KPD should not be overlooked. For them, upheaval apparently ranked higher than ideological purity.[147]

Some leaders became involved in activist conspiracies away from the immediate pressures of public speaking. In autumn 1931 senior figures in both the Hessian party and the SA planned a rising[148] which was eventually betrayed by one of their number to the authorities.[149] This plot, dubbed the Boxheim Plans after the farming estate on which it was conceived, was condemned by much of the press for its brutality and its allegedly communist tendencies.[150] It envisaged handing ultimate state power to the SA, who would enforce day-to-day order through the death penalty, abolishing the money economy and private property, and their replacement by a rationing ticket system to cover the distribution of accommodation, food and clothing.[151] A police raid on an SA hostel in Schneidemühle, Pomerania, in December 1931 uncovered similar plans.[152] After the Röhm purge it was alleged that Heines, when commander of the Silesian SA, contemplated a rising shortly before the November 1932 election, when even the Munich Command was gripped by doubts over the policy of legality.[153] Written orders also frequently revealed the equivocal line adopted by some leaders. Heines's name arises again, for while demanding 'discipline and propriety' of his men, he exhorted them simultaneously with the words: 'If you are attacked defend yourselves with all means available.'[154]

Occasionally SA leaders lost patience completely with Hitler's policy of legality, and then the rebelling leaders either supported or purported to support their following's own activist sentiments. The Stennes Revolt of April 1931 was the most spectacular example of this,[155] although many SA commanders who supported Stennes, in principle, remained loyal to Röhm and Hitler in practice, and hence remained loyal to the policy of legality. Like many radical groups in German society, whether of the right or the left, the Stennes group rejected middle-class values and ideals,[156] especially Western liberalism:

> The bourgeois, consumed by the Western spirit of liberalism and infecting all sections of the population with whom he comes into contact (embourgeoisment of the working-class movement!) is almost a greater enemy to us than the political West, under whose imperialism and exploitative capitalism we find ourselves. This is because he joins us as a fellow countryman and begins to weaken the front from within.[157]

Unlike prewar movements, but more in the spirit of the Freikorps and the KPD during the early 1920s, the Stennes group regarded active resistance to the state and its institutions as integral to its ideology and condemned the Nazi Party for its compromises with the parliamentary system:

> All [the party's] measures against the SA in conjunction with the Political Office's proclamations: the pitiful legality twaddle, the coalition feelers with the once so despised, bourgeois parties, the links with Rome [the Church] . . . , demonstrate clearly to the SA the change in political direction and in goals.[158]

Similarly, impatience with the wearisome and indecisive run of elections contributed to the Stegmann Revolt of January 1933 in Franconia.[159]

When the *SA-Mann* celebrated Hitler's appointment as Chancellor with the triumphant words, 'That for which we have fought, starved and bled, our Reich, approaches its fulfilment',[160] it was doubtless speaking for the SA as a whole. However, the stormtroopers' fundamental activism and radicalism was not satisfied by the Nazi successes in spring 1933. At first the authorities were optimistic that the stormtroopers' expectations could be accommodated,[161] but too many stormtroopers demanded the removal of the old order and of various attributes of regulated, bureaucratic life. Precisely these demands were rendered impossible by Hitler's compromise with sections of the existing social and political élites.[162] Even by February 1933 non-fulfilment of the SA's admittedly inarticulate revolutionary aspirations was expected to create trouble. The Lower Franconian police reported:

> It is pointed out by Würzburg police headquarters that the SA and SS commanders have great difficulties with their men. The latter's patience will very probably expire if all that has been promised to them over the years as compensation for their tenacity and loyalty is not fulfilled, at least to a great extent.[163]

Unfulfilled promises combined with a sense of anti-climax as the stormtroopers saw their political enemies disappear from the streets. Their struggle against the existing order had found expression in political violence, and Heinrich Wilkenloh of Hessen-Nassau perhaps summed up the mood of 1933 when later recounting his feelings:

> After the election victory on 5 March those opponents remaining went to ground. We SA men didn't have any adversaries facing us any more. We got the impression that we were superfluous. I felt that too. After April 1933 I had to go through a phase which I can regard as the worst during the years now past.[164]

As they had done before 1933, the leaders reacted equivocally. They discouraged politically embarrassing violence, such as attacks on the police, the occupation of Stahlhelm work camps in mid-1933 and attacks on factories and commercial premises.[165] As Sauer remarks:

> Where SA activities contravened the [Nazi] plan of campaign, the higher echelons were generally able to stop them. Where this did not occur it must be assumed, until proven otherwise, that basically, the Brown Mobs' undertakings accorded with their leaders' intentions.[166]

This principle appears to hold good. The SA frequently contravened party policy and the stormtroopers contravened their leaders' policies, but these incidents tended to be spontaneous. Unlike the assault on the political left during early 1933, this uncoordinated violence was usually resolved relatively swiftly. Only in 1934 did the cumulative pressure of these outbreaks, combined with the SA leadership's political ambitions, become a threat to Hitler's overall strategy. Furthermore, although Röhm supported the arming of some SA units,[167] and although the confiscation of SA weapons after the 1934 purge revealed that almost all units acquired some firearms,[168] he opposed the bearing of firearms in public[169] and ordered that socio-economic needs take precedence over weapons. 'When sums of money are made available to the SA, they are not for purchasing superfluous weapons, but to finish uniforming and equipping penniless comrades.'[170]

Even so, from Röhm downwards the leaders still expressed radical feelings after Hitler's takeover, and sometimes egged their men on, at least verbally. In part, the leaders perceived the opportunity of exploiting rank-and-file radicalism for their own ends, including their military ambitions. In addition, Röhm's distaste for ordered life rose unmistakably to the surface when he realised that the policy of legality had brought Hitler to power without revolutionising the structure of society and political life in the cathartic way he desired. In September 1933, for instance, he reacted sharply to a campaign to clean up German morals, declaring: 'The SA's task does not include watching over people's clothing, makeup and chastity, but lies in arousing Germany through its free and revolutionary fighting ideology ... '[171]

This incident was partially symptomatic of Röhm's radicalism but, in addition, was prompted possibly by his difficult personal circumstances created by his homosexuality. By mid-1934, however, the fundamental opposition of Röhm and his entourage to the course events were taking made itself plain through overtly political outbursts. In May 1934 Röhm rejected any stagnation of the Nazi revolution:

> I regard the present situation with concern. Experience shows that sure enough, a certain stagnation sets in during revolutions after the first big rush.
> It is simply a question of the vanguard of the revolution, the fighting troops, stopping and overcoming this stagnation.
> ... The danger of the SA and SS being used purely as a propaganda troop is not to be ignored.
> I request that ... the soldierly ethic be emphatically brought to the fore once again.[172]

The SA leadership generally prided itself on being a populist revolutionary cadre (even if its aims differed from their following's) and for this reason, too, it opposed the growing accommodation between Hitler and conservative circles. In June 1934 the SA Central Office remarked:

> The reactionary ordering of society still exists, contrasting with the revolutionary popular will (and hence also with the SA). It is hoped that the Führer will one day call on the 'socialists', Reventlow, Gregor Strasser and Stöhr, to replace the 'capitalists', Göring, Schacht and Thyssen, the former then accomplishing true National Socialism along with Feder, Röhm and Hess. Should the Führer

not fulfil this hope, then the crisis of confidence would also extend to him personally.[173]

The articulation of such conditional loyalty to Hitler ceased with the Röhm purge, and efforts to calm sporadic violence and radical feeling became more thorough[174] except, occasionally, in the field of industrial relations.[175]

Therefore, the SA's leaders occupied a position between the party and their own membership. Both SA leaders and men were radical activists, and this was probably the strongest bond between them, but their contrasting socio-economic and political backgrounds lent their brands of radicalism a different content and direction. With the crucial exception of the army question, the leaders could agree with the party on many, if not all, political issues and therefore usually restrained their men's activism when it threatened the overall movement's interests. The Communist newspaper *Neue Zeitung* remarked on this tendency in September 1930 when writing: 'A sharp, class-based contradiction has developed between the misused proletarian and lower-middle-class SA men, on the one hand, and the Nazi leaders . . . on the other',[176] under which heading it included the SA's leaders.[177] The KPD must have been more than aggrieved that the SA leaders' political juggling act succeeded until Hitler was firmly in power. The purge of the SA in 1934 served to resolve this complex of tensions, but by then could be presented as a return to normality – the curbing of SA ambition and lawlessness – rather than as a setback to Nazism.

Notes

1 A. Milatz, *Wähler und Wahlen in der Weimarer Republik* (Bonn, 1968), p. 151.
2 ibid.
3 K. Rohe, *Das Reichsbanner Schwarz Rot Gold* (Stuttgart, 1965), pp. 224–6.
4 W. Sauer, *Die Mobilmachung der Gewalt*, Vol. 3 of K. D. Bracher, G. Schulz and W. Sauer, *Die Nationalsozialistische Machtergreifung* (Frankfurt-am-Main, Berlin and Vienna, 1974), chs 3 and 4.
5 K. D. Bracher, *The German Dictatorship* (London, 1973), pp. 300–1, 424; M. Broszat, *Der Staat Hitlers* (Munich, 1969), pp. 256–7; C. Bloch, *Die SA und die Krise den NS-Regimes 1934* (Frankfurt-am-Main, 1970), p. 70; H. Bennecke, *Hitler und die SA* (Munich, 1962), p. 151. Röhm discussed his views and earlier career in his autobiography published in 1933: E. Röhm, *Die Geschichte eines Hochverräters* (Munich, 1933).
6 Bloch, *SA*, p. 47.
7 *SA-Mann*, year 3, no. 17, 28 April 1934, p. 2.
8 ibid., year 2, no. 50, 16 December 1933, p. 1.
9 ibid., year 2, no 40, 7 October 1933, p. 5.
10 ibid., year 3, no 17, 28 April 1934, p. 4.
11 ibid., p. 1.
12 M. H. Kele, *Nazis and Workers* (Chapel Hill, NC, 1972), p. 143.

13 A. Werner, 'SA and NSDAP' (Dissertation, Friedrich Alexander Universität zu Erlangen, 1964), p. 590.
14 Sauer, *Die Mobilmachung der Gewalt* (see note 4), p. 259. Author's interview with Stennes, 14 May 1974 confirmed this. According to Stennes, he and Röhm met secretly in 1932. Röhm had become disillusioned with Hitler and wished to work for a monarchist Bavaria while offering to finance Stennes in working for a monarchist Prussia: 'I am blue-white, you are black-white.' Stennes distrusted Röhm because of his association with Hitler and turned down the offer.
15 A. Schweitzer, *Big Business in the Third Reich* (London, 1964), p. 35.
16 W. S. Allen, *The Nazi Seizure of Power* (Chicago, 1965), p. 51.
17 Bloch, *SA*, p. 46.
18 ibid., p. 145.
19 R. J. Bessel, 'Militarismus im innenpolitischen Leben der Weimarer Republik: Von den Freikorps zur SA', in K. -J. Müller and E. Opitz (eds), *Militär und Militarismus in der Weimarer Republik* (Düsseldorf, 1978), pp. 193–222.
20 J. Fest, *The Face of the Third Reich*, (London, 1972), p. 218.
21 ibid., p. 223.
22 See p. 206.
23 Fest, *Third Reich*, p. 220.
24 O. E. Schüddekopf, *Linke Leute von rechts. Die nationalrevolutionären Minderheiten und der Kommunismus in der Weimarer Republik* (Stuttgart, 1960), p. 375.
25 E. Rosenhaft, 'Working-class life and working-class politics: Communists, Nazis and the state in the battle for the streets, Berlin 1928–1932', in R. J. Bessel and E. J. Feuchtwanger (eds), *Social Change and Political Development in Weimar Germany* (London, 1981), pp. 207–40.
26 R. Diels, *Lucifer ante Portas* (Zurich, 1949), pp. 157–8.
27 ibid., p. 154.
28 ibid., pp. 155, 157–8. However, Diels is content to define the SA as revolutionary because of the mass criminality displayed by the body, especially in early 1933: ibid., p. 152.
29 *Weissbuch über die Erschiessungen des 30. Juni 1934* (Paris, 1935), p. 35.
30 ibid., pp. 45–8.
31 ibid., p. 49.
32 ibid., pp. 56–7.
33 ibid., p. 35.
34 K. Bredow, *Hitlerrast* (Saarbrücken, 1935), p. 27.
35 ibid., pp. 34–5.
36 BA, NS23/400. NSDAP, SA-Gruppe Nord, Abt. Ib, B.B. Nr. 1 802/31. Betr.: Bekleidung und Ausrüstung der SA. Hannover, den 9.11.31. gez. Lutze.
37 ibid.
38 BA, NS23/398. Untergruppe Hamburg. Tagesbefehl 3: Judenboycott. Hamburg, den 11.4.1933. gez. Böckenhauer; BA, NS23/125. OSAF IV Nr. 1240/33. Betr.: Einkauf bei jüdischen Firmen. München, den 3.6.33.
39 BA, NS23/262. SA der NSDAP, Brigade 50 (Starkenburg). Lagebericht: Berichtszeit, 15. August bis 15. Dezember 1934. Darmstadt, den 17.12.1934.
40 NWHStA, Ge 46,688. R. S., born 1899, res. Essen, occ. electrician, father's occ. unknown.
41 NWHStA, Ge 30,169. P. M., born 1893, res. Krefeld, occ. plumber, father's occ. unknown.
42 NWHStA, Ge 42,365s, 19,368.
43 BA, NS23/349. SA der NSDAP. Der Führer der Gruppe Hansa. Tagesbefehl! Hamburg, 26.9.1935. gez. Fust.
44 HHW, Abt. 483/NSDAP 2199. Sturmmann Karl Stenger, born 1911, res. Frankfurt-am-Main, occ. worker, father's occ. packer.
45 HHW, Abt. 483/NSDAP 2188. Ausführungen des SAA und Pg. Wilhelm

Schecker, Frankfurt M. zu der ihm gestellten Frage: Warum wurde ich SA Mann? Frankfurt M., den 15. Oktober 1933.

46 HHW, Abt. 483/NSDAP 2149. SA man Fritz Kleinhenz, born?, res. Frankfurt-am-Main, occ. worker, father's occ. municipal worker. 'Warum bin ich in die SA?' Frankfurt-am-Main, Niederrad, 16 November 33.

47 HHW, Abt. 483/NSDAP 2194. SA man Ludwig Schucherd, born 1904, res. Frankfurt-am-Main, occ. worker, father's occ. unknown. Personal Recollections. Frankfurt-am-Main, 12 July 1933.

48 BDC, SA 797. SA man Hermann Feige, born 1885, res. Oberröblingen a/S., Bavaria, occ. worker, father's occ. unknown. Personal Recollections.

49 BDC, SA 857. Truppführer Roman Fischer, born 1900, res. Ansbach, occ. salaried employee, father's occ. notary's clerk. Personal Recollections.

50 BDC, SA 794. SA man Christian Fehr, born 1910, res. Wollrode, Hessen, occ. farmer's son. Personal Recollections.

51 Thus: BDC, SA 814. Sturmmann Ernst Feucht, Jr, born 1914, res. Korntal, occ. joiner (in family business), father's occ. master joiner. Personal Recollections; NWHStA, RW 23. Sturmmann Johann Mohren, born 1902, res. Würselen, occ. coal miner, father's occ. coal miner. Personal Recollections; NWHStA, RW 23. SA man Severin Errenst, born 1914, res. Würselen, occ. electrician, father's occ. electrical mounter. Personal Recollections; NWHStA, RW 23. Sturmmann Josef Giltz, born 1908, res. Würselen, occ. technician, father's occ. police officer. Personal Recollections; NWHStA, RW 23. SA man Hubert Errenst, (brother of Severin, E.), born 1912, res. Würselen, occ. trained as fitter (Maschinenfabrik H. J. Schmitz) worked as mine worker, Goulay pit. Father's occ. electrical mounter. Personal Recollections; BDC, SA 868. SA man Ulrich Fleiner, born 1915, res. Augsburg, occ. agricultural student, father's occ. farmer. Personal Recollections; BDC, SA 870. SA man Franz Fleischmann, born 1909, res. Regensburg, occ. junior barrister, father's occ. doctor. Personal Recollections; BDC, SA 799. SA man Georg Feinauer, born 1916, res. Petersdorf, Franconia, occ. farm labourer, father's occ. tailor. Personal Recollections; BDC, SA 849. SA man Jakob Fischer, born 1915, res. Zellbrüglingen, Franconia, occ. farm labourer, father's occ. unknown. Personal Recollections; BDC, SA 820. SA man Martin Fiedling, born 1912, res. Berlin, occ. metal worker (at Lorenz A. G.), father's occ. tailor. Personal Recollections; BDC, SA 825. SA man Andreas Fink, born 1902, res. Nenzenheim, Franconia, occ. farmer, father's occ. farmer. Personal Recollections.

52 NWHStA, Ge 34,434. SA man J. H., born 1886, res. Essen, occ. fitter (Krupp), father's occ. unknown.

53 NWHStA, RW 23. SA probationer Hans Funken, born 1913, res. Würselen, occ. office clerk, father's occ. sample weaver. Personal Recollections.

54 HHW, Abt. 483/NSDAP 2204. SA man Heinrich Vollberg, born 1912, res. Frankfurt-am-Main, occ. worker, father's occ. worker. Personal Recollections. Frankfurt-am-Main, 31 October 1933.

55 BA, NS23/376. Standarte 76. Standartenbefehl Nr. 4. Verbotene Lieder. Hamburg, den 12.5.1931.

56 NWHStA, Ge 46,478. J. F., born 1906, res. Essen, occ. worker, father's occ. unknown.

57 BHStA, Abt. I, So. I/1554A. Polizeidirektion, Ref. VIa F. 1429/31. Betreff: Stegmaier, Georg, led. Schreiner, geb. 14.8.1910. München, den 7.7.31.

58 BHStA, Abt. I, So. I/1554A. Polizeidirektion, Ref. VIa F. 2729/30. München, den 20. Dez. 1931.

59 HHW, Abt. 483/NSDAP 2241. SA man Josef Kinateder, born 1909, res. Niederursel, Hessen-Nassau, occ. farmworker, father's occ. unknown. Personal Recollections.

60 HHW, Abt. 483/NSDAP 2171. Rottenführer Franz Noth, born ?, res. Frankfurt-am-Main, occ. worker, father's occ. unknown. 'Warum wurde ich SA-Mann?'

61   BDC, SA 812. Geheime Staatspolizei, Staatspolizeistelle Würzburg. Würzburg, den 22.7.1938. Fessel, Wilhelm Georg, verh., Schumacher, geb. 15.10.1904 in Würzburg, Sohn des Arbeiterseheleute Wilhelm und Franziska ...

62   R. N. Hunt, *German Social Democracy, 1918–1933* (Chicago, 1970), pp. 101–2; S. Neumann, *Die Parteien der Weimarer Republik* (Stuttgart, Berlin, Cologne and Mainz, 1965), p. 88.

63   BDC, SA 829. SA man Gustav Finkbeiner, born, 1908, res. Pforzheim, occ. mechanic, father's occ. driver. Personal Recollections.

64   HHW, Abt. 483/NSDAP 2267. SA man Adolf Selig, born ?, res. Frankfurt-am-Main, occ. building joiner. 'Warum trat ich in die SA ein?'

65   HHW, Abt. 483/NSDAP 2539. SA probationer Heinrich Weimann, born 1902, res. Frankfurt-am-Main, occ. fireman (formerly fitter), father's occ. bookbinder. Personal Recollections. Frankfurt-am-Main, 17 September 1933.

66   HHW, Abt. 483/NSDAP 2215. SA probationer Wilhelm Desheimer, born 1903, res. Frankfurt-am-Main, occ. worker, father's occ. worker. 'Warum gehe ich zur SA'.

67   HHW, Abt. 483/NSDAP 2540. SA probationer August Wenzel, born 1915, res. Frankfurt-am-Main, occ. apprentice (German Railways), father's occ. packer. Personal Recollections. Frankfurt-am-Main, 4 September 1933.

68   HHW, Abt. 483/NSDAP 2277. SA probationer Herm. Theisen, born 1909, res. Frankfurt-am-Main, occ. electrical mounter (Firma Karl Diehl), father's occ. compositor. Personal Recollections.

69   See pp. 158–9, 193–5.

70   BDC, SA 852. Karl Fischer, born 1911, res. Stockhausen, Hessen, occ. joiner, father's occ. miller.

71   HHW, Abt. 483/NSDAP 2235. SA man Richard Hock, born 1913, res. Frankfurt-am-Main, occ. worker, father's occ. factory worker. 'Warum trat ich in die SA ein?'.

72   SM, NSDAP 792. Sturm 24/25, Trupp IV. Trupp Befehl. 13. Juni 1934.

73   IfZ, MA 131, 3545–3629 (SA III – Mitgliederwesen). SA Standarten 132, 203, 199 u.a. an zuständ. Polizeistellen, Aug. 1934–Juni 1937. Ausschlüsse aus d. SA m. Namen und Begrundungen.

74   SM, NSDAP 803. SA Sturmbann II/4, Sturm 17/4, Neuötting. Stärkemeldungen.

75   HHW, Abt. 483/NSDAP 2522–2524, 2100–2213, 2214–2284 (SA Regiments 25, 81 and 99). Reasons for leaving: 22·9% for reasons of health; 17·8% because of the 'reduction in size of the SA'; 14·4% to join the labour service; 14·1% because of the demands of their jobs (shift-work, etc.); 11·9% because of their failings in SA service; 5·9% to join the army; 3·5% 'at their own request'; 1·9% because of poverty; 1·6% because of party commitments; 1·5% because of membership of the police; 1·0% because of membership of the fire brigade; 0·6% for political reasons; 0·5% because of death; 2·4% for other reasons.

76   W. Böhnke, *Die NSDAP im Ruhrgebiet, 1920–1933* (Bonn–Bad Godesberg, 1974), p. 154.

77   See pp. 145–6.

78   See pp. 13, 18–19, 51–2.

79   HHW, Abt. 483/NSDAP 2119. SA man Adolf Fischer, born 1912, res. Frankfurt-am-Main, occ. fitter, father's occ. worker. Personal Recollections.

80   IfZ, MA 616/20, 73796–73819 (SA III – Ausschreitungen). Incidents in which SA members were either killed or injured, June–October 1932. See p. 115 and Chapter 5, note 43.

81   BHStA, Abt. I, M. Inn./73721. Report of the Prussian Ministry of the Interior, 8 January 1929, concerning political violence and other activities, pp. 5–6.

82   BHStA, Abt. I, M. Inn/73721. Sachsen, Polizeibericht, III. Zusammenstösse (Jan.–Sept. 1928).

83   BA, NS26/523. Aufstellung der beim Kommando befindlichen Unterlagen aus der Kampfzeit der NS-Bewegung.

84 BA, NS26/522. Aufstellung. Betrifft: Sammlung geschichtlicher Unterlagen aus der Kampfzeit der nationalsozialistischen Bewegung. Altona, den 8. Februar 1937.

85 GStAM, MA 100426. Zu Nr. 2013g.11. Übersicht über die in Bayern in der Zeit vom 1. Januar bis 31. Dezember 1931 verübten politischen Gewalttaten.

86 W. E. Williams, 'Versuch einer Definition paramilitärischer Organisationen', in V. R. Berghahn (ed.), *Militarismus*, (Cologne, 1975), pp. 141–2.

87 BA, NS26/315. *Front-Appell. Zeitschrift der oppositionellen Mitglieder der NSDAP (SA und SS)*, Nr. 2, München, Februar '32.

88 BA, NS26/315. *Sturmbanner. Sprachrohr der revolutionären SA und SS Kameraden*, Nr. 1, Ende November 1932, p. 1.

89 ibid.

90 BA, R45IV/24. Politische Gesamtübersicht (Staatsstreich in Preussen). Zusammenfassung der – zum Teil mündlich gegebenen – Einzelberichte, p. 3.

91 BHStA, Abt. I, So. I/1774. Abdruck. Amtsvorstand. Bezirksamt Bergzabern. Betreff: Vorbereitungen der NSDAP für den Wahltag. Bergzabern, den 27. Juli 1932.

92 BHStA, Abt. I, So. I/1774. Polizeibericht. München 3.8.32.

93 BA, Sch 404. Aus dem Lagebericht Nr. 112a der Polizei-Direktion München vom 20. Oktober 1932. Militärähnliche Organisationen der NSDAP.

94 GStAM, MA 106670. Nr. 283. Halbmonatsbericht des Regierungs-Präsidiums von Oberbayern (15. mit 31. Januar 1933). München, 6.2.1933.

95 Whether this latter comment stemmed from the authorities or was being attributed by the authorities to the SA group concerned is not clear. Source as for note 94.

96 R. J. Bessel, 'The SA in the Eastern Regions of Germany, 1925 to 1934' (D. Phil., Oxford University, 1980), ch. 4.

97 Geheimstaatsarchiv Berlin-Dahlem (GStABD), Bestand Grauert Rep. 77 (Rep. 77), Nr. 14. Der Gruppenführer Schlesien. Gruppenbefehl Nr. 32. Breslau, den 24. April 1933. gez. Heines.

98 GStABD, Rep. 77, Nr. 14. Entwurf. Telegramm an alle SA, SS und Stahlhelm Formationen von Ostpreussen, Schlesien und Grenzmark, 26.4.[1933].

99 BHStA, Abt. I, So. I/1573. Bayerische Politische Polizei. Bericht über geplanten Einfall von SA- und SS-Formationen nach Tirol. München, den 13. Juni 1933.

100 BA, NS26/306. Der Oberste SA-Führer I Nr. 5156/31. Betrifft: Weltanschauliche und politische Schulung der SA. München, den 31. August 1931. gez. Röhm.

101 BA, NS23/470. Aus den Mitteilungen des Landeskriminalpolizeiamtes (IA), Berlin vom 15. Juli 1931, Nr. 14, p. 3. I. Rechtsradikale Bewegung. 1. NSDAP (a) SA, (aa) Allgemeines und Organisation.

102 BA, NS23/401. Untergruppe Hamburg. Abt. 1c. 15.12.1932; BA, NS23/474. SA der NSDAP. Der Gruppenführer Franken. I Nr. 4 geh. Betrifft: Stimmungsbericht. Schillingsfürst, Mfr., den 21. September 1932. See also Bloch, *SA*, p. 42; F. L. Carsten, *The Reichswehr and Politics 1918–1933* (Oxford, 1966), pp. 377–80.

103 NHStA, Hann. 310 I N10. SA der NSDAP. Führervorschule der Untergruppe Hannover-Ost. Stammrollen Nr. 90 u. 100. Achterberg, den 5. August 1933.

104 BA, NS26/1240. 'Was wird aus der SA? – Unterredung mit dem Chef des Stabes', *Frankfurter Oder-Zeitung*, 6 July 1934.

105 BA, NS23/206. [Cutting] aus Folge 41 vom 13. Oktober 1934 der Zeitschrift *Der SA-Mann*. 'Reinigung der SA'.

106 SM, NSDAP 792. SA der NSDAP, Stuba III/25. An alle Stürme des Stubas III/25. Betreff: Politische Schulung der SA. Altötting, 26. November 1934.

107 LAS, Z 1293 Nr. 11. Trupp Jettenbach. Bewertung der weltanschaulichen Prüfung am 2. August 1935. Trupp A-1 Wolfstein. Bewertung der weltanschaulichen Prüfung am 12. August 1935. Trupp J-SA-Wolfstein. Bewertung der weltanschaulichen Prüfung am 16. August 1935.

108 GStABD, Preussisches Staatsministerium – Gestapo (90P): 83/2. III. Allgemeine Übersicht über die politische Lage im Monat August 1935 im Bezirk der Staatspolzeistelle für den Regierungsbezirk Arnsberg in Dortmund. A. Allgemeines.
109 ibid.
110 GLAK, Abt. 465d/1311. SA Brigade 155, Hohenlohe-Odenwald. Brigade Befehl Nr. 5/34. Heilbronn, den 27. April 1934.
111 BA, NS23/358. SA der NSDAP. Der Führer der Gruppe Hansa. Abtlg. Napo. Pu/ Zy. Besondere Anordnung: Betr.: Werbung für die Zeitschrift *Der SA-Mann*. Hamburg, am 2. Okt. 1935. gez. Fust.
112 BA, NS26/1111. Zeitung, *Der SA-Mann*. Auflageziffern.
113 BHStA, Abt. I, So. I/1545. Abschrift. NSDAP, Der Oberste SA-Führer. Der Generalinspekteur. B.B. Nr. 284/31. Bericht über die Stimmung in der SA (hauptsächlich aus dem Westen und Süden). Kassel, den 22.7.1931. gez. Ulrich.
114 IfZ, Fa 105/106, Blatt 3 (SA III – Verh. z. KPD). NSDAP SA, Gruppe Westfalen. Abteilung Ia. Br. B. Nr. 231/32. An Oberste SA-Führung München. Münster i.W., den 5. August 1932. gez. v. Fichte.
115 BA, NS23/474. SA der NSDAP. Der Gruppenführer Franken. 1 Nr. 4 geh. Betrifft: Stimmungsbericht. Schillingsfürst, Mfr., den 21. September 1932. See also E. G. Reiche, 'The Development of the SA in Nuremberg, 1922 to 1934' (Dissertation, University of Delaware, 1972), pp. 186–204, where he discusses the build up of this crisis to the point where the Franconian SA mutinied in early 1933.
116 BA, NS23/474. SA der NSDAP. Der Gruppenführer Franken. I Nr. 4 geh. Betrifft: Stimmungsbericht. Schillingsfürst, Mfr., den 21. September 1932. (2) Zu- und Abgänge der SA.
117 BA, NS23/474. SA der NSDAP, Untergruppe Oberschlesien. Stimmungsbericht. Oppeln, 22.9.32. p. 2.
118 BA, NS23/474: Gruppe Niederrhein. Stimmungsbericht. Wesel a. Rh., 21.9.32; Untergruppe Essen. An die OSAF München. Essen, den 21.9.1932; SA der NSDAP. Der Gruppenführer Mitte. Stimmungsbericht. Dessau/Anhalt. 22.9.1932; SA der NSDAP. SA-Gruppe Niedersachsen. Stimmungsbericht. Hannover, 22.9.32; SA der NSDAP. Untergruppe Gaust. Hannover Ost. Hermannsburg b. Celle. 23.9.32.
119 BA, NS23/474. Untergruppe Westfalen-Süd. Stimmung der SA. Bochum, den 21.9.32; SA Untergruppe Weser Ems. Stimmung der SA. Oldenburg, 22.9.32. NSDAP. Der Untergruppenführer Chemnitz. Betr.: Stimmungsbericht. Tgb. Nr. 727/32. Chemnitz, 22.9.32.
120 BA, NS23/474. Gruppe Ostsee. An die OSAF München. Stettin, 22.9.32. Many other units also judged that the announcement of fresh elections had raised morale, but there were exceptions, such as the Sub-Group Hamburg: BA, NS23/474. SA der NSDAP, Untergruppe Hamburg. Abschrift. Betr.: Stimmungsbericht. Hamburg, den 23.9.32. p. 2.
121 BA, NS23/474. SA der NSDAP. Der Führer der Gruppe Thüringen. Briefbuch Nr. 1141/32. Betrifft: Stimmungsbericht. Weimar, den 21. September 1932. gez. v. Jagow; Der Führer der SA-Untergruppe Braunschweig. Abt. Ia. Briefbuch Nr. 463/32. Braunschweig, den 22. Septbr. 1932; SA der NSDAP, Untergruppe Baden. Betrifft: Stimmungsbericht. Karlsruhe, den 22.9.32; SA der NSDAP, Untergruppe Hannover. Briefb. Nr. 917/32. Betrifft: Stimmungsbericht. Hannover, den 24. Sept. 1932. (1). cf. Werner, 'SA und NSDAP', p. 584, who detects no clear pattern in SA morale during autumn 1932.
122 BA, NS23/474. Gruppe Südwest. Stimmung der SA. Stuttgart, den 21.9.1932. gez. v. Jagow.
123 BA, NS23/474. SA der NSDAP. Der Führer der Gruppe Thüringen. Briefbuch Nr. 1141/32. Betrifft: Stimmungsbericht. Weimar, den 21. September 1932.
124 BA, NS23/474. Der Führer der SA-Untergruppe Braunschweig. Abt. Ia. Briefb. Nr. 463/32. Braunschweig, den 22. Septbr. 1932.

125 BA, NS23/474. SA der NSDAP, Untergruppe Baden. Betrifft: Stimmungsbericht. Karlsruhe, den 22.9.32.
126 BA, NS23/474. SA der NSDAP, Untergruppe Gaust, Hannover Ost. Hermanns-burg b. Celle, 23.9.1932.
127 BA, NS23/474. SA der NSDAP, Untergruppe Göttingen. Göttingen, den 24.9.1932. Punkt 1.
128 BHStA, Abt. I, So. I/1508. Zum Akt: SA (NSDAP). München, den 25.IV.1931. Polizeidirektion. gez. Wenzel. 'Scheringer an die Scheringer-SA, Ulm. Schluss mit Hitler! Vorwärts mit der KPD! SA Proleterwache!', *Neue Zeitung*, 14 April 1931.
129 BHStA, Abt. I, So. I/1548. *Münchner Post*, No. 262, 12 November 1931.
130 BHStA, Abt. I, So. I/1508. 'Ein Riss durchs Braune Haus', *Münchner Post*, No. 235, 10 October 1932; BA, Sch 404. Aus dem Lagebericht Nr. 112a der Polizei Direktion München vom 20. Oktober 1932. Militärähnliche Organisationen der NSDAP.
131 BHStA, Abt. I, So. I/1508. As in note 130.
132 ibid.
133 BHStA, Abt. I, So. I/1558. 'Die illegale SA', *Bayerischer Kurier*, No. 101, 10 April 1932; Bessel, 'Militarismus'; Werner, 'SA und NSDAP', pp. 519, 535–43.
134 BA, NS23/474. SA der NSDAP. Untergruppe Mittelschlesien-Süd. Stimmungs-bericht. Reichenbach, den 26.9.32.
135 P. H. Merkl, *Political Violence under the Swastika* (Princeton, NJ, 1975), pp. 581–4, 590–8.
136 BA, NS23/398. 'SA-Männer und SA-Führer der Untergruppe Hamburg!', Tagesbefehl. Hamburg, den 24.2.1932. gez. Böckenhauer.
137 BHStA, Abt. I, So. I/1552. PND Nr. 780. Zusammenkunft des ehemaligen SA-Sturms 14 im Wittelsbachergarten am 15.6.32.
138 BA, NS23/470. As in note 101.
139 BHStA, Abt. 1, So. I/1554A. SA-Untergruppe (Gausturm) München-Oberbayern. Untergruppenbefehl Nr. 4/31. München, den 4. Mai 1931. gez. Kallenbach.
140 BHStA, Abt. I, So. I/1553. 'Nationalsozialisten nehmt Euch in acht! Provokateure am Werk!', *Völkischer Beobachter* (April 1932), cutting no. 37 in police file.
141 BHStA, Abt. I, So. I/1552. PND Nr. 786. Appell des Sturms 14 der SA der NSDAP am 10.8.32 im Wittelsbachergarten.
142 BA, NS23/124. OSAF Ch/II Nr. 2950/32. Betr.: Versammlungen der DNVP. München, den 13.10.1932. gez. Röhm.
143 BA, NS23/124. Der Oberste SA-Führer Ch. Nr. 1980/32. Lagenbericht. München, den 4. August 1932. gez. Röhm.
144 BA, NS26/1355. Abschrift. Der Regierungs-Präsident. 15.K.Nr. 503 v. 504 Pol. Betrifft: Präventivverbot von Versammlungen. Magdeburg, den 31. März 1932. See also: BHStA, Abt. I, So. I/1774. Abdruck Nr. 6833. Polizeidirektion Kaisers-lautern. Betreff: Nationalsozialisten. Kaiserslautern, den 21. September 1932. gez. Beck.
145 BHStA, Abt. I, So. I/1550. '"Schluss mit der ewigen Legalität". Revolutionäre Drohungen eines SA-Häuptlings', *Münchner Post*, No. 248, 25 October 1932.
146 BHStA, Abt. I, So. I/1558. 'Revolution mit einer Million Gewehren', *Münchner Post*, No. 256, 4 November 1932.
147 See W. F. Williams, 'Versuch einer Definition paramilitärischer Organisationen', in V. R. Berghahn (ed.), *Militarismus* (Cologne, 1975), pp. 141–2.
148 E. Schön, *Die Entstehung des Nationalsozialismus in Hessen* (Miesenheim am Glan, 1972), pp. 131–4.
149 BHStA, Abt. I, So. I/1558. 'Die Vorbereitung zum nationalsozialistischen Ums-turz', *Bayrischer Kurier*, No. 331, 27 November 1931.
150 BHStA, Abt. I, So. I/1558. 'Hochverrat der hessischen Nationalsozialisten. Vor-bereitungen zur Nazi-Diktatur', *Münchner Post*, No. 274, 26 November 1931; *Berliner Tageblatt*, Morgenausgabe, No. 559, 27 November 1931 (no title with

cutting); 'Staatsbolschewismus', *Bayrischer Kurier*, No. 336, 2 December 1931; 'Die Putschpläne der Hakenkreuzler', *Neue Freie Presse*, No. 24140, Darmstadt, 27 November 1931.

151   BHStA, Abt. I, So. I/1558. 'Vision des Dritten Reichs', *Berliner Tageblatt*, Abend Ausgabe, Donnerstag, 26 November 1931, p. 1.
152   BHStA, Abt. I, So. I/1588. 'Neues Material gegen die Nationalsozialisten', *Bayrischer Kurier*, No 353, 19 December 1931.
153   BA, NS26/328. 'Röhm und sein Anhang'. Hans Kallenbach. München, den 4.7.1934. p. 6.
154   IfZ, MA 616/21, 73875 (SA III – Einsatz). Der Gruppenführer Schlesien. Gruppenbefehl Nr. 13. Breslau, den 5.8.1932. gez. Heines.
155   BA, NS26/83. 'Anleitung für den Aufbau der SA', *Die Front der Arbeiter Bauern Soldaten Nachrichtenblatt der 'National-Sozialistischen Kampfbewegung Deutschlands'*, No. 1, Berlin, 15 September 1931, pp. 4–5; 'Lage und Forderung', *Die Front der Arbeiter Bauern Soldaten*, No. 2, Berlin, 26 September 1931, p. 2.
156   BA, NS26/597. *Arbeiter Bauern Soldaten. Kampfblatt der Nationalsozialisten*, A.B.S. No. 3, Berlin, 18 April 1931, pp. 1–2; BA, NS26/83. 'Wie es zur Stennes-Aktion kam!', herausgegeben von Walter Stennes, p. 8.
157   BA, NS26/597. As in note 156.
158   BA, NS26/83. 'Wie es zur Stennes Aktion kam!'
159   Reiche, 'SA in Nuremberg', ch. 5.
160   *SA-Mann*, year 2, no. 5, 4 February 1933, p. 1.
161   GStAM, MA 106670. Nr. 842. Halbmonatsbericht des Regierungs-Präsidiums von Oberbayern (1. mit 15. März 1933). München, 20.3.1933; GStAM, R276/1. Nr. 802, Abdruck. Regierungspräsidium von Unterfranken und Aschaffenburg. An das Staatsministerium des Innern. Betr.: Halbmonatsbericht 1 für Juli 1933. 1. Allgemeine politische Lage.
162   Bloch, *SA*, pp. 44, 47, 50–3.
163   GStAM, MA 106680. Nr. 190, Abdruck. Regierungspräsidium von Unterfranken und Aschaffenburg. Würzburg, den 20. Februar 1933.
164   BA, NS26/531. Heinrich Wilkenloh, Personal Recollections, Hessen-Nassau, December 1936.
165   BHStA, Abt. I, So. I/1552. PND Nr. 802. Appell des Sturms 24/III/L am 1. Febr. 33 im Gasthaus Gärtnerplatz; BA, NS23/399. SA der NSDAP. Der Gruppenführer Nordsee. An die SA Untergruppen Weser Ems, Hannover Ost, Hamburg. Bremen, den 26.6.1933; BA, NS23/125. Der Oberste SA-Führer, Ch. Nr. 1314/33. Betreff: Verhalten der SA und SS gegen den Stahlhelm. München, 27.6.33. gez. Röhm. cf. Bloch, *SA*, pp. 54–5, where he discusses Röhm's attitude to rank-and-file activism, confirming the equivocal nature of Röhm's position.
166   Sauer, *Die Mobilmachung der Gewalt* (see note 4), p. 245.
167   H. Krausnick, 'Der 30. Juni 1934', *Aus Politik und Zeitgeschichte*, Vol. 25, no. 54, 30 June 1954, p. 318.
168   Various folders in BA, NS23 contain details of the confiscation process. For instance: NS23/254 for Hessen and the Bavarian Palatinate; NS23/266 for Hessen-Nassau; NS23/298 for Hessen and Hessen-Nassau.
169   BA, NS23/125. OSAF I Nr. 1172/33. Betr.: Tragen von Seitengewehren. München, den 13.5.33. gez. Röhm; BHStA, Abt. I, M. Inn/72425. Abdruck Nr. 9045.9125. Betreff: Führung von Schusswaffen durch die SA und SS. An die Staatsanwaltschaft für den Landgerichtsbezirk Würzburg. Polizeidirektion. Würzburg, den 13. Juli 1933. gez. Eder.
170   BA, NS23/125. OSAF I Nr. 1172/33 II Ang. München. 27.5.33. gez. Röhm.
171   BA, NS23/125. Der Oberste SA-Führer, Ch. Nr. 1499/33. Betreff: Ausbreitung des Muckertums. München, den 8.9.1933. gez. Röhm.
172   BA, NS26/328. Der Oberste SA-Führer, Ch. Nr. 1227/33. Betrifft: Auffassung über die Lage. München, den 30.5.1933. gez. Röhm; see also BA, Sch 403. SA

der NSDAP. Der Oberste SA-Führer. P 1455. München, den 16. Mai 1934. gez. Röhm.

173 BA, NS23/1. Der Oberste SA-Führer, Zentralamt. 'Kampf gegen die SA'. München, den 14. Juni 1934, pp. 4–5.

174 BA, NS23/2. OSAF F2 Nr. 34312. Betreff: NSDFB (Stahlhelm). München, den 23.11.1934. gez. Lutze; GStAM, R276/2. Nr. 1891, Abdruck. Monatsbericht des Regierungs-Präsidenten von Schwaben und Neuburg; BA, NS23/349. SA der NSDAP! Der Führer der Gruppe Hansa. Tagesbefehl! Hamburg, 26.9.1935. gez. Fust; GStAM, R280/3. Nr. 1499, Abdruck. Lagebericht des Regierungspräsidenten von Oberfranken und Mittelfranken. (August und September 1935). Ansbach, 10.10.1935. p. 6.

175 See pp. 100–01.

176 BHStA, Abt. I, So. I/1550. 'Hitlers Garden meutern!', *Neue Zeitung*, No. 197, 2 September 1930.

177 BA, R45IV/9. Bericht über Versammlungstour in Nordbayern (vom 9. Nov. bis 8. Dez. 1929), Berlin, 9.12.1929. gez. Ewert. p. 2; BA, R45IV/6. Beppo Römer. Dienstag, 14.6.32. Öffentliche Versammlung in Finkenbach-Hinterbach.

7   *Targets for SA Radicalism*

The intense material suffering of most stormtroopers indubitably sharpened and lent a bitter edge to their radicalism, but this radicalism's amorphous, negative nature was probably its most dangerous characteristic. While the crypto-millenarianist vision of the Third Reich clearly absorbed a great deal of their energy, the stormtroopers' ill-defined ideology demanded a search for scapegoats and enemies on whom their wrath and outrage could be vented.[1] Their analysis lacked sophistication at least partly because their leaders had rather different ideological preoccupations and, therefore, generally refrained from raising the bitter resentment of the stormtroopers on to any abstract philosophical plane. The stormtroopers' enemies arose, consequently, out of their immediate environment, even if these targets were considered part and parcel of the Weimar 'system': local employers, the local civil service, the trade unions, the conventional parties, landlords, policemen, Jews, churchmen, wealthy individuals, and so on. The SA's aggressiveness assumed an all-pervasive, symbolic importance in itself which also led to competition with, and attacks on, other groups opposed to Weimar, notably the KPD.

The almost universal nature of this outrage is seen in the SA's hatred for bodies as diverse as the monarchist Stahlhelm, the SPD and the Free Trade Unions, and, when the stormtroopers suspected that the NSDAP was leaving the brunt of the physical struggle to them before 1933 and was not interested in destroying entirely the old society after 1933, the NSDAP itself. The distinctly different fates of the Stahlhelm and the SPD demonstrate the effectiveness of the SA's leaders' manipulation of their following. The Freikorps veterans leading the SA, like the senior party men, were more selective in choosing their enemies. They wished to destroy Weimar but, despite Röhm's tirades, not the entire social and economic apparatus of that society – as their following's violence would have done. The stormtroopers' activities were therefore channelled along lines acceptable to their leaders and to the wider Nazi movement, and particular groups and institutions bore the brunt of the SA's wrath.

The Social Democratic Movement

The SA's confrontation with the Social Democratic movement was uniquely single-minded and intense. True, relations with the KPD were often more violent, and usually hostile, but the SA and Communist movement sometimes came to understandings and, in general, the confrontation was qualitatively different from that between the SA and

Social Democrats. SA–KPD relations are, therefore, considered in a separate chapter. The record of political violence before 1933 bears ample witness to the stormy relations between the SA and the Social Democratic movement, ranging from the SPD to the Reichsbanner and the Free Trade Unions (ADGB).[2] However, the most intense period of terror followed the NSDAP's election victory on 5 March as the Nazis eliminated their political rivals by means fair and foul.[3] In the wave of SA brutality which subsequently swept Germany the Social Democratic movement was particularly vulnerable because the stormtroopers, their leaders and the party agreed on the desirability of eliminating Social Democracy, and the composite Nazi aim coincided with that of their conservative allies. There were no holds barred and, therefore, the SA's anti-socialist measures in effect resulted in a relatively systematic purge of the Social Democratic movement.

The formidable socialist trade union movement saw its offices occupied by the SA and SS on 2 May 1933, but trade union offices had been a popular target for the SA's wrath well before this. The 2 May was little more than a symbolic, public confirmation of a process which had crippled the trade unions by the end of March. For instance, the Breslau ADGB complained bitterly to the German Vice-Chancellor, von Papen, of the SA's devastation of their headquarters on 8 March. Initially, the police had supervised a search of the building, treating property with scrupulous care, but:

> When the police then, in our opinion incomprehensibly, handed the conduct of the continuing search over to the auxiliary police and the SA, everything that could be destroyed by any means was destroyed. This occurred even though those reponsible for the building and the offices very willingly opened every room, each cupboard and every container as far as they were able . . .[4]

In another Silesian town, Liegnitz, the trade union buildings were similarly wrecked in the small hours of 10 March by stormtroopers under the command of Oberführer Koch. In a report to sub-*Gau* headquarters, a Nazi party official wrote that 'the trade union offices present a scene of utter destruction; at the moment Oberführer Koch is having piles of archival material taken down to the boilers in baskets and burned'.[5] The towns of Silesia witnessed some of the most extreme measures in this brutal process of *Gleichschaltung*, for the SA in many other cities showed at least a modicum of restraint. Following the occupation of the trade union buildings in Munich on 11 March, the unions' welfare activities were, in contrast with Silesia, allowed to continue.[6] In Westphalia, the local SA commander, Schepmann, was swift to occupy all the premises of the socialist and communist organisations in March and, in a report to the Prussian Interior Minister,

Göring, requested that the buildings concerned be handed to the SA.[7] None the less, as in Munich, the unions were allowed to maintain a temporary shadow existence as welfare organisations. Schepmann wrote:

> To protect that part of the working class concerned from personal harm, I have permitted the trade union buildings to resume exclusively social-political work subject to certain guarantees. A natural condition here was their refraining from any activities beneficial to the Marxist parties, and the renunciation of any thoughts of class struggle, even in social-political trade union work.[8]

Even this small concession ended with the formal elimination of the unions in May.

Individual members of the Social Democratic movement also suffered at the SA's hands, and underground left-wing literature painted a chilling picture of the resulting brutality:

> In Berlin alone thousands of SPD and KPD functionaries were dragged from their beds at night ... and led away to SA barracks. There they were worked over with boot and whip, beaten with steel rods and rubber truncheons until they collapsed unconscious and blood spurted under their skin. Many were forced to drink castor oil or had urine directed into their mouths; others had their bones broken. Working-class functionaries were tortured to death and public figures slaughtered savagely by these and similar methods of torture ...[9]

Official reports confirm that some stormtroopers were capable of atrocities of the first order, and not only in the cities. In the small Palatine town of Dürkheim a mob of SA, SS and VLS members, assisted by some civilians, brutally arrested two Jews and three Social Democrats:

> All five were beaten when arrested, largely with shoulder straps and belts, but also with hard objects ...
> On entering their homes, doors were pushed in and windows smashed. The detainees were not even allowed to dress ...
> Two officers of the Dürkheim gendarmerie arrived as the arrests took place. They were constrained to restrict themselves to protecting the arrested from further violence and to ensuring that they reached hospital.[10]

With so widespread a persecution of Social Democracy, it seems clear that a large proportion of the stormtroopers were involved in the campaign and, given its thoroughness and brutality, willingly involved. The reasons for this are not quite so clear. Lower-middle-class resentment and fear of the working class partly explains the growth and activities of the Nazi movement in the early 1930s, but the stormtroopers' social background invalidates this explanation in their case. At best, around a third of the stormtroopers were lower middle class (and then often clerical staff) which means that the SA was barely more middle class than the party was working class.[11] Why should the stormtroopers, then, have vented their wrath on people apparently from a similar background to themselves?

As with the SA itself, a helpful distinction can be made between the SPD's functionaries and its mass membership. Most accounts concerning attacks on the SPD speak of functionaries, and Bavarian records show (perhaps not surprisingly) that most of the political internees in Dachau concentration camp during 1933 were functionaries or prominent members of left-wing or Catholic organisations.[12] The SA's social composition does, in fact, help explain the body's antipathy to SPD functionaries, given that most of its membership was unemployed. Looking at the years before 1933, when SA attitudes were being formed, some had formerly belonged to Social Democratic organisations and others would have joined had their training led them into a skilled manual or white-collar job rather than to the dole queue. Social Democracy's failure to protect the working class from economic catastrophe and its attendant social misery was serious enough; equally serious was its failure to take drastic steps to remedy the crisis.

The SPD and unions were, by their nature, ill-equipped to do so. They had become well-entrenched bureaucratic organisations and were too closely involved in the day-to-day administration of society to step outside it and oppose it.[13] Hence the embittered stormtroopers (and KPD members!) condemned Social Democracy as part of the establishment and blamed it for political and economic developments since 1918. The NSDAP and SA leadership nurtured this attitude, drumming home the message that the Social Democrats' Weimar Republic was, along with the victor powers, largely responsible for Germany's misery. The ordinary workers were not to blame, indeed they were more commonly represented as betrayed by their leaders who, in turn, were blamed for society's failings. Not only were they accused of mismanaging or even betraying Germany, but of enjoying power and privilege; the Nazi leadership dubbed them *Bonzen* (big-wigs). The charge contained a grain of truth, for the great majority of Social Democratic leaders, from Reichstag members to junior Reichsbanner leaders were middle class, or had obtained jobs normally regarded as middle class.[14] True, the same could be said of SA leaders, but they were not ensconced cosily behind office desks, and were seen by their men as fighting the crisis on the streets of Germany.

The NSBO, whose membership overlapped with the SA's,[15] also drummed home this message, arguing that Social Democracy's aims conflicted with the workers':

> Marxism is responsible for the impoverishment of the working class because of its community of interest with the Brüning government. This community of interest is a defensive and offensive alliance against National Socialism. Therefore National Socialism has the right to take over the position occupied until now by the Reds in the factories and to organise the betrayed working classes' struggle for freedom.[16]

Similarly, when advertising a meeting for BMW workers in March 1931, the NSBO declared: 'Show that you have recognised the enemy and are determined to defend your right to an existence, to destroy the exploiting classes and seize the socialist state.'[17] Thus, ironically, the NSBO had adopted an ideological stance not entirely dissimilar to the KPD's interpretation of Social Democracy as being an element of the capitalist system, and hence 'social fascist'. Buchloh demonstrates the effectiveness of this approach in its own right in the Ruhr District,[18] and some stormtroopers would have been familiar with these ideas and introduced them into the SA.

However, the jobless stormtroopers no longer regarded employers as an immediate manifestation of authority and social repression. Their penchant for violence and the resulting arrests by the police led many stormtroopers to perceive the involvement of Social Democrats with the enforcement and execution of the law. It probably escaped their notice that the authorities, and particularly the courts, were showing far greater severity in dealing with voilence on the left of politics. SA man Kurt Becker of Company 33, Berlin, wrote to his unit from Moabit prison in June 1931:

> I hope that our innocence comes to light one day, because you too must know that my comrades and I must rot here innocent, because we defended ourselves against the murdering Red bandits. I hope their little game will be ended soon. It's really amazing that SA members are given deterrent sentences while the Red murdering dictatorship's bandits always have extenuating circumstances. But the day will come.[19]

When the day did come the SA found some police forces sufficiently influenced by Social Democracy to delay briefly their revenge until they took matters into their own hands. The problem was not universal – by no means all police forces contained Social Democrats – but the Hamburg area, for one, did have police forces containing socialists. The 15th

Regiment in Bergedorf, east of Hamburg, complained on 18 March 1933 to Sub-Group Hamburg of ineffectual police measures against the Reichsbanner. It then explained:

> Since most of the Bergedorf police are still active in the Reichsbanner, this organisation can continue its machinations unhindered. Training exercises are carried out especially zealously. All measures taken by the police command are illusory because the Reichsbanner unit commanders are themselves in the police.[20]

Battalion I/76 in Hamburg itself reported that the 2,000-strong military sport section of their local police force consisted 'almost entirely of Marxists',[21] and similar circumstances were reported elsewhere, for example, in Stettin, Pomerania.[22] No doubt the claims were exaggerated, but the resulting hostility felt by the stormtroopers to the police was presumably real enough.

The high unemployment rates within the SA in themselves set its membership somewhat apart from the relatively more fortunate SPD membership, but in more general terms the identification of the Social Democratic movement with authority characterised the SA's overall attitude to political parties and old-established, bureaucratised political movements which symbolised order, institutionalisation and authority. The implications of this stretched beyond the realm of politics. The personal experiences of SA members, coupled with their leaders' distaste for institutionalised life, resulted in a comprehensive attack by the SA against all spheres of authority, both on an individual and an institutional level. Strikes and agitation in industry, attacks on the police, the Church, and on political parties were cases in point.

The Catholic Movement

The NSDAP's electoral triumphs centred largely on Protestant Germany, with Catholic constituencies producing poorer results, at least until March 1933. Similarly, the SA sometimes expanded more slowly in Catholic districts and this rankled with many stormtroopers. They concentrated on attacking the youth movements and paramilitary expressions of political Catholicism, a pattern repeated in attacks on other political persuasions.[23] The SA's activist, ill-defined political creed, which usually confined the stormtroopers' perception of enemies to groups whose activities impinged on their own, accounts for this, and the vigorous Catholic youth organisations, notably the Catholic Male Youth League (KJMV), and the paramilitary Bayernwacht and Pfalzwacht became especially serious rivals for the SA.[24]

Friction arose well before 1933 and was not invariably initiated by the SA. The Church itself sometimes openly attacked Nazism, nationally and locally, to assert political dominance within Catholic areas. Paul Hainbach, a stormtrooper from Frankfurt-am-Main, recalled the beginnings of this confrontation in mid-1929:

> However, not only the Marxists, but also the Centre Party tried to snuff us out. In mid-1929 it was indeed the Centre Party which began a real campaign of lies against us to attribute to us heathen practices and the wish to end Christian teaching.[25]

In this atmosphere violent clashes could and did occur,[26] but matters reached a pitch in the changed political circumstances following Hitler's takeover.

The SA now strove to dominate the paramilitary scene and persistent, often successful, Catholic resistance, particularly by the KJMV, created friction and provoked some physical violence. The problem lay partly in the SA's failure to wean all its members from political Catholicism, for some stormtroopers hedged their bets by also remaining in the Catholic Youth. In April 1934 the 25th Regiment of Garching, Upper Bavaria, for one, tried regulating this situation by pressing stormtroopers to choose between Catholicism and Nazism: 'Since much of the Catholic clergy is at least hostile to the Third Reich, simultaneous membership of a Catholic youth organisation cannot be combined with a revolutionary oriented SA man's duties.'[27] Whether or not this particular unit sorted out its problems, difficulties persisted elsewhere in Bavaria. In May 1934 the SA man Martin Huber, a fitter from Kelheim, was arrested for founding a Catholic paramilitary youth group,[28] while as late as March 1935 Catholic organisations in Bavarian Swabia were recruiting successfully from the SA.[29]

Those SA members and units who were committed anti-Catholics often resorted to violence, either spontaneous or under junior leaders, in response to this glaring challenge to their dominance. After their village's poor showing in the November 1933 plebiscite, stormtroopers in Langenreichen, Bavarian Swabia, attacked a KJMV meeting,[30] while in other instances individual Catholic functionaries were attacked. In April 1934 a report by the authorities described how a Catholic mayor became one such victim:

> According to a report from the District Office in Krumbach, about fifty SA men gathered in front of the mayor's dwelling in Bayersried-Ursberg. He was formerly a member of the BVP. They demanded that he resign his office as mayor and apparently shouted 'traitor' in unison.[31]

Other attacks resulted more from the general antipathy between paramilitary rivals. For instance, on 26 February 1933 an SA unit clashed with members of the Pfalzwacht in Eppstein near Frankenthal, and since mounted stormtroopers became involved in the fighting, at least junior leaders were presumably present.[32] On the other hand, a mob of stormtroopers who attacked the vicarage in Landau an der Isar, Bavaria, clashed undirected with the Bayernwacht, who were 'accommodated inappropriately in a vicarage office'.[33] In this instance the local priest refused to be intimidated and drove off the stormtroopers with a firearm despite a barrage of abuse. In other communities the SA's relative isolation and their resulting resentment led to outbreaks of spontaneous violence. This occurred in Hiltenfingen, Bavarian Swabia, in August 1934:

> The mill owner, Kurz, a respected man and front-line veteran, was roughly mishandled in Hiltenfingen, Schwabmünchen District, on 12 August 1934 by four SA men. There was widespread anger about this. On the evening of Sunday 16 August several farmers were discussing the SA at an inn because of this incident. A slight scuffle with SA members resulted ... The commander of Company 54/3 who was called from Schwabmünchen was able initially to restore peace. However when he said that Kurz had needed beating up and that the SA in Hiltenfingen was disgruntled because there were still too many 'blacks' [political Catholics], there was renewed violence.[34]

During 1935 the intensity of this confrontation diminished.[35] This partly reflected the SA's own declining importance and stature, but was also symptomatic of a progressive restriction by the authorities of Church activities to within the 'four walls of the Church'. In preceding years both the SA and HJ had, with official acquiescence, contributed to this process by seizing or confiscating Catholic Youth property in much of southern Germany. Following the occupation and confiscation of Catholic property in Lower Bavaria and the Oberpfalz in August 1933, the Catholic Youth in these areas appealed for official intervention, complaining that 'Catholic organisations' hostels, especially those of the Catholic Youth, have been occupied by the SA in several towns and their property confiscated'.[36]

Of course, in the world of paramilitary activism force was not simply a negative weapon. Some Nazis remarked in personal recollections that shows of strength also served to attract recruits from rival groups or from the humdrum life of conventional politics,[37] and Bennecke recounts this when describing street marches as a means of attracting support to a cause.[38] The conflicts between the SA and the Catholic activists were not so much directed against the individual opponent, but against his loyalty to an opposing creed. The individual himself could usually switch loyalties, whether through a change in convictions or for reasons of expediency and this possibility was still more important in the SA's relations with its rivals of the left.

The Conservative Right

Relations between the SA and the conservative right were equally poor. Although violence between the SA and DNVP was relatively infrequent, there was little love lost between the two bodies before or after the Nazi takeover, whatever agreements Hitler made with the Nationalist leaders. Unlike the paramilitary groups, the DNVP posed no immediate, tangible challenge to the SA, but its very existence was none the less offensive to the stormtroopers. It embodied and symbolised traditional privilege – social, political and material – and therefore represented everything that the SA was not and some of the things the stormtroopers wished to destroy.

The commander of Sub-Group Pfalz-Saar wrote in September 1932 of his men's unease at the prospect of Hitler participating in a conservative government and of their relief when this came to nothing.[39] This mood was reflected throughout the SA and doubtless intensified as the DNVP mounted a bitter election campaign against the Nazis in autumn 1932. DNVP election pamphlets likened the Nazi movement to communism: 'Internally the NSDAP is nothing but an appendage of Marxism, riddled with communist ideas and incapable of pursuing its own nationalist goals.'[40] Another leaflet raged: 'We have established that the urban *Untermenschentum*, that shady rabble which was found formerly only in the KPD's ranks, has evidently now found refuge in the NSDAP.'[41] The SA's unemployed, blue-collar workers were thus the very social group the DNVP apparently despised most. Despite the previous infrequency of violent confrontations, ill-feeling had always been present and as the November 1932 election approached there was a flurry of violence. In October 1932 the chief mayor of Stolp in Pomerania accused National Socialists of 'hindering and disrupting DNVP meetings in an illegal fashion, evidently in a systematic manner',[42] while a similar incident in Stuttgart on 27 October prompted police intervention.[43] The SA High Command knew of such incidents, but its disapproval suggests that these were locally inspired.[44] The atmosphere remained poor after January 1933, but with the disappearance of the DNVP on 27 June, the stormtroopers' aversion to the German Nationalists focused entirely on paramilitary expressions of traditional conservatism such as the Tannenberg League and, in particular, the Stahlhelm.

Relations between the SA and Stahlhelm had begun to deteriorate before 1933, but until 1931 were often tolerably good. Stormtroopers in at least one *Gau* participated in the Stahlhelm's military sport training during 1931, a practice which Röhm eventually condemned and for-bade.[45] In the extreme east of Germany the SA and Stahlhelm were both involved in the army's defence organisation on the Polish border, the Grenzschutz, but relations between them within this organisation were sometimes cool.[46] If anything the ordinary Stahlhelmer were better disposed to the SA than vice versa,[47] with a trickle of Stahlhelmer into the SA by 1931. Bavarian Stahlhelm leaders complained of the SA poaching their members, to which Röhm retorted that the SA could not 'neglect, alongside its drive into the Marxist camp, to win members from the so-called patriotic camp'.[48]

The differing political tendencies of the SA and Stahlhelm led subsequently to mounting conflict. Some stormtroopers even baulked at affiliation to the NSDAP, but they regarded the Stahlhelm's association with the conservative, traditionally minded DNVP as utterly unacceptable. Fighting between stormtroopers and Stahlhelmer in Güstrow on New Year's eve 1931/2 was attributed to the Stahlhelm's politics,[49] while SA reports from many towns during 1932 spoke of friction between the SA and Stahlhelm because of the latter's liaison with the DNVP.[50] A Hamburg SA report, compiled in December, commented:

Alongside the usual military sport activities, the Stahlhelm threw itself almost unreservedly behind the DNVP during the last election. This naturally sharpened the antagonism between the Stahlhelm and NSDAP still further.[51]

Here too, however, the ordinary Stahlhelmer were less anti-Nazi than their leaders, suggesting that the more radical SA was attractive to some of them.

While the left-wing, and eventually the Catholic, paramilitary organisations were obliterated after the Nazi takeover, Hitler's accommodation with the right demanded different treatment of the Stahlhelm. It was partially absorbed into the SA, but the process was not straight-forward, only commencing after a struggle between the two senior Stahlhelm leaders, Seldte and Duesterberg.[52] Seldte, who sought integration with the Nazi movement, triumphed and the gradual transfer of the Stahlhelm into the SA followed an initial agreement in April 1933.[53] The Stahlhelm's membership was divided into two groups, those aged 35 and younger and those older than this.[54] The younger, Fighting Stahlhelm (Wehrstahlhelm) was to be integrated by 31 October,[55] but the older, Core Stahlhelm (Kernstahlhelm) was to remain autonomous, 'with its own units alongside the SA and SS'.[56] The Core Stahlhelm was subsequently renamed the National Socialist German Front-Line Fighter League (NSDFB) and its members encouraged, but not forced, to join special Reserve SA units designated SAR I.[57] This special treatment created resentment in the regular SA[58] and failed simultaneously to absorb the Stahlhelm, with integration anything but complete in 1935. Perhaps half the Stahlhelmer actually joined the SA.

Between January and July 1933 relations were generally poor with links between the Stahlhelm and the DNVP continuing to trigger incidents, as in Bavarian Swabia in April.[59] The unauthorised occupation of Stahlhelm camps by stormtroopers were sometimes complemented by the confiscation of Stahlhelm property or even weapons, as in Altötting, Upper Bavaria, in June.[60] Orders from the High Command to groups and sub-groups to maintain close surveillance of Stahlhelm formations inevitably involved the ordinary stormtroopers and only aggravated matters.[61] As early as February 1933 Seldte felt sufficiently threatened to try, unsuccessfully, to persuade Hitler to pre-empt any SA rising.[62]

Relations remained poor during the Stahlhelm's integration into the SA during late 1933 and early 1934. The approach of the Röhm purge saw Seldte among the advocates of a decisive blow against the SA,[63] whose overbearing attitude had become almost intolerable. The Stahlhelm resented deeply the purging of its leaders in certain districts as units were absorbed into the SA, and a Stahlhelm leader from Warstede-Hemoor, Lower Saxony, complained in December 1933 that 95 per cent of his district's leadership had been removed in this way.[64]

None the less, the Stahlhelm itself was not entirely blameless. The SA felt threatened as the Stahlhelm continued recruiting new members and even establishing new branches. Some of its recruits were former left-wingers seeking a safe, non-Nazi haven and Röhm complained bitterly that the Stahlhelm was recruiting 'many obvious opponents of the NSDAP: Freemasons, half-Jews and similar elements', adding that 'particularly in rural areas [the new Stahlhelm units] were becoming reservoirs for discontented elements'.[65] In addition, the Stahlhelm attempted to prevent members joining the SAR I and tried to reclaim former members from this body, claiming that the Stahlhelm was the only true front-soldier organisation.[66] In May 1934 Röhm grumbled that 'the language in the former Stahlhelm's newspapers and in Stahlhelm orders must often be regarded as hostile to the SA',[67] but he preferred to keep the conflict verbal. The SA Command restricted its hostility to a stream of vitriolic statements[68] and in May 1934 Röhm forbade rank-and-file attacks on the Stahlhelm.[69]

This followed months of local violence. In parts of Lower Bavaria fighting broke out between stormtroopers and Stahlhelmer in September 1933,[70] whilst the authorities reported tension in Upper Bavaria in January 1934.[71] In both cases the trouble was attributed to Stahlhelm recruiting activity, which presents an interesting parallel with friction between the SA and Catholic Youth. In addition, the memory of the Stahlhelm's association with the DNVP, and the relative affluence and privilege its members both represented and enjoyed rankled with the

SA. Veteran stormtroopers in Küstrin, Pomerania, regarded the appointment of former Stahlhelmer (among others) over their heads as the last straw: 'We all know how the Stahlhelm fought; they wore two coats.'[72] A Gestapo report from Schleswig-Holstein, written in January 1934, caught the rank and file's mood excellently. The belief that the ordinary SS members in Schleswig-Holstein thought similarly is intriguing:

> Things cannot continue as they are at present on the west coast of Holstein. Büsum, Heide and Wesselburen appear to be aiming to become strongholds of the Tannenberg League and the Reaction. In these towns the SA's struggle was especially hard; not because of meeting hall and street fights, but because of the underhand methods used by the Tannenberger and Stahlhelmer who stick together like Siamese twins. It is not understood here why these crooked-shooting estate owners should not be dealt with in the same way as workers reluctant to fall in. Thought has been given as to what would have become of the organisers and participants if these forbidden meetings were not held by reactionary property owners, but by workers and Communists. The morale in veteran party circles (SA and SS) is desolate. They feel utterly abandoned, and any authority on the pulse of life in Schleswig-Holstein can imagine for himself the consequences of the present policy.[73]

After the Röhm purge the stormtroopers' attitude to the Stahlhelm remained similar and the basic causes of friction changed little. Lutze, the new SA Chief of Staff, was aware of the continued ill-feeling and urged restraint,[74] but despite a decline in open violence, the tension persisted, due both to the Stahlhelm's dogged advocacy of traditional conservative politics and its continued recruiting drive. Lower Franconian SA units were agitated by the Stahlhelm's monarchist sympathies in late 1934,[75] while the commander of the 22nd Regiment, Zweibrücken, reported in December that the mood in the Palatinate was tense:

> The rumours circulating about the revival of the Stahlhelm are causing disquiet. The fact cannot be denied that the Reaction was embodied in the Stahlhelm and that this will not be forgotten very quickly. The SA veterans are asking; 'Shall the Reaction really obtain a defence troop again?'.[76]

The Stahlhelm was regarded as an unwelcome bastion of traditional conservative interests in other areas too, such as Hessen-Nassau and the Saarland.[77]

Despite SA hostility, the Stahlhelm continued to proselytise during 1935 and in May pro-conservative utterances by the Upper Bavarian Stahlhelm leader provoked the banning of Stahlhelm public functions by the Bavarian political police.[78] The Stahlhelm's recruitment drive angered the Rheinhessen SA among others. Here the Stahlhelm not only recruited discharged stormtroopers, who possibly sought some compensation for their loss of SA membership, but tried to recruit from within the SA itself.[79] While this did little more than irritate the Rheinhessen SA, the problem was a national one. In January 1935 the SA Command expressed its displeasure, noting renewed tension between the SA and Stahlhelm: 'The grounds [for this] lie primarily in its attempt to become comparable once again with the old Stahlhelm; organisationally, in terms of size and role, and to win back all former Stahlhelm members.'[80]

Given the longstanding hostility between the Stahlhelm and SA, it was fortunate for the Stahlhelm that the NSDAP's need to accommodate itself with the traditional right led to the restraining of the stormtroopers during the early years of the Third Reich.

Regulated Society: Authority, Institutions and Privilege

The SA's violence extended beyond this confrontation with political organisations, to take in most symbols of conventional authority, institutionalisation and privilege. The broader Nazi movement shared the SA's hostility to existing public institutions before 1933 and, consequently, Hitler often sympathised with his SA commanders' feelings on this issue; for instance, regarding relations between the SA and police.[81] However, even before 1933 there were revealing differences in outlook, leading to friction between the SA and party.[82] The party and its close allies, such as the SS, were already developing an alternative administrative structure to Weimar's, but the SA equated the destruction of Weimar with the permanent removal of routinised, bureaucratically structured society.[83] The policy of legality served simply as the first step towards the fundamental transformation of Germany, and stormtroopers and their leaders were in basic agreement on this, however much their detailed perceptions differed.

Of course, the SA's leaders saw some merit in tactical co-operation with sections of authority and differentiated between essentially friendly and hostile elements in authority. In late 1931, for instance, the SA in Wassertrudingen, Franconia, analysed its relations with dominant forces in the town's everyday life. Railway officials, the gendarmerie and the civil service were considered generally friendly, but the Finance Office, the District Court and the banks were hostile. The Protestant church was believed friendly, but the Catholic church hostile.[84] In other areas, the police were considered friendly on some occasions. The Hamburg SA was far fonder of the police in late 1929 than it became in 1933, reporting:

> The SA is concerned to maintain good relations [with the police] under the circumstances. This is easy because the police have suffered forty-five injuries from the KPD in the past eight weeks.[85]

Brigade 50 of Darmstadt noted that individual sympathies differed within the police force, listing twenty-one policemen who had assisted the Nazi movement before the takeover made such action opportune.[86]

The NSDAP itself believed that a generation gap within the Prussian police determined its attitude to Nazism. In October 1932 the NSDAP's adviser for police affairs commented that senior Prussian officers were 'Red or strongly democratic', while the junior police officers were pro-Nazi – although how far this goodwill applied to the SA is unclear. The same adviser's assessment of the Bavarian police, which he deemed pro-Nazi but unprepared to tolerate any illegal acts, provides a clue.[87]

In practice, the SA's manifestly generous interpretation of legality provoked mounting conflict with the police before Hitler's takeover. In Dortmund, for example, the police were involved in sixteen clashes with the SA between 1930 and 1933[88] and while friction generally occurred around marches, demonstrations and political meetings, the SA sometimes carried the attack to the police. In November 1932 an SA mob attacked the police guardroom at the Schweidnitz Court House, Silesia, hurling a 5lb stone into the room in the process.[89] Understandably the police responded, thus disturbing relations still further. The NSDAP in Schleswig-Holstein warned of police infiltrators who were seeking evidence to incriminate the SA during the SA ban in April 1932.[90] In the same month Sub-Group Hamburg warned of imminent police raids on SA leaders' homes and SA offices.[91]

The Nazi takeover only changed matters slowly. Police forces were purged of more outspokenly anti-Nazi members, while policemen who had previously sympathised privately with the SA could now support the organisation publicly. The 168th Regiment of Offenbach/Main, for one, reported that seven police officers actually joined it during early 1933.[92] Furthermore, the police helped to train stormtroopers for the auxiliary police force,[93] but while this body proved extremely useful to the NSDAP as it eliminated rival institutions during early 1933, it subsequently demonstrated that its value was limited largely to destructive and disruptive tasks.[94]

Moreover, stormtroopers continued attacking the regular police force. In Upper and Mid-Franconia the authorities complained of the SA's widespread disregard for the police and the law in June 1933:

> Highly unpleasant participation by SA men in fights. Attacks on police officers and the freeing of prisoners by force of arms. Public ridicule of gendarmerie officers and the threat of 'Dachau' for gendarmes are reported from the districts of Stadtsteinach, Lauf and especially Wunsiedel.[95]

This pattern was widespread throughout Germany, as Diels among others observes, when noting that police authority was virtually non-existent in Silesia and some western industrial areas by December 1933.[96]

The writings of individual stormtroopers confirm this unequivocal rejection of existing authority, with justice and the police symbolising much that they hated. Paul Maikowski of the 33rd Berlin Company had reason to be bitter. In June 1931, while serving a prison sentence for violent activities, he wrote: 'We will show the people who locked us up what legal Nazi revenge is; some of them will certainly be taken by the devil.'[97] In October he wrote similarly: 'Times can't stay as they are for ever; when they change in our favour we'll control justice and use it against them as they used it against us.'[98] After the Nazi takeover SA veteran Heinz-Hermann Horn of Giessen recalled a Nazi meeting where police rode down and clubbed participants in 1930,[99] illustrating that the SA opposed the police as much from experience as through conviction. Heinz Mai, an SA veteran from Frankfurt-am-Main, believed that the police had discriminated against stormtroopers in more sinister ways:

> Police tactics were, by arresting as many SA men as possible, to prevent them from arriving at their workplace on time and thereby to deprive them of their living. Unfortunately this worked all too often.[100]

In fact, the SA's opposition to authority fed upon itself. As stormtroopers expressed their hostility through open violence or other acts of lawlessness, society's counter-measures reinforced their original convictions. These specific grievances complemented their joblessness and the consequent feeling that society had failed them.

Some sections of the SA developed more elaborate criticisms of society which transcended immediate issues. SA leaders, whose relatively abstracted and relatively positive proposals were none the less appealing to a wider and presumably sympathetic SA audience, made many such attacks. Perhaps the most notable of these leaders was

Stennes, who wrote profusely on his views of society in his news-sheet *Arbeiter, Bauern, Soldaten* (Workers, Peasants, Soldiers) after his break with Hitler. In April 1931 he declared:

We know that this state must be reorganised both on national and socialist lines. We reject the liberal thesis of the necessity of freedom of action for private capitalists. We demand that the state as the highest executive of the people has the right to subordinate its members to its best judgement and conscience.[101]

In September he elaborated on these policies:

Nationalisation of the big banks. Resettling of the industrial proletariat which is still capable of making a living on the land (at least 20 to 50 acres). State monopoly of foreign trade ... Cuts in the cost of living (price cuts, elimination of cartel price-fixing, rent cuts). Relentless action against export of capital, corruption and treason.[102]

Other attacks, apparently developed by ordinary stormtroopers, were generally more negative, containing fewer concrete proposals for the future. A wave of such publications followed the Nazi takeover, as many stormtroopers watched developments with mounting unease. A radical Hamburg group, whose writings resembled sufficiently those of the KPD to suggest some kind of link, wrote of their growing disappointment on 16 March 1933:

The hectic election days are over. The torchlight processions and the enthusiasm of recent days seemed to us to be the beginning of a new Germany. We believed that at last our struggle and sacrifice was beginning to bear fruit. The tension in our ranks was huge. We all believed that the first government measure after the election would be aimed against finance capital. We all believed that Papen, Hugenberg and Seldte would be booted out of the Cabinet on 6 March. Capitalist Germany had brought us hunger and suffering; we wanted a free and socialist Germany at last ... The Social Democratic functionaries hadn't found the nerve to sweep away the capitalist system ... People are already afraid of us; we are only to be armed if we crush the Commune for the 'System'. Otherwise they will not give us weapons, they fear we would go beyond all these half-measures and precipitate serious struggle. If the Commune is troublesome for finance capital, we don't see why we should take over the elimination of this enemy of finance capital. On the contrary, we call for struggle against the capitalist system.[103]

Attacks on banks, commercial institutions and factories became wide-spread and raised fears in establishment circles that the SA was running out of control.[104] However, the risk of the stormtroopers' wrath seriously endangering capitalist interests was small. Not only did the NSDAP support the socio-economic *status quo*, but the SA's own leaders could not usually identify with this set of rank-an-file aspirations. Consequently, the attacks normally remained unorganised and undirected and could be resisted piecemeal by the authorities and even by the SA leaders themselves.

The Nazi Party

Once Hitler and the party began to co-operate with the establishment and to ape its forms and structures within the Nazi movement, the SA began to regard even them as enemies. This hostility transcended internal Nazi quarrels concerning finance and the bureaucratisation of the movement, although these particular quarrels were undoubtedly symptomatic of the wider SA attitude. The new conflicts involved the mainstream SA, but the body's ultra-radical fringe attacked the NSDAP even more strongly. Stormtroopers challenged the party on social and economic issues, before and after the takeover.

Within the mainstream SA, some criticism developed shortly before the Stennes Revolt, but it intensified during autumn 1932. For instance, the commander of the 5th Regiment in Danzig wrote in September:

> The tough social measures which were introduced in Danzig with the sanction of the NSDAP worked like a kick in the teeth for some SA men. The NSDAP now also stands in opposition to the bourgeois government in Danzig, and the morale in the SA has consequently improved.[105]

Following Hitler's takeover, the Upper Bavarian authorities remarked in February 1933 that SA circles opposed Hitler's capitalist leanings,[106] while in June 1933 the Hamburg SA Command learnt of uniformed SA men distributing pamphlets declaring, 'Comrades, our Leader has betrayed us!'[107] The outcome of checks subsequently ordered are unavailable. Stormtroopers also criticised individually the Nazi movement and even the SA Command because of unsatisfactory social conditions. One incident in Schlüchtern near Frankfurt-am-Main involved the SA man Heinerich Hohmann, whose commander reported:

> On 29 June 1934 I received a letter from the District President's Office in Schlüchtern, saying that Hohmann had made disparaging

remarks about the Leader and the SA . . . I arrested Hohmann in his house and handed him over to the brigade guardroom. On the way to the guardroom Hohmann said: 'It's a scandal that you have to send your wife home to her parents so that she does not starve in the city. It really was better before.'[108]

Local commanders sometimes agreed openly with their men's sentiments, at least until the Röhm purge. For instance, an SA colonel in Düsseldorf shouted during a confrontation between the SA and the party in June 1934: 'When the second wave of the Revolution comes we won't shoot any more Communists; instead we'll know our duty in purging our own ranks of functionaries and other rubbish.'[109]

Ultra-radical elements within the SA opposed vociferously the party's line rather earlier, with a particularly bitter flysheet appearing in Berlin on 31 May 1931:

We proletarian elements of the movement are indeed absolutely thrilled! Oh, we're so easily satisfied and through our delight over the beautiful SA memorial, as Hitler once called the Brown House, we can forget our grumbling stomachs.[110]

The flysheet continued by attacking Hitler's links with capitalist circles:

The deeper grounds for Hitler's behaviour lie in his close relations with industry. A National Socialist Workers' Party which is beholden to industry and the banking circles behind the latter cannot blame the largely working-class, north German SA men if they accuse Hitler of betraying the programme of social justice.[111]

Similar leaflets appeared throughout 1931 and 1932, for example in Leipzig and Berlin, and continued after the Nazi takeover. One of the latter, dated May 1933, read:

Where has any cleft whatsoever been made into the rule of the capitalist exploitative order, let alone attempted? Herr Hugenberg is economic dictator, Herr Schacht financial dictator of this 'Revolution'. Comrades, don't you realise what we have always said: There will be no National Socialism with Hugenberg and Schacht!)Emphasis in original)[112]

Some political opponents of Nazism merely reported these splits between the party and SA, either noting the immediate cause of the individual incidents, or offering no explanation at all. Thus the Social Democratic *Münchner Post* reported SA dissatisfaction with the policy of legality in September 1931[113] and an 'open rebellion of the SA and SS' in Schleswig-Holstein in late 1932.[114]

However, the KPD probed deeper and, perhaps predictably, argued that class contradictions between the party and SA lay behind the trouble. This analysis generally placed SA leaders on the party's side which, in class terms and to a qualified degree in terms of ideology, was basically accurate. Thus the KPD interpreted unrest in the Berlin SA during autumn 1930 as a class struggle between a working class and a lower-middle-class SA and a middle-class Nazi leadership.[115] In April 1931 Scheringer modified the conventional Communist line on the SA when warning the stormtroopers that Hitler was betraying Nazi principles to Jewish capitalism and that the NSDAP was in fact the party of international capital. He continued that Röhm agreed fully with this course and therefore urged the 'SA proletarian guard' to break with the NSDAP and, like him (a former Nazi), join the KPD.[116]

Immediately after the Nazi takeover the KPD maintained this ideological offensive, discussing discord within the Nazi movement in terms of class contradictions. On 2 February the *Neue Zeitung* wrote: 'Hugenberg Stomach Aches in SS and SA. SA Proletarians, only the KPD is leading the Working People to Battle for Social and National Liberation.'[117] The Hamburg KPD reported a shooting incident between SA units in Breslau on 7 April 1933 in similar terms:

> NSDAP Storm Troop units fought out a gun battle between themselves. The realisation is growing among the working-class members of the SA of Hitler's terrible betrayal of the interests of the working people; [Hitler] being the Reich Governor of the capitalists. The shots in Breslau demonstrate the social split in the NSDAP's following.[118]

Other evidence suggests that the KPD's interpretation of events was not wholly inaccurate but, although some stormtroopers may have grumbled, hopes of a fundamental split in the Nazi movement were premature. Not only did the SA expand rapidly during 1933, but it possibly became more working class.[119] Even though the content of the SA's radicalism made it eminently unsuitable for any long-term role in the (admittedly chaotic) bureaucratic Nazi state,[120] in the short term the SA's radical membership could therefore be exploited by the Nazi leadership and certainly, as Röhm himself understood, prevented from joining any sustained, populist anti-Nazi insurrection.[121]

Individuals

Stormtroopers often turned on prominent individuals in the local community as the most immediate manifestation of authority rather than on the institutions they represented, which is understandable given their lack of philosophical acumen. If potential victims happened to be Jewish, an attack was all the more likely. These assaults, like most SA violence, peaked between the Nazi takeover and the Röhm purge. Social and political motives probably underlay a series of incidents in the Palatinate village of Wolfstein on 22 June 1933. While three of the four victims were Stahlhelm members, all were prominent in the community: the pastor, a tax consultant, a merchant and a senior justice official. The attacks assumed something of a mass character and local officials subsequently complained that their gendarmerie 'apparently feels powerless in the face of developments'. One SA leader present obviously felt that he was leading a popular insurrection of sorts, declaring before one attack: 'The people wish it.'[122]

Violence sometimes involved less prominent figures: an innkeeper from Fischbach near Nuremberg was beaten senseless by two stormtroopers for drunken, anti-Nazi utterances in June 1933.[123] Much of the violence verged on straightforward criminality or involved personal revenge. By July, Röhm was sufficiently alarmed by the scale of this violence to condemn publicly 'the settling of personal scores, unacceptable brutality, robbery, theft and looting' by stormtroopers.[124] However, the violence continued. A pensioner from Nuremberg was savagely beaten for anti-Nazi remarks in October 1933,[125] while the mayor and a municipal official were 'crudely insulted' in Steinbühl, Lower Bavaria, after church on 26 November 1933. The crowd, led by a stormtrooper, then 'ransacked the files of the district offices'.[126] In April 1934 the Protestant vicarage in Memmelsdorf, Lower Franconia, was attacked by the SA and sixty window-panes smashed.[127]

Some Nazis, both party members and stormtroopers, had qualms over the wave of terror, and anonymous letters began to arrive in government ministries in late 1933. A party member from a village near Brunswick gave one of the frankest accounts when writing to the Ministry of Popular Enlightenment and Propaganda in December 1933:

> We veteran party members have already experienced all kinds of things here which contravene any sense of human decency. I am thinking of the inhuman maltreatment and torture in the SA cellar. If we intervened on behalf of the people being tortured beyond reasonable limits [!], we were threatened with concentration camp, or tortured ourselves. You will be aware that various people ended up in hospital, including Nationalist citizens and Stahlhelm members.[128]

Poor labour relations also caused mass violence during this period, provoking attacks on employers and management.[129] In August 1933 twenty-four stormtroopers attacked the estate of Baron Riederer von

Paar of Schönau in Lower Bavaria because, as the authorities commented:

> Two trainees on the estate who belong to the Schönau SA were dismissed recently by the manager, Reutschler. The dismissals occurred because of insubordination to the estate manager. The SA accuses Reutschler of treating the workers and trainees ruthlessly, and of showing himself to be spiteful and violent with his subordinates.[130]

The SA's particular target was, therefore, Reutschler, whose house was surrounded and its windows stoned. The attack was determined and thorough, the perpetrators taking care to destroy the estate's telephone lines before mounting their attack. The local gendarmerie were powerless to stop the attack, requiring the intervention of the local SA commander. Similarly, in September 1933 a large crowd of stormtroopers gathered before the house of the local trade bank director in Straubing, Lower Bavaria, intending to arrest him after he sacked one of their comrades, a bank clerk. In this case, the police restored order[131] with help from the local SA commissar.[132]

Landlords and tenants frequently fail to see eye to eye, and during the hard years of the depression this was especially so. Justly or unjustly, some landlords incurred the displeasure of stormtroopers who, after Hitler's takeover, felt free to exact retribution. In a particularly brutal incident in Düsseldorf-Gerresheim on 31 August 1933, the landlord K. M. was attacked and beaten in his own home. His subsequent complaint to the local SA commander simultaneously provides an intriguing insight into the political life of the locality:

> I obtained a court order for the eviction of four malicious tenants for drunkenness, breach of the peace and threats against my life. All the tenants belonged to the KPD. As I discovered, most of the SA men involved in the attack were still KPD members until 5 March. A lively intercourse has been observable for weeks between SA men and my tenants. On the very day of the attack an SA man visited and remained with the tenants for a long time ... The attack occurred on Tuesday. Men from the 30th SA Company were involved, most of whom work at the glassworks and who were formally KPD members.[133]

Despite the political ramifications surrounding the incident, no record survives of the official reaction, although the Gestapo was informed.

The Röhm purge contained the worst excesses and reduced petty violence, but failed to eliminate it completely. Attacks on individuals continued into 1935 although, judging from the diminished space devoted to the topic in official reports, on a reduced scale.[134] Moreover, the authorities seemed to be well in control of events by this time. Thus after an attack by stormtroopers in uniform on a former public official in Bad Tölz, Upper Bavaria, the attackers were prosecuted,[135] rather than the authorities simply restraining the attack as best they could, as so often happened in 1933 and early 1934. The violence and fury of the stormtroopers died away, incapable of achieving its ends in a society where bureaucratised violence was playing a progressively greater role.

Clearly the stormtroopers' anger was intense. However, they lashed out in piecemeal fashion against a wide range of targets which, they felt, represented a society that had failed or even betrayed them. This lack of selectiveness resembled a stampede which, for all its destructiveness, bypassed more serious obstacles lying in its path. Soft targets were the norm and the SA displayed few heroics. This reduced significantly any likelihood of a concerted frontal assault on the institutions of the state, however much stormtroopers may have despised that state – even if individuals such as policemen suffered abuse or even violence at the SA's hands.

It was the scale as much as the direction of SA activity which made it intolerable to Hitler and the government after the Nazi takeover. The sheer volume of intimidation, violence and disruption threatened to discredit and even to undermine the new administration, not least by exasperating its conservative allies, including the army. The depth of feeling behind the violence prevented any easy solution to the problem. The SA promised to remain in acute embarrassment to Hitler, either until it was brought forcibly to heel, or until the grievances of its members were redressed. In mid-1934, with the purge of the SA's leaders and the announcement of cutbacks in the SA's numerical strength, Hitler chose the former course.

Notes

1 For further discussion of this phenomenon see: E. Frenkel-Brunswik, 'Sex, people and self as seen through the interviews', in T. W. Adorno *et al.*, *The Authoritarian Personality* (New York, 1969), pp. 409–11.

2 For instance, GStAM, MA 100426. Zu Nr. 2013g.11. Übersicht über die in Bayern in der Zeit vom 1. Januar bis 31. Dezember 1931 verübten politischen Gewalttaten. For a national picture during the period before 1933, and especially June–October 1932, see IfZ, MA 616/20, 73794–73819 (SA III – Ausschreitungen).

3 The pattern of terror is described by W. Sauer, *Die Mobilmachung der Gewalt,*

200   *Stormtroopers*

Vol. 3 of K. D. Bracher, G. Schulz and W. Sauer, *Die nationalsozialistische Machtergreifung*, (Frankfurt-am-Main, Berlin and Vienna, 1974), pp. 235–55.

4   GStABD, Rep. 77, Nr. 23. ?-tsausschuss Breslau des Allgemeinen Deutschen Gewerkschaftsbundes. Herrn Vizekanzler Franz von Papen, Berlin. Breslau, den 8. März 1933. This communication was passed subsequently by Papen's office to Göring. There is no record of Göring's response.

5   GStABD, Rep. 77, Nr. 32. Nationalsozialistische Deutsche Arbeiter-Partei Kreisleitung Liegnitz, Stadt-Land. Der Kreisleiter. An die Untergauleitung Niederschlesien, Untergauleiter. Liegnitz, den 12. März 1933.

6   GStAM, R37. Der Beauftragte der Reichsregierung. Rundfunkmeldung. München, 11.3.33.

7   GStABD, Rep. 77, Nr. 32. SA der NSDAP. Der Führer der Gruppe Westfalen. B.B. Nr. 721/33. Betrifft: Staatliche Enteignung marxistischer parteieigener Gebäude. An den Preussischen Innenminister Göring. Bochum, den 30. März 1933. gez. Schepmann.

8   ibid.

9   GStABD, Rep. 77, Nr. 32. Achtung! Lesen! Weitergeben! Hitlers Taten. 36. Kampfgruppe revolutionäre Marxisten.

10 BHStA, Abt. I, M. Inn/71715. Abschrift zu Nr. II 38836a vom 22.7.1933. A.V.E. 811–814/33. Tgb. Nr. 1399. Der Oberstaatsanwalt bei dem Landgerichte. Betreff: Besondere Vorkommnisse, hier Ausschreitungen in Dürkheim am 25./26. VI. 1933. Frankenthal, den 14. Juli 1933.

11 See pp. 1, 25–45.

12 Of 263 KPD internees, 155 were described as functionaries and 40 as leading activists; of 4 SPD internees, 3 were functionaries; of 9 Reichsbanner internees, 8 were functionaries and the other a leading activist; of 2 Iron Front internees, 1 was a functionary: BHStA, M. Inn, Bd. 22/73690. Verzeichnis der Schutzgefangenen in Bayern, die länger als 3 Monate verwahrt sind. München, 1.8.1933. Of 4,152 people in protective custody on 5 August 1933 in Bavaria, 2,218 were in Dachau concentration camp: BHStA, Abt. I, M. Inn/73690. Staatsministerium des Innern. Betreff: Schutzhaft. An den Herrn Staatsminister des Innern, München. München, den 5. August 1933.

13 R. N. Hunt, *German Social Democracy, 1918–1933* (Chicago, 1970), pp. 7–63.

14 For Reichstag members: Hunt, *Social Democracy*, pp. 92–3, tables 4 and 5. For members of the Reichsbanner National Committee, of which none were working class: BA, Sch 273. Polizeidirektion Nürnberg-Fürth. Sonderbericht Nr. 162/11/29, Anlage 3. Nürnberg, 24.10.1929. For the Reichsbanner's middle-ranking and junior leadership: K. Rohe, *Das Reichsbanner Schwarz Rot Gold* (Stuttgart, 1965), p. 272.

15 Of the group of 1,650 stormtroopers from the Frankfurt-am-Main SA (30 June 1934), for instance, 68 had definitely belonged to the NSBO – more undoubtedly did so. Source: HHW, as for Frankfurt SA sources.

16 BHStA, Abt. I, So. I/1867. 'Wesen und Zweck der NSBO', *Der Betriebs-Stürmer. Zeitschrift der nationalsozialistischen Betriebszellen-Organisation, Gau* München-Oberbayern, No. 2, 6 March 1931, p. 6.

17 ibid., p. 8.

18 I. Buchloh, *Die nationalsozialistische Machtergreifung in Duisburg*, (Duisburg, 1980), pp. 54–61.

19 BA, NS26/323. Letter dated 18 June 1931 from SA man Kurt Becker, Company 33, from inside Moabit prison.

20 BA, NS23/401. Standarte 15. Abt. Ic. Betr.: Bericht über Polizei in Bergedorf. Der SA Untergruppe Hamburg. Hamburg, den 18.3.33.

21 BA, NS23/401. Standarte 76. Der SA Untergruppe Hamburg. Betr.: Wehrsportabteilung der Polizei. Hamburg, den 4.5.1933.

22 GStABD, Rep. 77, Nr. 32. NSDAP Gauleitung Pommern. Gaupropagandaleiter. Stettin, den 20.III.1933.

23 For instance, although the DNVP was for social reasons especially obnoxious in stormtroopers' eyes, its paramilitary ally, the Stahlhelm, was involved in a far greater number of confrontations with the SA both before and after 1933. See pp. 186–90.

24 The Bayernwacht and Pfalzwacht were the paramilitary wings of the Centre Party's Bavarian sister party, the Bavarian People's Party, or BVP.

25 BA, NS26/532. Paul Hainbach, Personal Recollections. Frankfurt-am-Main. 1 January 1937. Although Frankfurt-am-Main was predominantly Protestant, some surrounding areas were Catholic and hence the explanation for Hainbach's concern over this party.

26 There were even several resulting SA deaths. For instance: BA, NS26/523. Gestapo Saarbrücken. Betrifft: Mord an den SA-Mann Josef Wiesheier . . . 28.1.1937.

27 SM, NSDAP 803. Abdruck. SA der NSDAP, Standarte 25. B.B. Nr. 856/34. Betreff: Kath. Burschen- und Gesellenvereine. An die Sturmbanne I, II, III/25. Garching, den 24.4.1934.

28 GStAM, R281. Auszug aus dem Rapport der Bayerischen Politischen Polizei vom 4. Mai 1934. Festnahmen.

29 GStAM, R276/2. Nr. 453, Abdruck. Lagebericht (Monatsbericht) des Regierungs-Präsidenten von Schwaben und Neuburg. Augsburg, den 7. März 1935.

30 GStAM, R276/1. Nr. 2030, Abdruck. Augsburg, den 21. November 1933.

31 GStAM, R276/2. Nr. 746, Abdruck. Lagebericht (Halbmonatsbericht) des Regierungs-Präsidenten von Schwaben und Neuburg. Augsburg, 17.4.34.

32 BA, NS26/519. Eppstein, 26.II.1933. The SA's access to horses, albeit of indeterminate numbers, confirms that the SA did have some links with the farming community. SA leaders, in particular, who came from a farming background were able to provide horses for occasional SA use. Similarly, the SA relied on the owners of motor vehicles – whether cars, vans, lorries or motor bikes – to provide its small motorised section with vehicles.

33 GStAM, MA 106672. Nr. 352. Halbmonatsbericht des Regierungspräsidiums von Niederbayern und der Oberpfalz. Regensburg, 20.3.1933.

34 GStAM, R276/2. Nr. 1891, Abdruck. Monatsbericht des Regierungspräsidenten von Schwaben und Neuburg. [Autumn 1934].

35 Minor incidents none the less persisted. For instance, in Upper Bavaria there were scuffles between the SA and the local population over whether the Bavarian or the Nazi flag would fly on the maypoles! See GStAM, R280/3. Nr. 1055. Der Regierungspräsident von Oberbayern. Betr.: Lagebericht für April/Mai 1935.

36 GStAM, MA 106672. Nr. 915. Halbmonatsbericht des Regierungspräsidiums von Niederbayern u. der Oberpfalz. Regensburg, 7.8.1933.

37 For instance, SAG, Rep. 240/C61b(1). Ortsgruppe Widminnen.

38 H. Bennecke, *Hitler und die SA* (Munich, 1962), p. 126.

39 BA, NS23/474. Untergruppe Pfalz-Saar. Stimmungsbericht. Neustadt an der Haardt, 21.9.32. gez. Schwitzgebel.

40 NHStA, Hann. 310 I E3. Anlage zum 6. Wahlrundschreiben vom 28. Oktober 1932. Unsere Partei. 15.9.32.

41 ibid., Nr. 19. 1.10.32.

42 BA, NS26/523. Zu Schreiben an die NSDAP. Ortsgruppe Stolp. 19.10.1932. gez. Oberbürgermeister als Ortspolizeibehörde.

43 BA, NS26/1405. Berichte der Staatspolizei Württemberg zur politischen Lage den 29.10.1932 und den 27.10.32, Stuttgart, (a).

44 See p. 164.

45 BA, NS23/123. OSAF 1a Nr. 3047/31. Betrifft: Teilnahme an Übungen von Wehrverbänden. München, den 2.6.31. gez. Röhm.

46 R. J. Bessel, 'The SA in the Eastern Regions of Germany, 1925 to 1934' (D. Phil., Oxford University, 1980), p. 170.

47 BA, NS23/401. Ic. Lagen-Bericht der Untergruppe Hamburg. 10.12.1932. V. Stahlhelm.

48 BA, NS23/123. OSAF I Nr. 6193/31. An den Führer des Bayer. Stahlhelm, München. München, 24.10.1931. gez. Röhm.

49 BA, NS26/523. Geheime Staatspolizei. Schwerin, den 20. Oktober 1937.

50 For instance: BA, NS23/474. SA der NSDAP, Untergruppe Halle-Merseburg. Stimmungsbericht. An die OSAF, München. Halle a.S., 24.9.32; BA, NS23/474. SA der NSDAP, Untergruppe Göttingen. Göttingen, den 24.9.1932. Punkt 9.

51 BA, NS23/401. As in note 47.

52 K. D. Bracher, *The German Dictatorship* (London, 1973), pp. 281–2.

53 ibid. See also: BA, Sch 470. 'Der Jungstahlhelm unter Befehl der OSAF', *Völkischer Beobachter*, No. 174, 23 June 1933; BA, Sch 470. Der Oberste SA-Führer, Ch. Nr. 1336/33. Betrifft: Eingliederung des Stahlhelms in die SA. Verfügung. München, den 6.7.1933. gez. Röhm.

54 BA, Sch 470. Der Stahlhelm. Bund der Frontsoldaten. Der Bundesführer. Bundesbefehl für die Neugliederung des Stahlhelm B.d.F. Berlin, den 18. Juli 1933. gez. Seldte.

55 BA, NS26/308. Der Oberste SA-Führer, Ch. Nr. 1540/33. Betreff: Stahlhelm. München, 26.9.33. gez. Röhm.

56 As above, and BA, Sch 470. Der Stahlhelm B.d.F. B.Befehl für den Stahlhelm, B.d.F. Berlin, den 20. Juli 1933. gez. v. Stephani. Here it is stated that at the age of 36, Wehrstahlhelmer who had been transferred to the SA would return to the Stahlhelm.

57 BA, Sch 470. Stahlhelm B.d.F. Der Bundeshauptmann. Abt. Ia. B. Befehl für den Stahlhelm, B.d.F. Berlin, d. 20. Juli 1933. This order refers specifically to the NSDFB and also mentions the SA Reserve. However, frequent references to the SAR I elsewhere, and the context in which these were made, indicates that the Core Stahlhelm did either enter the SAR I or remain in the NSDFB.

58 GLAK, Abt. 465d/1282. SA der NSDAP. Der Führer der Brigade 150, Rheinhessen. Vierteljahresbericht für das 1. Vierteljahr 1934. gez. Schönborn, IX.

59 GStAM, MA 106682. Nr. 693, Abdruck. Lagebericht (Halbmonatsbericht) des Regierungs-Präsidenten von Schwaben und Neuburg. Augsburg, den 22.4.1933.

60 See p. 167, and GStAM, MA 106670. Nr. 2213. Halbmonatsbericht des Regierungs-Präsidiums von Oberbayern (1. mit 15. Juni 1933).

61 BA, NS23/124. Der Oberste SA-Führer I Nr. 956/1933. Betrifft: Feststellung der politischen Haltung des 'Stahlhelms' und seiner Mitglieder. München, den 7.4.1933. gez. Hühnlein; BA, NS23/409. Abteilung Ic. Der Untergruppe Hamburg. Betrifft: Stahlhelm. Hamburg, den 3. Juli 1933.

62 BHStA, Abt. I, So. I/1774. Präsidium der Bayr. Regierung von Oberfranken und Mittelfranken. An das Staatsministerium des Innern. Hd. des Herrn Ministerialdirektors Zetlmeier in München. Betr.: Politische Polizei. Ansbach, 17. Februar 1933.

63 BA, NS23/1. Der Oberste SA-Führer. Zentralamt. 'Kampf gegen die SA'. München, den 14. Juni 1934. p. 3.

64 BA, NS23/158. Abschrift. NSDAP Gauleitung Ost-Hannover. An die Standarte 26, Belum. Otterndorf, den 8. Dezember 1933.

65 BA, Sch 470. Der OSAF. Betr.: Aufnahme in den Stahlhelm. München, den 15.12.33. gez. Röhm.

66 BA, NS23/1. Der Oberste SA-Führer. Polit. Amt. Abtlg. Pol. Nr. 4668. Berlin, den 11. Mai 1934. gez. Röhm.

67 ibid.

68 BA, NS23/271. Der Oberste SA-Führer. Politisches Amt. Briefb. Nr. 5504. Berlin, den 13. Juni 1934. gez. v. Detten; BA, NS23/1. Der Oberste SA-Führer. Zentralamt. 'Kampf gegen die SA'. München, den 14. Juni 1934. p. 1. At this point, Brigade 12 of Hamburg forbade dual membership of the SA and NSDFB. See BA, NS23/391. SA der NSDAP, Brigade 12 (Hamburg). Betr. NSDFB (Stahlhelm). Hamburg, den 19.6.1934.

69 BA, NS23/1. As in note 66.
70 GStAM, R276/1. Nr. 1063. Halbmonatsbericht des Regierungspräsidiums von Niederbayern und der Oberpfalz. Regensburg. 19.9.1933.
71 GStAM, R276/1. Nr. 99. Halbmonatsbericht des Regierungspräsidiums von Oberbayern. (1. mit 15. Januar 1934). München, 17.1.1934. p. 2.
72 BA, NS23/158. Unser geliebter Stabschef! gez. Die ersten Kämpfer der Küstriner SA. Küstrin, den 1. Juni 1934.
73 BA, NS23/216. Geheim. An den SS-Standartenführer Diehls, Ministerialrat und Inspekteur der Geheimen Staatspolizei Berlin. Vorfälle in Schleswig-Holstein, den 17.1.1934. See also, a discussion of the case of a DNVP official from Marienburg, West Prussia, who was beaten up by the SA because of his anti-Nazi activities: GStABD, Rep. 77, Nr. 32, Sheet Nr. 48. Entwurf. Der Staatssekretär im Preuss. M.d.J. Berlin, den 27. September 1933.
74 BA, NS23/2. OSAF, F2 Nr. 34312. Betreff: NSDFB (Stahlhelm). München, den 23.11.1934. gez. Lutze. For other cases of ill-feeling and violence see: GStABD, 90P: 80/3. III. Allgemeine Übersicht über die politische Lage im Monat April 1935 im Bezirk der Staatspolizeistelle für den Regierungsbezirk Arnsberg in Dortmund: NSDFB (Stahlhelm); GStABD, 90P: 83/1. Staatspolizeistelle für den Regierungsbezirk Aachen. Betrifft: Lagebericht für den Monat August 1935. Aachen, den 5. September 1935, p. 47.
75 GStAM, R276/2. Nr. 1191, Abdruck. Regierungspräsidium von Unterfranken und Aschaffenburg. Betr.: Monatsbericht für Oktober 1934. Würzburg, 7.11.1934.
76 BA, NS23/265. Standarte 22. 4. Vierteljahresbericht 1934. Zweibrücken, 26.12.34.
77 BA, NS23/265. SA Brigade 250. Vierteljahresbericht. Offenbach/Main, 9.1.1935. The report concerned Wiesbaden; BA, NS23/265. Vierteljahresbericht. SA St. 70. II. Vierteljahr 1935. Miesenbach. gez. Schenkel.
78 BA, Sch 470. Bayerische Politische Polizei. Betr.: NS-Deutscher Frontkämpferbund (Stahlhelm). München, den 27.5.1935. i.V. gez. Stepp.
79 BA, NS23/262. SA der NSDAP. Führer der Brigade 150, Rheinhessen. Lagebericht für das 4. Vierteljahr 1934 (Okt/Dez). Mainz, 19.12.34.
80 BA, NS23/262. OSAF. Stabsabteilung. Bericht Nr. 19. München, 28.1.35. p. 8.
81 BHStA, Abt. I, So. I/1545. Auszug aus dem L. Nr. 105 vom 23. Oktober 1931, München.
82 This friction is well documented: A. Werner, 'SA und NSDAP' (Dissertation, Friedrich Alexander Universität zu Erlangen, 1964), pp. 478–516; Bennecke, 'Hitler und SA', pp. 147–52; E. Schön, *Die Entstehung des Nationalsozialismus in Hessen* (Miesenheim am Glan, 1972), pp. 126–31.
83 P. Hüttenberger, *Die Gauleiter* (Stuttgart, 1969), p. 68; Werner, 'SA und NSDAP', pp. 464, 518–19.
84 BHStA, Abt. I, So. I/1773. Bericht. 2.1.31. Wassertrudingen.
85 BA, NS23/407. NSDAP, Gau Hamburg. An Osaf Stellv. Nord, Hannover. Hamburg, den 26.11.1929.
86 BA, NS23/306. Brigade 50, (Starkenburg) Darmstadt. An Gruppe Kurpfalz. 20.12.34. gez. Lindenfels.
87 BHStA, Abt. I, So. I/1553. Aus dem Lagebericht Nr. 112a der Pol. Direktion, München vom 20. Oktober 1932.
88 BA, NS26/522. Stapostelle Dortmund. Aufgestellt Dortmund, den 12. Mai 1938.
89 BHStA, Abt. I, So. I/1550. 'Schwere Naziunruhen in Schweidnitz', *Münchner Post*, No. 260, 16 November 1932.
90 BA, NS23/399. Gau-Propaganda und Schulungsleiter. II. Gau Schleswig-Holstein. Rundschreiben Nr. 2. Itzehoe, den 27. April 1932.
91 BA, NS23/401. Untergruppe Hamburg. Abt. 1c. Warnung. 5.4.1932. gez. Böckenhauer.
92 BA, NS23/298. SA der NSDAP. Der Führer der Standarte 168. An die Brigade 250, Offenbach/Main. Offenbach a. Main, 15.12.34.

93 BA, NS23/399. Untergruppe Hamburg. An die SA-Gruppe Nordsee, Bremen. Hamburg, den 4 Juli 1933.

94 J. Klenner, *Verhältnis von Partei und Staat 1933–1945* (Munich, 1974), pp. 78–9; Sauer, *Die Mobilmachung der Gewalt* (see note 3), pp. 239–56.

95 GStAM, MA 106677. Halbmonatsbericht des Regierungspräsidiums von Oberfranken und Mittelfranken. Ansbach, den 21.6.1933.

96 R. Diels, *Lucifer ante Portas* (Zurich, 1949), pp. 159–67.

97 BA, NS26/323. Letter dated 12 June 1931 from gaoled SA man Paul Maikowski, Company 33, Berlin.

98 BA, NS26/323. Letter to 'Bubi' dated 19 October 1931 from Paul Maikowski, Company 33, Berlin.

99 BA, NS26/528. H. H. Horn, Personal Recollections. Giessen, 29 December 36.

100 BA, NS26/528. Heinz Mai, Personal Recollections. Frankfurt-am-Main, 6 August 1934.

101 BA, NS26/597. *Arbeiter Bauern Soldaten. Kampblatt der Nationalsozialisten*, A. B.S. No. 3, Berlin, 18 April 1931, p. 2.

102 BA, NS26/83. 'Anleitung für den Aufbau der SA', *Die Front der Arbeiter Bauern Soldaten. Nachrichtenblatt der 'National-Sozialistischen Kampfbewegung Deutschlands'*, No. 1, Berlin, 15 September 1931, p. 2.

103 BA, Sch 330. 16. März 1933. [No heading] gez. SA Untergruppe Hamburg. Opposition.

104 M. Jamin, 'Zur Rolle der SA im nationalsozialistischen Herrschaftssystem', in G. Hirschfeld and L. Kettenacker (eds), *The 'Führer State'* (Stuttgart, 1981), pp. 334–8.

105 BA, NS23/474. SA der NSDAP. Der Führer der Standarte 5, Danzig. Tgb. Nr. 4008/32. Betr.: Stimmungsbericht. Danzig, den 24. September 1932. p. 1.

106 GStAM, MA 106670. Nr. 283. Halbmonatsbericht des Regierungs-Präsidiums von Oberbayern (15. mit 31. Januar 1933). München, 6.2.1933.

107 BA, Sch 330. Hamburg Ic. 3.6.1933. gez. Moeller.

108 HHW, Abt. 483/NSDAP 2236. SA der NSDAP. Sanitätstrupp der Standarte 99. Betrifft: SA-Anwärter Heinerich Hohmann. Frankfurt-am-Main, den 14. Juli 1934.

109 NWHStA, Ge 5523. H.-J. A., born 10 July 1902. res. Düsseldorf. Landesrat, Dr. Phil., SA-Standartenführer.

110 BA, NS26/322. 'Pg., SA Kameraden!', Berlin, den 31. Mai 1931. Further leaflets in same file. See also BA, NS26/315. *Sturmbanner. Sprachrohr der revolutionären SA und SS Kameraden*, No. 1, end November 1932, p. 1.

111 ibid.

112 BA, Sch 330. Mai 1933. 'Geht es dem Volk besser? Kameraden der SA und SS . . . '

113 BHStA, Abt. I, So. I/1550. 'Aufruhr in der SA', *Münchner Post*, No. 215, 18 September 1931.

114 BHStA, Abt. I, So. I/1508. 'Gewaltige Rebellion im Hitlerlager', *Münchner Post*, No. 3, 4 January 1933.

115 BHStA, Abt. I, So. I/1550. ('Hitlers Garden meutern!', *Neue Zeitung*, No. 197, 2 September 1930.

116 BHStA, Abt. I, So. I/1508. Zum Akt: SA (NSDAP). München, den 25.IV.1931. Polizeidirektion. gez. Wenzel. 'Scheringer an die Scheringer-SA, Ulm. Schluss mit Hitler! Vorwärts mit der KPD! SA Proleterwache!', *Neue Zeitung*, 14. April 1931.

117 BHStA, Abt. I, So. I/1522. 'Hugenberg-Bauchschmerzen bei SS u. SA. SA Proleten, nur die KPD führt das werktätige Volk zum Kampf um die soziale und nationale Befreiung', *Neue Zeitung*, No. 27, 2 February 1933.

118 BA, Sch 331. KPD Wasserkante.

119 See pp. 32 and 35–6.

120 Against the concept of parasitical dynamism within the Nazi state, J. Caplan has recently argued that the Nazi state's failure to reproduce itself as a viable political system was not so much due to its fundamentally anti-bureaucratic nature but, rather, to a range of specific historical circumstances. J. Caplan, 'Bureaucracy,

205 Targets for SA Radicalism

politics and the National Socialist State', in P. D. Stachura (ed.), *The Shaping of the Nazi State* (London, 1978), pp. 234–56.

121 M. Weissbecker, 'Nationalsozialistische Deutsche Arbeiterpartei (NSDAP) 1919–1945', in D. Fricke, *et al.* (eds), *Die bürgerlichen Parteien in Deutschland* (Leipzig, 1970), p. 403; BA, NS23/1. As note 63. pp. 3–4.

122 BHStA, Abt. I, M. Inn/71715. Abschrift zu Nr. II 36650 vom 4. Juli 1933. T.B. 728/33. Staatsanwaltschaft für den Landgerichtsbezirk Kaiserslautern. Betreff: Vorgänge in Wolfstein, den 27. Juni 1933.

123 BHStA, Abt. I, M. Inn/71719. Abschrift. 1. Anklageschrift zum Amtsgericht b. Nbg. d. St. A. IX Nr. 2375/6/1933.

124 BA, NS23/125. OSAF, Ch. Nr. 1415/33. Betr.: Disziplin. München, den 31.7.1933. gez. Röhm.

125 BHStA, Abt. I, M. Inn/71719. Staatsanwaltschaft bei dem Landgerichte Nürnberg-Fürth. A.B. Nr. IX 2287/1933. Betreff: Misshandlung des 72-jährigen Rentners Georg Hauffenmayer von Nürnberg durch 2 unbekannte Männer in SA-Uniform. Nürnberg, den 5. Oktober 1933.

126 GStAM, R276/1. Nr. 1299. Halbmonatsbericht des Regierungspräsidiums von Niederbayern und der Oberpfalz. (1) Allgemeine politische Lage. Regensburg, den 4. Dezember 1933.

127 GStAM, R276/2. Nr. 445, Abdruck. Regierungspräsidium von Unterfranken und Aschaffenburg. An das Staatsministerium des Innern. Halbmonatsbericht 1 für April 1934.

128 BA, NS23/158. Anonymous letter. Helmstedt, 30 December 1933. Received in Reichsministerium für Volksaufklärung u. Propaganda, 3 January 1934.

129 See pp. 99–101.

130 GStAM, MA 106672. As in note 36.

131 GStAM, R276/1. As in note 70.

132 SA commissars were not locally based SA leaders, but representatives of the SA High Command seconded by Röhm to government and administrative departments throughout Bavaria. This process was not matched in the remainder of the Reich. See O. Domröse, *Der NS-Staat in Bayern von der Machtergreifung bis zum Röhm Putsch* (Munich, 1974), pp. 287–8.

133 NWHStA, Ge 12594. K.M., Düsseldorf-Gerresheim, 31.8.1933. An den Herrn Standartenführer Hauptmann a.D. Lohbeck.

134 For instance: GStAM, R276/2. Nr. 1891, Abdruck. Monatsbericht des Regierungspräsidenten von Schwaben und Neuburg. Augsburg, den 6. Oktober 1934; GStAM, R276/2. Nr. 2148. Monatsbericht des Regierungspräsidiums von Oberbayern (Nov. '34). München, 8.12.1934; BA, NS23/216. Geheimes Staatspolizei Br. Nr. II 1 H2 (981/35). Kz. Betr.: Gruss der Fahnen der SA. An die Oberste SA-Führung. Berlin, den 12. Juli 1935; BHStA, Abt. I, M. Inn/736686. Nr. 2168 a 20, 23, 25, 19, 30. Betreff: Ausschreitungen. Vormerkung über die Feststellung in den Regierungsberichten (ausgenommen Oberbayern). München, November 1935.

135 GStAM, R276/2. Nr. 606. Monatsbericht des Regierungspräsidiums von Oberbayern (März 1935). München, den 8. April 1935.

8 *The SA in the Radical Camp: Stormtroopers and Communists*

The SA found it relatively easy to outpoint activist groups which supported the republican or the pre-republican order. The economic crisis largely discredited the advocates of the *status quo*, particularly in the eyes of the unemployed, while youth usually rejected any return to a bygone age of monarchist grandeur. The SA lost these advantages when competing with other radical activist groups which, like itself, rejected the liberal and social democratic values of Weimar and also traditional, national–conservative values. Among these groups the KPD/Red Front featured prominently, being regarded by Röhm as the SA's main rival.[1]

On one level the KPD, like the SPD, was a target for SA radicalism and much of the political violence during the early 1930s involved clashes between Communists and stormtroopers. However, some recent research has noted appreciable transfers of membership between the SA and KPD.[2] Communist–SA rivalry was, therefore, possibly produced by competition for the same social groups rather than (as was often assumed previously) the product of direct class conflict. It is recognised that the economic crisis exacerbated existing political divisions, and created new ideological rifts within the working-class movement. These ideological differences acquired a more distinctly socio-economic basis than previously: a division between the haves and have-nots, with the SPD and KPD most commonly quoted in this context.[3] The SA was arguably an additional element in the equation, providing an alternative for the unemployed working classes to the KPD's style of anti-Weimar politics.[4] The membership of the KPD and SA was not identical, with the SA tending to attract skilled workers and a sizeable minority of clerical staff and some farmers and the KPD larger numbers of unskilled workers.[5] None the less, the two bodies' social profiles overlapped substantially, especially since the SA and KPD were, in contrast with the SPD, youthful bodies[6] and, returning to the effects of the economic crisis, both above all attracted the unemployed.[7] Therefore in social terms transfers between the two organisations would not have been particularly strange, while their members' ideologically confused, but none the less powerful, urge for social and economic change sometimes made such transfers of loyalty imperative.

The stormtroopers' material suffering and resulting sense of outrage, like that of most other contemporary radical activists,[8] was not only vented on parties, institutions and individuals, but also demanded the elimination of the republic itself.[9] This implied, however vaguely it was expounded, that fundamental social and political changes would follow.[10] The precise nature of these changes was, arguably, of secondary importance, but the combination of intense material suffering and moral outrage made speed of the essence. Relations between the SA and KPD, and also the SA's own prospects for success, revolved as much around this issue as anything else.

Spectacular electoral gains between 1929 and mid-1932 vindicated Hitler's policy of legality and most, but not all, stormtroopers believed that victory was imminent and that decisive social and political changes were at hand. For instance, a gaoled Berlin stormtrooper wrote to his unit in June 1931:

> My hope and my belief in our victory and the belief in our Idea has not left me for a single day. On the contrary, it has strengthened daily, for our victory is just around the corner.[11]

The imperatives of moral wrath and material desperation produced a massive commitment by stormtroopers to victory during summer 1932.[12] The Bavarian authorities later reported that, 'The members shouldered these considerable demands, both materially and physically, in the certain hope that they would thereby help their party to final victory and themselves to a job'.[13] However, this report appeared in October 1932 as the likelihood of a Nazi victory faded and it therefore also spoke of mounting disillusionment following the dashing of these hopes.

Indeed, the SA's triumph in early 1933 led contemporaries, and has led more recent observers, to ignore the tenuousness of its advance which was dependent on the correct or mistaken belief in imminent Nazi victory at the polls. Just as electoral success triggered upsurges in SA recruitment, so setbacks or stagnation generally created crises of some kind.[14] Even though the Stennes Revolt of April 1931 and the crisis which preceded it occurred during a period of rapid Nazi electoral advance, the incident does illustrate this process. Stennes, with the impatience typical of a radical activist, argued that failure to achieve total victory in the September 1930 election demonstrated that the parliamentary road was leading the NSDAP into a blind alley.[15] While this contradicted the prevailing mood that the NSDAP's policy of legality was proving extraordinarily successful, the origins and possible implications of the Stennes Revolt appeared disturbing enough. Stennes warned Röhm of a looming showdown in February 1931 as demoralisation grew throughout the SA formations under his command:

> All the [SA's problems] are leading, under pressure from the wretched economic situation and from political prospects which are, for the immediate future barely encouraging, to growing disgruntlement in the SA . . . From the middle-ranking leadership right down

to the last SA man, nobody understands the measures of the last six months.[16]

Material deprivation, frustrated hopes for political change, and the consequent need to act quickly were the potentially explosive forces at work.

When the revolt occurred in April 1931 the mainstream Nazi movement contained it with relative ease.[17] The authorities recognised this and discounted any immediate serious damage to the Nazi movement, but they regarded potential gains for the KPD from future such occurrences with concern:

> Much more serious attention should be paid to those voices who point to the danger of an exodus to the Communists caused by this fragmentation. The official Russian press is already concerning itself with this possibility.[18]

This report also cited the German press, including the *Kölnische Zeitung* of 8 April 1931, which was not alone in fearing that the KPD might gain most from the Stennes Revolt:

> If Hitler decides to expel all unreliable elements from the Storm Troops, then he must be clear that those expelled will be forced on the road to communism. The Communists could achieve no greater gain than if these largely unexploited activist forces fell into their hands.[19]

Ironically, Stennes himself argued that his revolt was intended to prevent this very process: 'Today we are fighting to preserve the betrayed and despairing party members from migrating to the ranks of the Commune'[20] – thereby recognising the threat to Nazism's activist appeal should its dynamism wane.

Of course, Stennes misjudged the political climate of the moment and, unlike Stegmann in January 1933,[21] failed to involve many ordinary stormtroopers in the revolt. The official NSDAP with its formidable, broadly based organisation remained the most convincing vehicle for fundamental change and the SA continued to grow rapidly in most of Germany. None the less, although premature, Stennes's fears were proven real enough in principle when, despite countless promises to the stormtroopers of imminent victory, the NSDAP failed to win an absolute majority at the polls in July 1932. Not only did this create discord in the SA, but initiated a drift of stormtroopers into the KPD. The commander of the Franconian SA, Stegmann, who was shortly to revolt with his men against the party, reported tersely in September 1932: 'Recruitment to the SA has dropped off for the first time during

August. Transfers from the SA's ranks to the KPD are increasing.'[22] Sub-Group Leine in Lower Saxony experienced similar problems. It attributed its recruitment of 'Marxists' partly to the SA's superior material benefits, but considered it equally important that these recruits 'expected the NSDAP would achieve more rapidly an alteration of the existing situation'.[23] With the collapse of Nazi confidence in autumn 1932, at least some of the ex-left-wingers evidently reverted to their former loyalties.[24]

This propensity to switch sides with changes in electoral fortunes features in the writings of many SA recruits. Thus the stormtrooper R. G., a worker from Essen, accounted in a very matter-of-fact way for his switch from the republican SPD to Nazism: 'Before the [Nazi] takeover I voted SPD and later, when I realised that the NSDAP was winning, I voted NSDAP.'[25] The apparent banality of his explanation would doubtless have been lost on him. Under the circumstances the SA Command was anxious to maintain the dynamic of success and, when this faltered, at least to keep up appearances. Thus as rival groups highlighted the SA's difficulties during autumn 1932, the High Command remarked: 'In order to dampen this howl of triumph somewhat, it would appear useful to counter these bodies with the same material.'[26]

The Central Committee of the KPD soon learned from provincial reports that the political stalemate of mid-1932 was demoralising the SA. Writing of mounting Nazi disillusionment after the July election, the Thuringian KPD noted that, 'Especially in SA and SS circles one finds increasingly expressions of exasperation with "the whole bloody mess"',[27] while the KPD in Magdeburg-Anhalt detected a similar mood:

> In Calbe and Genthin Nazis (SA) are declaring that Hitler has broken his promises and that it was all a bluff. According to reports, SA men engaged on the Reckleben Estate near Atzendorf are on strike.[28]

This was welcome news for the KPD, which had long since tried to attract working-class and lower-middle-class Nazis, seeking among other things to present itself as the champion of German nationalism. In 1930 the KPD somewhat incongruously branded the NSDAP as an unpatriotic, internationalist party. The Central Committee declared:

> We accuse the Hitler party of selling out the workers and salaried employees, the civil servants, the *Mittelständler*, and farmers a million times over through lies and treachery to the imperialist foreign powers.[29]

Similarly, *Rote Fahne* accused the NSDAP of being as pro-Western as the SPD:

> The Central Committee of the KPD has published a proclamation against Versailles and the Young Plan, to achieve social and national [!] liberation through the dictatorship of the proletariat. Everyone, from Hitler to Wels, rejected the Communist proposals to suspend the tribute burden. The worst agents of the capitalists and the Versailles imperialists are the NSDAP and SPD.[30]

Since the Versailles powers had opposed the extension of communism in Europe, the KPD's nationalism was not purely expedient, but for a nationalist-minded potential activist the SA was doubtless a more convincing alternative. The KPD's pro-Soviet propaganda and the well-publicised, if exaggerated, reports on Comintern activities made the KPD's claim to be a truly nationalist party ring hollow.

Once the SA faced problems in autumn 1932, the KPD was not content to remain a passive observer. Instead it acted wherever possible to accelerate the process. For instance, the KPD in Cologne discovered that it could easily exploit the SA's discomfiture:

> Through systematic subversive activity, we have achieved a situation in Cologne which exceeds the degree of subversion in the rest of the [Central Rhine] district. We have received reports that fights developed between the SA and SS in two Cologne SA hostels on election night. In the course of these, SA companies were disbanded.
>
> In Bonn an SA company tore up its flag in public on election night.
>
> The ideological work has recommenced at once, based on the election result.[31]

The KPD enjoyed similar success elsewhere after the November 6 election as the SA's morale and discipline throughout Germany deteriorated. The KPD noted the SA's mounting problems in north-west Germany.[32] A Munich police report observed as late as 21 January 1933 that the Munich SA was in rapid decline: 'No fewer than thirty-five men were expelled from SA Company 1 in December 1932, and fifteen during January, because they were no longer attending to duties.'[33] In Franconia, too, events were coming to a head in January. The SA commander, Stegmann, declared that Nazism, 'had missed its historic opportunity of coming to power through legal means', and emphasised the need for 'a more brutal and revolutionary fight'.[34] Only days before Hitler achieved power, Stegmann and many of his men left the Nazi movement.

Thus immediately before Hitler's takeover transformed its fortunes literally overnight, the SA was nearing collapse. There is little virtue in speculating on the possible consequences for German political life had

Hitler not become Reich Chancellor in January 1933, but the SA's prospects during another long year of opposition and, possibly, electoral decline, would have been bleak.

If the SA faced times of crisis the KPD had even greater difficulties and, after the Nazi takeover, it faced virtual disintegration in some areas at rank-and-file level. Except during the great crisis of late 1932, the SA's leaders had coped pragmatically and successfully with the challenges of radical activism. Their attitude to the specific problem of recruitment from the left was similarly pragmatic, although tempered with caution. Naturally, the senior leaders were uncompromisingly hostile to organised communism and the same usually applied to the middle and lower echelons of the leadership. However, the SA Command strove to recruit both individual KPD members and whole units, as well as Social Democrats – as Röhm himself testified[35] – and boasted successes well before the Nazi takeover.[36]

The SA's ability to attract former left-wingers also features in the personal recollections of many stormtroopers and evidently even predated the Nazi electoral breakthrough of 1929 and 1930. For instance, Georg Thomas of Worms wrote that in 1925, 'The Communists were no longer allowed to attend our meetings by their party, for the Jewish leaders soon realised that people were usually lost to communism when they had visited two or three meetings'.[37] More specifically, the stormtrooper Rudolf Bergmann recorded his success in winning over Communist workers in Suhl during 1927.[38] These scattered incidents probably reflected genuine changes in conviction or local factors, for the transfer rates certainly accelerated markedly when the Nazis achieved their electoral breakthrough. Albert Geis of Offenbach/Main recounted that the struggle between SA and KPD intensified during 1929 and 1930 as 'a leader and longstanding member of the KPD switched over to us',[39] while in his memoirs, Paul Then, an SA leader from Frankfurt-am-Main recalled that in a new SA unit which he founded in 1932, 'half of [the recruits] formerly belonged to the enemy camp'.[40]

Naturally, success itself was far more convincing than the prospect of success, however bright, and after Hitler's takeover the SA not only attracted the previously uncommitted in large numbers, but broke decisively into the ranks of their left-wing opponents, especially the KPD.[41] Diels writes, although perhaps self-interestedly, of the flood of former KPD members recruited by the Berlin SA during 1933,[42] and the process was repeated elsewhere. For instance, in 1936 the stormtrooper Karl Bund of Hessen-Nassau recalled the effects of the Nazi takeover: 'On 5 March the decisive election which secured the movement's seizure of power took place. On 6 March the Reichsbanner and Red Front joined up with the SA and donned the brown shirt.'[43] The alacrity of such conversions to the SA both here and elsewhere, in the northern Rhine basin for example, often startled existing stormtroopers who had fought the same individuals in the streets just days, if not hours, earlier.[44]

However, the SA's corporate consciousness was geared to such developments and its capacity for attracting former rivals became enshrined in its own mythology. An SA marching song, *Brüder in Zechen und Gruben*, contained the lines: 'Once we were Marxists, Red Front and SPD/Today Nazis, Fighters for the NSDAP', although the first line had run, 'Once we were Communists, Stahlhelm and SPD', until the Stahlhelm objected to being mentioned 'in the same breath' as the Communists![45]

Naturally, expediency of an immediate and pressing nature assisted changes in loyalty. Unemployed Reichsbanner[46] and Red Front members must have feared for their prospects of finding or keeping jobs if they remained openly hostile to the Nazi movement, not to mention fears for their physical safety. However, this type of expediency explains insufficiently the spectacular SA breakthrough of 1933, for although the process reached a climax at that point, it had begun long before and was inherent in radical activism.

This fluidity of membership between paramilitary organisations of the extreme left and right was reflected in elections where unemployed voters displayed a similar style of pragmatism. This behaviour was significant for the shaping of paramilitary politics since it provided the radical paramilitary organisations with ideologically malleable recruits who could, and did, fit in well. Above all, the destruction of conventional political norms, even in the electoral arena, provided the SA with a vast pool of potential recruits and, with Hitler's triumph in early 1933, with a flood of actual recruits.

Electoral analyses and forecasts by the KPD provide some graphic examples of this process. In April 1932, shortly before the second round of the German presidential elections, a KPD report concluded that in Württemberg, at least, the SPD retained the loyalty of most employed workers, but the Communists could take comfort from the clear lead that their candidate Thälmann enjoyed over Hitler among the employed voters. However, the report showed that things were very different among the jobless. The KPD believed that as many jobless workers planned to vote for Hitler as for Thälmann and the incumbent President, Hindenburg, (backed, among others, by the SPD) combined. The author of the report, a Central Committee member, commented:

> Most of those who wished to vote for Hitler were types who said to me, 'The SPD has betrayed us, you Communists are doing nothing, so we'll try voting for Hitler'. Perhaps things'll get worse; then we'll smash everything to pieces and Bolshevism can take over.[47]

Similarly, if slightly less melodramatically, two unaffiliated workers commented to a KPD functionary in Bielendorf, Silesia:

> What the Communists want is all absolutely right and communism will win in the end; but that's all taking much too long and you've got to do something at once. Although we sympathise with communism, we will therefore certainly vote National Socialist. Either Hitler will have to act, or everything will get going all the faster.[48]

Perhaps the belief of some elements within the KPD that a Nazi victory would only hasten the ultimate demise of capitalism is therefore understandable. However, the extent of the SA's expansion during 1933, and the measure of political control this would give the Nazi movement over so substantial a section of Germany's unemployed, were not foreseen in early 1932.

None the less, other signs suggested that not only were political loyalties becoming extremely unstable, but that outright confusion was growing. Typical was a report on the position in Gross-Rühden, Lower Saxony, during April 1932, when a KPD official noted his party's failure to penetrate the SPD-dominated factories of the area, but added that: 'In contrast, the divide between us and the Nazis has become fairly blurred, something that amounts of course to a great source of danger for us politically and organisationally.'[49] Another official, this time in Frankfurt-am-Main, was equally concerned by signs of ideological confusion which was beginning to penetrate the factories. Reporting on the position in the Kostheim Plastics Works he remarked:

> The Nazis have made advances recently in the factory. Six workers are known to be Nazi party members. Their influence among the staff is stronger. Since the beginning of the year the Nazis have published a factory news-sheet monthly, which bears the title 'The Revolutionary' and the sub-title 'The Militant Voice against Fascism'.[50]

Thus many of the unemployed and even some of the employed, who had stood aside from paramilitary politics until 1933, but had lost faith in the political order and abandoned any hope of an economic recovery, joined the SA during 1933 in accordance with a previously held philosophy. Had the KPD triumphed in early 1933 it is arguable that the same people within the brown-shirted stormtroopers who ransacked trade-union buildings would have meted out similar treatment to big business and finance in the name of communism. The exit ticket from Weimar was the immediate, vital issue and for a time the ultimate destination seemed unimportant.[51]

The SA's great triumph was, therefore, in a key sense triggered by developments on a national level. However, the preconditions for this breakthrough were as much the products of local as national developments, and no paramilitary organisation enjoyed uniform success throughout Germany. The KPD, for instance, believed that its efforts to win over the unemployed working classes had failed badly in rural northern Germany while the SA and NSDAP had fared better in attracting jobless workers in the same areas.[52] Nazism's appeal to the values of the 'national community' or *Volksgemeinschaft* is well understood, but equally recruits to the SA – and arguably any paramilitary activist organisation – sought the comradeship and communal solidarity of their immediate circle. This comradeship was partly created by the common struggle for material survival in an impoverished society, but a paramilitary activist understood that fights with the authorities and with rival activist groups who ostensibly opposed his own group's politics would also form an integral part of life in the paramilitary community. Since the finer points of ideology seldom counted for much in practice, the activist sought the most effective vehicle for change on a local as well as a national level. Joining a group which was weak in his area and, therefore, impotent made little sense, unless its undisputed nationwide strength compensated for this local inferiority.

Thus local SA formations realised that a struggle with rival radical activist groups was an inevitable part of establishing themselves in new areas, and local SA histories stressed the early fights, which evidently acquired both a symbolic and a practical importance. This is illustrated by a history of the Heidelberg SA which described a first, bloody fight that failed to establish an SA presence in the 'Red' district of Kirchheim. However, it continued that 'the SA march of 19 January 1930 was the beginning of the struggle for 'Red' Kirchheim. We came again and again and drummed until Kirchheim, too, was ours'.[53] The methods used by the SA to extend its influence reinforces the impression that a clear demonstration of strength was necessary to attract recruits in significant numbers. The SA operated from its strongholds into a hostile area until it had been subdued. This violent behaviour was not perceived as a totally negative, destructive process, for sometimes the very people the SA hoped to, and did, recruit through violent struggle were their erstwhile adversaries.[54] The party history of the Widminnen party branch, East Prussia, wrote of its SA:

Now the SA. While the NSDAP voters were mainly from the middle classes, the SA were mainly the sons of workers, or their fathers were petty officials. These were anything but an élite, which was an advantage, since they didn't tag along with routine. Instead they occupied themselves disrupting SPD meetings and beating up their opponents, the Reichsbanner men – thoroughly and often at that.

They achieved in this way what could not be achieved in meetings. They impressed the workers, and once again, especially the young ones.[55]

Stormtroopers themselves appreciated the central role of day-to-day violence in radical activist politics and believed that the KPD's violence against themselves often resulted from their success among social groups which the KPD claimed to represent. Karl Memberger later wrote of the pre-takeover years in Wiesbaden:

> At first [the KPD] tried to win us over and gave us the *Red Flag* and so on free and tried to talk politics with us. When they realised that they were getting nowhere ideologically, they began to beat up individual SA men at the labour exchange ...[56]

Willi Madré of Friedberg in Hessen ascribed similar motives to Communist threats of violence delivered in mid-1930:

> In June we played so strongly on our opponents' nerves that they stopped at nothing to weaken or prevent our propaganda work. Several anonymous notes gave me the kind advice to switch propaganda activity from the towns to the countryside if I wanted to do well, since greater success and less resistance were to be expected there.[57]

A similar reactive process occurred in Berlin where Hermann Jung recalled events in the Alexanderplatz district of the city: 'When the Communist leaders noticed that some of their men marched with us under the swastika flag behind Horst Wessel, they couldn't contain their rage any longer.'[58] In Munich, too, vigorous SA recruiting activity, such as the leafleting of the working-class Laim district in April 1930, provoked immediate KPD retaliation. After distributing leaflets stormtroopers found a decidedly menacing communication delivered to their own addresses:

> You hireling Jewish mercenaries of the Nazi assassin squads! – called the SA. If you want to hear yourselves scream, come to our block again. But don't forget your life insurance. Bring the papers along so that your marvellous contributions can be signed up for the last time.
> Guaranteeing your certain eradication,
> The Revolutionary Working Class.[59]

The same pattern occurred until Hitler's election victory in March 1933, with each side reacting in turn. For instance, the SA in Wuppertal-Barmen reported in April 1931 that, 'Communists have formed small terror groups for several months now, which set upon and beat up individual SA men. Suitable counter-measures by us have settled this little game'.[60] Similar incidents were reported from most parts of Germany with a rising spiral of fights, injuries and occasionally deaths.[61]

The picture was, not surprisingly, similar when viewed from the perspective of rival paramilitary activist groups. At local and national levels they were uncomfortably aware of the powerful impression created by the SA, and the KPD paid particularly close attention to the SA's activities. For instance, in June 1930 the Berlin KPD reported that 'the Nazis are now attempting to conquer the streets and also the factories through the terror of their Storm Troops'.[62] Even when the SA was not overtly violent, the potent impression given by the relatively well-disciplined and more or less uniformly dressed SA indicated that a compelling presence could count for more than political debate. A KPD official touring Hessen during the campaign for the July 1932 Reichstag elections wrote that he bettered the Nazis ideologically at a meeting attended by 225 unaffiliated workers and 220 to 225 Nazis. However, he emphasised the limited effectiveness of his debating success remarking: 'The tighter organisation of the Nazis under the command of their SA leaders was very apparent, in contrast to the disorganised collection of workers.'[63]

The KPD's leaders revealingly and understandably strove to develop a credible alternative to the SA's activism which, in essence, sought to fight fire with fire. The merging of the KPD's paramilitary and political functions following the banning of the Red Front often makes it hard to distinguish between parliamentary and activist campaigns. The two were more closely interrelated than within the Nazi movement, where the SA distanced itself from the party on principle, despite its close involvement in election work. Thus, when assessing the results of the July 1932 Reichstag election, the KPD's Greater Thuringia district discussed activist operations, as much as the humdrum of routine electoral work:

> The party directed unemployment campaigns in thirty-two towns; it established Mass Self-Defence Formations in fifty-four towns. A large number of Social Democratic workers were won for these bodies as well as for the struggles; indeed alongside the unaffiliated workers, Nazi workers were won for the unemployment campaigns. This means that the Anti-Fascist Action was and is a powerful United Front movement.[64]

The recruitment of Fascists to an anti-Fascist movement might appear incongruous, but it was common enough and here, too, the activist mentality need not have found such a move especially difficult.

In its confrontation with the SA, conspicuous success and dynamism were even more important to the KPD. In November 1931 the Württemberg police noted the problems of the Militant League against Fascism (Kampfbund gegen den Faschismus) in their area.

> After initial successes in the first months following its establishment, an unmistakable stagnation in the Kampfbund's development has set in . . .
> . . . Because of this situation, an irritable mood has arisen. This has found expression in continual personal disputes at the league's group evenings, and in many resignations from dissatisfied leaders and members and in desertions to the SA of the NSDAP. In September 1931, among other cases, the leader of the Stuttgart-Stockach group went over to the SA in unison with many of his men.[65]

This reaction is immensely revealing. In terms of party-based ideology the switch from Communism to Nazism is barely credible, but within the context of radical activism, with the SA doing well in Württemberg,[66] the move was almost obvious.[67]

The Nazi takeover in spring 1933 assured the SA's ultimate victory over its rivals, with the combination of manifest political success and SA terror overwhelming them totally. None the less the takeover created as many problems as it solved. Social and economic hardships continued to dog the stormtroopers and, as shown, perpetuated political instability within the SA, but the moral outrage, which equally fuelled the urge for drastic change, also remained unsatiated by the onslaught on left-wing institutions and by the other, less systematic violence. The stormtroopers had always regarded with hostility the traditional right and the institutions of society. Their call for a 'second revolution' consequently involved a final, thoroughgoing assault on the social, economic and political institutions on which they blamed their misfortunes.

For a time the party and the SA's leadership exploited successfully the stormtroopers for their own interests, but their usefulness to both could only be temporary. As early as February 1933 the Prussian Minister of the Interior noted that stormtroopers, and people posing as stormtroopers, had been involved in shootouts and urged the regional authorities to take necessary counter-measures.[68] In October 1933 the Reich Minister of the Interior complained that despite repeated announcements by Hitler and despite his own many circulars, 'New attacks by junior SA leaders and ordinary stormtroopers have been reported over and over again'.[69] The time was coming to remove the SA from the streets, but whether the stormtroopers were moved to well-paid jobs, punishing labour projects or, later, the armed forces was a matter of some indifference. While the SA leaders sported certain ill-defined emancipatory ideals, their main political interests after January 1933 focused on the army question[76] and their attempts to help the stormtroopers socially and economically were, at best, partially successful. Under the circumstances, pressures built up from below within the SA which threatened to exceed anything the body had witnessed before 1933,[71] but the leaders realised that this pressure might be used as a bargaining counter to further their ambition of creating a popular army.

Their unwillingness or inability either to fulfil their followers' demands or to control their membership weighed heavily in the decision to purge the SA's leadership in mid-1934. In public Hitler declared that the purge had been designed merely to remove a few morally and materially corrupt SA leaders and at a Cabinet meeting on 3 July he began by repeating this claim.[72] Röhm was a known homosexual (although this had not bothered Hitler or the electorate up until 1933), but the accusations of corruption were somewhat far-fetched. Only days earlier on 8 June, the Reich Ministry of the Interior had concluded that the SA was administering the state finances it received honestly and well.[73] Later, in the same Cabinet meeting, Hitler betrayed his real motives: 'It had not simply been a matter of snuffing out the Revolt through the example [made of the SA leaders] which he had sanctioned, but instead to make it clear to every single leader and SA man that he risked his neck if he conspired in any way whatsoever against the existing régime.'[74] Of course, Hitler knew that talk of an impending organised revolt was nonsense, but he had to admit in the relative privacy of the Cabinet room that the NSDAP's paramilitary wing, of which he was Commander-in-Chief, was, at best, utterly unreliable and, at worst, politically disloyal. Subsequently, a new, compliant SA Command struggled to restore its cowed but embittered membership to a mainstream society in which meaningful political rights had disappeared, and which was hard-pressed to provide them even with the 'bread and games' which Hitler had once contemptuously declared to characterise the aspirations of the working classes.[75]

Notes

1 M. Weissbecker, 'Nationalsozialistische Deutsche Arbeiterpartei (NSDAP) 1919–1945', in D. Fricke, *et al.* (eds), *Die bürgerlichen Parteien in Deutschland* (Leipzig, 1970), p. 403. See also p. 187.
2 For instance, W. Böhnke, *Die NSDAP im Ruhrgebiet, 1920–1933* (Bonn–Bad Godesberg, 1974), p. 154, note 73.
3 O. K. Flechtheim, *Die KPD in der Weimarer Republik* (Frankfurt-am-Main, 1976), pp. 316–17.

4   See S. Neumann, *Die Parteien der Weimarer Republik* (Stuttgart, Berlin, Cologne and Mainz, 1965), p. 87.
5   For SA see pp 25–45. For KPD, Flechtheim, *KPD*, pp. 314–17; Neumann, *Parteien*, pp. 94–5. Both, however, emphasise that the KPD also attracted its share of skilled workers, even during the depression.
6   For SA see pp. 48–50. For KPD, S. Bahne, 'Die Kommunistische Partei Deutschlands', in E. Matthias and R. Morsey, (eds), *Das Ende der Parteien*, (Düsseldorf, 1966), p. 660.
7   For SA see pp. 45–81. For KPD, Flechtheim, *KPD*, pp. 316–17.
8   For a discussion of this phenomenon within the wider Nazi movement see B. Moore, Jr., *Injustice* (London, 1978), pp. 411–20.
9   See pp. 155–7.
10 See A. Schweitzer, *Big Business in the Third Reich* (London, 1964), pp. 35, 113–19, 125; and C. Bloch, *Die SA und die Krise des NS-Regimes 1934* (Frankfurt-am-Main, 1970), p. 46, who perceive this demand for fundamental change, but interpret it as being lower middle class and specifically reactionary in nature.
11 BA, NS26/323. Letter dated 14 June 1931 from a gaoled SA man (anon.) in Berlin.
12 BHStA, Abt. I, So. I/1774. Abdruck. Amtsvorstand. Bezirksamt Bergzabern. Betreff: Vorbereitungen der NSDAP für den Wahltag. Bergzabern, den 27. Juli 1932; BA, NS23/474. SA der NSDAP, Untergruppe Magdeburg-Anhalt. Stimmungsbericht. Dessau, den 22.9.32.
13 BA, Sch 404. Aus dem Lagebericht Nr. 112a der Polizei-Direktion München vom 20. Oktober 1932. Militärähnliche Organisationen der NSDAP.
14 See pp. 158, 162–9.
15 BA, NS26/325. Abschrift 1161/31 St/v.B. An die Oberste SA-Führung z. Hd. des Herrn Oberstleutnant Röhm. 28. Februar 1931. gez. Stennes.
16 ibid.
17 A. Werner, 'SA und NSDAP' (Dissertation, Friedrich Alexander Universität zu Erlangen, 1964), pp. 531–5.
18 BHStA, Abt. I, So. I/1551. Zu IAN 2100 a 2, SH 1/13.5. Gründe und Auswirkungen des Zwistes Hitler-Stennes, pp. 11–13. Quote from p. 12.
19 ibid., p. 13.
20 BA, NS26/83. 'Wie es zur Stennes-Aktion kam!', herausgegeben von Walter Stennes, p. 16.
21 E. G. Reiche, 'The Development of the SA in Nuremberg, 1922 to 1934' (Dissertation, University of Delaware, 1972), ch. 5.
22 BA, NS23/474. SA der NSDAP. Der Gruppenführer Franken. I Nr. 4 geh. Betrifft: Stimmungsbericht. Schillingsfürst, Mfr., den 21. September 1932. (2) Zu- und Abgänge der SA.
23 BA, NS23/474. NSDAP. Der Führer der SA-Untergruppe Leine. Abt. IIb. Briefb. Nr. 756/32. Betrifft: Stimmungsbericht. Hameln, den 22. September 1932. (1) Stimmung in der SA.
24 ibid.
25 NWHStA, Ge 48,726. R. G., worker, born 19 December 1899. res. Essen. See also HHW, Abt. 483/NSDAP 2267. SA man Adolf Selig, factory-employed joiner, SA Regiment 99, Frankfurt-am-Main. 'Warum trat ich in die SA ein?', dated April 1933.
26 BA, NS23/124. Der Oberste SA-Führer. Abt. P. Nr. 3771/32. Betrifft: Zersetzungserscheinungen im feindlichen Lager. München, den 20. Dezember 1932.
27 BA, R451V/22. Bericht über meine Tätigkeit als Instrukteur während der Wahlperiode im UB 8. [Aue/Eibenstock, July 1932].
28 BA, R45IV/21. KPD analysis of July 1932 Reichstag election. Bezirk Magdeburg-Anhalt, p. 3.
29 BA, NS26/810. Entwurf. Deklaration des Zentralkommitees der KPD gegen die Tributsklaverei des deutschen Volkes ... , p. 4.

30 BA, NS26/1169. Pressebericht der Hauptorgane der Gegner. *Die Rote Fahne*, 12 March 1932.
31 BA, R45IV/21. KPD analysis of July 1932 Reichstag election. Bezirk Mittelrhein, p. 12.
32 BA, R45IV/44. Resolution des Bezirksparteitages über das XII Plenum des EKKI und die Aufgaben der Parteiorganisation in Nordwest. November 1932. pp. 11–12.
33 BHStA, Abt. I/So. I/1774. Police report, unsigned. Munich, 21 January 1933.
34 Reiche, 'SA in Nuremberg', p. 199.
35 See p. 187.
36 The party, too, had some successes in this field. For instance see: SAG, Rep. 240/C34d. NSDAP Bezirk Westpreussen. Tätigkeitsbericht des Bezirkes Westpreussen der NSDAP für Monat Februar 1931. Riesenburg, den 14.3.1931. gez. K. Schmidtke; SAG, Rep. 240/C38c2. Gauleitung der NSDAP. Propaganda. Königsberg Pr. 27.5.32.
37 BA, NS26/528. Georg Thomas, Personal Recollections. Worms, 24 November 1936.
38 BA, NS26/533. Rudolf Bergmann, Personal Recollections. Bad Orb, 28 December 1936.
39 BA, NS26/529. Albert Geis, Personal Recollections. Offenbach/M, 1 December 1936.
40 BA, NS26/532. Paul Then, Personal Recollections. Frankfurt-am-Main, 3 May 1937. Some SA recruits here and elsewhere were certainly Social Democrats rather than Communists. However, the assertion by an SA deserter to the KPD in Berlin that up to 30 per cent of the SA there were former Reichsbanner and SPD members appears very high: BA, R45IV/16. Berichte der Arbeiterkorrespondenten über die Lage in den Grossbetrieben unter der Militärdiktatur und dem Ausnahmezustand. (Von 20. – 26. Juli [1932]). p. 17, Siemens.
41 See pp. 56–7.
42 R. Diels, *Lucifer ante Portas* (Zurich, 1949), pp. 152–3.
43 BA, NS26/529. Karl Bund, Personal Recollections. Hessen-Nassau, 19 December 1936.
44 BA, NS23/9. Meldung von 1101. An V 99. Stimmungsbericht der SA Anwärter und NSBO. Opladen, den 11.7.33.
45 BA, NS23/125. Oberste SA-Führung. Der Chef des Stabes Z2 Nr. 1391/33. Betrifft: Aenderung eines Liedtextes. München, den 25. Juli 1933. gez. Seydel.
46 The activist, Schufo units of the Reichsbanner had particularly high proportions of unemployed within them: K. Rohe, *Das Reichsbanner Schwarz Rot Gold* (Stuttgart, 1965), pp. 272–3.
47 BA, R45IV/21. Bericht Nr. 2 (Württemberg). 16. April 1932.
48 BA, R45IV/21. Abschrift. Bericht für die BL Schlesien über den Unterbezirk Langenbielau. April '32. gez. Z.K. Instrukteur Richard Schulz.
49 BA, R45IV/21. Bericht über die Versammlungen im Bezirk Niedersachsen. April 1932. gez. Handke.
50 BA, R45IV/21. Versammlungsberichte. Frankfurt-am-Main, 7.–9.4.1932. gez. Werner.
51 cf. BA, R45IV/21. Bericht. 17.4–24.4.32. Schlesien. gez. Ziegler: 'Liegnitz: . . . The Nazis are very strong. The population does not know what the Nazis are and what they want. The attitude is as follows: All parties have let us down so far. Hitler has not been in power yet, he must have his chance. If he fails, then there is still plenty of time to go over to the Communists.'
52 BA, R45IV/5. Abschrift. Bericht Mecklenburg. Öffentliche Versammlung Lübz. Richthofen [1932]. gez. Hi; BA, R45IV/25. Protokoll der erweiterten Sekretariatssitzung der B.L. Pommern vom 26. April 1932. An Z.K. Sekretariat, p. 3, Diskussion – Genosse Wiesner (Stralsund); BA, R45IV/5. Bericht über Wahlversammlung in Mecklenburg. Berlin, den 30.5.1932. p. 3. gez. Edwin Hoenicke; BA, R45IV/5. An ZK, KPD Sekretariat. Bericht über Versammlungen in Oldenburg. Mannheim,

den 30.5.1932. gez. Paul Schreck; BA, R45IV/11. Bericht über den Bezirk Halle-Merseburg (2.–6. Mai 1932). p. 3. gez. Werner; BA, R45IV/21. Bericht über Wahlversammlung in Hessen. Mannheim, 19.6.1932. 15.6.32, Öffentliche Versammlung in Niederflörsheim. gez. Paul Schreck. cf. Chapter 3, note 257.

53 GLAK, 465d/1293. Aus dem Kampf der Heidelberger SA. Pfingsten 1925–März 1933. Tagebuchblätter von Oberführer Ziegler. 19.1.1930.

54 H. Bennecke, *Hitler und die SA* (Munich, 1962), p. 126.

55 SAG, Rep. 240/C61b(1). Die Geschichte der Bewegung der NSDAP, Ortsgruppe Widminnen.

56 BA, NS26/530. Karl Memberger, Personal Recollections. Wiesbaden, 5 December 1936, p. 2.

57 BA, NS26/529. Willi Madré, Personal Recollections. Friedberg, 7 December 1937.

58 BA, NS26/532. Hermann Jung, Personal Recollections. Frankfurt-am-Main, January 1937.

59 Text: BHStA, Abt. I, So. I/1554A. 'Achtung! Achtung! Achtung!'. gez. Die revolutionäre Arbeiterschaft. For interpretation of text: BHStA, Abt. I, So. I/1554A. Polizeidirektion Ref. VIa F. Betreff: Aigner, verh. Hilfsarbeiter. München, den 16. April 1930. Aigner was one of the Nazis who received the leaflet. Here he is giving evidence against a member of the KPD who had allegedly circulated the leaflets.

60 BHStA, Abt. I, So. I/1545. Abschrift. NSDAP/SA. Bri. III Dü. Wuppertal-Barmen, 7.4.1931. gez. Keller. Zu VII. See also, U. Klein, 'SA-Terror und Bevölkerung in Wuppertal 1933/34', in D. Peukert and J. Reulecke (eds), *Die Reihen fast geschlossen* (Wuppertal, 1981), pp. 46–7.

61 For instance: BA, NS26/522. Der Bürgermeister als Ortspolizeibehörde. Betr.: Inhaltsangabe des Angriffs der Kommunisten auf das braune Haus der NSDAP in Frechen. Frechen, den 26.1.1937. The incident described occurred on 31 January 1933; BA, NS26/528. Kampfbericht von Eugen Weyrauch, Worms, Turnerstrasse 9. This mentions KPD activity after 30 January 1933; BA, NS26/522. Der Bürgermeister der Stadt Immenstadt (Allgäu). Immenstadt, den 12.12.1936. 2. Politische Zusammenstösse am 10. Juli 1932.

62 BA, R45IV/26. Bezirksleitung Berlin-Brandenburg-Lausitz. An alle Strassenzellen in Gross-Berlin. Berlin, 2.6.1930. p. 2.

63 BA, R45IV/6. Karl Schulz – Neukölln. An das ZK der KPD, Berlin. Bericht über Versammlungstour im Hessen-Wahlkampf v. 10.–18. Juni 1932. Berlin, den 22. Juni 1932. p. 1.

64 BA, R45IV/21. Abschrift. Bezirk Grossthüringen. Bericht der Bezirksleitung Grossthüringen über die Arbeit zur Reichstagwahl 1932. pp. 2–3.

65 BA, NS26/1404. Berichte der Staatspolizei Württembergs zur politischen Lage. 25.11.1931.

66 SA growth in Württemberg, membership 1931 – January: 2,581; April: 4,396; October: 5,979; November: 6,522; December: 7,224. Sources: January and April: BA, Sch 415. Stärke der SA und SS nach dem Stande vom 1.4.1931. München, den 18. Mai 1931; October and November: BA, NS26/307. Der Oberste SA-Führer. Betrifft: Stand der SA nach dem Stande der letzten Stärkemeldung (15.12.31). München, den 11.1.1932; December: BA, NS26/307. Der Oberste SA-Führer. 1b Nr. 316/32. Betrifft: Stand der letzten Stärkemeldung (15.1.32). München, den 1. Februar 1932.

67 This is not to claim that all KPD, or SA, members were indifferent, ideologically speaking, as to which organisation they belonged. The point at issue is whether or not a sizeable proportion of each organisation's members would swap sides, despite the existence of a politically conscious core in each organisation. For a further assessment of this problem *vis à vis* the KPD see Neumann, *Parteien*, pp. 87, 94–5, and R. N. Hunt, *German Social Democracy, 1918–1933* (Chicago, 1970), pp. 101–2. The latter compares the SPD's highly stable party membership with the chronically unstable membership of the KPD. On this latter point see also Neumann, *Parteien*, p. 88.

68 NWHStA, Regierung Aachen 22757. Der Preussische Minister des Innern. I 1272/9.2.33. An die Herren Regierungspräsidenten. Berlin, den 15. Februar 1933.

69 BA, R43II/1202. Reichsminister des Innern. IA 2000/29.9. An die Herren Reichsstatthalter und die Landesregierungen. Berlin, den 6. Oktober 1933.

70 H. Bennecke, 'Die Reichswehr und der "Rohm Putsch"', *Politische Studien* (Munich, 1964); H. Krausnick, 'Der 30. Juni 1934', *Aus Politik und Zeitgeschichte*, vol. 25, no. 54, 30 June 1954; R. J. O'Neill, *The Germany Army and the Nazi Party, 1933–1939* (London, 1966), ch. 3.

71 For a general account see C. Bloch, *Die SA und die Krise des NS-Regimes 1934* (Frankfurt-am-Main, 1970), ch. 3.

72 BA, R43II/1202. Auszug aus der Niederschrift über die Ministerbesprechung vom 3. Juli 1934. Betr.: Politische Lage.

73 BA, R2/11913a. Zu IB 370/34. Bericht über die Prüfung der Vereinnahmung der der Obersten SA-Führung (OSAF) vom Reichsministerium des Innern im Rechnungsjahr 1933 aus dem Ausgabekapitel V E 16 Titel 15 (SA-Hilfswerk) überwiesenen Reichsgelder und über die Prüfung der Verwendung dieser Gelder. Potsdam, den 8. Juni 1934, p. 10.

74 BA, R43II/1202. As in note 72. p. 5.

75 K. D. Bracher, *The German Dictatorship* (London, 1973), p. 199.

9 Conclusion

Militarism featured in German political life long before the great crisis of the early 1930s and had involved substantial sections of the population. During this earlier period the social divisions within paramilitary politics reflected, by and large, those in conventional political life. Before the First World War, largely middle-class nationalist youth movements, which anticipated the paramilitary groups of later years, were formed to counteract the increasingly influential SPD youth movement as part of a wider right-wing response to mounting socialist electoral strength. Defeat after a long, costly war which was followed by the socialist revolution in late 1918 galvanised the right further, precipitating the formation of paramilitary organisations – notably the Freikorps, citizens' defence associations, and patriotic leagues, such as the Stahlhelm, which mainly attracted members of the middle classes.

The SPD-led government found a short-term use for the Freikorps and the defence associations in containing the radical left, but some right-wing paramilitary groups, including by 1921 the newly formed SA, quickly turned their attention to destroying the republic itself. The republican Reichsbanner and the Communist Red Front were formed in 1924 as a response to these right-wing formations, although the effectiveness of the Reichsbanner, in particular, has sometimes been questioned. During the mid-1920s the importance of paramilitary politics declined temporarily but, in essence, large sections of middle-class Germany regarded the nationalist paramilitary groups as an important element in right-wing opposition to the republic, while several million workers joined the Reichsbanner to help protect the republic.

Within the SA's history, only that of its leadership fitted relatively well into this process by the early 1930s. The leaders were products of the (lower) middle-class experience in the trenches of the Great War and of (lower) middle-class insecurity in the postwar era. However, their hostility to Marxian socialism was combined with a suspicion of traditional imperial society, which moulded them into right-wing populists – albeit without a clear conception of social reorganisation. The same cannot be said for the ordinary stormtroopers during the SA's heyday. The latter's growth during the radically altered social and political circumstances of the depression brought substantial numbers of working-class recruits to the paramilitary right. It appealed to the most politically vulnerable section of the working class, the young unemployed, who formed the core of the SA's membership. Unlike their parents, they took for granted the social and political advances achieved by Weimar, but experienced its economic failings at first hand. These recruits sought relief from the intense material suffering of the period and an outlet for the sense of outrage which the loss of their work, well-being and self-respect had created. Conventional political activity and conventional ideologies seemed less suited to their needs than the activism and violence which they found in the SA.

The depression, therefore, had brought together the leaders and men. The leaders' organisational capacity provided an institutional framework capable of absorbing a huge membership. The ability of the leaders and the wider Nazi movement to provide the material benefits sought by the stormtroopers, albeit in piecemeal fashion, was extremely important. The leaders' activism, inherited from the war and the Freikorps era was combined with a political outlook which differed from that of the ordinary stormtroopers, but it provided the method of political mobilisation which appeared most effective to the latter during the crisis years of the early 1930s.

The SA contributed substantially to the Nazi takeover. Some working-class Nazis and many working-class Nazi voters were not SA members, but the SA represented the most significant organised Nazi presence within many working-class areas. The stormtroopers' brand of politics – the marching, fighting, rallying, leafletting and proselytising – and the welfare available within the SA undoubtedly enhanced the National Socialist impact on the urban and town-dwelling working class, and within the more fragmented non-urban working classes. This not only attracted impressive numbers of recruits to the SA, but won more passive support for Nazism from social groups to which its appeal was not immediately evident.

Therefore, the SA blurred the political options available to the unemployed working class, and the polarisation of politics on class lines during the depression was by no means absolute. Of course, many jobless workers did move to the extreme left during the depression. The Reichsbanner's more active units contained many unemployed workers. The KPD's growing membership was drawn largely from the jobless by 1932 and much of its electoral support derived from similar circles, but the SA's success placed limits on this growth.

Consequently, the National Socialist takeover occurred while some of the potentially revolutionary elements in society were organised within the Nazi movement. Any possible opposition to Hitler's takeover was weakened from the outset and the SA's credibility as a radical, activist institution was sufficient to attract a spectacular wave of new recruits during 1933 – to the mounting dismay of Nazism's opponents. Far from obstructing the National Socialist takeover, the very people whom the KPD had sought to recruit and organise during the early 1930s actually assisted it, not least through their assault on the main labour organisations.

This is not to say that these groups had been found a long-term role within the Nazi movement. National Socialism had always been shot through with contradictions which, eventually, had to be resolved either through the NSDAP's collapse or through the sacrifice of part of the movement. The ambitions of most senior leaders, Hitler included, held no brief for either socio-economic revolution or retribution, focusing instead on a racialist Social Darwinism. Therefore, once Hitler's government had established itself, the broader coalition of social interests created during the drive for power and maintained during its consolidation had to break up. The Röhm purge was part of this process. It demonstrated the diminishing usefulness of the SA to the NSDAP which wished to govern Germany in co-operation with the army, civil service and industry.

If the Röhm purge ended any prospects of an active political role for the SA, it retained an important social function for a time. It provided the NSDAP with an organisational focus for the unemployed, both to keep them off the streets and under surveillance, and to provide a measure of care and vocational retraining. This final service to the NSDAP ended in 1936 as an expanding economy and conscription combined to soak up the remaining hard-core jobless. A greatly reduced SA was then accorded a secondary role in rallies and other propaganda displays and in ideological and pre-military training.

Its significance in German history was, therefore, brief but crucial. In many industrial societies the middle classes remained staunch defenders of the *status quo* during the interwar years, but Weimar received little help from this quarter. Democratic republicanism was not popular among a largely right-wing middle class. Consequently, Weimar was sandwiched after 1929 between a politically hostile and economically insecure middle class and an alienated, embittered, working-class younger generation. These two groups shared few common goals beyond the destruction of Weimar, but the SA, by attracting so many young workers, provided the basis for temporary co-operation between them and the middle-class members of other Nazi and nationalist organisations to achieve the demise of the republic and the initial consolidation of National Socialism.

Sources

Primary Sources

Note: Inconsistencies in presentation of both dates and abbreviations in primary sources in the notes reflect the usage of the original documents and have been retained to facilitate reference to these.

Archival sources were consulted as follows:

Bayerisches Hauptstaatsarchiv München (BHStA)

> Abteilung I (Abt. I)
> Sonderabgabe I (So. I) [NSDAP Hauptarchiv]
> Staatsministerium des Innern, Band 22 (M. Inn)
>
> Geheimes Staatsarchiv München (GStAM)
> Monatsberichte der Regierungspräsidenten/Lageberichte (MA)
> Reichsstatthalter Epp, 1933–1945 (R)
>
> Staatsarchiv München (SM)
> NSDAP

Berlin Document Center (BDC)

> SA Archive

Bundesarchiv Koblenz (BA)

> NS23 (SA Archiv)
> NS26 (NSDAP Hauptarchiv)
> Sammlung Schumacher
> R1 (Reichsschatzmeister der NSDAP)
> R2 (Reichsfinanzministerium)
> R36 (Deutscher Gemeindetag)
> R41 (Reichsarbeitsministerium)
> R43I, II (Reichskanzlei)
> R45IV (KPD Archiv)

Geheimstaatsarchiv Berlin-Dahlem (GStABD)

> Bestand Rep. 90P, Preussisches Staatsministerium – Gestapo
> Bestand Rep. 77, Grauert.

Generallandesarchiv Karlsruhe (GLAK)

> Bestand Abt. 233 (Badische Staatskanzlei)

Bestand Abt. 460 (Arbeitsämter)
Bestand Abt. 465d (NSDAP)

Hessisches Hauptstaatsarchiv Wiesbaden (HHW)

Abt. 405 (Preussische Regierung Wiesbaden)
Abt. 483 (NSDAP Gauleitung Hessen-Nassau)

Institut für Zeitgeschichte (IfZ)

SA I (Allgemeines)
SA II (Dienststellen)
SA III (Sachliches)
SA IV (Gruppe Schlesien)

Landesarchiv Speyer (LAS)

Akten Rep. 71 I: H33, H37, Z1293

Niedersächsisches Hauptstaatsarchiv (NHStA)

Hann. 80, Hann. II. Polizeisachen
Hann. 80, Lün. III. Polizeisachen
Hann. 310 I NSDAP. Gau Südhannover-Braunschweig und Gau Osthan-
nover, ihre Gliederungen und angeschlossene Verbände 1919–1945
Landratsamt Hameln-Pyrmont

Nordrhein-Westfälisches Hauptstaatsarchiv (NWHStA)

Bestand RW 23 (SA)
Gestapo(leit)stelle Düsseldorf (Ge)
Regierung Aachen
Regierung Düsseldorf (BR 1021)

Staatliches Archivlager Göttingen, (Staatsarchiv Königsberg (Archivbestände Preussischer Kulturbesitz)) (SAG)

Rep. 240A, Reichsleitung der NSDAP
Rep. 240 B, Gauleitung Ostpreussen der NSDAP
Rep. 240 C, Territoriale Gliederung der NSDAP Ostpreussen
Rep. 240 D, Nachträge aus den ungeordneten Material des Gauarchivs
    Ostpreussen der NSDAP
Rep. 17, Polizeipräsidium Königsberg
Rep. 18, Landrat Rosenberg
Rep. 36, Landgericht Königsberg
Rep. 37, Staatsanwaltschaft Königsberg
Rep. 37a, Staatsanwaltschaft Allenstein
Rep. 38a, Amtsgerichte Königsberg
Rep. 39, Amtsgerichte Verschiedene
Nürnberger Prozess, SA Akten (NI, NIK)

228   *Stormtroopers*

Staatsarchiv Bremen (SB)

Rep. 7, 1066/62–1. (D52)

Wiener Library London

Der SA-Mann, Organ der OSAF der NSDAP. 7 January 1933 to 30 June 1934.

Secondary Sources

Secondary sources have been cited as follows:

Abraham, D., *The Collapse of the Weimar Republic – Political Economy and Crisis* (Princeton, NJ, 1981).

Adorno, T. W., *et al.*, *The Authoritarian Personality* (New York, 1969 edn).

Allen, W. S., *The Nazi Seizure of Power. The Experience of a Single German Town. 1930–1935* (Chicago, 1965).

Bahne, S., 'Die Kommunistische Partei Deutschlands', in E. Matthias and R. Morsey (eds), *Das Ende der Parteien* (Düsseldorf, 1966), pp. 655–739.

Balogh, T., 'The national economy of Germany', *Economic Journal* (September 1938), pp. 461–97.

Bennecke, H., 'Die Reichswehr und der "Röhm Putsch"', Beiheft 2, *Politische Studien* (Munich, 1964).

Bennecke, H., *Hitler und die SA* (Munich, 1962).

Benz, W., 'Vom freiwilligen Arbeitsdienst zur Arbeitsdienstpflicht', *Vierteljahreshefte für Zeitgeschichte*, year 16, no. 4 (1968), pp. 317–46.

Berghahn, V. R. (ed.), *Militarismus* (Cologne, 1975).

Berghahn, V. R., *Der Stahlhelm, Bund der Frontsoldaten 1918–1935* (Düsseldorf, 1966).

Bergsträsser, L., *Geschichte der politischen Parteien in Deutschland* (Munich and Vienna, 1965).

Bessel, R. J., 'Militarismus im innenpolitischen Leben der Weimarer Republik: Von den Freikorps zur SA', in K.-J. Müller and E. Opitz (eds), *Militär und Militarismus in der Weimarer Republik* (Düsseldorf, 1978), pp. 193–222.

Bessel, R. J., 'The SA in the Eastern Regions of Germany, 1925 to 1934' (D. Phil., Oxford University 1980).

Bessel, R. J., and Feuchtwanger, E. J. (eds), *Social Change and Political Development in Weimar Germany* (London, 1981).

Bessel, R. J., and Jamin, M., 'Nazis, workers and the uses of quantitative evidence', *Social History*, vol. 4, no. 1 (1979), pp. 111–16.

Blackbourn, D., *Class, Religion and Local Politics in Wilhelmine Germany. The Centre Party in Württemberg before 1914* (New Haven, Conn. and London, 1980).

Bloch, C., *Die SA und die Krise des NS-Regimes 1934* (Frankfurt-am-Main, 1970).

Boelitz, O., *Der Aufbau des preussischen Bildungswesens nach der Staatsumwälzung* (Leipzig, 1925).

Böhnke, W., *Die NSDAP im Ruhrgebiet, 1920–1933* (Bonn–Bad Godesberg, 1974).

Bracher, K. D., *The German Dictatorship. The Origins, Structure and Consequences of National Socialism*, trans. J. Steinberg (London, 1973 and London, 1971). Latter used in ch. 3.

Bracher, K. D., Schulz, G., and Sauer, W., *Die nationalsozialistische Machter-greifung. Studien zur Errichtung des totalitären Herrschaftssystems in Deutschland 1933/34* (Frankfurt-am-Main, Berlin and Vienna, 1974).

Bredow, K., *Hitlerrast. Die Bluttragödie des 30. Juni 1934. Ablauf, Vorgeschichte und Hintergründe* (Saarbrücken, 1935).

Broszat, M., *Der Staat Hitlers. Grundlegung und Entwicklung seiner inneren Verfassung* (Munich, 1969).

Buchloh, I., *Die nationalsozialistische Machtergreifung in Duisburg. Eine Fallstudie* (Duisburg, 1980).

Caplan, J., 'Bureaucracy, politics and the National Socialist State', in P. D. Stachura (ed.), *The Shaping of the Nazi State* (London, 1978), pp. 234–56.

Carsten, F. L., *Fascist Movements in Austria: From Schönerer to Hitler* (London, 1977).

Carsten, F. L., *The Reichswehr and Politics 1918–1933* (Oxford, 1966).

Carsten, F. L., *The Rise of Fascism* (London, 1976).

Childers, T., 'The social bases of the National Socialist vote', *Journal of Contemporary History*, vol. 11, no. 4 (1976), pp. 17–42.

Craig, G. A., *The Politics of the Prussian Army, 1640–1945* (Oxford, 1975).

Czichon, E., *Wer Verhalf Hitler zur Macht? Zum Anteil der deutschen Industrie an der Zerstörung der Weimarer Republik* (Cologne, 1967).

Diehl, J. M., *Paramilitary Politics in Weimar Germany* (Bloomington, Ind. and London, 1977).

Diels, R., *Lucifer ante Portas. Zwischen Severing und Heydrich* (Zurich, 1949).

Domröse, O., *Der NS-Staat in Bayern von der Machtergreifung bis zum Röhm Putsch* (Munich, 1974).

Eley, G., 'The Wilhelmine right: how it changed', in R. J. Evans (ed.), *Society and Politics in Wilhelmine Germany*, (London, 1978).

Evans, R. J. (ed.), *Society and Politics in Wilhelmine Germany* (London, 1978).

Fest, J., *The Face of the Third Reich*, trans. M. Bullock (London, 1972).

Fetscher, I., 'Faschismus und Nationalsozialismus', *Politische Jahresschrift*, vol. 3 (1962), pp. 42ff.

Fetscher, I., 'Zur Kritik des sowjetmarxistischen Faschismusbegriffs', in G. Jasper (ed.), *Von Weimar zu Hitler, 1930–1933* (Cologne and Berlin, 1968).

Fischer, C., and Hicks, C., 'Statistics and the historian; the occupational profile of the SA of the NSDAP', *Social History*, vol. 5, no. 1 (1980), pp. 131–8.

Flechtheim, O. K., *Die KPD in der Weimarer Republik* (Frankfurt-am-Main, 1976).

Frenkel-Brunswik, E., 'Sex, people and self as seen through the interviews', in T. W. Adorno *et al.* in *The Authoritarian Personality*, (New York, 1969), pp. 390–441.

Fricke, D., *et al.*, *Die bürgerlichen Parteien in Deutschland. Handbuch der Geschichte der bürgerlichen Parteien und anderen bürgerlichen Interessenorganisationen vom Vormärz bis zum Jahre 1945* (Leipzig, 1970).

Fröhlich, E., 'Die Partei auf lokaler Ebene. Zwischen gesellschaftlicher Assimilation und Veränderungsdynamik', in G. Hirschfeld and L. Kettenacker (eds), *The 'Führer State': Myth and Reality. Studies on the Structure and Politics of the Third Reich* (Stuttgart, 1981), pp. 255–69.

Führ. C., *Zur Schulpolitik der Weimarer Republik. Die Zusammenarbeit von Reich und Ländern im Reichsschulausschuss (1919–1923), und im Ausschuss für das Unterrichtswesen (1924–1933)* (Weinheim, Berlin and Basle, 1970).

Gallo, M., *Der Schwarze Freitag der SA. Die Vernichtung des revolutionären Flügels der NSDAP durch Hitlers SS im Juni 1934* (Cologne and Hamburg, 1972).

Geiger, T., *Die Klassengesellschaft im Schmelztiegel* (Cologne and Hagen, 1949).

Gellately, R., *The Politics of Economic Despair. Shopkeepers and German Politics 1890–1914* (London, 1974).

Gimbel, A., *So kämpften wir* (Frankfurt-am-Main, 1941).

Gossweiler, K., 'Der Übergang von der Weltwirtschaftskrise zur Rüstungskonjunktur in Deutschland 1933 bis 1934. Ein historischer Beitrag zur Problematik staatsmonopolistischer "Krisenüberwindung"', *Jahrbuch für Wirtschaftsgeschichte*, vol. 2 (1968), pp. 55–116.

Hallgarten, G., and Radkau, J., *Deutsche Industrie und Politik von Bismarck bis heute* (Frankfurt-am-Main, 1974).

Hamilton, R. F., *Who Voted for Hitler?* (Princeton, NJ, 1982).

Heberle, R., *Landbevölkerung und Nationalsozialismus. Eine soziologische Untersuchung der politischen Willensbildung in Schleswig-Holstein 1918–1932* (Stuttgart, 1963).

Heiden, K., *Der Fuehrer. Hitler's Rise to Power*, trans. R. Manheim (London, 1967).

Hentschel, V., *Weimars letzte Monate. Hitler und der Untergang der Republik* (Düsseldorf, 1978).

Hirschfeld, G., and Kettenacker, L., (eds), *The 'Führer State': Myth and Reality. Studies on the Structure and Politics of the Third Reich* (Stuttgart, 1981).

Hunt, R. N., *German Social Democracy, 1918–1933* (Chicago, 1970).

Hüttenberger, P., *Die Gauleiter. Studie zum Wandel des Machtgefüges in der NSDAP* (Stuttgart, 1969).

Jamin, M., 'Zur Rolle der SA im nationalsozialistischen Herrschaftssystem', in G. Hirschfeld and L. Kettenacker (eds), *The 'Führer State': Myth and Reality. Studies on the Structure and Politics of the Third Reich* (Stuttgart, 1981), pp. 329–60.

Jamin, M., 'Zwischen den Klassen. Eine quantitative Untersuchung zur Sozialstruktur der SA-Führerschaft' (Dissertation, Rühr-Universität-Bochum, 1982).

Jasper, G., (ed.), *Von Weimar zu Hitler, 1930–1933* (Cologne and Berlin, 1968).

Kater, M. H., 'Ansätze zu einer Soziologie der SA bis zur Röhm Krise', in U. Engelhardt *et al.* (eds) *Soziale Bewegung und politische Verfassung*, (Stuttgart, 1976), pp. 798–831.

Kater, M. H., 'Sozialer Wandel in der NSDAP im Zuge der nationalsozialistischen Machtergreifung', in W. Schieder (ed.), *Faschismus als soziale Bewegung*, (Hamburg, 1976), pp. 25–67.

Kater, M. H., 'Zum gegenseitigen Verhältnis von SA und SS in der Sozialgeschichte des Nationalsozialismus von 1925 bis 1939', *Vierteljahresschrift für Sozial – und Wirtschaftsgeschichte*, vol. 62, no. 3 (1975), pp. 339–79.

Kater, M. H., 'Zur Soziographie der frühen NSDAP', *Vierteljahreshefte für Zeitgeschichte*, vol. 19, no. 2 (1971), pp. 124–59.

Kele, M. H., *Nazis and Workers. National Socialist Appeals to German Labor, 1919–1933* (Chapel Hill, NC, 1972).

Kershaw, I., 'The Führer image and political integration: the popular conception of Hitler in Bavaria during the Third Reich', in G. Hirschfeld and L. Kettenacker (eds), *The 'Führer State': Myth and Reality. Studies on the Structure and Politics of the Third Reich*, (Stuttgart, 1981), pp. 133–63.

Klein, U., 'SA-Terror und Bevölkerung in Wuppertal 1933/34', in D. Peukert and J. Reulecke (eds) *Die Reihen fast geschlossen* (Wuppertal, 1981), pp. 45–64.

Klenner, J., *Verhältnis von Partei und Staat 1933–1945. Dargestellt am Beispiel Bayerns* (Munich, 1974).

Krausnick, H., 'Der 30. Juni 1934 – Bedeutung – Hintergründe – Verlauf', *Aus Politik und Zeitgeschichte – Beilage zur Wochenzeitung, 'Das Parlament'*, vol. 25, no. 54, 30 June 1954.

Kuczynski, J., *A Short History of Labour Conditions under Industrial Capitalism. Vol. 3, Part 1: Germany 1800 to the Present Day* (London, 1945).

Larsen, S. U. (ed.), *Who Were the Fascists? Social Roots of European Fascism* (Oslo, 1980).

Mason, T. W., *Arbeiterklasse und Volksgemeinschaft. Dokumente und Materialien zur deutschen Arbeiterpolitik 1936–1939* (Opladen, 1975).

Mason, T. W., 'The coming of the Nazis', *Times Literary Supplement*, no. 3,752, 1 February 1974, pp. 93–6.

Mason, T. W., 'Labour in the Third Reich 1933–1939', *Past and Present* (1966), pp. 112–41.

Matthias, E., and Morsey, R., (eds), *Das Ende der Parteien* (Düsseldorf, 1966).

Merkl, P. H., *The Making of a Stormtrooper* (Princeton, NJ, 1980).

Merkl, P. H., *Political Violence under the Swastika. 581 Early Nazis* (Princeton, NJ, 1975).

Milatz, A., *Wähler und Wahlen in der Weimarer Republik* (Bonn, 1968).

Moore, Jr, B., *Injustice. The Social Bases of Obedience and Revolt* (London, 1978).

Mühlberger, D., 'The sociology of the NSDAP: the question of working class membership', *Journal of Contemporary History*, vol. 15, no. 3 (1980), pp. 493–511.

Müller, K. J., and Opitz, E. (eds), *Militär und Militarismus in der Weimarer Republik* (Düsseldorf, 1978).

Neumann, S., *Die Parteien der Weimarer Republik* (Stuttgart, Berlin, Cologne and Mainz, 1965).

Noakes, J., *The Nazi Party in Lower Saxony, 1921–1933* (Oxford, 1971).

O'Neill, R. J., *The German Army and the Nazi Party, 1933–1939* (London, 1966).

Peukert, D., and Reulecke, J., (eds), *Die Reihen fast geschlossen* (Wuppertal, 1981).

Preller, L., *Sozialpolitik in der Weimarer Republik* (Düsseldorf, 1978).

Reiche, E. G., 'The Development of the SA in Nuremberg, 1922 to 1934' (Dissertation, University of Delaware, 1972).

Reichsorganisationsleiter der NSDAP (ed.), *Partei-Statistik. Stand 1. Januar 1935* (Munich, 1935).

Roberts, S. H., *The House that Hitler Built*, 12th edn (London, 1945).

Rohe, K., *Das Reichsbanner Schwarz Rot Gold. Ein Beitrag zur Geschichte und Struktur der politischen Kampfverbände zur Zeit der Weimarer Republik* (Stuttgart, 1965).

Röhm, E., *Die Geschichte eines Hochverräters* (Munich, 1933).

Rosenberg, A., *Imperial Germany. The Birth of the German Republic, 1871–1918*, trans. I. F. D. Morrow (Oxford, 1970).

Rosenhaft, E., 'Working-class life and working-class politics: Communists, Nazis and the state in the battle for the streets, Berlin 1928–1932', in R. J. Bessel and E. J. Feuchtwanger (eds), *Social Change and Political Development in Weimar Germany* (London, 1981).

Schieder, W. (ed.), *Faschismus als soziale Bewegung* (Hamburg, 1976).

Schön, E., *Die Entstehung des Nationalsozialismus in Hessen* (Miesenheim am Glan, 1972).

Schüddekopf, O. E., *Linke Leute von rechts. Die nationalrevolutionären Minderheiten und der Kommunismus in der Weimarer Republik* (Stuttgart, 1960).

Schweitzer, A., *Big Business in the Third Reich* (London, 1964).

Stephenson, J., *The Nazi Organisation of Women* (London, 1980).

Stachura, P. D., (ed.), *The Shaping of the Nazi State* (London, 1978).

Starke, G., *NSBO und Deutsche Arbeitsfront* (Berlin, 1934).

Statistisches Jahrbuch für das deutsche Reich, 1934 (Berlin, 1934).

Stegmann, D., Die Erben Bismarcks (Cologne, 1970).

Stokes, L. D., 'The social composition of the Nazi Party in Eutin, 1925–32', *International Review of Social History*, vol. 23, pt 1 (1978), pp. 1–32.

Strasser, O., *Sonnabend 30. Juni: Vorgeschichte, Verlauf, Folgen* (Prague, date unknown).

Tormin, W., *Geschichte der deutschen Parteien seit 1848* (Stuttgart, Berlin, Cologne and Mainz, 1968).

Turner, H. A., *Faschismus und Kapitalismus in Deutschland. Studien zum Verhältnis zwischen Nationalsozialismus und Wirtschaft* (Göttingen, 1972).

Turner, H. A., 'Grossunternehmertum und Nationalsozialismus 1930–1933. Kritisches und Ergänzendes zu zwei neuen Forschungsbeiträgen', *Historische Zeitschrift*, vol. 221, no. 1 (August 1975), pp. 18–68.

Weber, H., *Völker hört die Signale. Der deutsche Kommunismus, 1916–1966* (Munich, 1967).

Weissbecker, M., 'Nationalsozialistische Deutsche Arbeiterpartei (NSDAP) 1919–1945', in D. Fricke *et al.* (eds), *Die bürgerlichen Parteien in Deutschland* (Leipzig, 1970).

Weissbuch über die Erschiessungen des 30. Juni 1934 (Paris, 1935).

Werner, A., 'SA und NSDAP. SA: "Wehrverband", "Parteitruppe" oder "Revolutionsarmee"? Studien zur Geschichte der SA und der NSDAP, 1920–1933 (Dissertation, Friedrich Alexander Universität zu Erlangen, 1964).

Wickham, J., 'The Working Class Movement in Frankfurt-am-Main during the Weimar Republic' (D. Phil., University of Sussex, 1979).

Williams, W. E., 'Versuch einer Definition paramilitärischer Organisationen', in V. R. Berghahn (ed.), *Militarismus* (Cologne, 1975), pp. 139–51.

Winkler, H. A., *Mittelstand, Demokratie und Nationalsozialismus. Die politische Entwicklung von Handwerk und Kleinhandel in der Weimarer Republik* (Cologne, 1972).

Index